The Quick Resume & Cover Letter Book

WRITE AND USE AN EFFECTIVE RESUME IN ONLY ONE DAY

Third Edition

Michael Farr

JIST Works
America's Career Publisher

The Quick Resume & Cover Letter Book, Third Edition

Published by JIST Works, an imprint of JIST Publishing, Inc.
8902 Otis Avenue
Indianapolis, IN 46216-1033
Phone: 1-800-648-JIST Fax: 1-800-JIST-FAX E-mail: info@jist.com

Visit our Web site at **www.jist.com** for information on JIST, free job search tips, book chapters, and ordering instructions for our many products! For free information on 14,000 job titles, visit **www.careeroink.com**.

Quantity discounts are available for JIST books. Please call our Sales Department at 1-800-648-5478 for a free catalog and more information.

Acquisitions and Project Editor: Lori Cates Hand
Development Editor: L. Michelle Tullier, Editorial Eyes
Interior Design and Page Layout: Aleata Howard
Cover Design: designLab, Seattle
Proofreader: David Faust
Indexer: Tina Trettin

Printed in Canada
09 08 07 06 05 9 8 7 6 5 4 3 2

Library of Congress Cataloging-in-Publication Data

Farr, J. Michael.
The quick resume & cover letter book : write and use an effective resume in only one day / Michael Farr.-- 3rd ed.
p. cm.
Includes bibliographical references and index.
ISBN 1-59357-089-9 (alk. paper)
1. Résumés (Employment) 2. Cover letters. I. Title: Quick resume and cover letter book. II. Title: Resume & cover letter book. III. Title.
HF5383.F32 2005
650.14'2--dc22

2004029997

ISBN 1-59357-089-9

You Don't Have to Read This Whole Book!

Read Just the First Section and Have a Resume Today!

This is a big book, but you really don't have to read it all. Writing a resume does not have to be difficult. A simple one can be created in about an hour, and a few more hours will give you a very nice resume. That is what Section One is about: getting an acceptable resume finished quickly. And that may be all the resume information you need.

I include essential resume-writing information in Section One, along with some job search tips. My point is to help you get your resume done today, so that you can get started on your job search tomorrow—or this afternoon. After all, your desire is not to do a perfect resume—it is to get a perfect job.

But this book consists of a lot more than Section One. After you've finished your resume, read the job search tips in Section Five. That section will give you brief but solid advice that can dramatically reduce the time it takes to get a good job.

Other sections will provide you with lots of sample resumes plus information on writing a superior resume, defining your perfect job, and much more. Review the Table of Contents to see what's inside, and read only those things that interest you.

So, yes, this is a pretty big book, but its approach is still "quick." Good luck!

Contents

Section Five: Getting a Good Job in Less Time..............337

While this is a resume book, your interest in writing a resume exists because you are looking for the right job. So this may be one of the most important sections of the book. It presents basic techniques for getting the right job in less time and on using the Internet effectively in your job search.

Appendices...381

Quick Tips on How to Use This Book

I did not write this book for it to be read in order from cover to cover. Instead, I suggest you skip around to use only those sections you need most or that interest you. Since you obviously want to put together a resume, I assume that you are also looking for a job or are thinking about doing so. That being the case, here are my suggestions on the best way to use this book:

1. **Read the Table of Contents.** This will introduce you to the content of the book and its chapters so that you can start to select the parts most relevant to your needs.
2. **Complete a basic resume as described in Section One.** This short section will show you how to put together a resume that will be fine for most situations—and help you do this in just a few hours. You might also want to review the sample resumes in Section Three to help you do your own resume.
3. **Begin looking for a job.** Once you have a basic resume, read Section Five for a quick review of self-directed job search techniques. These techniques can reduce the time it takes to find a job. Then go out looking for your next job.
4. **Do the activities in Section Two.** Besides being helpful in writing a good resume, Section Two provides activities and tips that will help you plan your career, handle interviews, and get a better job than you might otherwise. You may find some chapters more important to you than others; so, again, do what you think is best.
5. **If you really need to, and as time permits, write a great resume.** While it will take more time, you may want to revise your resume and create one that is, well, better. This book provides lots of good information and sample resumes to help you in this task. But keep in mind that your priority is to get a good job and *not* to stay home working on your resume.

There you are. I've written this book to help you over the resume hurdle. It will help you get a resume done quickly and go about the more important task of getting a job. I hope it helps.

Preface

A thousand or more resume books are probably available, so you might ask why yet another is needed. The answer is that most resume books misrepresent themselves. They typically argue that the way to get a good job is to do the following:

1. Create an outstanding resume.
2. Put it in front of lots of people who have job openings.

But, if you take that advice (which seems reasonable enough), you will probably be making a big mistake.

The reason is that the logic is flawed. Those authors assume that you should conduct your job search in the traditional way by sending out lots of resumes to human resource (HR) offices, search firms, or hiring managers, in response to an available opening. And they assume that the resume, if only done well enough, will help you stand out from the pile of resumes that employers get by mail or can find on the Internet. It all seems to make sense, *but most of the labor market does not work this way anymore!*

The fact is that most jobs are filled by people employers know before a job is ever advertised. For the relatively few jobs that are advertised (and the research indicates that only about 15 to 25 percent are), half of these jobs are filled by people who never read the ads. While the Internet is changing this for some technology-oriented jobs and in some organizations, it is still true for most hires.

So, if you believe that the way to get a job is to send in your resume for an available job opening or to post it on the Internet, you are missing out on most job opportunities. Sending your "dynamite" resume in the conventional way or over the Internet will cause you to miss about 75 percent of the jobs—the ones that are never advertised at all.

You could, of course, send your dynamite resume to lots of employers and hope for the best—and this has worked for some people. Or you could put it on the Internet's many resume databases and wait. But, you might be waiting a long time. There is a better way and that is what this book is about. Since you obviously think you need a resume (and you probably do), then the thing to do is to get one together quickly. This approach avoids the all-too-common problem of taking a week or more to work on your resume before getting started on your job search. Then, as time permits, you can work on writing a better resume.

That is how this book is arranged. I have included in Section One directions for creating and using a resume in several hours, including an electronic form of your resume for posting or transmitting online. Section Two provides a more detailed approach that will help you sort out your skills, job objective, and other matters and provides a form of career counseling. This section will, of course, teach you much more about writing a good resume. Section Three provides sample resumes written by resume-writing professionals. Section Four gives you information and examples for other job search correspondence such as cover letters and thank-you notes. Finally, Section Five offers a quick review of job search methods that have been proven to cut the time it takes to get a job as well as tips on job seeking on the Internet.

This thoroughly updated Third Edition retains the successful approach of the First and Second Editions. Among its many changes and enhancements are the following:

- More (over 80!) sample resumes from professional resume writers.
- Up-to-date information on using the Internet in your job search, reflecting the latest technology issues and hiring trends.
- Updated information throughout on using personal computers, laser printers, e-mail addresses, voice mail, and more.
- Updated information on print and online resources for choosing a career direction and finding your ideal job.

So this is a real resume book, and it will teach you many things about resumes. Unlike most resume books, it will show you how to create a resume in stages, beginning with a simple one that you can write in about an hour all the way up to more sophisticated ones. You can decide which approach is right for you. But the real difference in this resume book is that I have spent over 25 years studying, teaching, and writing about job-seeking skills, with an emphasis on techniques that work. For this reason, I do something that few resume books do—provide the facts about what a resume can and can't do:

- A resume will not get you a job—an interview can.
- A resume is not a particularly good tool for getting interviews. Direct contacts and leads given to you by those you know—or can come to know—are far more important.
- A good resume can help you in your job search, but many people get good jobs without using a resume at all.
- A simple, error-free resume is a far more effective job search tool than an elegant one that you are working on while you should be out getting interviews.

I hope you like the book and, more importantly, that it helps you get the job you want.

Best of "luck" in your job search and your life.

Mike Farr

P.S.: Please send me your resume and stories about how you got your job. I'd like to collect them for use in a future book. Write to info@jist.com.

Section One

The Same-Day Resume

This section is short and sweet. It will help you put together a resume in a matter of hours. And that is precisely the point—a simple resume may be all you need to get started on your job search.

I have learned in my many years of studying and teaching job-seeking skills that too many people worry about (and work on) their resumes when they should be out there networking and getting interviews. I'm not saying that some people should not take the time to do a particularly good resume. I'm suggesting that you will be far better off spending more of your time getting out there to connect with people who can give you interviews or can lead you to the people who will interview you.

So I wrote this section to help you quickly put together a resume that will work just fine in most situations. This section even includes tips on using your resume to get a job in less time.

Later, as time permits, you can read Section Two to create a more advanced resume. You can also browse through the book's many sample resumes to get ideas for your own resume and use the other sections to learn much more about yourself, resumes, and job hunting. But, if you want to keep things simple, this first section may be all you really need to put together today the resume that you can use tomorrow.

Chapters in This Section

Chapter 1: Quick Tips for Creating and Using a Resume

Provides specific information on how to create and use a resume in your search for a new job.

Chapter 2: Create a Simple Resume in About an Hour

Presents an "Instant Resume Worksheet" and a variety of tips to develop a basic resume that will give you a quick start on your job search.

Chapter 3: Write a Skills Resume in Just a Few Hours

Shows you how to write a resume that will emphasize your skills and that offers, for some, significant advantages over a more traditional chronological resume format.

Chapter 4: Develop an Electronic Resume in Less Than an Hour

Explains why you need a different version of your resume for most online job hunting and how to convert your regular resume document to an electronic version.

Chapter 1

Quick Tips for Creating and Using a Resume

This chapter provides basic information on how to write and use a resume. You should read it as an introduction to the book because it will give you an overview of my opinions on resumes and how to use them during your search. Additional information on career planning, job-seeking skills, Internet resumes, and related topics is included in other chapters.

As I mentioned in the preface, this book's objective is to help you get a good job in less time. Creating a superior resume will not get you a job. No matter how good your resume is, you will still have to get interviews and do well in them before getting a job offer.

So, a legitimate question might be "Why have a resume at all?" This chapter answers that question by presenting both sides of the argument as well as my own conclusions. I also give you an overview of some guidelines for writing your resume and tips on how to use it.

While all topics in this chapter are covered in more detail later, this chapter is an introduction that will help you understand the basics of writing and using a resume as one tool in your search for a new job.

What Is a Resume?

As a first step in creating a resume, examine what a resume is and consider what it can and cannot do. The word "resume" describes a one- or two-page summary of your life and employment history. While traditionally submitted on paper, resumes also are sent in electronic form over the Internet. Whatever a resume's form, the idea is to highlight specific parts of your past that demonstrate that you can do a particular job well.

A resume presents you to prospective employers who—based on their response to the resume—may or may not grant you an interview. Along with the application form, the resume is the tool employers use most to screen job seekers.

So, a resume is clearly a tool to use in getting a job, right? The answer to this is both yes and no.

Some People Say You Don't Need a Resume

For a variety of reasons, many career professionals suggest that resumes aren't needed at all. Some of these reasons make a lot of sense and are detailed in the following sections.

Resumes Aren't Good Job Search Tools

It's true: Resumes don't do a good job of getting you an interview. Other methods (as discussed in Sections Four and Five) do a better job. When used in the traditional way, your resume is more likely to get you screened out than screened in.

Some Jobs Don't Require Resumes

Employers seeking to fill office, managerial, professional, and technical positions often want the details provided in a resume. But for many jobs, particularly some entry-level, trade, or unskilled positions, resumes typically aren't required. Often, completing an application is all that's required.

Some Job Search Methods Don't Require Resumes

Many people get jobs without using a resume at all. In most cases, these people get interviews because they are known to the employer or are referred by someone. In these situations, a resume might help; but the employer might not even ask for it.

Some Resume Experts Call a Resume by Another Name

Many other names are used in place of the word "resume," including "professional job power report," "curriculum vitae or CV," "employment proposal," and other terms. One resume book author, for example, advises you not to use a resume. Instead, he advises you to use a "qualifications brief." In all their forms, though, they are really various types of resumes.

Some Good Reasons Why You Should Have a Resume

Although there are some legitimate arguments for why a resume isn't all that important, the reality is that most job seekers will need to have a resume. In my opinion, there are several good reasons why this is so.

Employers Usually Ask for Resumes

If an employer asks for a resume, why make excuses? This alone is reason enough to have one.

Resumes Help Structure Your Communications

A good resume requires you to clarify your job objective; select related skills, education, work, or other experiences; and list accomplishments—and present all this in a short format. Doing this is an essential step in the job search, even if you don't use the resume. If you've put some effort into writing your resume, you'll find that you're that much better prepared to speak about yourself in networking situations and interviews.

If Used Properly, a Resume Can Be an Effective Job Search Tool

A well-done resume presents details of your experiences efficiently so that an employer can refer to them as needed. It can also be used as a tool to present the skills you have to support your job objective and to present details that are often not solicited in a preliminary interview. In other words, the resume helps you tell the employer what you want them to know about you.

A Big Problem with Resumes Is That Everyone Is an Expert

A resume is one of those things that almost everyone seems to know more about than you do. If you were to show your resume to any three people, you would probably get three different suggestions on how to improve it.

One person might tell you that you really only need a one-page resume ("And how come no references are listed?"). Another will tell you that you should list all your hobbies plus your spelling bee victory from the sixth grade. The third may tell you that your resume is boring and that you should hand print it in red ink on a brown paper bag to get attention.

QUICK TIP

Few experts agree on the best way to prepare your resume. This means that *you* will have to become your own expert and make some decisions on how to present your qualifications. I'm here to help.

Resume Basics—for Print and Electronic Formats

I've developed some basic guidelines you should consider as you develop your resume. While these aren't hard-and-fast rules, they are based on many years of experience and make good common sense.

Many of these guidelines assume a traditional, printed-on-paper format rather than a resume submitted electronically (you can read more on resumes for the Internet and other electronic uses in Chapter 4). But you will likely need a paper resume *and* an electronic resume, and this advice will help in either case.

Length: Make Every Word Count

Opinions differ on length, but one to two pages are usually enough. If you are seeking a managerial, professional, or technical position and have at least several years of experience, if not more, two pages is the norm. In most cases, a busy person will not read all of a resume that is longer than two or three pages. Shorter resumes are often more difficult to write, but when done properly, they can pay off.

If you can't get everything on one page without crowding, you are better off going on to two pages. Just be sure that if you end up having only about a page and a half of content, that you spread the text over the two pages to fill up those two pages and not leave a lot of white space.

Quick Alert

Surveys have consistently shown that most employers and recruiters read resumes in only 10 to 30 seconds. That's all! The more unnecessary words you include in your resume, the more likely it is that the important information won't get read at all. So, keep your resume short and concise.

Honesty Is the Best Policy

Some people lie on their resumes and claim credentials that they don't have, hoping that no one will find out. Many organizations now verify this information, sometimes long after a person is hired.

(continued)

(continued)

> People lose their jobs over such lies. So never lie on your resume. That does not mean that you have to present negative information! Make sure that everything you put in your resume is positive and supports your job objective in some direct way. If you really can do the job you are seeking, someone will hire you. You will sleep better, too.

Eliminate Errors

I am amazed how often an otherwise good resume has typographical, grammatical, or punctuation errors. Employers who notice will not think kindly of you. So dont have any! (Actually, this should be "don't have any!" which, if you did not notice, should encourage you to pay attention here.)

Even if you are good at proofreading, find someone else who is good at proofreading and ask this person to review your resume. Carefully. If possible, wait at least one day (or longer, if you can) before reading your draft to approach it with fresh eyes.

QUICK TIP

A day's delay will allow you to notice what your resume says, rather than what you think it says.

Then, after you've read your resume, read it again to make sure you catch the errors. Then go over it again.

Use Action Words and Stress Accomplishments—Don't Be Humble!

Most resumes are boring. So don't simply list what your duties were; emphasize what you got done! Employers want to know what you can do for them—how you can help them solve their problems, reach their goals, and edge out the competition. If you only tell them your basic past duties, you aren't distinguishing yourself from other job seekers. All resumes can start to sound alike. But, if you highlight accomplishments, you will set yourself apart from your competition by showing employers how you can add value. Like an interview, your resume is no place to be humble. If you don't communicate what you can do, who will?

Quick Alert

Make sure that you mention specific skills you have to do the job, as well as any accomplishments and credentials. Even a resume put together quickly can include some of these elements, as you will soon see.

The list entitled "Use Action Words and Phrases" in Chapter 2 will give you ideas on how to word your accomplishments, as will the sample resumes throughout the book.

Make Every Word Count

Write a long rough draft and then edit, edit, edit. If a word or phrase does not support your job objective, consider dropping it. Force yourself to shorten your resume to include only those words that build a case for why you should get an interview. You can start by putting down too much information to make sure you're not leaving anything out or shortchanging yourself. But then you need to boil it all down to only the essential information.

Write It Yourself

Although I expect you to use ideas and even words or phrases you like from the sample resumes in this book, it is most important that your resume represent *you* and not someone else. Present your own skills and experience, and support them with your own accomplishments.

If you do not have good written communication skills, get help from someone who does. Just make sure that your resume ends up sounding like you wrote it.

Appearance: Make It Look Good

Your resume's overall appearance will affect an employer's opinion of you. In a matter of seconds, the employer will form either a positive or a negative opinion. Is your resume well laid out? Is it crisp and professional looking? Does it include good use of white space?

Photocopying and Printing

Almost all printed resumes are produced on high-quality ink-jet or laser printers with word-processing software such as Word or WordPerfect. If you don't have a computer and printer that can produce high-quality print, have the production done by someone who does. Your resume *must* be of the highest quality, so don't even consider using an old printer that does not produce excellent print. When you're satisfied with your resume, you may want to print larger quantities than one-by-one on your computer printer. In that case, consider having a print shop make good quality photocopies of your resume from a laser-printed original or your word-processing file.

Most quick-print shops, including the national chains such as FedEx Kinko's and PIP Printing, will do the word processing and printing for a modest fee, or you can pay an hourly rental fee to do it yourself on their equipment. Ask to see samples of their work and fees—and be willing to go to a few places to get the quality you want.

Quick Alert

Don't print too many copies of your resume at one time. Start with about 25 to 50 or even fewer because you'll probably want to make changes to it as you go along and apply for different jobs. You might be tempted to make hundreds of copies to do a large mailing, but resist that temptation. Mass mailings are usually not an effective job search method.

Use Good Paper

Never print your resume on cheap, thin paper like that typically used for photocopies. Papers come in different qualities, and employers can see the difference. Papers that include cotton fibers have a richer texture and feel that is appropriate for a professional-looking resume.

Most stationery and office-supply stores carry better papers, as do quick-print shops.

Although most resumes are printed on white, off-white, bone, or ivory colored paper, you can also use other very light colors in shades of tan or gray, but I do not recommend red, pink, or green tints. Also avoid heavily textured, dark papers; they will not produce clean copies and will not show up well if your resume is scanned

Once you've selected your paper, get matching envelopes. You may also find matching "Monarch" size papers and envelopes. This smaller-sized paper, when folded once, makes for an inexpensive and perfectly acceptable thank-you note.

The Most Important Rule of All

Making contacts and getting interviews is far more important than having a "perfect" resume. So your task is to create a simple but acceptable resume quickly—then use it in an active job search. You can create a better resume later but use your simple one to get started on your job search without delay.

Three Types of Resumes

To keep this simple, I'm going to discuss only three types of resumes. There are other, more specialized types, but these are generally the most useful: the chronological resume, the skills resume, and the combination resume.

The Chronological Resume

The word "chronology" refers to a sequence of events in time, and the primary feature of this type of resume is the listing of jobs you've held from the most recent to the least recent. This is the simplest of resumes and can be an effective format if you use it properly. Chapter 2 shows you how to create this basic type of resume.

The Skills, or Functional, Resume

Instead of listing your experience under each job, this resume style clusters your experiences under major skill areas. For example, if you are strong in "communication skills," you could list a variety of work and other experiences under that heading. You would also include listings for several other of your major skill areas.

This format would make little sense, of course, unless your job objective *requires* these skills. For this reason and others, a skills resume is often more difficult to write than a simple chronological resume. But if you have limited paid work experience, are changing careers, or have not worked for a while, a skills resume may be a superior way to present your strengths and avoid displaying your weaknesses.

The Combination, or Creative, Resume

You can combine elements of both the chronological and skills formats in various ways to improve the clarity or presentation of your resume. There are also creative formats that defy categorization but that are clever and have worked for some people. I've seen handwritten resumes (usually *not* a good idea); unusual paper colors, sizes, and shapes; resumes with tasteful drawings and borders; and lots of other ideas. Some of these resumes were well done and well received; others were not.

Weird Resume Formats

For your entertainment, here are some resume formats and presentations that I have seen or know of. Please, if you ever credit me for this list, be sure to mention that I thought many of these were bad ideas. But, then again, some of them did work.

- A cluster of helium-filled balloons, each with a copy of the same resume attached and a note saying, "Please hire me!"
- A small gift bag containing a handwritten resume and a stuffed bear. The bear was holding the candidate's JIST Card (which you will learn about in Chapter 3).
- A box of candy with a resume inside.

- A 24-x-24-inch box, shipped overnight, with a balloon and confetti inside. As the recipient opened the box, the balloon floated up and spread confetti around. This, of course, was intended to surprise and delight. The balloon had a resume attached to a string. This one got some laughs but no job, other than cleaning up the confetti.
- And, yes, I really have seen a resume handwritten on a melon that was painted white.

I could keep going, but I don't want to encourage these types of resumes. They certainly get attention, and some people insist that they helped them land jobs. Such resumes might even make some sense in certain creative jobs such as marketing, graphic design, or sales—or in creative industries and organizations. But, for most situations, my advice is to stick to less outrageous approaches.

"Send Your Resume to Lots of Strangers and, if It Is Good Enough, You Will Get Job Offers" and Other Fairy Tales

You've probably gotten the message loud and clear by now that your resume is only as good as how you use it. That is why I suggest doing a simple resume early in your job search—one you can create in a few hours. This approach allows you to get on with actively getting interviews rather than sitting at home working on a better resume. Later, you can do an improved one.

Resumes Don't Get Jobs

Contrary to the advice of many people who write resume books, writing a "dynamite" or "perfect" (or whatever) resume will rarely get you the job you want. That will happen only following an interview, with just a few odd exceptions. So the task in the job search is to get interviews and to do well in them. Sending out lots of resumes to people you don't know—and most other traditional resume advice—is a lot of baloney (or, if you prefer, bologna).

Seven Steps to Getting the Job You Want

Although I can't teach you all there is to know about getting a job in this book, I have included some information in Section Five that will help. For those of you who are particularly anxious to get on with your job search without delay, following are some basic tips on getting a good job that I have learned over many years.

1. **Know your skills and their value.** If you don't know what you are good at and what difference you can make to an employer, how can you expect anyone else to figure it out? One employer survey found that about 80 percent of those who made it to the interview did not do a good job presenting the skills they had to do the job. If you don't know your skills and accomplishments and how they relate to a particular job, you can't write a good resume or perform well in an interview, and are unlikely to get a good job.

2. **Have a clear job objective.** If you don't know where you want to go, it will be most difficult to get there. You can write a resume without having a job objective, but it won't be a good one. Section Two will help you with this issue.

3. **Know where and how to look.** Since three out of four jobs are not advertised, you will have to use other job search techniques to find them. Section Five provides additional information on the techniques I recommend you use in your search for a job.

4. **Spend at least 30 to 40 hours a week looking if you're unemployed and about 10 to 15 hours a week if you're currently employed.** Most job seekers spend far less than this and, as a result, take much longer to find a new job than they need to. So, if you want to get a better job in less time, plan on spending more time on your job search.

5. **Get two interviews a day.** It sounds impossible but this *can* be done once you redefine what counts as an interview. Section Five will help you do this and get those two interviews a day.

Compare getting two interviews a day to the average job seeker's activity level of four or five interviews a *month,* and you see how it can make a big difference.

6. **Do well in interviews.** You are unlikely to get a job offer unless you do well in this critical situation. I've reviewed the research on what it takes to do well in an interview and found, happily, that you can improve your interview performance relatively easily. Knowing what skills you have and being able to support them with examples is a good start. Section Two includes a chapter on identifying your key skills and helps to prepare you for interviews—as well as for writing a superior resume.

7. **Follow up on all contacts.** Following up can make a big difference in the results you get in your search for a new job. Tips for sending thank-you notes appear in Section Four and other tips for following up are provided in Section Five and elsewhere.

No one should ever say that looking for a job is easy. But I have learned that you can take steps to make the process a bit easier and shorter than it typically is. Getting your resume together is something that hangs many people up for entirely too long. The next two chapters help you solve that problem.

Chapter 2

Create a Simple Resume in About an Hour

You can write a basic resume in about an hour. It will not be a fancy one, and you may want to write a better one later, but I suggest you develop the simple one first. Even if you decide to create a more sophisticated resume later, doing a quick one now will allow you to use it in your job search within 24 hours.

The activities in this chapter will also prepare you to take better advantage of the material in other chapters. So don't resist—get out your pen and get to work.

Keeping things simple has its advantages. This chapter does just that by presenting information, examples, and an Instant Resume Worksheet to help you write a basic chronological resume in about an hour. It also includes tips to improve your basic resume that would, for most, be worth an extra bit of time.

A chronological resume is easy to develop, which gives this format a big advantage over other styles. It works best for those who have had several years of experience in the same type of job they are seeking now. This is because a chronological resume clearly displays your recent work experience. If you want to change careers, have been out of the workforce recently, or do not have much paid work experience related to the job you want, a chronological resume may not be the best format for you. In these instances, you might want to use a skills resume, which is presented in Chapter 3.

Most employers will find a chronological resume perfectly acceptable, as long as it is neat and has no errors. You can use it early in your job search while you work on a more sophisticated resume.

Quick Tip

The important point is to get an acceptable resume together quickly so you won't be sitting at home worrying about your resume instead of being out job hunting.

Two Chronological Resume Samples

Before your own chronological resume, you might find it helpful to see a couple of samples. Two sample resumes for the same person follow, and both use a chronological format. The first (figure 2-1) is a simple one, but it works well enough in this situation because Judith is looking for a job in her present career field, has a good job history, and has related education and training. Note that she wants to move up in responsibility and emphasizes the skills and education that will help her do so.

Figure 2-1: A simple chronological resume.

Judith J. Jones

115 South Hawthorne Avenue
Chicago, Illinois 66204
tel: (312) 653-9217
email: jj@earthlink.com

JOB OBJECTIVE

A position in the office management, accounting, or administrative assistant area, requiring initiative and ability to multi-task.

EDUCATION AND TRAINING

Acme Business College, Lincoln, IL
Graduate of a one-year business program.

John Adams High School, South Bend, IN
Diploma, business education.

U.S. Army
Financial procedures, accounting functions.

Other: Continuing-education classes and workshops in business communication, spreadsheet and database applications, scheduling systems, and customer relations.

EXPERIENCE

2003–present—Claims Processor, Blue Spear Insurance Co., Wilmette, IL. Process customer medical claims, develop management reports based on created spreadsheets and develop management reports based on those forms, exceed productivity goals.

2002–2003—Returned to school to upgrade business and computer skills. Completed courses in advanced accounting, spreadsheet and database programs, office management, human relations, and new office techniques.

1999–2002—E4, U.S. Army. Assigned to various stations as a specialist in finance operations. Promoted prior to honorable discharge.

1998–1999—Sandy's Boutique, Wilmette, IL. Responsible for counter sales, display design, cash register, and other tasks.

1996–1998—Held part-time and summer jobs throughout high school.

STRENGTHS AND SKILLS

Reliable, hardworking, and good with people. General ledger, accounts payable, and accounts receivable. Proficient in Microsoft Word, WordPerfect, Excel, and Outlook.

One nice feature is that this job seeker put her recent business schooling in both the education and experience sections. Doing this filled a job gap and allows her to present recent training as equivalent to work experience. This resume also includes a "Strengths and Skills" section, where Judy presents some special qualifications and technical skills.

This same resume is then improved in the second example (figure 2-2). The improved resume adds a number of features, including a more thorough job objective, a "Special Skills and Abilities" section, and more accomplishments and skills. Notice, for example, the impact of the numbers she adds to this resume in statements such as "top 30% of class" and "decreased department labor costs by more than $30,000 a year."

You should be able to do a resume like the one in figure 2-2 with an hour or two of additional work over the one in figure 2-1. As I think you will realize, most employers will be impressed by the additional positive information it provides.

Quick Tip

Besides being fairly quick to create, these two resumes have an added benefit in an Internet-oriented world. If you will be submitting your resume to an online database or via e-mail, this format will require only minor modification. Fancier resumes with graphics, bullets, borders, and other special formatting must be stripped of their more decorative elements to become an electronic resume. In Chapter 4, you'll find much more detail on writing and formatting your resume for use on the Internet. That chapter also discusses the importance of including many "keywords" (or buzzwords) in your resume.

Figure 2-2: The improved chronological resume.

Judith J. Jones

115 South Hawthorne Avenue
Chicago, Illinois 66204

jj@earthlink.com
(312) 653-9217

JOB OBJECTIVE

Seeking a position requiring excellent business management expertise in an office environment. Position should require a variety of skills, including office management, word processing, and spreadsheet and database application use.

EDUCATION AND TRAINING

Acme Business College, Lincoln, IL
Completed one-year program in Professional Office Management. Achieved GPA in top 30% of class. Courses included word processing, accounting theory and systems, advanced spreadsheet and database applications, graphics design, time management, and supervision.

John Adams High School, South Bend, IN
Graduated with emphasis on business courses. Earned excellent grades in all business topics and won top award for word-processing speed and accuracy.

Other: Continuing-education programs at own expense, including business communications, customer relations, computer applications, and sales techniques.

EXPERIENCE

2003–present—**Claims Processor, Blue Spear Insurance Company,** Wilmette, IL. Process 50 complex medical insurance claims per day, almost 20% above department average. Created a spreadsheet report process that decreased department labor costs by more than $30,000 a year. Received two merit raises for performance.

2002–2003—**Returned to business school to gain advanced office skills.**

1999–2002—**Finance Specialist (E4), U.S. Army.** Systematically processed more than 200 invoices per day from commercial vendors. Trained and supervised eight employees. Devised internal system allowing 15% increase in invoices processed with a decrease in personnel. Managed department with a budget equivalent of more than $350,000 a year. Honorable discharge.

1998–1999—**Sales Associate promoted to Assistant Manager, Sandy's Boutique,** Wilmette, IL. Made direct sales and supervised four employees. Managed daily cash balances and deposits, made purchasing and inventory decisions, and handled all management functions during owner's absence. Sales increased 26% and profits doubled during tenure.

1996–1998—**Held various part-time and summer jobs through high school while maintaining GPA 3.0/4.0.** Earned enough to pay all personal expenses, including car insurance. Learned to deal with customers, meet deadlines, work hard, and handle multiple priorities.

STRENGTHS AND SKILLS

Reliable, with strong work ethic. Excellent interpersonal, written, and oral communication and math skills. Accept supervision well, effectively supervise others, and work well as a team member. General ledger, accounts payable, and accounts receivable expertise. Proficient in Microsoft Word, WordPerfect, Excel, and Outlook.

The Major Sections of a Chronological Resume

Now that you have seen what both basic and improved chronological resumes look like, it is time to create your own chronological resume. An Instant Resume Worksheet follows this section. I encourage you to use it to complete each part of your basic chronological resume.

Quick Tip

You may find it helpful to complete each worksheet section after you read its related tips here. I will direct you to do so.

Heading

Often, the top of a resume includes the word "Resume," just in case the reader didn't know what it was. But, since everyone will know what it is, the heading "resume" is really not necessary. However, if you are employed now and don't want your employer to know of your job search, put "Confidential Resume" at the top and hope the reader honors it.

Name

This one seems obvious, but you want to avoid some things. For example, don't use a nickname—you need to present a professional image. Even if you have to modify your name a bit from the way you typically introduce yourself, it's important to sound professional by using your full name.

Quick Reference

Refer to the appropriate chapter in Section Two for substantial additional information on handling any specific part of a resume. You should also look at the many sample resumes in Section Three to see how others have handled various situations.

Address

Don't abbreviate words such as "Street" or "Avenue." Do include your ZIP code. If you move during your job search, or expect that you might, ask a relative, friend, or neighbor in the new location if you can temporarily use his or her address for your mail. Forwarded mail will be delayed and can cause you to lose an opportunity. Get an address at the new location so that you appear to be settled there.

Quick Tip

If you're looking for a job in another location and don't know anyone there whose address you could use on your resume, look into the option of having a drop box that gives a real street address rather than a post office box. These are available for a small fee through local office-supply shops and national shipping chains such as The UPS Store.

Phone Numbers and E-mail Address

An employer is more likely to phone or e-mail you than to contact you by mail, so giving an employer this contact information is essential.

Let's start with the telephone. Use a phone number that will be answered throughout your job search. Always include your area code. Since you often will be gone (at your current job or out job-seeking, right?), you must have an answering machine or voice-mail service.

Quick Alert

Keep in mind that an employer could call at any time. Make sure that anyone who will pick up the phone knows to answer professionally and take an accurate message, including a phone number. Practice with these people if you need to, since nothing is as maddening as a garbled message with the wrong number.

I suggest that you call your answering machine or voicemail. Listen to what the outgoing message says, and how. If it has some cute, boring, or less-than-professional message, change it to one you would like your next employer to hear. You can go back to your standard howling-wolves answer after you get your next job.

As you look at this book's sample resumes, notice that some provide more than one phone number or an explanation following the number. For example, "555-299-3643 (messages)" quickly communicates that the caller is likely to be asked to leave a message rather than reach you in person. Adding "555-264-3720 (cell)" will give employers another calling option.

If you have an e-mail address, definitely include it. If you don't have an e-mail account, give serious consideration to getting one. Many services, such as Hotmail.com and Yahoo.com offer free e-mail. Even if you don't have Internet access at home, you can check your mail at a public library or on a friend's computer. Just be sure that if you do give out an e-mail address, you will check it regularly to see whether you've received any mail.

Do It Now

Now, take a moment to complete the identification section in the Instant Resume Worksheet on page 33.

Job Objective

Although you could put together a simple resume without a job objective, it is wise to include one. Doing so will allow you to select resume content that will directly support the job you want. In a more advanced version of your resume, you might choose to omit the objective and include a Summary of Qualifications section instead, but for now the objective will help you focus your thinking and create a sharply focused resume.

Carefully write your job objective so that it does not exclude you from jobs you would consider. For example, if you use a job title like "administrative assistant," ask yourself whether doing so would exclude you from other jobs you would consider. Look at how Judith Jones presented her job objective in her basic resume (figure 2-1):

> A position in the office management, accounting, or administrative assistant area, requiring initiative and ability to multi-task.

This resume keeps her options open more than saying "administrative assistant." And her improved resume's job objective says even more:

> Seeking a position requiring excellent business management expertise in an office environment. Position should require a variety of skills, including office management, word processing, and spreadsheet and database application use.

A good job objective allows you to be considered for more responsible jobs than you have held in the past, or to accept positions with different job titles that use similar skills.

I see many objectives that emphasize what the person wants but that do not provide information on what he or she offers the employer. For example, an objective that says "Interested in a position that allows me to be creative and that offers adequate pay and advancement opportunities" is not good. Who cares? This objective, a real one that someone wrote, displays a self-centered, "gimme" approach that will turn off most employers. Yours should emphasize what you can do, your skills, and where you want to use them.

Refer to the following examples of simple but useful job objectives. Most provide some information on the type of job sought as well as on the skills offered.

Quick Tip

The best objectives avoid a narrow job title and position you to be considered for a range of appropriate jobs.

The sample resumes throughout this book include job objectives that you can review to see how others have phrased them. Browse these objectives for ideas.

Do It Now

Jot down your own draft job objective and refine it until it "feels good." Then rewrite it on page 33 of the Instant Resume Worksheet.

Sample Job Objectives

Responsible general office position to utilize solid clerical and computer skills in a fast-paced, medium-sized organization.

Management position in the warehousing industry requiring supervisory, problem-solving, and organizational skills.

Computer programmer or systems analyst position. Prefer an accounting-oriented emphasis and a solution-oriented organization.

Medical assistant or coordinator in a physician's office, hospital, or other health services environment.

Responsible position that requires skills in public relations, writing, and reporting.

An aggressive and success-oriented professional, seeking a sales position offering both challenge and growth.

Desire position in office management requiring flexibility, strong organizational skills, and an ability to interact with people at all levels of the organization.

Education and Training

Lead with your strengths. Recent graduates or those with good academic or training credentials but weak work experience should put their education and training toward the top because it represents a more important part of their experience. More experienced workers with work history related to their job objective can put their education and training toward the end.

You can drop the Education and Training section if it doesn't support your job objective or if you don't have the credentials typically expected of those seeking similar positions. This is particularly true if you have lots of work experience in your career area. Usually, though, you should emphasize the most recent or highest level of education or training that relates to the job.

Quick Tip

Drop or downplay details that don't support your job objective. For example, if you possess related education but not a degree, tell employers what you do have. Include details of relevant courses, good grades, related extracurricular activities, and accomplishments.

Depending on your situation, your education and training could be the most important part of your resume, so beef it up with details if you need to.

Do It Now

Look at the sample resumes in Section Three for ideas. Then, on a separate piece of paper, rough out your Education and Training section. Then edit it to its final form and write it on pages 33–34 of the Instant Resume Worksheet.

Use Action Words and Phrases

Use active rather than passive words and phrases throughout your resume. Here is a short list of active words to give you some ideas:

Achieved	Established priorities	Organized
Administered	Expanded	Planned
Analyzed	Implemented	Presented
Controlled	Improved	Promoted
Coordinated	Increased productivity (profits)	Reduced expenses
Created	Initiated	Researched
Designed	Innovated	Scheduled
Developed	Instructed	Solved
Diagnosed	Modified	Supervised
Directed	Negotiated	Trained
Established policy		

Work Experience

This resume section provides the details of your work history, starting with the most recent job. If you have significant work history, list each job along with details of what you accomplished and special skills you used. Emphasize skills that directly relate to the job objective on your resume.

Volunteer and military work experience are usually listed in separate sections after your paid civilian work history. You may, however, include volunteer work in the regular Work Experience section if you have limited paid work experience or if the volunteer work is highly relevant to your job objective. Similarly, you may include military experience in the Work Experience section if you consider your military experience to be a significant part of your career history.

Previous/Current Job Titles

You can modify the titles you've had to more accurately reflect your responsibilities. For example, if your title was sales clerk but you frequently opened and closed the store and were often left in charge, you might use the more descriptive title of Night Sales Manager. Always check with your previous supervisors to make sure they approve of this and will back you up when a prospective employer checks your references.

Quick Tip

If you were promoted, handle the promotion as a separate job, listing the dates that you held each position to show how you progressed with one organization.

Previous/Current Employers

Provide the organization's name and list the city, state, or province in which it was located. A street address or supervisor's name is not necessary—you can provide those details on a separate sheet of references if you are asked for them.

Employment Dates

If you have large gaps in employment that are not easily explained, use full years to avoid emphasizing the gaps, instead of mentioning the months in which you started and left. Additional information on handling this and other problems is covered in Chapter 8. If there was a significant period when you did not work, did you do anything that could explain it in a positive way? School? Travel? Raise a family? Self-employment? Even if you mowed lawns and painted houses for money while you were unemployed, that could count as self-employment. It's much better than saying you were unemployed.

Duties and Accomplishments

In writing about your work experience, be sure to use action words and emphasize what you accomplished. Quantify what you did and provide evidence that you did it well. Take particular care to mention skills that directly relate to doing well in the job you want now.

If your previous jobs are not directly related to what you want to do now, emphasize skills you used in previous jobs that could be used in the new job. For example, someone who waits on tables has to deal with people and work quickly under pressure—skills needed in many other jobs such as accounting and managing.

Quick Tip

Look up the descriptions of jobs you have held in the past and jobs you want now in a book titled the *Occupational Outlook Handbook (OOH)*. Available in most libraries, this book will tell you the skills needed to succeed in the new job. Emphasize these and similar skills in your resume. (See Chapter 7 for more about the *OOH*.) You can also access the *OOH* online at www.careeroink.com or www.bls.gov/oco.

Do It Now

Use separate sheets of paper to write rough drafts of what you will use in your resume. Edit it so that every word contributes something. When you're done, transfer your statements to pages 36–38 of the Instant Resume Worksheet.

Professional Organizations

This is an optional section where you can list your activities with job-related professional, humanitarian, or other groups. These activities may be worth mentioning, particularly if you were an officer or were active in some other way. Mention accomplishments or awards you earned during these affiliations. Many of the sample resumes in this book include statements about accomplishments to show you how to do this.

Quick Tip

Emphasize accomplishments! Think about the things you accomplished in jobs, school, the military, and other settings. Make sure that you emphasize these things in your resume, even if it seems like bragging.

Do It Now

Go to page 38 in the Instant Resume Worksheet and list your job-related efforts in professional organizations and other groups.

Recognition and Awards

If you have received any formal honors or awards that support your job objective, consider mentioning them. You may create a separate section for your awards if you have at least two to list, or you can put them in the Work Experience, Skills, Education, or Personal section.

Personal Information

Years ago, resumes included personal details such as height, weight, marital status, hobbies, leisure activities, and other trivia. Please do not do this. Current laws do not allow an employer to base hiring decisions on certain points, so providing this information can cause some employers to toss your resume. For the same reason, do not include a photo of yourself.

Quick Reminder

Remember my earlier advice to make every word count. If something does not support your job objective, delete it. If you think the information can help you, go ahead and use it. Look at the sample resumes in Section Three for ideas and decide for yourself.

Although a Personal section is optional, I sometimes like to end a resume on a personal note. Some resumes provide a touch of humor or playfulness as well as selected positives from outside school and work. This section is also a good place to list significant community involvements, a willingness to relocate, or personal characteristics an employer might like. But keep it short.

Do It Now

Turn to page 38 in the Instant Resume Worksheet and list any personal information that you feel is appropriate and relevant.

References

It is not necessary to include the names of your references on a resume. You can do better things with the precious space. It's also not necessary to state "references available on request" at the bottom of your resume, because that is obvious. If an employer wants your references, he or she knows to ask you for them.

Line up references in advance. Pick people who know your work as an employee, volunteer, or student. Make sure that they will express nice things about you by asking what they would say if asked. Push for negatives and don't feel hurt if you get some. Nobody is perfect, and it gives you a chance to delete references before they do you damage. Once you know who to include, type a list of references on a separate sheet. Include names, addresses, phone numbers, and details of why they are on your list. You can give this to employers who ask for references.

Be aware that some employers are not allowed to give references over the phone. I have refused to hire people who probably had good references but about whom I could not get information. If this is the case with a previous employer, ask the employer to write a letter of reference for you to photocopy as needed. This is a good idea in general, so you may want to ask employers for one even if they have no rules against phone references.

The Final Draft

At this point you should have completed the Instant Resume Worksheet on pages 33–38. Carefully review dates, addresses, phone numbers, spelling, and other details. You can use the worksheet as a guide for preparing a better-than-average chronological resume.

Use the sample chronological resumes from this chapter as the basis for creating your resume. Additional examples of resumes appear in Chapters 3, 4, 10, and 11. Look them over for writing and formatting ideas. The sample resumes in Chapter 3 tend to be simpler and easier to write and format than some of the more advanced samples found in Chapters 10 and 11 and will provide better models for creating a resume quickly.

Quick Reminder

Remember that your initial objective is not to do a wonderful, powerful, or creative resume. That can come later. You first need an acceptable resume, one that you can use tomorrow to begin an active job search. So keep your first resume simple. Set a tight deadline so that the lack of a resume does not become a barrier in your job search.

Once you have completed the Instant Resume Worksheet, you have the information you need for a basic resume. If you have access to a computer, go ahead and put the information into the form of a resume. Most word-processing programs have resume templates or "wizards" that will help make it look good.

If you do not have access to a computer, have someone else type and format your resume. But whether you do it yourself or have it done, carefully review it for typographical or other errors that may have slipped in. Then, when you are certain that everything is correct, have the final version prepared.

INSTANT RESUME WORKSHEET

Identification

Name ______________________________

Home address ______________________________

______________________________ ZIP code ____________

Phone number and description (if any) (   ) ______________________________

____

Alternate phone number and description (   ) ______________________________

____

E-mail address ______________________________

Your Job Objective

____

____

____

____

____

____

Education and Training

Highest Level/Most Recent Education or Training

Institution name ______________________________

City, state/province (optional) ______________________________

Certificate or degree ______________________________

Specific courses or programs that relate to your job objective ______________________________

____

____

(continued)

(continued)

Related awards, achievements, and extracurricular activities ______________________

____

____

Anything else that might support your job objective, like good grades ____________

____

____

____

____

College/Post High School

Institution name ____

City, state/province (optional) ____________________________________

Certificate or degree ____

____

Specific courses or programs that relate to your job objective ______________________

____

____

Related awards, achievements, and extracurricular activities ______________________

____

____

Anything else that might support your job objective, like good grades ____________

____

____

____

____

High School

Institution name ____

City, state/province (optional) ____________________________________

Certificate or degree ______________________

Specific courses or programs that relate to your job objective ______________________

Related awards, achievements, and extracurricular activities ______________________

Anything else that might support your job objective, like good grades ______________________

Armed Services Training and Other Training or Certification

Institution name ______________________

Specific courses or programs that relate to your job objective ______________________

Related awards, achievements, and extracurricular activities ______________________

Anything else that might support your job objective, like good grades ______________________

(continued)

(continued)

Related Workshops, Seminars, Informal Learning, or Any Other Training

____

____

____

____

____

____

Experience

Most Recent Position

Dates: from ______________ to ______________

Organization name ______________________

City, state/province ______________________

Your job title(s) ______________________

Duties ______________________

____

____

Skills ______________________

____

____

Equipment or software you used ______________________

____

____

Promotions, accomplishments, and anything else positive ______________

____

____

Next Most Recent Position

Dates: from ______________________ to ______________________

Organization name ______________________

City, state/province ______________________

Your job title(s) ______________________

Duties ______________________

____

____

Skills ______________________

____

____

Equipment or software you used ______________________

____

____

Promotions, accomplishments, and anything else positive ______________________

____

____

Next Most Recent Position

Dates: from ______________________ to ______________________

Organization name ______________________

City, state/province ______________________

Your job title(s) ______________________

Duties ______________________

____

____

(continued)

(continued)

Skills____

Equipment or software you used __________________________

Promotions, accomplishments, and anything else positive ______________

Any Other Work or Volunteer Experience

Professional Organizations

Personal Information

Chapter 3

Write a Skills Resume in Just a Few Hours

Although it takes a bit longer to develop a skills resume than it does a chronological resume, you should consider writing one for a variety of reasons. This chapter will show you why a skills resume may be good to consider and how to write one.

Be sure to read Chapter 1 and do the activities in Chapter 2 (particularly the Instant Resume Worksheet) before completing the skills resume described here.

This chapter shows you how to write a resume that is organized around the key skills you have that are needed in the job you want.

Quick Alert

In its simplest form, a chronological resume is little more than a list of job titles and other details. If you want to change your career or increase your responsibility, the chronological style can often be ineffective. This chapter will help you highlight your skills that can be used to transition to a new career or promotion.

Employers and recruiters usually look for candidates with a work history that fits the position they have to fill. If they want to hire a cost accountant, they look for someone who has done this work. If you are a recent graduate or have little experience in the career or at the level you now want, you will find that a simple chronological resume emphasizes your lack of related experience rather than your ability to do the job.

A skills resume avoids these problems by highlighting what you have done under specific skills headings rather than under past jobs. If you hitchhiked across the country for two years, a skills resume won't necessarily display this as an employment gap. Instead, you could say "Traveled extensively throughout the country and am familiar with most major market areas." That could be very useful experience for certain positions.

Quick Alert

Because a skills resume can hide your problems, some employers do not like it. But if a chronological resume highlights a weakness, a skills resume may help get you an interview (with an employer who doesn't dislike skills resumes) rather than get screened out. Who wins? You do.

Even if you don't have anything to hide, a skills resume emphasizes your key skills and experiences more clearly. And you can always include a chronological list of jobs as one part of your skills resume, as shown in some of the examples in this book. So everyone should consider a skills resume.

A Sample Skills Resume

Following is a basic skills resume (figure 3-1). The example is for a recent high school graduate whose only paid work experience has been in fast food. Read it and ask yourself: If you were an employer, would you consider interviewing Lisa? For most people, the answer is yes.

Quick Reference

This resume is a good example of how a skills resume can help someone who does not have the best credentials. It allows the job seeker to present school and extracurricular activities to good effect. It is a strong format choice because it lets her highlight strengths without emphasizing her limited work experience. It doesn't say where she worked or for how long, yet it gives her a shot at many jobs.

Although the sample resume is simple, it presents Lisa in a positive way. She is looking for an entry-level job in a nontechnical area, so many employers will be more interested in her skills than in her job-specific experience. What work experience she does have is presented as a plus. And notice how she listed her gymnastics experience next to "Hardworking."

You may have more work experience than shown in this sample. If so, look at the sample resumes at the end of this chapter and at those in Section Three—there are examples of skills resumes for people with more education and experience.

Quick Alert

You'll get the best results from a skills resume by using it when you have a referral to an organization instead of using it to apply cold or to an ad. Since the skills resume usually doesn't list specifics of work history, many employers will toss it out in favor of your competitors' resumes that do. So, stick with using the skills resume primarily when you're networking for a job.

Figure 3-1: A sample skills resume.

Lisa M. Rhodes

813 Lava Court • Denver, CO 81613
Home: (413) 643-2173 (leave message)
Cell: (413) 442-1659
lrhodes@netcom.net

Objective

Sales-oriented position in a retail sales or distribution business.

Skills and Abilities

Communications	Good written and verbal presentation skills. Use proper grammar and have a good speaking voice.
Interpersonal Skills	Able to get along well with coworkers and accept supervision. Received positive evaluations from previous supervisors.
Flexible	Willing to try new things and am interested in improving efficiency on assigned tasks.
Attention to Detail	Concerned with quality. Produce work that is orderly and attractive. Ensure tasks are completed correctly and on time.
Hardworking	Throughout high school, worked long hours in strenuous activities while attending school full-time. Often managed as many as 65 hours a week in school and other structured activities while maintaining above-average grades.
Customer Service	Routinely handled as many as 500 customer contacts a day (10,000 per month) in a busy retail outlet. Averaged lower than a .001% complaint rate and was given the "Employee of the Month" award in second month of employment. Received two merit increases.
Cash Sales	Handled more than $2,000 a day ($40,000 a month) in cash sales. Balanced register and prepared daily sales summary and deposits.
Reliable	Excellent attendance record; trusted to deliver daily cash deposits totaling more than $40,000 a month.

Education

Franklin High School, 2001–2004. Classes included advanced English. Member of award-winning band. Excellent attendance record. Superior communication skills. Graduated in top 30% of class.

Other

Active gymnastics competitor for four years. Learned discipline, teamwork, how to follow instructions, and hard work. Ambitious, outgoing, reliable, and have solid work ethic.

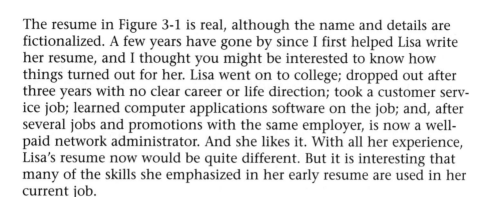

The resume in Figure 3-1 is real, although the name and details are fictionalized. A few years have gone by since I first helped Lisa write her resume, and I thought you might be interested to know how things turned out for her. Lisa went on to college; dropped out after three years with no clear career or life direction; took a customer service job; learned computer applications software on the job; and, after several jobs and promotions with the same employer, is now a well-paid network administrator. And she likes it. With all her experience, Lisa's resume now would be quite different. But it is interesting that many of the skills she emphasized in her early resume are used in her current job.

Writing a Skills Resume

The skills resume format uses a number of sections similar to those in a chronological resume. I discuss only those sections that are substantially different—the Job Objective and Skills sections. Refer to Chapter 2 for information on sections that are common to both types of resumes. The samples at the end of this chapter will give you ideas on skills resume language, organization, and layout, and how to handle special problems.

Don't be afraid to use a little creativity in writing your skills resume. You are allowed to break some rules if it makes sense.

Quick Fact

It is essential that your resume emphasize the skills you have that directly support the job you want. You will benefit greatly from the skills identification activities in Chapter 4. These include lists of skills that are of particular value in a skills resume.

Job Objective

Whereas a simple chronological resume does not require a career objective, a skills resume does. Without a reasonably clear job objective, it is not possible to select and organize the key skills you have to support that job objective. It may be that the job objective you wrote for your chronological resume is good as is, but for a skills resume, your job objective statement should answer the following questions:

- **What sort of position, title, or area of specialization do you seek?** After reading the information on job objectives in Chapter 2, you should know how to present the type of job you are seeking. Is your objective too narrow and specific? Is it so broad or vague as to be meaningless? If necessary, turn to Chapter 6 to identify your job objective more clearly.
- **What level of responsibility interests you?** Job objectives often indicate a level of responsibility, particularly for supervisory or management roles. If in doubt, always try to keep open the possibility of getting a job with a higher level of responsibility (and, often, salary) than your previous or current one. Write your job objective to include this possibility.
- **What are your most important skills?** What are the two or three most important skills or personal characteristics needed to succeed on the job you've targeted? These are often mentioned in a job objective.

QUICK REFERENCE

Review the "Sample Job Objectives" in Chapter 2 and look over the sample resumes at the end of this chapter and in Section Three. Notice that some resumes use headings such as "Position Desired" or "Career Objective" to introduce the job objective section. Many people think that these headings sound more professional than "Job Objective." It's up to you to choose the wording that works best for your situation.

The Skills Section

This section can be called "Areas of Accomplishment," "Summary of Qualifications," "Areas of Expertise and Ability," or other titles. Whatever you choose to call it, this section is what makes a skills resume. To construct it, you must carefully consider which skills you want to emphasize.

Your task is to feature the skills that are essential to success on the job you want and the skills that you have and want to use. You probably have a good idea of which skills meet both criteria, but you may find it helpful to review Chapter 5 on developing your skills language.

Note that some resumes in this book emphasize skills that are not specific to a particular job. For example, "well organized" is an important skill in many jobs. In your resume, you should provide specific examples of situations or accomplishments that show you possess such skills. You can do this by including examples from previous work or other experiences.

Key Skills List

On the next page is a list of skills considered key for success on most jobs. It is based on research on the skills employers look for in employees. So, if you have to emphasize some skills over others, include these—assuming you have them, of course.

Key Skills Needed for Success in Most Jobs

Basic Skills *Considered the Minimum to Keep a Job*	**Key Transferable Skills** *That Transfer from Job to Job and Are Most Likely to Be Needed in Jobs with Higher Pay and Responsibility*
Basic academic skills	Instructing others
Accepting supervision	Managing money and budgets
Following instructions	Managing people
Getting along well with coworkers	Meeting the public
Meeting deadlines	Working effectively as part of a team
Good attendance	Negotiating
Punctuality	Organizing/managing projects
Good work ethic	Public speaking
Productivity	Communicating orally and in writing
Honesty	Organizational effectiveness and leadership
	Self-motivation and goal setting
	Creative thinking and problem solving

In addition to the skills in the list, most jobs require skills that are specific to that particular job. For example, an accountant needs to know how to set up a general ledger, use accounting software, and develop income and expense reports. These job-specific skills are called job-content skills and can be quite important in qualifying for a job.

If you want to identify more job-specific skills, Chapter 5 will work you to distraction. You can probably write a fine skills resume without Chapter 5 and the other material in Section Two, but many will find the activities helpful.

Identify Your Key Transferable Skills

Look over the preceding key skills list and write down any skills you have and that are particularly important for the job you want. Add other skills you possess that you feel must be communicated to an employer to get the job you want. Write at least three, but no more than six, of these most important skills:

1. ______________________________

2. ______________________________

3. ______________________________

4. ______________________________

5. ______________________________

6. ______________________________

Prove Your Key Skills with a Story

Now, write each skill you listed above on a separate sheet. For each skill, write two detailed examples of when you used it. If possible, you should use work situations; but you can use other situations such as volunteer work, school activities, or other life experiences. Try to quantify the examples by giving numbers such as money saved, sales increased, or other measures to support those skills. Emphasize results you achieved and any accomplishments.

An example of what one person wrote for a key skill follows and may give you an idea of how to document your own skills.

EXAMPLE OF A KEY SKILL STORY

Key skill: Meeting deadlines

I volunteered to help my social organization raise money. I found out about special government funds, but the proposal deadline was only 24 hours away. So I stayed up all night and submitted it on time. We were one of only three whose proposals were approved, and we were awarded over $100,000 to fund a youth program for a whole year.

Edit Your Key Skills Proofs

If you carefully consider the skills needed in the story above, there are quite a few. Here are the most obvious ones: hard work, meeting deadlines, willing to help others, good written communication skills, persuasive, problem solver.

QUICK TIP

In a similar way, you can use your proof stories to demonstrate in your resume and in an interview that you have the skills to do a particular job.

Review each "proof sheet" and select those proofs that are particularly valuable in supporting your job objective. You should have at least two proof stories for each skill area. Once you have selected your proofs, rewrite them using action words and short sentences. Write the skills you needed to do these things in the margins.

When done, write statements you can use in your resume. Rewrite your proof statements and delete anything that does not reinforce the key skills you want to support.

Following is a rewrite of the proof story I provided earlier. Do a similar editing job on each of your own proofs until they are clear, short, and powerful. You can then use these statements in your resume, modifying them as needed.

Key skill rewrite

Key skill: Meeting deadlines

On 24-hour notice, submitted a complex proposal that successfully obtained over $100,000 in funding.

You could easily use this same proof story to support other skills I listed earlier, such as hard work. So, as you write and revise your proof stories, consider which key skills they can best support. Use those proofs to support those key skills in your resume.

Tips for Editing Your Draft Resume into Final Form

Before you make a final draft of your skills resume, look over the samples that follow for ideas on content and format. Several show interesting techniques that may be useful for your situation. For example, if you have a good work history, you can include a brief chronological listing of jobs. This jobs list could be before or after your skills section. If you have substantial work history, you could begin your skills resume with a summary of experience to provide the basis for details that follow.

When you have the content from the proof stories that you need for your skills resume, write your first draft. Rewrite and edit it until the resume communicates what you really want to say about yourself. Cut anything that does not support your objective. When you are done, ask someone to review it *very carefully* for typographical and other errors.

If you are having someone else prepare your resume, have someone other than yourself review the "final" copy for errors you may have overlooked. Only after you are certain that your resume contains no errors should you prepare the final version.

Your objective is to get a good job, not to keep working on your resume. So avoid the temptation to make a "perfect" resume and, instead, get this one done. Today. Then use it tomorrow. If all goes well, as I hope it does, you may never need a "better" resume.

QUICK REFERENCE

If you plan to search for jobs using the Internet, keep in mind that you'll need to use a special format. Chapter 4 describes electronic resumes and provides information on modifying your resume to this format.

More Sample Skills Resumes (and JIST Cards®)

Look over the sample resumes that follow to see how others have adapted the basic skills format to fit their situations. These examples are based on real resumes (although the names and other details are not real). I have included comments to help you understand details that may not be apparent.

The formats and designs of the resumes are intentionally basic and can be done with any word processing software. Many other skills resumes are in Section Three, including many with fancier graphics and designs. But remember that it is better to have a simple and error-free resume—and be out there using it—than to be at home working on a more elaborate one.

If all goes well, as I hope it does, you may never need a "better" resume.

A JIST Card precedes each skills resume. The JIST Card is a job search tool I developed many years ago. It is a mini-resume you can use in a variety of ways. You can attach JIST Cards to applications or resumes; give them to friends and other people in your network of contacts; enclose them in thank-you notes before or after an interview; and even put them on car windshields (really, this has been done, and with good results).

Employers like JIST Cards. The cards are short, quick to read, and present essential information in a positive way. And the many, many people who have used them tend to have good stories about how well they work.

Quick Tip

The more JIST Cards you have in circulation, the better they work. If you want to learn more about JIST Cards, refer to Chapter 13.

A JIST Card and Resume for a Career Changer

Figure 3-3 is a resume of a career changer with substantial work experience in another occupation. After working for an alarm and security systems company and at a variety of other jobs, Darrel went back to school and learned computer programming. The skills format allows him to emphasize his past business experience to support his current job objective. His resume includes no chronological jobs listing and no education dates, so it is not obvious that he is a recent graduate with little formal work experience as a programmer.

Darrel does a good job of presenting previous work experience and includes numbers to support his skills and accomplishments. Even so, the relationship between his previous work and current objective could be improved. For example, collecting bad debts requires discipline, persistence, and attention to detail—the same skills required in programming. And, although he is good at sales, his resume does not relate the skills required for sales to his new job objective of programming.

Darrel's job objective could be improved. If Darrel were here to discuss it, I'd ask him if he wants to use his selling skills *and* his programming skills in a new job. If so, he could modify his job objective to include jobs such as selling technology or computer consulting services. Or, if he wants to be a programmer, I would suggest he emphasize other transferable skills that directly support his programming objective, such as his history of meeting deadlines. Still, this resume is effective in relating his past business experience to his ability to be a programmer in a business environment.

You will notice that a JIST Card is quite small. Darrel has to pack a lot of information in a very small space. This means that every word has to support his objective. Note, for example, that the first sentence does not mention he is a new graduate, but it indicates that he is very experienced. The next few sentences present his "credentials," followed by the last line, which lists several key transferable skills.

Postscript: Darrel got a job as a programmer–systems analyst and is doing fine in his new career. He is learning new skills, including designing his company's Web site. His sales and customer service experience helped him design the site, and out-of-area Internet sales are increasing rapidly. The skills approach was effective in helping him get started in a new field.

Figure 3-2: Darrel's JIST Card.

Darrel Craig **(412) 437-6217**
Message: (412) 464-1273

Position Desired: Programmer/Systems Analyst

Skills: More than 10 years of combined education and work experience in business, data processing, and related fields. Proficient with UNIX, Java, C++, and BASIC. Certified Microsoft Systems Engineer. Knowledge of various database and applications programs in networked PC and mainframe environments. Substantial business experience including accounting, management, sales, and public relations.

Dedicated, self-starter, creative, dependable, and willing to relocate.

A Combination Skills/Chronological Resume (with JIST Card)

The resume in figure 3-5 combines elements of the chronological and skills formats. Thomas's resume breaks some "rules," but for good reasons.

Figure 3-3: Darrel's resume.

Darrel Craig

Career Objective	Challenging position in programming or related areas that would best use expertise in the business environment. Position should have opportunities for a dedicated individual with leadership abilities.
Programming Skills	Experience with business program design including payroll, inventory, database management, sales, marketing, accounting,and loan amortization reports. Knowledgeable in program design, coding, implementation, debugging, and file maintenance. Familiar with distributed PC network systems (LAN and WAN) and working knowledge of DOS, UNIX, BASIC, FORTRAN, C, and LISP, plus UML, Java, C++, and Visual Basic.
Applications and Network Software	Microsoft Certified Systems Engineer familiar with a variety of applications, including Lotus Notes, Novell NetWare, and MS Windows NT network systems, database and spreadsheet programs, and accounting and other software.
Communication and Problem Solving	Interpersonal communication strengths, public relations capabilities, innovative problem solving, and analytical talents.
Sales	A total of eight years of experience in sales and sales management. Sold security products to distributors and alarm dealers. Increased company's sales from $36,000 to more than $320,000 per month. Organized creative sales and marketing concepts. Trained sales personnel in prospecting techniques and service personnel in more efficient and consumer-friendly installation methods. Result: 90% of all new business was generated through referrals from existing customers.
Management	Managed security systems company for four years while increasing profits yearly. Supervised 20 personnel in all office, sales, accounting, inventory, and installation positions. Worked as assistant credit manager, responsible for more than $2 million per year in sales. Handled semi-annual inventory of five branch stores totaling millions of dollars.
Accounting	Balanced all books and prepared tax return forms for security systems company. Four years of experience in credit and collections. Collection rates were more than 98% each year; was able to collect a bad debt in excess of $250,000 deemed "uncollectible."
Education	School of Computer Technology, Pittsburgh, PA Graduate of two-year Business Application Programming/TECH EXEC Program—3.97 GPA Robert Morris College, Pittsburgh, PA Associate degree in Accounting, minor in Management

2306 Cincinnati St., Kingsford, PA 15171
(412) 437-6217
(412) 464-1273 (leave message)
Dcraig1273@aol.com

Thomas has kept his job objective quite broad and does not limit it to a particular industry or job title. Because he sees himself as a business manager, it does not matter to him in what kind of business or industry he works. He prefers a larger organization, as his job objective indicates. His education is near the top because he thinks it is one of his strengths.

Thomas has worked with one employer for many years, but he presents each job there as a separate one. This allows him to provide more details about his accomplishments within each position and more clearly indicate that these were promotions to increasingly responsible jobs. His military experience, while not recent, is listed under a separate heading because he thinks it is important. Note how he presented his military experience using civilian language.

This resume could have been two pages, and doing so would allow him to provide additional details on his job at Hayfield Publishing and in other areas. The extra space could also be used for more white space and a less crowded look, although the resume works fine as is.

Postscript: Thomas got a job in a smaller company as vice president of operations. The company's owner also had a military background and, once Thomas explained how that experience taught him skills in business, the owner offered him the job.

Figure 3-4: Thomas's JIST Card.

Thomas Marrin

Cell: (716) 223-4705; E-mail: tmarrin@techconnect.com

Objective: Business-management position requiring skills in problem solving, planning, organizing, and cost management.

Skills: Bachelor's degree in Business Administration and more than 10 years of management experience in progressively responsible positions. Managed as many as 40 staff and budgets in excess of $6 million a year. Consistent record of getting results. Excellent communication skills. Thorough knowledge of budgeting, cost savings, and computerized database and spreadsheet programs. Enjoy challenges, meet deadlines, and accept responsibility.

Willing to relocate.

Results-oriented, self-motivated, good problem-solving skills, energetic.

Figure 3-5: Thomas's resume.

THOMAS P. MARRIN

80 Harrison Ave. • Baldwin L.I., New York 11563
Cell: (716) 223-4705
tmarrin@techconnect.com

POSITION DESIRED

Mid- to upper-level management position with responsibilities including problem solving, planning, organizing, and budget management.

EDUCATION

University of Notre Dame, B.S. in Business Administration. Course emphasis on accounting, supervision, and marketing. Upper 25% of class. Additional advanced training: time management, organizational behavior, and cost control.

PROFESSIONAL EXPERIENCE

Wills Express Transit Co., Inc., Mineola, NY
Promoted to Vice President, Corporate Equipment—2003 to Present

Control purchase, maintenance, and disposal of 1100 trailers and 65 company cars with more than $8 million operating and $26 million capital expense responsibilities.

- Schedule trailer purchases for six divisions.
- Operated 2.3% under planned maintenance budget in company's second best profit year while operating revenues declined 2.5%.
- Originated schedule to correlate drivers' preferences with available trailers, decreasing driver turnover 20%.
- Developed systematic Purchase and Disposal Plan for company-car fleet.
- Restructured company-car policy, saving 15% on per-car cost.

Promoted to Assistant Vice President, Corporate Operations—1999 to 2003

Coordinated activities of six sections of Corporate Operations with an operating budget more than $10 million.

- Directed implementation of zero-base budgeting.
- Developed and prepared executive officer analyses detailing achievable cost reduction measures. Resulted in cost reduction of more than $600,000 in first two years.
- Designed policy and procedure for special equipment leasing program during peak seasons. Cut capital purchases by more than $1 million.

Promoted to Manager of Communications—1997 to 1999

Directed and managed $1.4 million communication network involving 650 phones, 75 WATS lines, 3 switchboards, and 15 employees.

- Installed computerized WATS Control System. Optimized utilization of WATS lines and pinpointed personal abuse. Achieved 100% system payback six months earlier than projected.
- Devised procedures that allowed simultaneous 20% increase in WATS calls and a $75,000/year savings.

Hayfield Publishing Company, Hempstead, NY
Communications Administrator—1995 to 1997

Managed daily operations of a large communications center. Reduced costs 12% and improved services.

MILITARY EXPERIENCE

U.S. Army—2nd Infantry Division, 1993 to 1995. First Lieutenant and platoon leader stationed in Korea and Ft. Knox, Kentucky. Supervised an annual budget equivalent of nearly $9 million and equipment valued at more than $60 million. Responsible for training, scheduling, supervision, mission planning, and activities of as many as 40 staff. Received several commendations.
Honorable discharge.

Another Combination Resume and JIST Card

Peter lost his factory job when the plant where he worked closed. He got a survival job as a truck driver and now wants to make truck driving his career because it pays well and he likes the work.

Notice how his resume (figure 3-7) emphasizes skills from previous jobs and other experiences that are essential for success as a truck driver. This resume uses a combination format since it includes elements from both skills and chronological resumes. The skills approach allows him to emphasize specific skills that support his job objective, and the chronological list of jobs allows him to display a stable work history.

The jobs he had years ago are clustered under one grouping because they are not as important as more recent experience. Also, doing so does not reveal that he is older. Yes, I realize employers are not supposed to discriminate based on age, but Peter doesn't want to take a chance because it's been known to happen.

For the same reason, Peter does not include dates for his military experience or high school graduation, nor does he separate them into categories such as "Military Experience" or "Education." They just aren't as important in supporting his job objective as they might be for a younger person.

Unusual elements are comments about health and not smoking or drinking. These comments work for his objective. Peter figures that an employer will think that a healthy and sober truck driver is better than the alternative. Note how he presented his military experience as another job, with an emphasis on the truck driving and diesel experience.

Quick Tip

Peter has another version of this resume that changed his job objective to include the supervision and management of trucking operations and added a few details to support this. When it made sense, he used the other version. If you are considering a promotion as one of your options, you can use this strategy, too.

Postscript: Peter got a job in a smaller long-distance trucking company, driving a regular route that lets him be home on weekends. After about six months, he was promoted and supervises other drivers and fills in as needed. Life is good.

Figure 3-6: Peter's JIST Card.

Peter Neely Messages: (237) 649-1234
Beeper: (237) 765-9876 (anywhere in the USA)

Position: Short- or Long-Distance Truck Driver

Background and Skills: More than 15 years of stable work history, including no traffic citations or accidents. Formal training in diesel mechanics and electrical systems. Familiar with most major destinations and have excellent map-reading and problem-solving abilities. Track record of getting things done and handling responsibility.

Excellent health, good work history, dependable.

A Resume for a Recent High School Graduate

This resume (figure 3-9) uses a simple format with few words and lots of white space. It looks better, I think, than more crowded resumes. I would like to see more numbers used to indicate performance or accomplishments. For example, what was the result of the more efficient record-keeping system she developed? And why did she receive the employee-of-the-month awards?

As a recent high school graduate, Andrea does not have substantial experience in her field, having had only one full-time job since graduation. This resume's skills format allows her to present her strengths better than a chronological resume would. Because she has formal training in retail sales, she could have given more details about specific courses she took or other school-related activities that would support her objective. Even so, her resume does a good job of presenting her basic skills to an employer in an attractive format.

Figure 3-7: Peter's resume.

Peter Neely
203 Evergreen Rd.
Houston, TX 39127
Messages: (237) 649-1234   Beeper: (237) 765-9876 (anywhere in the country)

POSITION DESIRED: Short- or Long-Distance Truck Driver

Summary of Work Experience: More than 15 years of stable work history, including substantial experience with diesel engines, electrical systems, and driving all types of trucks and heavy equipment.

SKILLS

Driving Record/ Licenses: Have current Commercial Driving License and Chauffeur's License and am qualified and able to drive anything that rolls. No traffic citations or accidents for more than 20 years.

Vehicle Maintenance: Maintain correct maintenance schedules and avoid most breakdowns as a result. Substantial mechanical and electrical systems training and experience enable me to repair many breakdowns immediately and avoid towing.

Record Keeping: Excellent attention to detail. Familiar with recording procedures and submit required records on a timely basis.

Routing: Thorough knowledge of most major interstate routes, with good map reading and route-planning skills. Get there on time and without incident.

Other: Not afraid of hard work, flexible, get along well with others, meet deadlines, excellent attendance, responsible.

WORK EXPERIENCE

2002–Present: CAPITAL TRUCK CENTER, Houston, TX
Pick up and deliver all types of commercial vehicles from across the United States. Entrusted with handling large sums of money and complex truck purchasing transactions.

1998–2002: QUALITY PLATING CO., Houston, TX
Promoted from production to Quality Control. Developed numerous production improvements, resulting in substantial cost savings.

1988–1998: BLUE CROSS MANUFACTURING, Houston, TX
Received several increases in salary and responsibility before leaving for a more challenging position.

Prior to 1988: Truck delivery of food products to destinations throughout the South. Also responsible for up to 12 drivers and equipment-maintenance personnel.

OTHER

Four years of experience in the U.S. Air Force, driving and operating truck-mounted diesel power plants. Responsible for monitoring and maintenance on a rigid 24-hour schedule. Stationed in Alaska, California, Wyoming, and other states. Honorable discharge.

High school graduate plus training in diesel engines and electrical systems. Excellent health, love the outdoors, stable family life, nonsmoker, and nondrinker.

Andrea's JIST Card uses the same education and experience with more emphasis on skills needed to make a transition to higher-paying marketing or sales jobs. She did a resume to support this job objective as well, although I did not include it here.

Postscript: When she wrote this resume, Andrea was interested in a marketing-oriented position. But she was not sure her credentials were strong enough. She wrote well, but the computer skills noted on her JIST Card (and her other resume) were mostly self-taught. To her surprise, her marketing-and-computer-skills JIST Card helped her get more interviews than did this sample resume. She got a job helping a small business upgrade its computerized accounting system; then she was promoted to work on its marketing and direct-mail activities. Andrea is now working full time and taking business courses at a local college.

Figure 3-8: Andrea's JIST Card.

Andrea Atwood **Home: (303) 447-2111**

Position Desired: A responsible position in retail sales or marketing.

Skills: Two years of sales and marketing training including promotional writing, advertising design, and business processes. Computer skills in desktop publishing, graphics design, word processing, and Web page design. Good written and verbal communication skills. Experienced in dealing with customers, direct sales, and problem solving. Punctual, honest, reliable, and hardworking.

Figure 3-9: Andrea's resume.

ANDREA ATWOOD
3231 East Harbor Road
Grand Rapids, Michigan 41103
Home: (303) 447-2111

Objective: A responsible position in retail sales or marketing.

Areas of Accomplishment:

Customer Service
- Communicate well with all age groups.
- Able to interpret customer concerns to help them find the items they want.
- Received six Employee-of-the-Month awards in 3 years.

Merchandise Display
- Developed display skills via in-house training and experience.
- Received Outstanding Trainee Award for Christmas toy display.
- Dress mannequins, arrange table displays, and organize sale merchandise.

Inventory Control
- Maintained and marked stock during department manager's 6-week illness.
- Developed more efficient record-keeping procedures.

Additional Skills
- Operate cash register and computerized accounting systems.
- Willing to work evenings and weekends.
- Punctual, honest, reliable, and hardworking.

Experience:
Harper's Department Store
Grand Rapids, Michigan
2003 to present

Education:
Central High School
Grand Rapids, Michigan
3.6/4.0 grade-point average
Honors Graduate in Distributive Education

Two years of retail sales training in Distributive Education. Also courses in business writing, computerized accounting, and word processing.

A Combination Resume with Lots of White Space and Brief Copy (and No Dates)

Linda's resume (figure 3-11) is based on one included in a book by David Swanson titled *The Resume Solution*. This resume shows the style that David prefers: lots of white space, short sentences, and brief but carefully edited narrative. Short. Like promotional copy. Like this.

This is another skills resume that breaks rules, since it uses a skills format but the skills are really ways to organize job-related tasks. Some skills include references to specific employers. So this would have to be called a combination resume, if you have to categorize it.

QUICK TIP

The design for this resume is based on a resume template from a popular word-processing program. Most programs offer several predetermined resume design options that include various typefaces and other simple but effective format and design elements. This makes resume creation much easier.

Linda's resume is short but presents good information to support her job objective. I would like to see some numbers or other measures of results, although it is clear that Linda is good at what she does.

Did you notice that this resume includes no dates? You probably wouldn't notice until you had formed a positive impression. Well, it turns out that Linda did this on purpose, to hide the fact that much of her work was as a self-employed freelancer. Linda is also a bit older. She thought these things could work against her in getting a job, so she left off the dates.

Postscript: Linda kept getting freelance writing assignments from people responding to her resume (which is not all bad but not what she had hoped for). She convinced one of the businesses that liked her freelance marketing work to hire her full time. She works about 20 hours a week at her office and 20 hours from home, writing copy and doing public relations for her employer. She has health insurance, vacation pay, coworkers to interact with, and other benefits. Things worked out; it just took a while.

Figure 3-10: Linda's JIST Card.

Linda Marsala-Winston / Voice Mail: (415) 555-1519 / lmw@netmail.net

Career Objective: Copywriter or account executive in an advertising or public relations agency

Skills: More than seven years of experience in promoting various products and services. Advanced education and training in journalism, advertising, writing, design, psychology, and communications. Excellent written communication skills; have won several awards for writing excellence. Am creative in solving problems and getting results.

Persuasive, innovative, meet deadlines.

Figure 3-11: Linda's resume.

Linda Marsala-Winston
6673 East Ave.
Lakeland, CA 94544
(415) 555-1519 (voice mail)
lmw@netmail.net

Objective: Copywriter or account executive in advertising or public relations agency

Professional Experience

Copywriter
Developed copy for direct-mail catalogs featuring collectible items, real estate developments, and agricultural machinery and equipment.

Writer
Wrote many articles for *Habitat* magazine. Specialized in architecture, contemporary lifestyles, and interior design.

Sales Promotion
Fullmer's Department Store, Detroit. Developed theme and copy for grand opening of new store in San Francisco Bay area.

Fabric Designer
Award-winning textile designer and importer of African and South American textiles.

Other Writing and Promotion
News bureau chief and feature writer for college newspaper, contributor to literary magazine. Script writer for fashion shows. Won creative writing fellowship to study in Mexico. Did public relations for International Cotton Conference. Summer graduate fellow in public information, United Nations, New York City.

Education

University of California, Berkeley
Bachelor of Arts Degree in English. Graduate study, 30 credits completed in Journalism.

California State University, Fresno
Master of Arts Degree in Guidance and Counseling.

Professional Membership

San Francisco Women in Advertising

A Two-Page Resume for a Candidate Without Recent Formal Experience

Figure 3-13 is a resume based on one in a book by Richard Lathrop titled *Who's Hiring Who*. While Richard calls it a "Qualifications Brief," this is a pure-form example of a skills resume.

This resume is unconventional in a variety of ways. It clearly takes advantage of the skills format by avoiding all mention of a chronology of past jobs. There are no references to specific employers, to employment dates, or even to job titles.

This is a clever example of how a well-done skills resume can present a person effectively in spite a lack of formal paid work experience—or to cover other problems. Students, career changers, and others can benefit in similar ways.

Postscript: If you read carefully, you may figure out that Sara's job history has been as a "domestic engineer." Yet you have to be impressed with how she presents this experience. I concluded that this would be one very smart person to have around. I don't know how she turned out, but I am certain she landed on her feet.

Figure 3-12: Sara's JIST Card.

Sara Smith **(416) 486-3874**

Job Objective: Program development, coordination, and administration

Skills: B.A. degree plus more than 15 years of experience in management, budgeting, and problem solving. Good financial management skills including cost control, purchasing, and disbursement. Able to organize and manage multiple tasks at one time and to meet deadlines. Excellent communication skills.

Well organized, efficient, can give and accept responsibility.

Figure 3-13: Sara's resume.

Sara Smith

1516 Sierra Way • Piedmont, CA 97435 • (416) 486-3874

OBJECTIVE

Program Development, Coordination, and Administration

...especially in a people-oriented organization where there is a need to ensure broad cooperative effort through the use of sound planning and strong administrative and persuasive skills to achieve common goals.

MAJOR AREAS OF EXPERIENCE AND ABILITY

Budgeting and Management for Sound Program Development

With partner, established new association devoted to maximum personal development and self-realization for each of its members. Over a period of time, administered budget totaling more than $1,000,000. Jointly planned growth of group and related expenditures, investments, programs, and development of property holdings to realize current and long-term goals. As a result, holdings increased twenty-fold over the period, reserves invested increased 1200%, and all major goals for members have been achieved or exceeded.

Purchasing to Ensure Smooth Flow of Needed Supplies and Services

Made purchasing decisions to ensure maximum production from available funds. Determined ongoing inventory needs, selected suppliers, and maintained a strong continuing line of credit while minimizing financing costs. No significant project was ever adversely affected by lack of necessary supplies, equipment, or services on time.

Personnel Development and Motivation

Developed resources to ensure maximum progress in achieving potential for development among all members of our group. Frequently engaged in intensive personnel counseling to achieve this. Sparked new community progress to help accomplish such results. Although arrangements with my partner gave me no say in selecting new members (I took them as they came), the results produced by this effort are a source of strong and continuing satisfaction to me. (See "Some Specific Results.")

Transportation Management

Determined transportation needs of our group and, in consultation with members, ensured specific transportation equipment acquisitions over a broad range of types (including seagoing). Contracted for additional transportation when necessary. Assured maximum utilization of limited motor pool to meet frequently conflicting requirements demanding arrival of the same vehicle at widely divergent points at the same moment. Negotiated resolution of such conflicts in the best interest of all concerned. In addition, arranged four major moves of all facilities, furnishings, and equipment to new locations.

Other Functions Performed

Duties periodically require my action in the following additional functional areas: crisis management; proposal preparation; political analysis; nutrition; recreation planning and administration; stock market operations; taxes; building and grounds maintenance; community organization; social affairs administration (including VIP entertaining); catering; landscaping (two awards for excellence); contract negotiations; teaching; and more.

Some Specific Results

Above experience gained in 10 years devoted to family development and household management in partnership with my husband, Harvey Smith, who is equally responsible for results produced. *Primary achievements:* Daughter Sue, 12, a leading candidate for the U.S. Junior Olympics team in gymnastics; a lovely home in Piedmont (social center for area teenagers). *Secondary achievements:* Vacation home at Newport, Oregon (on the beach); president of Piedmont High School PTA, two years; organized successful citizen protest to stop incursion of Oakland commercialism on Piedmont area.

PERSONAL DATA AND OTHER FACTS

Bachelor of Arts (Business Administration), Cody College, Cody, California. Highly active in community affairs. Have learned that there is a spark of genius in almost everyone that, when nurtured, can flare into dramatic achievement.

Chapter 4

Develop an Electronic Resume in Less Than an Hour

With the advent of the Internet, more and more people are looking for jobs online and posting their resumes on the Web for employers to view. This technology requires you to have an electronic version of your resume so that you can make your credentials available to more employers online. Resumes on the Web are stored in electronic databases that are designed to save space and will be viewed by employers with many variations in computers and software. This means that most resumes are *not* stored as graphic images but, instead, as text files. Simple text files take up much less space than graphic files and can be read easily by any word processor or database program. Text files can also be searched by employers for keywords, which I discuss later in this chapter.

Also, many employers take paper resumes they receive and scan them into electronic form. This lets employers put resume information into their own searchable databases. Scanning can introduce text errors and odd formatting due to the imperfect science of scanning technology. What this means is that your resume's carefully prepared format-and-design elements get stripped out, reducing your resume to a simple text format. So, you are better off making the modifications yourself if you know your resume will be scanned, if you will be submitting it to resume banks, or if you will be e-mailing it.

The Requirements of One Large Employer Are Typical

In addition to searching resume banks or databases on the Internet, employers are putting resumes they receive directly into their own electronic databases. This saves them time and money. Larger employers get thousands of resumes, so it is impractical for them to store and retrieve paper resumes as jobs open up. Yet employers do want to retrieve resumes as positions become available and, for specialized positions, they want to consider applicants who submitted resumes weeks or even months in the past. To show you how this works, here are the instructions from one large employer's Web site on how to submit a resume.

Instructions from a Large Employer on How to Submit Your Resume

Submitting Your Resume

For positions located at our various sites, we use an electronic applicant-tracking system that uses the latest in document imaging technology. The system allows us to receive your resume by e-mail, direct-line fax, or hard copy. This system will enhance your exposure to a wider variety of employment opportunities within Big Company. The one-time submission of your resume will make you eligible for consideration for any openings that occur within our organization for which you meet the minimum qualifications.

As your resume is input into our system, you will receive an acknowledgment by e-mail and your resume will be kept active in our database for a period of one year. As openings occur, our recruiters will query the database for those individuals whose qualifications and skills match the criteria needed for the open positions. If a match occurs, you will receive further notification regarding the specific opening.

Here's how to increase the effectiveness of your resume—be sure to clearly state your skills and experiences, educational background, work history, and specific salary information that you feel is important. In addition, please follow these directions when preparing your resume:

- Prepare your resume on white or light-colored 8½ by 11 paper (hard copy or faxing).
- Please use a standard paper weight so that the system will produce a quality image (hard copy or faxing).
- Avoid font treatments such as italics, underlining, and shadowing. Boldface type and/or capital letters are acceptable.
- Place your name at the top of the page on its own line, use a standard address format below your name, and list each phone number on a separate line.

You may submit your resume by one of the following methods:

- Electronic mail: The e-mail address is resume@bigcompany.com. You MUST put the word resume in the subject or reference line when e-mailing and submit it in ASCII text format. All information must be contained in the body of the message. We cannot accept attachments into this system.
- Fax: You may fax your information to XXX-XXX-XXXX. Please fax in fine mode.
- Postal mail: You may mail a hard copy of your resume to the following address: Corporate Recruitment, Big Company, Corporate Center, ZY 21211.

Big Company is an Equal Opportunity Employer.

Although these instructions aren't particularly friendly, the methods for submitting a resume are pretty clear: No matter what your resume looks like or how you get it to the employer, this company will convert your lovely resume into a simple text file. This means that the best way to ensure that a resume is handled well electronically is to revise it into the most universally accepted electronic form, as the example in figure 4-1 shows.

A Sample Text-Only Resume, with All Graphics and Format Removed

Look at the sample resume that follows, adapted from one by Susan Britton Whitcomb in *Résumé Magic* (JIST Publishing). This resume has had all formatting and graphic elements removed for submission in electronic or scannable form.

It has the following features:

- No graphics
- No lines (it uses equal signs instead)
- No bold, italic, or other text variations
- Only one easy-to-scan font (which is Courier)
- No tab indentations
- No line or paragraph indents
- Keywords are added.

Yes, this resume looks boring, but it has the advantage of being universally accepted into company or Web resume databases, whether submitted in paper form or e-mailed.

Figure 4-1: A scannable resume.

```
AMY RICCIUTTI
Greenville, ME
(203) 433-3322
aricciut@compuserve.com

PROFESSIONAL EXPERIENCE
========================================================================

ROCKWOOD INSURANCE, Augusta, ME
10/98-Present

Independent agency specializing in commercial coverage for
transportation and lumber industries.

Underwriting Manager ...

Recruited by partner/sales manager to manage underwriting in support of
aggressive expansion/business development campaign.  Liaison to five
agents and some 50 companies.  Underwrite $6 million in renewal coverage
and $200,000 in new business on a priority basis (commercial and
personal lines).  Collaborate with agents to protect loss ratios.
Aggressively process submissions to meet critical deadlines and offer
better premium to customers.

*** Contributions ***

+ Developed focus and structure for newly created position; established
underwriting and customer service infrastructure to support a projected
$500,000 increase in annual revenue.

+ Achieved new agency record for retaining renewal accounts.

+ Earned accolades from insurance companies for having "most complete
submissions."

+ Trained two Customer Representatives, equipping them with technical
knowledge to service complex accounts.

+ Designed and introduced Quote Worksheet and Agent Checklist to
standardize and streamline underwriting.

+ Diplomatically mitigated circumstances involving premium increases and
noncoverage of claims.


COAST INSURANCE SERVICES, Brunswick, ME
1995-1998

Senior Customer Service Representative ...

Accountable for policy maintenance, renewal retention, new business
submissions, claims, CSR training, and liaison work for independent
agency with $7 million in premiums.
```

(continued)

(continued)

*** Contributions ***

+ Assisted with AMS Novell network upgrade (resident expert for software installation, troubleshooting).

+ Took on several new books of business during tenure without need for additional support staff.

SUPPORTING SKILLS, INFORMATION
===

*** Education *** INS 21 (Principles of Insurance). INS 23 (Commercial Principles of Insurance). Personal Lines (Property and Auto). Commercial Lines (Property). E&O Coverage. Employee Practices Liability. Property & Casualty Agent (# 760923)

*** Computer *** Windows 3.1. Windows 95 and 98. MS Works. MS Office. WordPerfect. AMS Novell. DOS and UNIX-based programs. Redshaw. OIS and FSC Rating Systems. PS4 Proposal System.

*** Affiliations *** National Association of Insurance Women. National Association of Female Executives. Volunteer, Marine Mammal Center.

Quick Alert

It is important to provide a short, clear, and concise electronic resume! Some scanning systems and databases stop reading resumes after a certain number of lines, often after about one and a half pages, so be sure that your most important information appears early in the resume.

Adapting Your Resume for Electronic Use

You can easily take your existing resume and reformat it for electronic submission. Here are some quick guidelines to do so:

1. Open your regular resume file and select the Save As command on your toolbar, usually located under the File menu. Select Text Only, Plain Text, or ASCII as the type.
2. Close the file and then reopen it to make sure you are working from the new text-only version. You'll see that most graphic elements such as lines, images, and bullet point symbols have now been eliminated. But if they haven't, go ahead and delete them. You may use equal signs in place of lines or borders and replace bullet points with plus symbols (+), asterisks (*), or hyphens (-).
3. Limit your margins to no more than 65 characters wide.
4. Use an easy-to-scan sans-serif type font, such as Courier, Arial, or Helvetica.
5. Eliminate bold, italics, and underlining if any remain after saving as text-only.
6. Introduce major sections with words in all uppercase letters, rather than in bold, italics, or underlining.
7. Keep all text aligned to the left.
8. Instead of using bullets, use a standard keyboard character, such as the asterisk.

9. Instead of using the Tab key or paragraph indents, use the space key to indent.

10. When done, click Save or OK. Then reopen the file to see how it looks. Make any additional format changes as needed.

Now test your electronic resume by e-mailing it to a friend who uses a different Internet Service Provider. For example, if you use AOL, send it to a friend on Yahoo! or Hotmail. Also try sending it to someone who works in a large company to see how it transmits via their company e-mail system. When you send it, paste the electronic resume into the body of the e-mail rather than sending it as an attachment. That way, they will be able to tell you how it looks when it shows up in their e-mail system and whether it is legible. After getting their feedback, make any adjustments necessary to fix it.

Quick Tip

While changing your resume to a boring but electronically acceptable format will undermine your creative side, think of it as mashed potatoes: It can be very good if you do it right. Try to take satisfaction from that thought, OK?

The Importance of Keywords

Creating an electronic resume is more than just putting it into a plain format. This is because employers look for qualified applicants in a resume database by searching for what are called keywords. This being so, your task is to add keywords to your electronic resume so that your chance of being selected for appropriate jobs is increased.

Keywords and Scanning Technology

The technology used by databases to search for your resume is very sophisticated. Software first extracts keywords and sorts them into major categories such as education, work history, personal traits, job skills, job titles, and others. The keywords from your resume are then sorted into the appropriate category. This allows an employer to search thousands of resumes to find the ones that meet very specific criteria.

For example, an employer could start with major criteria such as only those with a job objective in human resources, four or more years of experience in the field, and a four-year college degree in a related area. From this group the employer could then sort for those with specific skills such as interviewing, fringe benefit administration, grievance complaint handling, and EEOC policy compliance. The database would then search for those resumes that met these criteria, overlooking others that did not specifically state these things (and, often, thereby passing over the best applicant who did not include the right words).

So if you plan on putting your resume on the Internet or submitting it to employers who will scan it, you should revise your resume to include as many key skill words as you can. Many resumes in Section Three include a keyword approach that will help them be selected from a resume database. Some consist almost entirely of keywords organized into groupings. This does not make for a very readable resume for humans, but can result in high "hit rates" for employers searching a database for someone with specific skills.

Quick Tips for Selecting Keywords to Include in Your Resume

You probably already have many terms in your regular resume that can be used in a keyword section in your electronic resume. Leave them where they are, but repeat some of the most important ones in a "Keywords" section near the top of your resume. In addition to using words you already have, here are some keyword tips for you to keep in mind:

- **Think like a prospective employer.** Think of the jobs you want, and then include the keywords you think an employer would use to find someone who can do what you can do. Emphasize technical terms, specific equipment or software names, certifications, and other specific terms an employer might use to fill the position. The job ads you read on the Internet or in newspapers are great ways to figure out what keywords employers are looking for.
- **Review job descriptions from major references.** Read the descriptions for the jobs you seek in major references like the

Occupational Outlook Handbook or the *O*NET Dictionary of Occupational Titles*. These and other references are described in Chapter 7 and are available in both print and online formats. They will give you a variety of keywords you can use in your electronic resume.

- **Include all your important skill words.** When you complete the exercises in Chapters 5 and 6, you will identify key skills that can help you develop keyword sections on your resume.
- **Look for examples of keywords in the sample resumes in Section Three.**

Some of the sample resumes in Section Three contain keywords. These are noted in the handwritten comments on the resumes. These resumes were specifically designed to be easily scanned, e-mailed, or posted to Web sites. Some provide a list of keywords in a separate section, in addition to the many keywords used throughout the resume. Look to them for inspiration on how to add more keywords to your own electronic resume.

Quick Tip

I've noticed a trend of resume writers using simpler and less graphic-oriented formats. This is particularly so for the resumes of people with computer and technology skills—the ones most likely to be scanned into databases or submitted via e-mail. As electronic submissions and scanning increase, most people will have two or more resumes—one that looks good to humans and another that scans and e-mails well. Having both, to be used in different situations, will give you a competitive edge.

What About Fancy Internet Resumes, Including Graphics, HTML, Video Clips, and More?

Remember that this is a quick book, so I've not included information on the many sophisticated things you can do with your resume on the Internet. Some job seekers have created their own interactive Web sites that include stunning resume graphics; video clips introducing themselves; samples of their work using digital images, video, or sound; copies of letters of reference; and many other features. Doing this would make sense for artists, Web designers, and people seeking technical or design-oriented positions that can be demonstrated or shown most effectively in this format. For most others, however, it may not be worth the bother, so use your judgment and do this only if you think an employer's impression of you will benefit greatly from the time you spend doing so.

Quick Reference

To learn about the more advanced things you can do with an electronic resume, look at the JIST book titled *Cyberspace Resume Kit* by Mary Nemnich and Fred Jandt. Or see Susan Britton Whitcomb and Pat Kendall's book, *e-Resumes: Everything You Need to Know About Using Electronic Resumes to Tap into Today's Hot Job Market.* Also, the Internet itself has lots of information on how to use electronic resumes most effectively, including the sites recommended at the end of Chapter 15.

Section Two

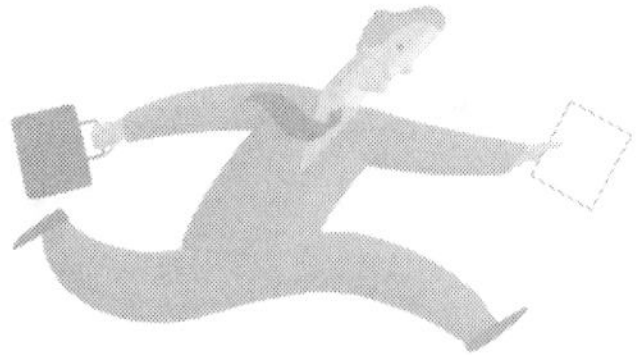

A More Thorough Approach to Resume Writing (and Career Planning)

You do not have to read or complete this section at all. As I said in Section One, all you may really need is a simple resume that allows you to get started on an active job search. Section One has enough information to help you create a respectable resume for both print and electronic uses. But, if you are motivated to develop a better resume and learn some important career planning tips, reading this section has some advantages.

You should know that this section is more than it may appear to be at first. It is all of the following:

- **A series of chapters that will help you build the contents of a superior resume.** Each chapter in this section will help you build specific content for a powerful resume. For example, Chapter 5 will show you how to identify the wide array of skills you possess and to select those that are most important to include in a resume.
- **A process to help your career and life planning.** While you are working on the activities needed to write a superior resume, you will also learn important things for your career and life planning. For example: What are you really good at? What sorts of things do you enjoy? What values do you need satisfied in your next job? What sort of job will you be looking for, specifically? These are just some of the issues the chapters in this section will help you explore. They are all important topics—far more important to you than "just" putting together a resume.

- **A series of activities that will help you tremendously throughout your job search—and beyond.** One big question you will have to answer in an interview is "Why should I hire you?" By doing the activities in this section, you will be able to better handle this essential interview question. This is but one example of how the process of writing a superior resume can benefit you in other ways. I have included activities and tips that will help you write a resume as well as help you in other, and surely more important, ways.

Chapters in This Section

Although you can complete just the chapters that seem most important to you, it is best to read them in order.

Chapter 5: Develop a Powerful New Skills Language
Helps identify key skills you have that you can use in your resume. These same skills are essential in making good career decisions and handling interview questions. Important!

Chapter 6: Document the Many Details of Your Work and Life Experience
Includes forms to collect information on your education, work, and other life experiences. These details will help you pull out special accomplishments and skills you can use in your resume. Later, this information will prove very helpful in interviews.

Chapter 7: Identify Your Perfect Job and Industry
Provides activities to help you define your ideal job. Also provides advice on researching and setting a specific job objective, exploring various job options, and writing your job objective.

Chapter 8: Present Strengths and Overcome "Problems" on Your Resume
Specific advice on handling a variety of problems, such as gaps in your job history or not having much experience.

Chapter 9: Write a Better Resume Now
Provides a more detailed resume worksheet than in Section One to help write a superior resume. It includes advice on editing, designing, and producing your final resume, and suggestions for using standard software for resume design.

Chapter 5

Develop a Powerful New Skills Language

This is an important chapter with some useful activities that are well worth your time. It provides a helpful list of skills to include on your resume. But this chapter is far more important than that. Knowing your skills is key to making good decisions about your future, interviewing effectively, and finding a job that matches what you do well.

Can You Communicate Your Skills?

Knowing what you do well is an essential part of writing a good resume. But it is also important to you in other ways. For example, unless you use skills you enjoy and are good at, it is unlikely you will be fully satisfied with your job.

Quick Alert

Most people are not good at telling others what skills they have. I can tell you this based on many years of working with groups of job seekers. When asked, few people can quickly tell me what they are good at and fewer yet can quickly present the specific skills they have that are needed to succeed in the jobs they want. So knowing your skills and communicating them well will give you an advantage over other job seekers.

Employers tell us that most job seekers don't present their skills effectively. Surveys of employers have often shown that as many as 80 percent of the people they interview cannot adequately define the skills they have to support their ability to do the job. They may *have* the necessary skills, but they can't communicate them. It is problem number one in the interview process. So, this chapter is designed to help you fix that problem—on your resume and in an interview.

Three Major Types of Skills: The Skills Triad

Analyzing skills for even a simple task can become quite complicated. But a useful way to organize skills is to divide them into three basic types, as shown in the Skills Triad in figure 5-1. Each type is explained briefly in the following sections. The rest of this chapter will help you identify your own key skills.

Adaptive Skills/Personality Traits

These are skills you use every day to survive and get along. They are called adaptive or self-management skills because they allow you to adapt or adjust to a variety of situations. Some of them also could be considered part of your basic personality. Examples of adaptive skills valued by employers include getting to work on time, honesty, enthusiasm, and interacting well with others.

Transferable Skills

These are general skills that can be useful in a variety of jobs. For example, writing clearly, good language skills, and the ability to organize and prioritize tasks would be desirable skills in many jobs. These are called transferable skills because they can be transferred from one job—or even one career—to another.

Figure 5-1: The Skills Triad.

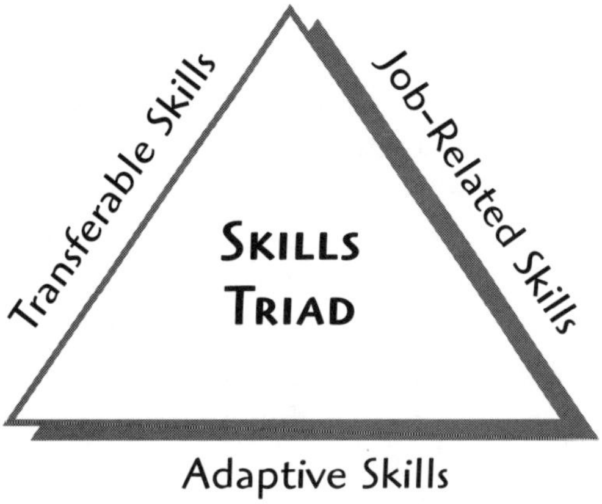

> **KEEP UP YOUR COMPUTER SKILLS**
>
> If you don't have computer skills, you are at a great disadvantage in the job market because employers require computer literacy at all levels. If you have not kept up with computer skills related to your career area, consider taking some classes on the applications used most in the jobs you want. This might be word processing, spreadsheet, database, graphics, Web design, or some other type of program. Local adult education and community colleges often offer low-cost courses. You should also read computer magazines to familiarize yourself with the concepts, capabilities, and language. Do it regularly!

Job-Related Skills

These are the skills people typically first think of when asked, "Do you have any skills?" These skills are related to a particular job or type of job. An auto mechanic, for example, needs to know how to tune engines and repair brakes. An accountant needs to know how to create a general ledger, use computerized accounting programs, and perform other activities related to that job.

Skills Categories Not Perfect But Still Useful

The system of dividing skills into three categories is not perfect because some overlap exists between the three skills categories. Some things, such as being trustworthy, dependable, and well organized, are not skills as much as they are personality traits. So, a skill such as being organized can be considered either adaptive or transferable. For our purposes, however, the Skills Triad is a very useful system for identifying skills that are important in the job search.

Identify Your Skills

Because it is so important to know your skills, I have included checklists and other activities in this chapter to help you identify the skills that will be most important to include on your resume. Completing the activities will help you develop a skills language that can be very useful during interviews and throughout your job search and, perhaps, your life.

Begin your skills identification process with the simple activity that follows.

Three Good Worker Traits

On the following lines, list three things about yourself that you think will make you a good worker. Take your time. Think about what an employer might like about you or the way you work.

1. ______________________________

2. ______________________________

3. ______________________________

The skills you just wrote may be among the most important points an employer will want to know about you. Most (but not all) people write adaptive skills when asked this question. Whatever you wrote, these are key details to mention in the interview and to back up with examples of how you've demonstrated these skills. In fact, presenting these skills well—and the examples that provide evidence of them—will often allow a less experienced job seeker to get the job over someone with better credentials. It's simple, I know, but this list may be the most critical element to remember from this whole book—but only if you learn how best to use the information.

Identify Your Adaptive Skills—Skills That Allow You to Adapt to New Situations

I have created a list of adaptive skills that are important to employers. The ones listed as "The Minimum" are those that most employers consider essential for a person to keep a job. Employers usually will not hire someone who has problems in these areas. The remaining adaptive skills are important to employers for a variety of reasons. Look over the list and put a check mark next to each adaptive skill you have. Put a second check mark next to those skills that are particularly important to use or include in your next job.

Adaptive Skills Checklist

The Minimum

- ❑ Follow instructions
- ❑ Get along with supervisor
- ❑ Get along with coworkers
- ❑ Good attendance
- ❑ Hardworking, productive
- ❑ Honest
- ❑ Meet deadlines
- ❑ Punctual

Other Adaptive Skills

- ❑ Able to coordinate
- ❑ Ambitious
- ❑ Apply new skills
- ❑ Assertive
- ❑ Capable
- ❑ Cheerful
- ❑ Competent
- ❑ Complete assignments
- ❑ Conscientious
- ❑ Creative
- ❑ Dependable
- ❑ Discreet
- ❑ Eager
- ❑ Efficient
- ❑ Energetic

(continued)

(continued)

- ❑ Enthusiastic
- ❑ Expressive
- ❑ Flexible
- ❑ Formal
- ❑ Friendly
- ❑ Good-natured
- ❑ Helpful
- ❑ Humble
- ❑ Imaginative
- ❑ Independent
- ❑ Industrious
- ❑ Informal
- ❑ Intelligent
- ❑ Intuitive
- ❑ Learn quickly
- ❑ Loyal
- ❑ Mature
- ❑ Methodical
- ❑ Modest
- ❑ Motivated
- ❑ Natural
- ❑ Open-minded
- ❑ Optimistic
- ❑ Original
- ❑ Patient
- ❑ Persistent
- ❑ Physically strong
- ❑ Reliable
- ❑ Resourceful
- ❑ Responsible
- ❑ Self-confident
- ❑ Sense of humor
- ❑ Sincere
- ❑ Solve problems
- ❑ Spontaneous
- ❑ Steady
- ❑ Tactful
- ❑ Take pride in work
- ❑ Tenacious
- ❑ Thrifty
- ❑ Trustworthy
- ❑ Versatile
- ❑ Well organized

Add Any Other Adaptive Skills That You Think Are Important

Include here any adaptive skills that you included in your "good worker traits" earlier.

- ❑ ____________________
- ❑ ____________________
- ❑ ____________________
- ❑ ____________________
- ❑ ____________________
- ❑ ____________________
- ❑ ____________________
- ❑ ____________________
- ❑ ____________________
- ❑ ____________________
- ❑ ____________________
- ❑ ____________________
- ❑ ____________________

Your Top Three Adaptive Skills

Carefully review the skills checklist you just completed and select the three adaptive skills you feel are most important to tell an employer about or that you most want to use in your next job. The three skills you choose for this list are extremely important to include in your resume and to present to an employer in an interview.

1. ______________________________

2. ______________________________

3. ______________________________

Transferable Skills Checklist—Skills That Transfer to Many Jobs

Over the years, I have assembled a list of transferable skills that are important in a wide variety of jobs. In the checklist that follows, the skills listed as "Key Transferable Skills" are those I consider to be most important to many employers. Hint: The key skills are also those often required in jobs with more responsibility and higher wages, so it pays to emphasize these skills if you have them.

The remaining transferable skills are grouped into categories that may be helpful to you. Check each skill you are strong in; then check twice the skills you want to use in your next job. When you are finished, you should have checked 10 to 20 skills at least once.

Transferable Skills Checklist

Key Transferable Skills

- ❏ Accept responsibility
- ❏ Control budgets
- ❏ Communicate in writing
- ❏ Increase sales or efficiency
- ❏ Instruct others
- ❏ Manage money or budgets
- ❏ Manage people
- ❏ Meet deadlines
- ❏ Meet the public
- ❏ Negotiate
- ❏ Organize/manage projects
- ❏ Plan
- ❏ Solve problems
- ❏ Speak in public
- ❏ Supervise others

Other Transferable Skills

Dealing with Things

- ❏ Assemble or make things
- ❏ Build, observe, inspect things
- ❏ Construct or repair buildings
- ❏ Drive or operate vehicles
- ❏ Operate tools and machinery
- ❏ Repair things
- ❏ Use complex equipment
- ❏ Use my hands

Dealing with Data

- ❏ Analyze data or facts
- ❏ Audit records
- ❏ Budget
- ❏ Calculate, compute
- ❏ Classify data
- ❏ Compare, inspect, or record facts
- ❏ Count, observe, compile
- ❏ Detail-oriented
- ❏ Evaluate
- ❏ Investigate
- ❏ Keep financial records
- ❏ Locate answers or information
- ❏ Manage money
- ❏ Negotiate
- ❏ Research
- ❏ Synthesize
- ❏ Take inventory

Working with People

- ❏ Administer
- ❏ Care for patients
- ❏ Confront others
- ❏ Counsel people
- ❏ Demonstrate
- ❏ Diplomatic
- ❏ Help others
- ❏ Interview others
- ❏ Insightful
- ❏ Kind
- ❏ Listen
- ❏ Negotiate
- ❏ Outgoing
- ❏ Patient
- ❏ Persuade
- ❏ Pleasant
- ❏ Sensitive
- ❏ Sociable
- ❏ Tactful
- ❏ Teach
- ❏ Tolerant
- ❏ Tough
- ❏ Trust
- ❏ Understand

Using Words, Ideas

- ❏ Articulate

❑ Communicate verbally
❑ Correspond with others
❑ Create new ideas
❑ Design
❑ Edit
❑ Inventive
❑ Logical
❑ Remember information
❑ Research
❑ Speak in public
❑ Write clearly

Leadership

❑ Arrange social functions
❑ Competitive
❑ Decisive
❑ Delegate
❑ Direct others
❑ Explain things to others
❑ Get results
❑ Mediate problems
❑ Motivate people
❑ Negotiate agreements
❑ Plan
❑ Run meetings
❑ Self-controlled
❑ Self-motivated
❑ Solve problems
❑ Supervise others
❑ Take risks

Creative, Artistic

❑ Artistic
❑ Dance, body movement
❑ Draw, sketch, render
❑ Expressive
❑ Music appreciation
❑ Perform, act
❑ Play instruments
❑ Present artistic ideas

Add Any Other Transferable Skills That You Think Are Important

Include here any transferable skills that you included in your "good worker traits" earlier.

❑ ____________________
❑ ____________________
❑ ____________________
❑ ____________________

Your Top Five Transferable Skills

List the five top transferable skills you want to use in your next job.

1. ____
2. ____
3. ____
4. ____
5. ____

Identify Your Job-Related Skills

Many jobs require skills that are specific to that occupation. An airline pilot will obviously need to know how to fly an airplane. Thankfully, good adaptive and transferable skills would not be enough to be considered for that job. You might have gained your job-related skills in a variety of ways, including education, training, work, hobbies, or other life experiences. Chapter 6 reviews your education, work, and other experiences and helps you use this as a basis for identifying your key job-related skills, which you can then present in your resume and interviews.

The Top Skills Employers Want

Based on a variety of research studies, here are the skills employers consider most important in the people they hire. Note that all but computer literacy are adaptive or transferable skills because once a person has the minimum required job-related skills, these skills are the ones an employer will look for in making a hire or no-hire decision. Are some of these on your skills lists?

- Analytical ability/critical thinking
- Computer literacy
- Decision-making
- Honesty/Integrity
- Interpersonal
- Leadership
- Motivation/Initiative/Enthusiasm
- Oral and written communication
- Organization/Coordination
- Problem-solving
- Results-orientation
- Self-confidence
- Strong work ethic
- Teamwork
- Time management
- Willingness to learn

Source: Surveys by the U.S. Department of Labor and QuintCareers.com.

Chapter 6

Document the Many Details of Your Work and Life Experience

All employers require you to provide information about what you have done in the past. Employers use applications, resumes, cover letters, e-mail interaction, phone contacts, and interviews to collect this information. If you can present yourself well in these ways, you are far more likely to be hired than if you do poorly. This chapter will help you collect the basic information needed to create a resume, but it will also encourage you to consider your accomplishments, identify additional skills, and develop specific examples of when and where you used those skills. These additions to the dry facts can make your resume a much more powerful tool for presenting yourself well.

I admit that this is a tedious chapter, with lots of worksheets to complete. For that reason, you would be forgiven for not wanting to do them all. But the details this chapter asks for will help you recollect specifics that later will help you develop a superior resume and, more importantly, better handle interviews. So filling out the worksheets in this chapter is worth your time.

Quick Tips for Completing the Forms

Several forms in this chapter ask for information on your education, training, work and volunteer history, and other life experiences. Although you may have provided some of this information in Section One, the forms in this chapter are considerably more detailed. When filling out these forms, emphasize the key skills you identified in Chapter 5. Those skills, as well as your accomplishments and results, are of particular interest to most employers.

Pay attention to experiences and accomplishments you really enjoyed; these often demonstrate skills that you should try to use in your next job. When possible, include numbers to describe your activities or their results. For example, "spoke to groups as large as 200 people" has more impact than "did presentations."

In some cases, you may want to write a first draft on a separate sheet before completing the forms. Use an erasable pen or pencil on the worksheets to allow for changes. In all sections, emphasize the skills and accomplishments that best support your ability to do the job you are seeking.

Education and Training Worksheet

High School

This worksheet is an important source of resume information for recent high school graduates. For those with more experience, it can still be helpful to emphasize highlights from this time, particularly those that support your doing the job you want now.

Name of school(s) and years attended ______________________________

____

Subjects you did well in or that directly relate to the job you want________________

____

____

____

____

Extracurricular activities ____

____

____

____

____

____

Accomplishments/things you did well in or out of school ______________________

____

____

____

____

Any related hobbies or recreational activities______________________________

____

____

____

____

Post High School Training (Other Than College)

List any training after or outside of high school that might relate to the job you want. Include military and on-the-job training, workshops, or informal training such as from a hobby.

Training/dates/certificates ____

____

____

____

____

____

(continued)

(continued)

Specific things you can do as a result ______

Specific things you learned or can do that relate to the job you want ______

College

If you graduated from college or took college classes, this will interest an employer. If you are a new graduate, these experiences are especially important. Consider those points that directly support your ability to do the job. For example, working your way through school proves that you are hardworking. If you took courses that specifically support your job, you can include details on these as well.

Name of school(s) and years attended ______

Courses related to job objective____

____

____

____

____

____

Extracurricular activities, including hobbies and leisure activities ______________

____

____

____

____

____

Accomplishments/things you did well in or out of school ____________________

____

____

____

____

Specific things you learned or can do related to the job you want ______________

____

____

____

____

Work and Volunteer History Worksheet

Virtually all resumes include information on work you have done in the past. Use this worksheet to list each major job you have held and information related to it. Begin with your most recent job.

Include military experience and unpaid work. Both are work and are particularly important if you do not have much paid civilian work experience. Create additional sheets to cover all of your significant jobs or unpaid experiences as needed. If you have been promoted, consider listing each position with that employer as a separate job.

Whenever possible, provide numbers to support what you did: number of people served over one or more years; number of transactions processed; percent sales increased; total inventory value you were responsible for; payroll of the staff you supervised; total budget you were responsible for; and other data. Think about any gauge you could use to measure your results on each job and, as much as possible, use numbers here, too.

I have provided four job worksheets, but if you need more, please feel free to photocopy extras.

Job 1

Name of organization ______________________________

Address ______________________________

____

Employed from ______________________________ to

Job title(s) ______________________________

Supervisor's name ______________________________

Phone number (   ) ______________________________

Machinery or equipment you used ______________________________

____

____

____

Computer skills developed or used, including software ______________________________

____

____

____

Data, information, or reports you created or used

People-oriented duties or responsibilities to coworkers, customers, others

Services you provided or goods you produced

Promotions or salary increases, if any

Details on anything you did to help the organization, such as increase productivity, simplify or reorganize job duties, decrease costs, increase profits, improve working conditions, reduce turnover, or other improvements. Quantify results when possible; for example, "Increased order processing by 50%, with no increase in staff costs."

(continued)

(continued)

Specific things you learned or can do that relate to the job you want________________

What would your supervisor say about you? ________________

Job 2

Name of organization ________________

Address ________________

Employed from ________________ to ________________

Job title(s) ________________

Supervisor's name ________________

Phone number (   ) ________________

Machinery or equipment you used ________________

Computer skills developed or used, including software ________________

Data, information, or reports you created or used

People-oriented duties or responsibilities to coworkers, customers, others

Services you provided or goods you produced

Promotions or salary increases, if any

Details on anything you did to help the organization, such as increase productivity, simplify or reorganize job duties, decrease costs, increase profits, improve working conditions, reduce turnover, or other improvements. Quantify results when possible; for example, "Increased order processing by 50%, with no increase in staff costs."

Specific things you learned or can do that relate to the job you want

(continued)

(continued)

What would your supervisor say about you? ______

Job 3

Name of organization ______

Address ______

Employed from ______ to ______

Job title(s) ______

Supervisor's name ______

Phone number (   ) ______

Machinery or equipment you used ______

Computer skills developed or used, including software ______

Data, information, or reports you created or used ______

People-oriented duties or responsibilities to coworkers, customers, others ____________

____

____

____

____

Services you provided or goods you produced ____________

____

____

____

____

Promotions or salary increases, if any ____________

____

____

Details on anything you did to help the organization, such as increase productivity, simplify or reorganize job duties, decrease costs, increase profits, improve working conditions, reduce turnover, or other improvements. Quantify results when possible; for example, "Increased order processing by 50%, with no increase in staff costs." ____________

____

____

____

____

____

Specific things you learned or can do that relate to the job you want____________

____

____

____

____

____

What would your supervisor say about you? ____________

____

(continued)

(continued)

____

____

____

____

Job 4

Name of organization ______________________________

Address ______________________________

____

Employed from ____________________ to ____________________

Job title(s) ______________________________

Supervisor's name ______________________________

Phone number (   ) ______________________________

Machinery or equipment you used ______________________________

____

____

____

Computer skills developed or used, including software ____________________

____

____

____

Data, information, or reports you created or used ____________________

____

____

____

People-oriented duties or responsibilities to coworkers, customers, others ____________

____

____

____

Services you provided or goods you produced ______________________________

____

____

____

____

Promotions or salary increases, if any ______________________________

____

____

Details on anything you did to help the organization, such as increase productivity, simplify or reorganize job duties, decrease costs, increase profits, improve working conditions, reduce turnover, or other improvements. Quantify results when possible; for example, "Increased order processing by 50%, with no increase in staff costs." ______________

____

____

____

____

____

Specific things you learned or can do that relate to the job you want______________

____

____

____

____

____

____

What would your supervisor say about you? ______________________________

____

____

____

____

____

____

Other Life Experiences Worksheet

Use this worksheet to describe accomplishments or other significant information from hobbies, family responsibilities, family business employment, recreational activities, travel, and any other experiences in your life. Write any that are particularly meaningful to you, and name the key skills that were involved in these accomplishments. Make extra copies of this sheet as needed.

Situation 1

____

____

____

____

Details and skills used ______________________________

____

____

Specific things you learned or can do that relate to the job you want__________

____

____

____

Situation 2

____

____

____

____

Details and skills used ______________________________

____

____

Specific things you learned or can do that relate to the job you want________________

____

____

____

Your Most Important Accomplishments and Skills to Tell an Employer

Here are three questions to help you consider which items from your history are most important to include in your resume and to mention in an interview.

1. What are the most important accomplishments and skills you can tell an employer regarding your education and training? ______________________

____

____

____

____

2. What are the most important accomplishments and skills you can present to an employer regarding your paid and unpaid work experiences?________________

____

____

____

____

(continued)

(continued)

3. What are the most important accomplishments and skills you can present to an employer regarding your other life experiences? ____________________

____

____

____

____

Emphasize these skills in your resume and in interviews!

Chapter 7

Identify Your Perfect Job and Industry

Whether or not you choose to include an actual Job Objective statement near the top of your resume, you should always have a clear job objective in mind. Even a general objective helps you to select details for your resume that best support what you want to do. If you have a very clear job objective, you could skip ahead to the next chapter; however, I do not recommend this. That's because this chapter will show you how to explore career and job alternatives you might not have considered.

This chapter will help you in the following ways:

- It will help you more clearly identify the range of jobs you can target in your job search.
- It will show you how to obtain more information related to jobs that interest you.
- It will help you write your resume's Job Objective statement and support it with skills and other details.
- It will assist you in making good career decisions.

Why Your Resume Needs a Job Objective

One of the worst things you can do with your resume is to try to make it work for "any" job. Although it is acceptable for you to consider a broad range of jobs, applicants who don't have a clear idea of what they want to do impress few employers. This means that all but the simplest resumes deserve to include a job objective.

Another mistake many people make on resumes is not emphasizing skills that support the job objective. So, if you are not clear about what sort of job you want, it will be most difficult to present the skills you have to do the job.

Quick Tip

As you may know, deciding on a job objective can be quite complicated. The U.S. Department of Labor defines over 12,000 job titles, and it would be impractical to consider all alternatives. You probably have some idea of jobs that either interest you or that you are most likely to consider. If you have no idea about what you want to do, you need to settle the matter (or make it appear as if you have settled it) when you write your resume.

This chapter will help you learn more about the job options available to you—and how to use career information sources in constructing your resume. If you are not sure of what sort of job you want or are considering additional education or training, plan to thoroughly explore your career options and consider this chapter as an introduction to a more thorough process.

Consider Jobs Within Clusters of Related Occupations

Most people overlook many job opportunities. They do this simply because they don't know about all the occupations that are suited to someone with their skills, interests, and experience. Most people go about their lives and their work with very little information about the universe of career and job possibilities. They may go to school and take courses that interest them, but later find jobs in a haphazard way. Their careers develop almost by accident. That is how it happened for me during my early years, and it was probably that way for you. Things simply happened.

But I think most of us can do better. I am not suggesting that career planning is a simple process; however, you can do a few simple things to make better decisions. And, in this chapter, I will present a few points that I think can be particularly helpful.

The first step is to introduce you to several ways that labor market experts have organized jobs and information about jobs. Fortunately, the over 12,000 job titles are not in random order. Someone has spent a lot of time arranging them into clusters of related jobs. Knowing these arrangements can help you identify possible job targets, prepare for interviews, consider long-term career plans, and of course, write a better resume.

The *Occupational Outlook Handbook*

I consider the *Occupational Outlook Handbook* (which I will now refer to as the *OOH*) to be one of the most helpful books on career information available. I urge you either to buy one or arrange for frequent access to it throughout your job search because it is so useful in a variety of ways.

The *OOH* provides descriptions for about 280 of America's most popular jobs, organized within *clusters* of related jobs. Although that may not sound like many jobs, about 87 percent of the workforce works in these jobs.

The *OOH* is updated every two years by the U.S. Department of Labor and provides the latest information on salaries, growth projections, related jobs, skills required, education or training needed, working conditions, and many other details. Each job is described in a readable, interesting format.

Quick Tip

I've included one job description from the *Occupational Outlook Handbook* in Appendix A for you to review. Although that particular job may not interest you, reading the description will help you understand how useful the *OOH* job descriptions can be.

Some Ways to Use the OOH

You can use the *OOH* in many ways. Here are some suggestions:

- **To identify the skills needed in the job you want.** Look up a job that interests you, and the *OOH* will tell you the transferable and job-related skills it requires. Assuming that you have these skills, you can then emphasize them in your resume and interviews.
- **To find skills from previous jobs to support your present objective.** Look up *OOH* descriptions for jobs you have had in the past. A careful read will help you identify skills that can be transferred and used in the new job. Even "minor" jobs can be valuable in this way. For example, if you waited on tables while going to school, you would discover that this requires the ability to work under pressure, deal with customers, and work quickly. If you are now looking for a job as an accountant, you can see how transferable skills used in an apparently unrelated past job can support your ability to do another job. If you are changing careers or don't have much work experience related to the job you want, describing your transferable skills can be very important.
- **To identify related job targets. Each major job described in the *OOH* lists other jobs that are closely related.** The description also provides information on positions that the job might lead to through promotion or experience. And, since the jobs are listed within clusters of similar jobs, you can easily browse descriptions of related jobs you may have overlooked. All of this detail gives you options to consider in your job search as well as information to include in the Job Objective section of your resume.
- **To find out the typical salary range, trends, and other details.** While you should never (well, almost never) list your salary requirements in a resume or cover letter, the *OOH* will help you

know what pay range to expect and which trends are affecting the job. Note that local pay averages and other details can differ significantly from the national information provided in the *OOH*.

- **To get more specific information on this and related jobs.** If a job interests you, it is important to learn more about it. Each *OOH* job description provides helpful sources, including a cross-reference to the O*NET career information, related professional associations, Internet sites, and other sources.

Quick Reference

Most libraries have the *Occupational Outlook Handbook,* but you probably won't be able to take it home. Another book titled *America's Top 300 Jobs* provides the same information (plus my job search tips) and is often available for circulation. You can order either book through JIST or most bookstores. These books should be used as reference tools frequently during your job search and after. You can also access the *OOH* information online at www.careeroink.com or at www.bls.gov/oco.

A Complete List of the 277 Jobs in the Occupational Outlook Handbook

Following are the jobs in the current edition of the *OOH,* arranged in the same clusters used there. The clusters will give you an idea of related jobs you might want to consider when writing your resume and conducting your job search.

Put a check mark by any job that interests you or that you have done in the past. Later, you can look up these jobs in the *OOH* and obtain additional information related to each.

List of Jobs in the *OOH* within Clusters of Related Jobs

Management and Business and Financial Operations Occupations

Management Occupations

Administrative services managers

Advertising, marketing, promotions, public relations, and sales managers

Computer and information systems managers

Construction managers

Education administrators

Engineering and natural sciences managers

Farmers, ranchers, and agricultural managers

Financial managers

Food service managers

Funeral directors

Human resources, training, and labor relations managers and specialists

Industrial production managers

Lodging managers

Medical and health services managers

Property, real estate, and community association managers

Purchasing managers, buyers, and purchasing agents

Top executives

Business and Financial Operations Occupations

Accountants and auditors

Budget analysts

Claims adjusters, appraisers, examiners, and investigators

Cost estimators

Financial analysts and personal financial advisors

Insurance underwriters

Loan counselors and officers

Management analysts

Tax examiners, collectors, and revenue agents

Professional and Related Occupations

Computer and Mathematical Occupations

Actuaries

Computer programmers

Computer software engineers

Computer support specialists and systems administrators

Mathematicians

Operations research analysts

Statisticians

Computer systems analysts, database administrators, and computer scientists

Architects, Surveyors, and Cartographers

Architects, except landscape and naval

Landscape architects

Surveyors, cartographers, photogrammetrists, and surveying technicians

Engineers

Aerospace engineers

Agricultural engineers

Biomedical engineers

Chemical engineers

Civil engineers

Computer hardware engineers

Electrical and electronics engineers, except computer

Environmental engineers

Industrial engineers, including health and safety
Materials engineers
Mechanical engineers
Mining and geological engineers, including mining safety engineers
Nuclear engineers
Petroleum engineers

Drafters and Engineering Technicians

Drafters
Engineering technicians

Life Scientists

Agricultural and food scientists
Biological scientists
Medical scientists
Conservation scientists and foresters

Physical Scientists

Atmospheric scientists
Chemists and materials scientists
Environmental scientists and geoscientists
Physicists and astronomers

Social Scientists and Related Occupations

Economists
Market and survey researchers
Psychologists
Urban and regional planners
Social scientists, other

Science Technicians

Community and Social Services Occupations

Clergy
    Protestant ministers
    Rabbis
    Roman Catholic priests
Counselors
Probational officers and correctional treatment specialists
Social and human service assistants
Social workers

Legal Occupations

Court reporters
Judges, magistrates, and other judicial workers
Lawyers
Paralegals and legal assistants

Education, Training, Library, and Museum Occupations

Archivists, curators, and museum technicians
Instructional coordinators
Librarians
Library technicians
Teacher assistants
Teachers—adult literacy and remedial and self-enrichment education
Teachers—postsecondary
Teachers—preschool, kindergarten, elementary, middle, and secondary
Teachers—special education

Arts and Design

Artists and related workers
Designers

Entertainers and Performers, Sports and Related Occupations

Actors, producers, and directors
Athletes, coaches, umpires, and related workers
Dancers and choreographers
Musicians, singers, and related workers

Media and Communications-Related Occupations

Announcers
Broadcast and sound engineering technicians and radio operators
Interpreters and translators
News analysts, reporters, and correspondents

(continued)

(continued)

List of Jobs in the *OOH* within Clusters of Related Jobs

Photographers
Public relations specialists
Television, video, and motion picture camera operators and editors
Writers and editors

Health Diagnosing and Treating Occupations

Audiologists
Chiropractors
Dentists
Dietitians and nutritionists
Occupational therapists
Optometrists
Pharmacists
Physical therapists
Physician assistants
Physicians and surgeons
Podiatrists
Recreational therapists
Registered nurses
Respiratory therapists
Speech-language pathologists
Veterinarians

Health Technologists and Technicians

Cardiovascular technologists and technicians
Clinical laboratory technologists and technicians
Dental hygienists
Diagnostic medical sonographers
Emergency medical technicians and paramedics
Licensed practical and licensed vocational nurses
Medical records and health information technicians
Nuclear medicine technologists
Occupational health and safety specialists and technicians
Opticians, dispensing
Pharmacy technicians
Radiologic technologists and technicians
Surgical technologists
Veterinary technologists and technicians

Service Occupations

Healthcare Support Occupations

Dental assistants
Medical assistants
Medical transcriptionists
Nursing, psychiatric, and home health aides
Occupational therapist assistants and aides
Pharmacy aides
Physical therapist assistants and aides

Protective Service Occupations

Correctional officers
Firefighting occupations
Police and detectives
Private detectives and investigators
Security guards and gaming surveillance officers

Food Preparation and Serving Related Occupations

Chefs, cooks, and food preparation workers
Food and beverage serving and related workers

Building and Grounds Cleaning and Maintenance Occupations

Building cleaning workers
Grounds maintenance workers

Pest control workers

Personal Care and Service Occupations

Animal care and service workers

Barbers, cosmetologists, and other personal appearance workers

Childcare workers

Flight attendants

Gaming services occupations

Personal and home care aides

Recreation and fitness workers

Sales and Related Occupations

Cashiers

Counter and rental clerks

Demonstrators, product promoters, and models

Insurance sales agents

Real estate brokers and sales agents

Retail salespersons

Sales engineers

Sales representatives, wholesale and manufacturing

Sales worker supervisors

Securities, commodities, and financial services sales agents

Travel agents

Office and Administrative Support Occupations

Communications equipment operators

Computer operators

Customer service representatives

Data entry and information processing workers

Desktop publishers

Financial clerks

Bill and account collectors

Billing and posting clerks and machine operators

Bookkeeping, accounting and auditing clerks

Gaming cage workers

Payroll and timekeeping clerks

Procurement clerks

Tellers

Information and record clerks

Brokerage clerks

Credit authorizers, checkers and clerks

File clerks

Hotel, motel and resort desk clerks

Human resources assistants, except payroll and timekeeping

Interviewers

Library assistants, clerical

Order clerks

Receptionists and information clerks

Reservation and transportation ticket agents and travel clerks

Material recording, scheduling, dispatching, and distributing occupations, except postal workers

Cargo and freight agents

Couriers and messengers

Dispatchers

Meter readers, utilities

Production, planning, and expediting clerks

Shipping, receiving, and traffic clerks

Stock clerks and order fillers

Weighers, measurers, checkers, and samplers, recordkeeping

Office and administrative support worker supervisors and managers

Office clerks, general

Postal service workers

Secretaries and administrative assistants

(continued)

(continued)

List of Jobs in the *OOH* within Clusters of Related Jobs

Farming, Fishing and Forestry Occupations

- Agricultural workers
- Fishers and fishing vessel operators
- Forest, conservation, and logging workers

Construction Trades and Related Workers

- Boilermakers
- Brickmasons, blockmasons, and stonemasons
- Carpenters
- Carpet, floor, and tile installers and finishers
- Cement masons, concrete finishers, segmental pavers, and terrazzo workers
- Construction and building inspectors
- Construction equipment operators
- Construction laborers
- Drywall installers, ceiling tile installers, and tapers
- Electricians
- Elevator installers and repairers
- Glaziers
- Hazardous materials removal workers
- Insulation workers
- Painters and paperhangers
- Pipelayers, plumbers, pipefitters, and steamfitters
- Plasterers and stucco masons
- Roofers
- Sheet metal workers
- Structural and reinforcing iron and metal workers

Installation, Maintenance and Repair Occupations

Electrical and Electronic Equipment Mechanics, Installers, and Repairers

- Computer, automated teller, and office machine repairers
- Electrical and electronics installers and repairers
- Electronic home entertainment equipment installers and repairers
- Radio and telecommunications equipment installers and repairers

Vehicle and Mobile Equipment Mechanics, Installers, and Repairers

- Aircraft and avionics equipment mechanics and service technicians
- Automotive body and related repairers
- Automotive service technicians and mechanics
- Diesel service technicians and mechanics
- Heavy vehicle and mobile equipment service technicians and mechanics
- Small engine mechanics

Other Installation, Maintenance, and Repair Occupations

- Coin, vending, and amusement machine servicers and repairers
- Heating, air-conditioning, and refrigeration mechanics and installers
- Home appliance repairers
- Industrial machinery installation, repair, and maintenance workers, except millwrights
- Line installers and repairers

Maintenance and repair workers, general

Millwrights

Precision instrument and equipment repairers

Production Occupations

Assemblers and Fabricators

Food Processing Occupations

Metal Workers and Plastic Workers

Computer-control programmers and operators

Machinists

Machine setters, operators and tenders—metal and plastics

Tool and die makers

Welding, soldering, and brazing workers

Printing Occupations

Bookbinders and bindery workers

Prepress technicians and workers

Printing machine operators

Textile, Apparel, and Furnishings Occupations

Woodworkers

Plant and System Operators

Power plant operators, distributors, and dispatchers

Stationary engineers and boiler operators

Water and liquid waste treatment plant and system operators

Other Production Occupations

Dental laboratory technicians

Inspectors, testers, sorters, samplers, and weighers

Jewelers and precious stone and metal workers

Ophthalmic laboratory technicians

Painting and coating workers, except construction and maintenance

Photographic process workers and processing machine operators

Semiconductor processors

Transportation and Material Moving Occupations

Air Transportation Occupations

Aircraft pilots and flight engineers

Air traffic controllers

Motor Vehicle Operators

Bus drivers

Taxi drivers and chauffeurs

Truck drivers and driver/sales workers

Rail Transportation Occupations

Water Transportation Occupations

Material Moving Occupations

Job Opportunities in the Armed Forces

Quick Tip

A very useful book titled the *Enhanced Occupational Outlook Handbook* includes the complete text of each job description in the current *OOH* plus brief descriptions for more than 1,100 O*NET jobs and more than 6,000 more specialized job descriptions from the *Dictionary of Occupational Titles*. This approach allows you to quickly identify the many specialized job titles in a simple-to-use format.

Other Important Sources of Occupational Information

There are a variety of useful career information sources and I present here the ones I consider most important.

*The Occupational Information Network—the O*NET*

The U.S. Department of Labor maintains an up-to-date computer-database of occupational information. Called the O*NET, it provides detailed information for almost 1,200 jobs. While the *OOH* is more useful for most situations, the O*NET describes many more jobs (and more specialized jobs) and provides more details on each one.

The O*NET database offers basic descriptions for each of its jobs, plus 450 additional data elements for each job. Keep in mind that the O*NET is a complex database and much of the detailed information it provides will not be of much use for most job seekers—it is simply too much and too detailed if used in its database form.

Quick Tip

Fortunately, career counselors have developed more helpful versions of the O*NET database. A book version published by JIST and titled the *O*NET Dictionary of Occupational Titles* was designed to provide the O*NET information of greatest value to most job seekers in an easy-to-use book format.

The job descriptions in this book are presented in an easy-to-use format that is packed with information, including the following:

- **O*NET Number.** Allows you to cross-reference other systems using this number.
- **O*NET Occupational Title.** The job title most often used for this job.
- **Related *OOH* Title/s.** Tells you the most closely related major job title in the *OOH*.

- **Number Employed.** Gives the total number of people who work in that job.
- **Number of Openings.** Provides the number of job openings per year projected for the job.
- **Earnings.** Provides the average annual earnings for people employed in the job.
- **O*NET Occupational Description.** A brief but useful review of what a person working in that job would typically do.
- **GOE Information.** Allows cross-reference to related jobs in the *Guide for Occupational Exploration*'s Interest Area and Work Group.
- **Personality Type.** Tells you what personality type the job best fits into in the system used in Holland's Self-Directed Search or other interest inventories.
- **Work Values.** Lists any of the job's 21 work values with high scores in the O*NET database.
- **Knowledge.** Areas of knowledge required to successfully perform in the occupation described. The knowledge may have been obtained from formal or informal sources, including high school or college courses or majors, training programs, self-employment, military, paid or volunteer work experience, or other life experience.
- **Physical Work Conditions.** Information on work hazards, environment, strength, and other measures.
- **Skills.** Lists a variety of skills needed to perform at above-average levels in each job. Depending on the occupation, some of these skills are quite complex, while others are relatively basic.
- **Work Activities.** Lists the general types of work activities needed to perform the job described.
- **Job Characteristics.** Includes several types of information such as interacting with others; mental processes; role relationships; communication methods; responsibility for others; and many more.
- **Experience.** Lists the work or other experience the job requires.

- **Job Preparation.** Provides specific information on the training or education level the job requires.
- **Related Classification of Instructional Programs.** A cross-reference to a system that provides information on the type of training and education typically required for entry into the occupation.
- **Related *Dictionary of Occupational Titles* Jobs.** Lists related job titles from the *DOT,* a standard reference book that describes more than 12,000 jobs.

The complete set of O*NET information is available on the Internet at http://online.onetcenter.org/. I recommend, however, that you use the *O*NET Dictionary of Occupational Titles* book because it was designed for career exploration and job seeking. Your library or school may have access to a CD-ROM version of the O*NET. This can be a useful tool as well.

Quick Tip

Look up the *OOH* or O*NET description of a job you will interview for and include keywords or skill sets for that job in your resume, cover letter, and interview. You will be much better prepared to target your presentation and give the specific strengths you have that are needed for the job.

The Guide for Occupational Exploration

After extensive research, the U.S. Department of Labor developed an easy-to-use system that organized all jobs by interest. For example, if you are interested in artistic activities, this system would allow you to identify the many jobs related to this area. This interest-based system is presented in a book titled the *Guide for Occupational Exploration (GOE)* and is used in a variety of print and computer career information systems.

The current edition of the *GOE* organizes all jobs into just 14 major interest areas. These areas are further divided into more specific groupings ("work groups") of related jobs. While the *GOE* system is easy to understand and use, it is powerful enough to allow thousands of job titles to be organized into its various work groups.

The *GOE* allows you to quickly identify groups of jobs that are most closely related to what you want to do. All along the way, from major interest areas to the more specific work groups, helpful information is provided related to each group of jobs. So, even if some jobs are not familiar to you, the *GOE* gives you enough information to help you understand the jobs within that group and what they require. In a quick and logical way, you can use the *GOE* to narrow down the thousands of job possibilities to the dozen or so that most closely match what you want to do and are good at.

Quick Tip

A good Internet site for free career information is located at www.careeroink.com. Maintained by JIST, it provides most of the information from the *OOH*, O*NET, and *GOE* sources mentioned in this chapter as well as sample resumes, crosswalks to job postings, and many other helpful resources.

The *GOE*'s Major Interest Areas

The current edition of the *Guide for Occupational Exploration* is published by JIST and includes the 14 major Interest Areas presented here.

The 14 Interest Areas in the Current GOE

1. Arts, Entertainment, and Media
2. Science, Math, and Engineering
3. Plants and Animals
4. Law, Law Enforcement, and Public Safety
5. Mechanics, Installers, and Repairers
6. Construction, Mining, and Drilling
7. Transportation
8. Industrial Production
9. Business Detail
10. Sales and Marketing
11. Recreation, Travel, and Other Personal Services
12. Education and Social Service
13. General Management and Support
14. Medical and Health Services

GOE Work Groups Provide a Quick Way to Find Related Jobs

Each of the *GOE*'s Interest Areas is broken down into more specific groups of related jobs. This is a very helpful approach because it allows you to quickly identify groups of jobs that are of most interest to you.

To show you how the *GOE*'s is organized, I've provided a sample listing of one *GOE* Interest Area here: "Arts, Entertainment, and Media." Under it, listed in bold text, are the various work groups for this Interest Area. In regular type following each work group name are the job titles from the O*NET that fit into each group. As you can see, this allows you to quickly find a work group that interests you and then review the job titles within that group. You can then use the *GOE* to read job descriptions for the jobs that interest you most or to get more details on the education, training, type of work, and other information for the jobs in that work group.

Subgroupings Within the GOE *Arts, Entertainment, and Media Interest Area*

GOE INTEREST AREA: 1. ARTS, ENTERTAINMENT, AND MEDIA

Work Group: Managerial Work

O*NET jobs: Agents and Business Managers of Artists, Performers, and Athletes; Art Directors; Producers; Program Directors; Technical Directors/Managers

Work Group: Writing and Editing

O*NET jobs: Editors; Technical Writers; Poets and Lyricists; Creative Writers; Copy Writers

Work Group: News, Broadcasting, and Public Relations

O*NET jobs: Broadcast News Analysts; Reporters and Correspondents; Public Relations Specialists; Caption Writers; Interpreters and Translators

Work Group: Visual Arts: Studio Art

O*NET jobs: Painters and Illustrators; Sketch Artists; Cartoonists; Sculptors

Work Group: Visual Arts: Design

O*NET jobs: Multi-media Artists and Animators; Commercial and Industrial Designers; Fashion Designers; Floral Designers; Graphic Designers; Interior Designers; Merchandise Displayers and Window Trimmers; Set Designers; Exhibit Designers

Work Group: Performing Arts: Drama: Directing, Performing, Narrating, and Announcing

O*NET jobs: Actors; Stage, Motion Pictures, Television, and Radio; Radio and Television Announcers; Public Address System and Other Announcers

Work Group: Performing Arts, Music: Directing, Composing and Arranging, and Performing

O*NET jobs: Talent Directors; Music Directors; Music Arrangers and Orchestrators; Composers; Singers; Musicians, Instrumental

Work Group: Performing Arts, Dance: Performing and Choreography

O*NET jobs: Dancers; Choreographers

Work Group: Craft Arts

O*NET jobs: Craft Artists; Glass Blowers, Molders, Benders, and Finishers; Potters

Work Group: Graphic Arts

O*NET jobs: Desktop Publishers; Paste-Up Workers; Photoengravers; Camera Operators; Dot Etchers; Electronic Masking System Operators; Precision Etchers and Engravers, Hand or Machine; Engravers/Carvers; Etchers; Pantograph Engravers; Etchers, Hand; Engravers, Hand

Work Group: Media Technology

O*NET jobs: Audio and Video Equipment Technicians; Broadcast Technicians; Radio Operators; Sound Engineering Technicians; Professional Photographers; Camera Operators, Television, Video, and Motion Picture; Film and Video Editors

(continued)

(continued)

Work Group: Modeling and Personal Appearance

O*NET jobs: Costume Attendants; Makeup Artists, Theatrical and Performance; Models

Work Group: Sports: Coaching, Instructing, Officiating, and Performing

O*NET jobs: Athletes and Sports Competitors; Coaches and Scouts; Umpires, Referees, and Other Sports Officials; Fitness Trainers and Aerobics Instructors

GOE in Book and Internet Format

The current edition of the *Guide for Occupational Exploration* includes descriptions for all jobs (more than 1,100) described in the O*NET, plus substantial additional information on the jobs in each Interest Area and work group. Among many other things, the *GOE* provides special crosswalks that allow you to identify jobs by your values, leisure activities, school subjects, work settings, skills required, special knowledge areas, abilities, and home activities. You should be able to find the *GOE* in most libraries, and the GOE system is also used in various computerized career information systems you may have access to. Much of its content is also available on the Internet at www.careeroink.com.

Also Consider Industries in Your Job Search

Although much of this chapter is devoted to occupational choices, the industry you work in can be just as important. For example, an information technology professional with an interest in health and wellness might be happier working in an IT role at a hospital rather than in aircraft manufacturing or some other industry of lesser interest.

> Your job search and career planning should consider both occupation and industry.

Look for an industry that interests you or that you know something about from your hobbies, family business, volunteer work, or other life experiences. Some industries also pay better than others for essentially the same work. Being clear about what industry you want to work in, and why, can give you a competitive edge over those who don't have a preference.

Following is a list of about 40 major industries from a book titled *Career Guide to America's Top Industries* by the U.S. Department of Labor. The book gives details on the nature of the industry, working conditions, employment opportunities, types of occupations it employs, training needed, earnings, outlook, and more for each industry.

Major Industries to Consider

Goods-Producing Industries

Agriculture, Mining, and Construction

Agriculture, forestry, and fishing
Construction
Mining
Oil and gas extraction

Manufacturing

Aerospace product and parts manufacturing
Apparel manufacturing
Chemical manufacturing, except pharmaceutical and medicine manufacturing
Computer and electronic product manufacturing
Food manufacturing
Motor vehicle and parts manufacturing
Pharmaceutical and medicine manufacturing
Printing
Steel manufacturing
Textile mills and products

Service-Producing Industries

Trade

Automobile dealers
Clothing, accessory, and general merchandise stores
Grocery stores
Wholesale trade

Transportation and utilities

Air transportation
Truck transportation and warehousing
Utilities

Information

Broadcasting
Motion picture and video industries
Publishing, except software
Software publishers
Telecommunications

Financial Activities

Banking
Insurance
Securities, commodities, and other investments

Professional and Business Services

Advertising and public relations services
Computer systems design and related services
Employment services
Management, scientific, and technical consulting services

Education and Health Services

Child daycare services
Educational services
Health services
Social assistance, except child daycare

Government

Federal government, excluding the Postal Service
State and local government, excluding education and hospitals

Values, Preferences, and Other Matters to Consider in Defining Your Job Objective

Following is a brief review of points that others have found important in making career plans. While this won't replace a thorough career planning process, you may find it helpful to consider a variety of issues that relate to deciding on a job objective, working on your resume, and making career plans.

Eight Quick Questions to Help You Define Your Ideal Job

If you were to develop a profile of your ideal job, just what would it include? As you probably realize, this includes more than picking out a job title. I have selected questions that you should consider in defining your ideal job. Of course, this involves a bit of reality (and I have included some of these elements), but dreams can never come true if you don't have them. So, I present the following very important but sometimes overlooked issues for you to consider in planning your job objective.

What Skills Do You Have That You Want to Use in Your Next Job?

Review the skills lists you worked on in Chapter 5. Think about those skills that you enjoy using and are particularly good at. Then list the five that you would most like to use in your next job.

1. ______________________________
2. ______________________________
3. ______________________________
4. ______________________________
5. ______________________________

What Type of Special Knowledge Do You Have That You Might Use in Your Next Job?

Perhaps you know how to fix radios, keep accounting records, or cook food. You don't need to have used these skills in a previous job to include them. Write down the things you have learned from schooling, training, hobbies, family experiences, and other sources. Perhaps one or more of them could make you a very competitive applicant in the right setting. For example, an accountant who knows a lot about fashion would be a very special candidate if he or she just happened to be interviewing for a job with an organization that sells clothing. Can you see the possibilities?

1. ______________________________

2. ______________________________

3. ______________________________

4. ______________________________

5. ______________________________

What Types of People Do You Prefer to Work With?

It is unlikely you will be happy in a job if you're surrounded by people you don't like. One way to approach this is to think about characteristics of people that you would not want to work with. The opposite characteristics are those that you probably would enjoy. For example, if you don't like a boss or coworkers that are negative and constantly complaining, you can say that you prefer to work with people who are positive about their work and a boss who provides positive feedback. List the preferred characteristics of your supervisor and coworkers here.

1. ______________________________

2. ______________________________

3. ______________________________

4. ______________________________

5. ______________________________

What Type of Work Environment Do You Prefer?

Do you want to work inside, outside, in a quiet place, in a busy place, in a clean place, or a place with a nice view? For example, I like variety in what I do (since I am easily bored), so I want a work environment with lots of action and diversity—and a window. Once again, you can review what you have disliked about past work environments for clues on what you would most appreciate. Write those things that are most important to have on your next job.

1. ______________________________

2. ______________________________

3. ______________________________

(continued)

(continued)

4. ______________________________
5. ______________________________

Where Do You Want Your Next Job to Be Located—in What City or Region?

This could be as simple as finding a job that allows you to live where you are now (because you want to stay near your relatives, for example). Or, you may prefer to work in an area near certain necessities or conveniences, such as one close to a child-care center. If you were able to live or work anywhere, what would your ideal community be like? List its characteristics here.

1. ______________________________
2. ______________________________
3. ______________________________
4. ______________________________
5. ______________________________

How Much Money Do You Hope to Make in Your Next Job?

Many people will take less money if the job is great in other ways—or if they just need a job to survive. Think about the minimum you would take as well as what you would eventually like to earn. Realistically, your next job will probably be somewhere between your minimum and maximum amounts.

How much money do you hope to get in your next job? ______________________________

What is the least you are willing to accept? ______________________________

How Much Responsibility Are You Willing to Accept?

In most organizations, those willing to accept more responsibility are often paid more—there is typically a relationship between the two. Higher levels of responsibility often require you to supervise others or to make decisions that affect the organization. Some people are willing to accept this responsibility; and others, understandably, would prefer not to.

Decide how much responsibility you are willing to accept and write that here. ________

____

____

You should also ask yourself if you prefer to work by yourself, be part of a group, or be in charge. If so, at what level? Jot down where you see yourself, in terms of accepting responsibility for others, and in other ways within an organization. ________________

____

____

The Top Ten Values Employers Want

In completing some of these questions, it might help you to know the values that are most often cited in surveys of employers as being important in the people they hire:

1. Honesty/integrity/morality
2. Adaptability/flexibility
3. Dedication/hardworking/work ethic/tenacity
4. Dependability/reliability/responsibility
5. Loyalty
6. Positive attitude/motivation/energy/passion
7. Professionalism
8. Self-confidence
9. Self-motivated/ability to work with little or no supervision
10. Willingness to learn

What Things Are Important or Have Meaning to You?

What are your values? I once had a job where the sole reason for the organization's existence was to make money. Not that this is wrong—it's just that I wanted to be involved in something I could believe in. If money is the thing for you, fine. But some people prefer working to help others, clean up our environment, build things, make machines work, gain power or prestige, care for animals or plants, or many other possibilities. I believe that all work is worthwhile if done well, so the issue here is what is important to include in your next job, if you can. Write these values below.

(continued)

(continued)

1. ______________________________
2. ______________________________
3. ______________________________
4. ______________________________
5. ______________________________

Your Ideal Job

Use the eight preceding questions as a basis for defining your ideal job. Think about each question and select the points most important to you. You may want to include other issues not covered by the questions but that are particularly important to you.

You don't have to be practical here, nor do you need to write a job objective as it might appear on your resume. Just dream.

Now, write the five to ten most important elements you would like to include in your next job, your ideal job, if only you could find it.

1. ______________________________
2. ______________________________
3. ______________________________
4. ______________________________
5. ______________________________
6. ______________________________
7. ______________________________
8. ______________________________
9. ______________________________
10. ______________________________

Write Your Resume's Job Objective

Once you have a good idea of your ideal job, you need to write the job objective you will use for your resume. For many, this can be more difficult than it might seem. It assumes, for example, that you have a good idea of the type of job or jobs you want.

You may need to spend more time researching career alternatives before settling on one you can use for your resume. If that is the case with you, consider putting together a resume around a broad job objective that makes the resume acceptable for a variety of jobs. Even if you are not sure that these are the ones you want long term, doing this allows you to conduct a job search while researching alternatives. In some cases, a job may present itself that is acceptable to you, even though it may be in a field you were not sure of. It happens.

It is also acceptable to create more than one resume, each with a different job objective. This approach allows you to write your resume's content to support each job objective in a specific way.

Quick Alert

If you still don't know what type of job you want, concentrate on what you want to do next. That might be working toward a long-term objective such as going back to school or starting your own business. In the meantime, you may also need to earn a living, so decide on a short-term job goal that you are qualified for and go after it. Make that short-term job goal the job objective for your resume.

Four Quick Tips for Writing a Good Job Objective

While the job objective you write should meet your specific needs, here are some things to consider in writing it:

1. **Avoid job titles.** Job titles such as "administrative assistant" or "marketing analyst" can involve very different activities in different organizations. The same job can often have different job titles in different places, and using a title may limit you from consideration for such jobs as "office manager" or "marketing assistant."

   It is best to use broad categories of jobs rather than specific titles. You can then be considered for a wide variety of jobs related to your skills. For example, instead of "administrative assistant," you could say "responsible office management, support, and coordination position" if that is what you would really consider—and qualify for.

2. **Define a "bracket of responsibility" to include the possibility of upward mobility.** Although you may be willing to accept a variety of jobs related to your skills, you should include those that require higher levels of responsibility and pay. In the preceding example, it keeps open the option to be considered for an office management position as well as clerical jobs.

(continued)

(continued)

In effect, you should define a "bracket of responsibility" in your objective that includes the range of jobs you are willing to accept. This bracket should include the lower range of jobs that you would consider as well as those requiring higher levels of responsibility, up to and including those that you think you could handle. Even if you have not handled those higher levels of responsibility in the past, many employers may consider you if you have the skills to support the objective.

3. **Include your most important skills.** What are the most important skills needed for the job you want? Consider including one or more of these as required for the job you seek. The implication here is that if you are looking for a job that requires "organizational skills," then you have those skills. Of course, your resume content should support those skills with specific examples.
4. **Include specifics if these are important to you.** If you have substantial experience in a particular industry (such as "computer-controlled machine tools") or have a narrow and specific objective that you really want (such as "art therapist with the mentally handicapped"), then it is fine to state this. But realize that by narrowing your alternatives, you will often not be considered for other jobs for which you might qualify. Still, if that is what you want, it just may be worth pursuing (although I would encourage you to have a second, more general resume just in case).

The Job Objective Worksheet

Use this worksheet to create a draft of your resume's job objective. This worksheet includes questions and activities to help you decide what to include.

What Sort of Position, Title, and Area of Specialization Do You Seek?

Write the type of job you want, as if you were explaining it to someone you know.

____

____

____

____

Define Your "Bracket of Responsibility"

Describe the range of jobs that you would accept at a minimum as well as those you might be able to handle if given the chance.

Name the Key Skills You Have That Are Important in This Job

Describe the two or three key skills that are particularly important for success in the job you seek. Select one or more of these that you are strong in and that you enjoy using. Write it (or them) here.

Name Specific Areas of Expertise or Strong Interests That You Want to Use in Your Next Job

If you have substantial interest, experience, or training in a specific area and want to include it in your job objective, list that here.

What Else Is Important to You?

Is there anything else you want to include in your job objective? This could include a value that is particularly important, such as "A position that allows me to affect families" or "Employment in an aggressive and results-oriented organization"; a preference for the size or type of organization such as "A small to mid-size business"; or some other consideration.

(continued)

(continued)

Finalize Your Resume's Job Objective Statement

Look over the sample resumes in Sections One and Three to see how others have written their job objectives. Some do not include all the elements that are presented in the Job Objective Worksheet, and that is perfectly acceptable. Some are very brief, providing just a job title or category of jobs; others are quite long and detailed. Others don't include a Job Objective statement at all—it's just implied by the resume's content.

There are no rigid rules for writing your resume's Job Objective statement. You should include only information that is essential for an employer to know in considering you; this means that the objective should be brief. Each and every word should be important in some way. Go ahead and write your job objective below just as you want it to appear on your resume. Edit it so that each word counts, and make certain that each word creates a positive impression.

Chapter 8

Present Strengths and Overcome "Problems" on Your Resume

In a perfect world, we would be considered solely on our ability to do the job. But the reality is that employers are subjective, and their personal feelings about someone enter into the hiring decision.

In this chapter, I present common resume concerns I have heard from job seekers over the years and try to give you a positive way to present problems to employers. Employers are people too, and most are more understanding than you might think.

Never Highlight a Negative

Although it may not be apparent in many of this book's resumes, a well-written resume often covers a job seeker's weaknesses or flaws. That is precisely the point. All of the resumes are based on real ones written for and by real people. These resumes follow a primary resume-writing rule: *Never highlight a negative.* Since everyone has less-than-perfect credentials for a given job, all resumes hide one thing or another to some degree. In some cases, I have written notes on the sample resumes that point out how the writers have handled job-seeker problems. Use these as examples of how you might handle similar problems in your resume.

Quick Tip

Although I couldn't list every dilemma job seekers face, what follows will help you handle problems that many people deal with during their job search. If you have a different issue, this chapter will help you figure out what to do.

Note that these often are not just resume problems—they are problems to resolve when completing applications or in interviews. While the solutions offered relate primarily to handling the problems on a resume, you should gain some insight on how to approach the same problems in other situations as well.

Deal with "Problems" in an Interview, Not on Your Resume

A resume should present your strengths, so include only content an employer can interpret as positive. Try to think like an employer and exclude anything that *you* might interpret as a negative. While you can't be dishonest, neither should you present negative information. In many cases, issues that concern or worry you may not be problems to employers at all.

If something does not support your job objective, you should eliminate it. No rule says you must include information in a resume that may not help you.

Quick Alert

If you feel strongly that an employer needs to know something potentially negative about you, don't present it until you're in the interview. Better yet, don't bring it up at all until the employer asks about it!

Some Problems Are Sensitive Subjects

Just mentioning that the issues covered here might be "problems" will upset some people. For example, some will object to any mention that people over 50 might experience discrimination in the labor market. Individuals over 50 know, however, that their age makes it harder to get a good job. Others will resent the implication that employers would consider such issues as race, religion, national origin, child-care arrangements, membership in the cigar-and-steak-lover's society, and other "politically sensitive" matters in evaluating people for employment.

So, with the certainty of offending someone, I have included information that is a bit sensitive for some. But I think that you, as a job seeker, need to accept reality and look for ways to overcome situations that some might consider to be problems. It can be done.

Quick Fact

It's well known that some employers are unfair. Some consider factors in their hiring decisions that should not be factors. For example, many older people do have a harder time getting jobs than younger ones. Many employers are interested in whether a young woman has children (or is planning to in the near future). People are sometimes unfair, and employers are people.

I realize that some of these things are controversial and that you may not agree with some of my advice. But it is better that you consider these matters in advance and have a way to respond to them if they come up—or if you think one or more of them could be an issue to a given employer. I am on your side, and that is why I have listed the problems that follow, along with some suggestions for handling them.

General Guidelines for Handling "Problems"

Most employers are good people trying to do their jobs. They want to select people who will stay on the job, be reliable, and do well. That is usually why employers want to know as much as they can about you. Why, for example, are you new to this area? Do you plan on staying? If you are "overqualified," are you likely to be unhappy and leave after a short period of time?

Quick Tip

Employers want to determine whether they can depend on you and, to find out, they want to know more about you. You can either help them to know that, yes, you are reliable (and greatly increase your chances for a job offer, in spite of their technically inappropriate questions) or tell them to jump in the lake (which will likely not result in a job offer).

Employers want to understand your true motivations. This can involve understanding issues such as how likely you are to stay in the area and other matters that are not work related.

Some of these points may arise when you're completing your resume, although they are often far more of an issue in an interview. In many cases, a cover letter provides additional details, but an interview is where most "problems" can be best addressed. In that context, I suggest that you consider your situation in advance and be able to present to the employer that, in your case, the issue is simply not a problem at all, but an advantage.

In any case, an interview—and not a resume—is where you deal with problems. A resume is simply a preliminary piece of paper, and it should never, never present a problem of any kind. If yours does, you need to rework it until that problem is not evident.

In the interview, be truthful and learn to present your problem as a potential advantage, should it come up. In that context, I hope that the following tips help you see that almost every problem has two sides.

Quick Tips for Handling Specific Problems on a Resume

Here is my advice for handling a variety of problem situations on your resume.

Gaps in Work History

Many people have gaps in their work history. If you have a legitimate reason for major gaps, such as going to school or having a child, you can simply state this on your resume. You could, in some situations, handle one of these gaps by putting the alternative activity on the resume, with dates, just as you would handle any other job.

Quick Tip

Minor gaps, such as being out of work for several months, do not need an explanation. You can often simply exclude any mention of months on your resume. Instead, refer to the years you were employed, such as "2003 to 2005."

Being Out of Work

Some of the most accomplished people I know have been out of work at one time or another. One out of five people in the workforce experiences some unemployment each year, so you will be in good company. It's not a sin, and many people who are bosses have experienced it themselves, as have I. But the tradition is to try to hide this on the resume.

One technique is to put something like "(year you started) to present" on your resume when referring to your most recent job. This approach makes it look like you are still employed. While this might be an acceptable approach in some cases, it may also require you to explain yourself early on in an interview. This soft deception can start you off on a negative note and may not end up helping you at all. Another alternative is to write the actual month that you left your last job or to write some interim activity, such as being self-employed. Even if that means that you are working at a temporary agency, doing odd jobs, or helping a friend with his or her business, it is better than being deceitful.

Quick Reminder

A resume is the place for presenting positive information. If something might be interpreted as negative, do not include it. Use your judgment, and if in doubt, cut it out.

Being Fired and Other Negatives in Your Work History

There is no reason for a resume to include details related to why you left previous jobs—unless, of course, they were positive reasons. For example, leaving to accept a more responsible job is to your credit, and your resume can say this. If you have been fired, analyze why. In most cases, it is for reasons that do not have to do with your performance. Most often, people are fired as a result of interpersonal conflicts. Personality clashes are quite common and do not mean you will have the same problem in a different situation. If your performance was the reason, you may have to explain why that would not be the case in a new job.

The resume itself should present what you did well in previous situations. Leave the discussion of problems for the interview, and take time in advance to practice what you will say about them if asked.

Job History Unrelated to Your Current Job Objective

If your previous work experience was in jobs that don't relate to what you want to do next, your best bet is to use a skills resume. This resume format was presented in Chapter 3, and you can see examples of it there and in Section Three. In this situation, using a traditional chronological resume will display an apparent lack of preparation for the job you want.

The advantage of the skills resume in this situation is that it allows you to emphasize those transferable skills that you have developed and used in other settings. If you carefully select skills that are needed in the job you want next, you can draw from work and life experiences to demonstrate that you have the needed skills. And, of course, you would emphasize any education, training, and other experiences that directly prepared you for the job you now seek.

Quick Reference

Interview skills, including how to answer problem questions, are a topic of another book I wrote titled *Next-Day Job Interview.* If you need more information on handling a problem that may come up in an interview, I humbly suggest that this book will help you handle most interview situations well.

Changing Careers

This is a situation related to the preceding one and would also be handled through a skills resume. A change in careers does require some justification on your part, so that it makes sense to an employer.

For example, a teacher who wants to become a real estate sales agent could point to his hobby of investing in and fixing up old houses. He could discuss his superior communications skills and his ability to get students to do what they were told in a classroom. And he could describe the many after-hours activities he has been involved in as a sign of a high energy level and a willingness to work the nights and weekends needed to sell real estate.

Recent Graduate

If you have recently graduated, you probably are competing against those with similar levels of education but with more work experience. If you don't have a lot of work experience related to the job you want, you will need to emphasize your recent education or training. This might include specific mention of courses you took and other activities that most directly relate to the job you now seek.

QUICK REFERENCE

The sample resumes in Chapter 11 will show you how recent graduates have presented their education, part-time jobs while in school, and other activities in a positive and convincing way via a skills resume.

New graduates need to look at their school work as the equivalent of work. Indeed, school work is real work in that it requires self-discipline, completion of a variety of tasks, and other activities similar to those required in many jobs. You also may have learned a variety of things that are directly related to doing the job you want. A skills resume will allow you to present these experiences in the same way you might present work experiences in a chronological resume.

You should play up the fact, if you can, that you are familiar with the latest trends and techniques in your field and can apply these skills right away to the new job. And, since you are experienced in studying and learning new material, you will be better able to quickly learn the new job than someone who has been out of school for a while, won't you?

A skills resume will also allow you to more effectively present transferable skills you used in other jobs (such as waiting on tables) that don't seem to directly relate to the job you now want. These jobs can provide a wealth of adaptive and transferable skills that you can use, with some thought, to support your resume's job objective.

Too Little Experience

Young people, including recent graduates, often have difficulty in getting the jobs they want since employers often prefer to hire someone with more experience. If this is your situation, you may want to emphasize your adaptive skills (see Chapter 5) that would tend to compensate for a lack of experience.

Once again, a skills resume allows you to present yourself in the best light. For example, emphasizing skills such as "hardworking" and "learn new things quickly" may impress an employer enough to consider you over more experienced workers. It happens more often than you may think.

Quick Tip

You should also consider expressing a willingness to accept difficult or less desirable conditions as one way to break into a field and gain experience. For example, "willing to work weekends and evenings" or "able to travel or relocate" may open up some possibilities.

Look for anything that might be acceptable as experience and emphasize it. This might include volunteer work, family responsibilities, education, training, military experience, or anything else you might present as legitimate activities that support your ability to do the work you believe you can do.

Overqualified

It doesn't seem to make sense that you could have too much experience, but some employers may think so. They may fear you will not be satisfied with the available job and that, after awhile, you will leave for a better one. So what they really need is some assurance of why this would not be the case for you.

Quick Alert

If, in fact, you are looking for a job with higher pay than the one you are applying for—and if you communicate this in some way to an employer—it is quite likely that he or she will not offer you a job for fear that the company will soon lose you. And they may be right.

After a period of unemployment, most people become more willing to settle for less than they had hoped for. If you are willing to accept jobs where you may be defined as overqualified, consider not including some of your educational or work-related credentials on your resume—although I do not necessarily recommend doing this. Be prepared to explain, in the interview, why you do want this particular job and how your wealth of experience is a positive and not a negative.

Race, Religion, or National Origin

There is simply no need to make this an issue on your resume. The most important issue is whether you can do the job well. For this reason, I discourage people from including details that refer to these issues.

Not Sure of Job Objective

As I have mentioned on several occasions, including a job objective on your resume is highly desirable. If you really can't settle on a long-term job objective, consider a short-term one, and use that on your resume. In some cases, you can also develop several resumes, each with its own job objective. This allows you to select information that will best support your various options.

Recently Moved

Employers are often concerned that someone who has recently moved to an area may soon leave. If you are new to the area, consider explaining this on your resume (or, better yet, in your cover letter). A simple statement such as "Relocated to Cincinnati to be closer to my family" or any other reasonable explanation will often be enough to present yourself as stable. Giving a reason will eliminate the concern for most employers.

No Degree or Less Education Than Typically Required

If you have the experience and skills to do a job that is often filled by someone with more education, you should take special care in preparing the Education and Experience sections of your resume.

For those with substantial work experience, you can simply not include an Education section. While this has the advantage of not presenting your lack of formal credentials in an obvious way, a better approach might be to present the education and training that you do have without indicating that you do not have a degree. For example, mention that you attended such-and-such college or program but don't mention that you did not complete it. Several sample resumes in Section Three take this approach (see pages 202, 204, 216, 238, 264, and 278). It avoids you being screened out unnecessarily and provides you with a chance at an interview you might not otherwise get.

Quick Tip

Note that I do not suggest you misrepresent yourself by overstating your qualifications or claiming a degree you do not have. That may result in your later being fired and is clearly not a good idea. But again, no law requires you to display your weaknesses. As I said earlier, the interview is where you can bring up any problems or explain any weaknesses.

Too Young

Young people need to present their youth as an advantage rather than as a disadvantage. So consider just what aspects of your youth might be seen as advantages. For example, perhaps you are willing to work for less money, accept less desirable tasks, work longer or less convenient hours, or do other things that a more experienced worker might not. If so, say so.

You need to realize that many employers prefer to hire workers with experience and demonstrated ability in jobs related to those they have available. Still, young people who present themselves effectively will often be considered over those with better credentials.

Too Old

Older workers need to present their wealth of experience and maturity as an advantage rather than as a disadvantage. If that sounds similar to the advice I offered for being "too young," you're right. In all cases, you need to look for ways to turn what someone might consider a negative into a positive. Older workers often have some things going for them that younger workers do not. On a resume, stress your years of experience as a plus, emphasize your loyalty to previous employers, and list accomplishments that occurred over time.

If you have more than 15 years or so of work experience, emphasize your more recent work experience. Once you have 10 or more years of work experience in a related field, you only need to write "More than 10 years of experience in accounting," rather than a more specific number that could be used to indicate your age.

QUICK TIP

If you are an older worker, select activities that best support your ability to do the job you are seeking and emphasize them on your resume. Unless it is clearly to your advantage, you don't need to provide many details on your work or other history from earlier times.

To avoid sounding "too old," you should consider not including graduation dates or any other date that can be used to indicate your age. You can cluster earlier jobs into one statement that covers them by saying something like "Various jobs requiring skills in engineering." In most cases, your more recent experiences will be more important to an employer anyway. Emphasize recent training, accomplishments, and responsibilities in your resume and include dates on these items as appropriate.

Family Status and Children

There is absolutely no need for your resume to mention your marital status or whether you have children. The employer doesn't need to know these details of your life, and by law is not allowed to ask, so don't volunteer the information on your resume.

Physical Limitations and Disabilities

I assume that you will not seek a job that you can't or should not do. This would be foolish. So that means you are looking for a job that you are capable of doing, right? And, that being the case, you don't have a disability related to doing this job at all.

For this reason, I see no need to mention any disability on your resume. Laws require employers to consider all applicants based on the requirements of the job and the ability of the applicant to do that job. This means that any disability you have is not supposed to be a limitation to being considered for a job that you are able to do.

Of course, employers are still able to use their judgment in selecting the best person for the job, and that means that people with disabilities will have to compete for jobs along with everyone else. That is fair, so you will need to present to a prospective employer a convincing argument for why the employer should hire you over someone else. But on your resume, you should never mention a disability. Instead, focus on your *ability* to do the job.

> A disability is not a disability if it does not prevent you from doing the job well.

Quick Reference

For more advice on seeking, getting, and keeping jobs, see *Job Search Handbook for People with Disabilities* by Dr. Daniel J. Ryan (JIST Publishing).

Negative References

Most employers will not contact your previous employers unless you are being considered seriously for the job. If you fear that a previous employer will not give you a positive reference, here are some things you can do:

- List someone other than your supervisor as a reference from that employer—someone who knew your work there and who will say nice things about you.
- Discuss the issue in advance with your previous employer and negotiate what this person will say. If what the former employer agrees to say is not good, at least you know this and can prepare potential employers.
- Get a written letter of reference. In many cases, employers will not give references over the phone—or negative references at all—for fear of being sued. Having a letter in advance allows you to give a copy to a prospective employer, and this may help the employer in making a decision.

Quick Tip

If you're worried about what your references are saying about you, ask a friend to pose as a prospective employer and call your references. Or, if you're willing to pay a fee to check on them, hire a service such as Allison & Taylor, Inc. (www.myreferences.com) or use Yahoo.com's fee-based service of a confidential background check. If any negatives turn up, this will give you a chance to negotiate a more positive reference with a past employer, provide alternate references, or explain things in a positive way to a potential employer.

Criminal Record

A resume should *never* include any negative information about you. So if you have ever been in trouble with the law, do not mention it in your resume. Labor laws prevent an employer from including such general questions on an application as "Have you ever been arrested?" and limit formal inquiries to "Have you ever been convicted of a felony?" since convictions for minor offenses are not supposed to be considered in a hiring decision.

In most cases, your criminal record would never be an issue on a resume, since you would not mention it. In this country, we are technically innocent until proven guilty, thank goodness, and that is why employers are not allowed to consider an arrest record in a hiring decision. Being arrested and being guilty are two different things.

Quick Alert

A felony conviction is a different matter. These crimes are more serious, and employment laws allow an employer to ask for and get this information—and to use it in making certain hiring decisions. For example, few employers would want to hire an accountant who had been convicted of stealing money from a previous employer.

If you have an arrest or conviction record that an employer has a legal right to inquire about, my advice is to avoid looking for jobs where your record would be a big negative. The accountant in the example should consider changing careers. I would advise people in this situation to avoid jobs where they could easily commit the same crime, since few employers would consider hiring them for that reason. Even if they did get such a job because they concealed their criminal history, they could be fired at any time for lying about it. Instead, I might suggest the above-mentioned accountant consider selling accounting software, starting his or her own business, or getting into a career completely unrelated to accounting.

> As you prove yourself and gain good work experience, your distant past becomes less important.

As always, your resume should reflect what you *can* do rather than what you can't. If you chose your career direction wisely and present a convincing argument that you can do the job well, many employers will, ultimately, overlook previous mistakes.

So a criminal history really isn't an issue for a resume. Instead, it is a career planning, job search, and interview issue.

Other Items to Include—or Not Include—on Your Resume

Here are some other items to include or not include on your resume.

A Heading, Such as "Resume"

Few people would confuse a resume with something else, so using a header is not necessary. In some cases, this is done to make the resume appear more formal or, at times, just because the writer wanted it that way, but you really don't need to include one.

A Way to Reach You by Phone or E-mail

Employers are most likely to try to reach you by phone or e-mail. For this reason, it is essential that you include a phone number and, if at all possible, an e-mail address.

Here are some essential things to consider for the phone number you include on your resume (e-mail will be covered separately):

- **The telephone must always be answered.** In most cases, employers will call you during their regular business hours. If you are actively out looking for a job, you may be gone too often to reliably receive phone calls. The solution is to use an answering machine or voice-mail service. While some people don't like leaving messages, most are used to it and are likely to leave a message asking you to return their call. This is far better than someone not being able to reach you.
- **The phone must be answered appropriately and reliably.** First impressions count, so make sure your phone is answered appropriately. If you are using your home phone, instruct anyone answering the phone during the day (when employers are most likely to call) to conduct themselves in a professional way. Make certain that anyone who answers the phone knows how to take reliable messages, including the name, organization, and phone number of the caller. And make certain your answering machine or voice-mail greeting is professional and clear. Keep in mind that an employer will hear this message, so be sure it presents you positively.

Quick Reminder

If needed, train anyone who might answer the phone until you are certain that the person can do it correctly and professionally.

- **Your telephone number must include an area code.** Always include the correct area code for your phone number, even if you don't want to move to another area. Resumes have a way of getting circulated widely and in ways that you might not expect. In some cases, you may get a call from an employer who lives out of your area (at a corporate office, for example), but who has the authority to offer you a job where you are.

Quick Alert

Many cities now have multiple area codes, so don't assume that someone will know yours.

- **The phone number must remain the same throughout your job search.** Resumes can be filed for quite some time, which can result in an employer trying to reach you long after your resume was first put into circulation. So include a long-term phone number. If you are in the process of moving, you might consider using an answering machine, voice-mail service, cell phone, or pager until you no longer need it. You can even arrange for a local phone number to be used in a distant location by obtaining one of these services there. This will avoid creating the impression that you are not readily available.

In many situations, it is wise to include more than one phone number on your resume, and some resume examples in this book include two numbers. This allows you to use your home number (for example) as the primary place to reach you, as well as provide the employer an alternate number should the first one be unavailable, busy, or no longer in service. As you can see in the various sample resumes, you can simply indicate each phone number's type with words such as the following:

- Daytime
- Messages
- Cell or Mobile
- Fax
- Office
- Evenings
- Answering Service
- Pager
- Voice Mail
- Home

Alternate Addresses

In most cases, including your home address is enough. Just be sure to give your complete address and ZIP code. In rare situations, you might want to include either no address or an alternate one. For example, perhaps you don't consider your home address to be positive because it is in a "bad area," you live out of the area, or for some other reason. Before you exclude an address, consider asking someone reliable to accept your mail at his or her address and forward it to you.

Your Resume Should Include Your E-mail Address!

Many employers prefer to use e-mail instead of the phone because it takes less of their time. This is reason enough to include an e-mail address on your resume. In addition, people who don't include an e-mail address will appear to many employers to be computer illiterate—not a good thing. Here are some tips on using your e-mail address to best effect:

- Handle your e-mail address just as you would your phone number, formatted in a similar way and placed near the top of your resume.
- If you don't want to use your personal e-mail address or if your regular address does not sound professional (like "snakelady.com" or whatever), set up a temporary address through a site like www.yahoo.com, www.msn.com, or www.hotmail.com.
- Check your e-mail daily throughout your job search and respond immediately to any employers who contact you that way.
- Remember that your e-mail response will create an impression, so make sure it is a positive one. Keep your e-mail responses short, professional, and friendly. And check them carefully to eliminate spelling and grammar errors.

If you are moving and know what the new address will be, you may list both the current and future locations. Add a statement like "Moving—Please mail all correspondence to new address below after July 15." This is not the best solution, but it can work.

Personal Information

There is no need to include personal information on your resume such as height, weight, or marital status. The reason is that these things have little or nothing to do with your ability to do the job. In addition, labor laws introduced in the past prevent an employer from considering many of these things in their hiring decisions. As a result, most employers will throw away resumes that include this sort of information, to reduce their chances of being sued for using the information in their screening process.

There are exceptions, of course: Some resumes do effectively include personal details that reinforce the candidates' ability to do the job or reflect positively on their personality or style. For example, mentioning certain leisure interests, hobbies, or volunteer activities may reinforce your ability to do the job in some way. But these same things may also harm you, so be cautious in what you include. For example, your mention of involvement in a social or political organization, or of being a fan of a particular sport or team, may help you with some employers but harm you with others.

Quick Tip

If personal information does not directly support your ability to do the job, it is best left out of your resume.

Photographs

Unless you are applying for a position in modeling or the performing arts, never include your photograph with your resume. A photograph gives an indication of your age, gender, attractiveness, race, and other characteristics that an employer may later be accused of using in screening applicants. For this reason, many employers will not consider resumes that have photos attached.

References

Some resumes include a statement such as "References Available on Request" at the bottom. Older resume books typically advise you to do this, but it is no longer necessary. Employers know they can ask for references if they want to check them out.

In some cases, if you feel you have particularly good references, you may add a statement such as "Excellent References Available" to indicate that you have a good work history and nothing to hide. Some resumes incorporate this statement as narrative in another section rather than listed at the bottom.

Quick Tip

Get letters of reference from previous employers before you begin your job search. Many employers will not give out information on your performance after you leave, so ask previous supervisors to write letters of reference you can copy and give to prospective employers who ask for references. You might consider writing a draft of the letter and then having your supervisor approve and sign it. Some previous employers might appreciate this because it saves them time, but others may take offense. Use your judgment.

While I don't suggest you list your references on your resume itself, I do suggest that you create a separate list of references. Having your references available in advance allows you to get them quickly to those employers who ask and conserves valuable space on your resume for use in documenting more important information.

A Final Few Words on Handling Problems

Thankfully, a variety of laws and regulations require employers to consider applicants on their ability to do a job rather than such personal attributes as race, religion, age, disability, gender, or other unrelated criteria. Most employers are wise enough to avoid making decisions based on points that should not matter. They are often just like you are (you know: intelligent, good looking, humble, and so on). They will try to hire someone who convinces them that they can do the job well.

For this reason, it is *your* responsibility to present to your next employer a convincing argument as to why he or she should hire you over someone else. Even if your "problem" does not come up in the interview, it may be to your advantage to bring it up and deal with it. This is particularly true if you think an employer might wonder about this issue or that it might hurt you if you don't address it.

However you handle the interview, the ultimate question you have to answer is "Why should I hire you?" So provide a good answer, even if the question is not asked quite so obviously.

Chapter 9

Write a Better Resume Now

After completing Chapters 5 through 8, you are ready to put together a "better" resume. By better, I mean one that is more carefully crafted than those you have already prepared, based on Section One.

This chapter will help you pull together what you have learned and create an effective resume. It also expands on the tips in Section One on how to design, produce, and use your resume to best effect.

Getting Started on a Better Resume

One decision I made in writing this book was to put all the basic information on how to do a resume in the first section. I said that Section One would be all that most people would need to write a resume—with the exception of looking at the sample resumes in Section Three, if desired.

So, because you are now reading this, you need to know that this chapter assumes that you have read and completed the activities in Chapters 1, 2, 3, and 4. I also assume that you finished a basic resume as outlined in those chapters, and I hope you took my advice to use it right away while you worked on creating a "better" resume as time permitted.

If that information is not fresh in your mind, what follows won't make much sense because it is supplemental to the information presented in the first four chapters. And if you've worked through Chapters 5 through 8, the results from that material will help you work through this chapter more easily. So now, I present you with additional and sometimes redundant information on writing an improved resume.

If You Aren't Good at Writing a Resume, Get Some Help

I begin this chapter with some advice: If you are not particularly good at writing and designing a resume, consider getting help. Here are several sources of assistance.

Professional Resume Writers

The fees that some resume writers charge are a bargain, while others charge entirely too much for what you get. Few regulations or requirements exist for setting up business as a resume writer, and the quality and pricing of services vary widely.

In reviewing a resume writer's capabilities, you need to have a good idea of the services you want and buy only those you need. For example, some resume writers have substantial experience and skills in career counseling and can help you clarify what you want to do. Helping you write your resume may be the end result of more expensive, time-consuming career counseling services that you may or may not need.

Most professional resume writers will ask you questions about your skills, experiences, and accomplishments so that they can use this information to improve your resume. This expertise will benefit almost everyone. But, in some cases, the writer is essentially a keyboarder who takes the information you provide and puts it into a simple format without asking questions. This service does not have the same value and obviously should cost less.

Quick Alert

Ask for prices and know exactly what is included before you commit to any resume-writing services.

Some resume writers provide additional services. These services include printing a number of resumes and matching envelopes, putting your resume on a computer disk (for future changes you can make), putting your resume into an electronic format for Internet posting, or posting your electronic resume on one or more Internet sites.

I said early in this book that writing a good resume will help you clarify what you want to do in your career. That process is not simple, and you might benefit greatly from the help of a true career-counseling professional who also happens to be a resume writer.

Quick Tip

A variety of excellent resume writers contributed sample resumes used in this book and you can find their contact information in Appendix B. Local resume writers are listed under "Resume Service" and similar headings in the Yellow Pages (although be sure to check that they have credentials). And many Internet career and job sites sell or provide links to resume services.

CHECK FOR PROFESSIONAL CREDENTIALS

There are four major associations of professional resume writers and each provides a Web site with links to professional writers:

- Professional Association of Résumé Writers & Career Coaches (PARW/CC; www.parw.com)
- National Résumé Writers' Association (NRWA; www.nrwa.com)
- Career Masters Institute (CMI; www.cminstitute.com)
- Professional Resume Writing and Research Association (PRWRA; www.prwra.com)

Each of these associations has a code of ethics, so someone who belongs to these groups offers better assurance of legitimate services than someone who does not. Better yet is someone who has a Certified Professional Resume Writer (CPRW), Nationally Certified Resume Writer (NCRW), Master Resume Writer (MRW), or similar designation, which they earned by passing resume-writing competency tests.

Members of these associations wrote many of the sample resumes in Section Three. As you can see, those writers are very good at what they do and will be happy to help you with your resume if you contact them.

In any situation, ask for the credentials of the person who will provide the service, get a clear quote on services included in their prices, and see examples of the person's work before you agree to anything.

Career or Job Search Counselors and Counseling Services

In your search for someone to help you with your resume, you may run into high-pressure efforts to sell you services. If so, buyer beware! Good, legitimate job search and career professionals are out there, and they are worth every bit of their reasonable fees. Many employers pay thousands of dollars for outplacement assistance to help those leaving find new jobs. But some career-counseling businesses prey on unsuspecting, vulnerable souls who are unemployed. Some "packages" can cost thousands of dollars and are not worth the price.

Quick Reference

Two reputable organizations that can refer you to a career counselor or job search coach in private practice are: Career Masters Institute (www.cminstitute.org) and the Career Planning and Adult Development Network (www.careernetwork.org).

I have said for years that many job seekers would gain more from reading a few good job search books than they might get from the less-than-legitimate businesses offering these services. But how do you tell the legitimate from the illegitimate? One clue is high-pressure sales and high fees—fees over $1,000 are clearly out of line for most situations. If this is the case, your best bet is to walk out quickly. Call the agency first and get some information on services offered and prices charged. If the agency requires that you come in to discuss this, assume that it is a high-pressure sales outfit and avoid it.

Quick Tip

Low-cost services often are available from local colleges or other organizations. These may consist of workshops and access to reading materials, assessment tests, and other services at a modest cost or even free. Consider these as an alternative to higher-priced services.

Print and Photocopy Shops

Some of these businesses offer substantial services, including resume design, high-quality output, resume copying and printing, and a selection of good paper and matching envelopes. Their prices are often quite reasonable, although few are capable of providing significant help in writing your resume.

Look in the Yellow Pages under "Photocopying," "Copying & Duplicating," or "Printers" for local services. Read their ads and call a few; you may be surprised at what they offer.

What Sort of Resume Will Work Best for You?

As you know, there are just a few basic resume types. But these types have many variations that could make sense for your situation. I covered the basic resume types in Section One, but here is a review, along with some additional information.

The Simple Chronological Resume

Chapter 2 provides examples of a simple chronological resume. As you know, this resume arranges your history in chronological order, beginning with your most recent work experience. Education and training may come before or after your work history, depending on your situation.

Use your judgment and this book's guidance about how to structure and write your resume.

Quick Alert

Since a chronological resume organizes information by your work experience, it highlights previous job titles, locations, dates employed, and tasks. This is fine if you are looking for the same type of job you have held in the past or are looking to move up in a related field. However, it is not ideal for some situations. For employers, the chronological resume presents a career progression and allows them to quickly screen out those applicants whose backgrounds are not conventional or do not fit the preferred profile.

The chronological format is often not good for those who have limited work experience (such as recent graduates), who want to do something different, or who have less-than-ideal work histories such as job gaps.

Consider a Modified Chronological Resume

While a basic, traditional chronological resume has limitations, you can add some information and modify its style in such a way that will help you. Here are some things you can do, depending on your situation:

Add a job objective. Although a chronological resume might not include a job objective, yours certainly can. Although this has the disadvantage of limiting your resume to certain types of jobs, you should be focusing your job search in this way for other reasons. And including a job objective allows you to focus your resume content to best support that objective.

Emphasize skills and accomplishments. Most chronological resumes simply provide a listing of tasks, duties, and responsibilities, but once you have included a job objective, you should clearly emphasize skills, accomplishments, and results that support your job objective.

Expand your education and training section. Let's say that you are a recent graduate who worked your way through school, earned decent grades (while working full time), and got involved in extracurricular activities. The standard listing of education would not do you justice, so consider expanding that section to include statements about your accomplishments while going to school.

Add new sections to highlight your strengths. There is no reason you can't add one or more sections to your resume to highlight something you think will help you. For example, let's say you have excellent references from previous employers. You might add a statement to that effect and even include one or more positive quotes. Or maybe you got exceptional performance reviews, wrote some articles, edited a newsletter, traveled extensively, or did something else that might support your job objective. If so, nothing prevents you from creating a special section or heading to highlight these activities.

Some sample resumes in Section Three break the "rules" and include features that make sense for the individual. And that is one rule that really matters—that your resume communicates your strengths in an effective way.

The Skills or Functional Resume

Chapter 3 reviews the basics of writing a skills resume. This resume style arranges content under major skills rather than jobs previously held. A well-done skills resume emphasizes skills that are most important to succeed in the job stated in the job objective. Of course, you should possess these skills. These resumes are sometimes called "functional" resumes because they use a functional design that is based on the skills needed for the job sought.

Quick Alert

A skills resume is often used in situations where the writer wants to avoid displaying obvious weaknesses that would be highlighted on a chronological resume. For example, someone who has been a teacher but who now wants a career in sales could clearly benefit from a skills resume.

A skills resume can help hide a variety of other weaknesses as well, such as limited work experience, gaps in job history, lack of educational credentials, and other flaws. This is one reason why some employers don't like skills resumes: They make it harder for them to quickly screen out applicants. Personally, I like skills resumes. Assuming that you honestly present what you can do, a skills resume often gives you the best opportunity to present your strengths in their best light.

The Combination Format

In a combination format, you might highlight your key skills related to your job objective and include a separate section that presents your work history in a conventional, chronological way. Some sample resumes in Chapter 11 have successfully merged the skills resume and chronological resume formats—a good idea for many situations (see pages 241, 248–249, and 251–252). Consider using this approach if it can present you well.

Creative Resumes

There is one other type of resume, and it defies easy description: These resumes use innovative formats and styles. Some use dramatic graphics, colors, and shapes. Graphic artists, for example, may use their resumes as examples of their work and include various graphic elements. An advertising or marketing person might use a writing style that approximates copywriting and a resume design that looks like a polished magazine ad.

I've seen all sorts of special resumes over the years; some are well done and create a good impression and some do not. I haven't included many examples of these resumes in this book since they do not lend themselves to a book's format (black ink on white paper). How, for example, could I do justice to the resume I once saw that was written on a watermelon?

Quick Alert

I've also seen many gimmicks such as a dollar bill attached to a resume with a statement that this person would help his employer make lots of money. Some gimmicks work and you can try them, but I encourage you to stick to the basics: Write a resume that shows you deserve the interview, instead of relying on gimmicks.

So use your judgment. In some cases, creative resumes can make sense and a few examples of them are included in Section Three. Good design can certainly help, particularly in professions where good design is the profession.

Portfolios and Enclosures

Some occupations typically require a portfolio of your work or some other concrete example of what you have accomplished. Artists, copywriters, advertising professionals, clothing designers, architects, radio and TV personalities, and many others know this and should take care to provide good examples of what they do. Examples can include writing samples, photographs of your work, articles you have written, sample audio or videotapes, artwork, a Web site you designed, and other samples of your work that support your job objective.

Curriculum Vitae (CVs) and Other Special Formats

Attorneys, college professors, physicians, scientists, and people in various other occupations have their own rules or guidelines for preparing a "Professional Vitae" or some other special format. If you are looking for a job in one of these specialized areas, you should learn how to prepare a resume to those specifications. These specialized and occupation-specific resumes are not within the scope of this book and examples are not included, but many books provide information on these special formats.

Gather Information and Emphasize Accomplishments, Skills, and Results

Section One included activities and a worksheet designed to gather basic information for your resume. Chapters in Section Two provided more detailed information and activities to help you gather facts about yourself, identify key skills, and consider alternative ways to present what you want to include in your resume.

Quick Tip

Much of Section Two does more than help you write a resume. It was also designed to help you in career planning. But, assuming that you did some or all of those activities, you now have to select the key elements to include in your resume.

I have provided an expanded worksheet in this chapter to help you gather the information that is most important to include in a resume. Some information is the same as that called for in the Instant Resume Worksheet in Chapter 2, but this new worksheet is considerably more thorough. If carefully completed, it will prepare you for the final step of writing a superior resume.

Comprehensive Resume Worksheet

General Instructions

Use this worksheet to write a draft of the material you will include in your resume. Use a writing style similar to that of your resume, emphasizing skills and accomplishments. Keep your narrative as brief as possible and make every word count.

Use a pencil or erasable pen to allow for changes. You may find it helpful to use a separate sheet of paper for drafting the information in some worksheet sections that follow. Once you have done that, go ahead and complete the worksheet in the book. The information you write on the worksheet should be pretty close to the information you will use to write your resume, so write it carefully. For some sections, you will probably need to refer back to the appropriate section of this book to find previously recorded information.

Personal Identification

Name ____

Home address ____

____

City, state or province, ZIP or postal code______________________________

____

Primary phone number ______________________________________

Comment ____

Alternate/cell phone number______________________________________

(continued)

(continued)

Comment ______________________________

E-mail address ______________________________

Job Objective Statement

Write your job objective here, as you would like it to appear on your resume. Writing a good job objective is tricky business and requires a good sense of what you want to do as well as the skills you have to offer. You may want to refer to the work you did in Chapter 7 and review sample resumes in Section Three before completing this. ________

____

____

____

____

In Just a Few Words, Why Should Someone Hire You?

A good resume will answer this question in some way. So, to clarify the essential reasons why someone should hire you over others, write a brief answer to the question in the space below. Then make sure that your resume gets this across in some way. ________

____

____

____

____

Key Adaptive Skills to Emphasize in Your Resume

What key adaptive skills do you have that support your stated job objective? Review Chapter 5 to identify your top adaptive skills and list those that best support your job objective in the spaces below. After each, write the accomplishments or experiences that best support those skills—your proof that you have these skills. Be brief and emphasize numbers and results when possible. Include some or all of these skills in your resume.

Adaptive skill ______________________________

____

Proof of this skill ______________________________

____

____

____

____

____

Adaptive skill ____

____

Proof of this skill ____

____

____

____

____

____

Adaptive skill ____

____

Proof of this skill ____

____

____

____

____

____

Key Transferable Skills to Emphasize in Your Resume

Select your transferable skills that best support your stated job objective. Refer to Chapter 5 as needed to help identify these skills and list them below, along with examples of when you used or demonstrated these skills. Use some or all of these in your resume.

Transferable skill ____

____

(continued)

(continued)

Proof of this skill ______

Transferable skill ______

Proof of this skill ______

Transferable skill ______

Proof of this skill ______

Transferable skill ______

Proof of this skill ______

Transferable skill ______________________

Proof of this skill ______________________

What Are the Key Job-Related Skills Needed in the Job You Want?

Refer to Chapter 7 to learn how to identify the key job-related skills needed in the job you want. If you have selected an appropriate job objective, you should have those very skills. Write the most important job-related skills below (and more if you know them), along with examples to support these skills—and include them in your resume.

Job-related skill ______________________

Proof of this skill ______________________

Job-related skill ______________________

Proof of this skill ______________________

(continued)

(continued)

Job-related skill ______________________________

Proof of this skill ______________________________

Job-related skill ______________________________

Proof of this skill ______________________________

Job-related skill ______________________________

Proof of this skill ______________________________

What Specific Work or Other Experience Do You Have That Supports Your Doing This Job?

If you completed the worksheets in Chapter 6, you have plenty of information to draw on in completing this section. If you are doing a chronological resume, you should organize the information below in order of the jobs you have held. If you are doing a skills resume, organize the information within major skill areas.

Space has been provided for both of these arrangements, and I suggest you complete both sections. In doing so, write the content as if you were writing it for use in your resume. You can, of course, further edit what you write here into its final form, but try to approximate the writing style you will use in your resume. Use short sentences. Include action words. Emphasize key skills. Include numbers to support your skills and emphasize accomplishments and results instead of simply listing your duties.

In previous jobs that don't relate well to what you want to do next, emphasize adaptive and transferable skills and accomplishments that relate to the job you want. Mention promotions, raises, or positive evaluations as appropriate. If you did more than your job title suggests, consider a title that is more descriptive (but not misleading) such as "head waiter and assistant manager," if that is what you were, instead of "waiter." If you had a number of short-term jobs, consider combining them all under one heading such as "Various Jobs While Attending College."

You may need to complete several drafts of this information before it begins to "feel good," so please use additional sheets of paper as needed.

Experiences Organized by Chronology

Most recent or present job title ______________________________

Dates (month/year) from ____________________ to ____________________

Organization name ______________________________

City, state or province, ZIP or postal code ______________________________

____

Duties, skills, responsibilities, accomplishments ______________________________

____

____

____

____

____

(continued)

(continued)

Next most recent job title ______________________________

Dates (month/year) from ____________________ to ____________________

Organization name ______________________________

City, state or province, ZIP or postal code ______________________________

____

Duties, skills, responsibilities, accomplishments ______________________________

____

____

____

____

____

Next most recent job title ______________________________

Dates (month/year) from ____________________ to ____________________

Organization name ______________________________

City, state or province, ZIP or postal code ______________________________

____

Duties, skills, responsibilities, accomplishments ______________________________

____

____

____

____

____

Next most recent job title ______________________________

Dates (month/year) from ____________________ to ____________________

Organization name ______________________________

City, state or province, ZIP or postal code ______________________________

____

Duties, skills, responsibilities, accomplishments ______________________________

____

____

____

____

____

Experience Organized by Skills

Look at the sample resumes in Section Three and you will see that some organize their experience under key skills needed for the job. These resumes often include statements regarding accomplishments and results as well as duties. They also often mention other skills that are related to or support the key skill as well as specific examples. These can be work-related experiences or can come from other life experiences.

Assume for now that your resume will organize your experience under key skills. Begin by listing the three to six skills you consider to be most important to succeed in the job you want.

I've included space for up to six such skills in the worksheet. Once you have decided on which ones to list, write examples of experiences and accomplishments that directly support these skills. Write this just as you want it to appear in your resume.

Key skill 1 ____

Resume statement to support this skill ______________________________________

____

____

____

____

Key skill 2 ____

Resume statement to support this skill ______________________________________

____

____

____

____

(continued)

(continued)

Key skill 3 ______________________________

Resume statement to support this skill ______________________________

____

____

____

____

Key skill 4 ______________________________

Resume statement to support this skill ______________________________

____

____

____

____

Key skill 5 ______________________________

Resume statement to support this skill ______________________________

____

____

____

____

Key skill 6 ______________________________

Resume statement to support this skill ______________________________

____

____

____

____

What Education or Training Supports Your Job Objective?

Chapter 6 provides a worksheet that organizes your education and training in a thorough way. Go back and review that information before completing this section. In writing your Education and Training section, be sure to include any additional information that supports your qualifications for your job objective. New graduates should emphasize their education and training more than experienced workers and include more details in this section.

Use the space that follows to write what you want to include on your resume under the Education and Training heading.

School or training institution attended ______________________________

Dates attended or graduated ______________________________

Degree or certification obtained ______________________________

____

Anything else that should be mentioned ______________________________

____

____

____

____

School or training institution attended ______________________________

Dates attended or graduated ______________________________

Degree or certification obtained ______________________________

Anything else that should be mentioned ______________________________

____

____

____

____

School or training institution attended ______________________________

Dates attended or graduated ______________________________

Degree or certification obtained ______________________________

(continued)

(continued)

Anything else that should be mentioned ______________________________

____

____

____

____

Other Formal or Informal Training That Supports Your Job Objective

____

____

____

Other Resume Sections

If you want to include other sections on your resume, go ahead and write their headings and whatever you want to include. Examples might be "Summary of Experience," "Special Accomplishments," or others. See the headings of this kind among the sample resumes in Section Three for inspiration.

____

____

____

____

____

____

____

____

____

More Quick Resume-Writing Tips

I covered the basics of writing a resume in Section One. Here are some additional tips and information you may find helpful.

As Much As Possible, Write Your Resume Yourself

I have come to realize that some people, even very smart people who are good writers, can't write or design a good resume. They just can't. And there is no good reason to force them to write one from start to finish. If you are one of these people, just decide that your skills are in other areas and don't go looking for a job as a resume writer. Get someone else, preferably a professional resume writer, to do it for you.

But, even if you don't write your own resume, you should do as much as possible yourself. The reason is that, if you don't, your resume won't be truly yours. Your resume may present you well, but it won't be you. Not only may your resume misrepresent you to at least some extent, you also will not have learned what you need to learn by going through the process of writing your resume. You will not have struggled with your job objective statement in the same way and may not have as clear a sense of what you want to do as a result. You won't have the same understanding of the skills you have to support your job objective. As a result, you probably won't do as well in an interview.

Quick Alert

While I encourage you to "borrow" ideas from this book's sample resumes, your resume must end up being yours. You have to be able to defend its content and prove each and every statement you've made.

Even if you end up hiring someone to help with your resume, you must provide this person with what to say and let him or her help you with how to say it. If you don't agree with something the writer does, ask the person to change it to your specifications. However you do it, make sure that your resume is *your* resume and that it represents you accurately.

Don't Lie or Exaggerate

Some job applicants misrepresent themselves. They lie about where they went to school or say that they have a degree that they do not have. They state previous salaries that are higher than they really were. They present themselves as having responsibilities and titles that are not close to the truth.

I do not recommend you do this. For one reason, it is simply not right, and that is reason enough. But there are also practical reasons for not doing so. The first is that you might get a job that you can't handle. If that were to happen, and you fail, it would serve you right. Another reason is that some employers check references and backgrounds more thoroughly than you might realize. Sometimes, this can occur years after you are employed and, if caught, you could lose your job, which would not be a pleasant experience. So, my advice is this: Honesty is the best policy.

Quick Reminder

Telling the truth does not mean you have to tell everything. Some things are better left unsaid, and a resume should present your strengths and not your weaknesses.

This Is No Place to Be Humble

Being honest on your resume does not mean you can't present the facts in the most positive way. A resume is not a place to be humble. So work on *what* you say and how you say it, so that you present your experiences and skills as positively as possible.

Use Short Sentences and Simple Words

Short sentences are easier to read. They communicate better than long ones. Simple words also communicate more clearly than long ones. So use short sentences and easy-to-understand words in your resume (like I've done in this paragraph).

Many people like to throw in words and phrases that are related to their field but are not used elsewhere. Some of this may be necessary, but too often I see language that is too specialized, which will turn off many employers. Good writing is easy to read and understand. It is harder to do but is worth the time.

Be careful in your use of jargon.

If It Doesn't Support Your Job Objective, You Should Probably Cut It Out

A resume is only one or two pages long, so you have to be careful in what you do and do not include. Review each and every word and ask yourself, "Does this support my ability to do the job in some clear way?" If that item does not support your job objective, it should go.

Include Numbers

Many sample resumes in Section Three include some numbers (see pages 190–191, 210, and 226–227). Numbers can be used to refer to the speed at which someone does word processing, the number of transactions processed per month, the percentage of increased sales, the dollar amount of costs cut, or some other numerical measure of performance.

Quick Fact

Numbers communicate in a special way, and you should include numbers to support key skills you have or that reflect your accomplishments or results.

Emphasize Skills

It should be obvious by now that you should emphasize skills in your resume. Besides listing the key skills needed to support your job objective in a skills resume, you should include a variety of skill statements in all narrative sections of your resume. In each case, select skills you have that support your job objective.

Highlight Accomplishments and Results

Anyone can go through the motions of doing a job, but employers want to know how *well* you have done things in the past. Did you accomplish anything out of the ordinary? What were the results you achieved? Chapter 5 includes many activities that will help you emphasize accomplishments and results from a variety of work and life situations.

The Importance of Doing Drafts

It will probably take you several rewrites before you are satisfied with your resume's content. And it will take even more changes before you are finished.

Quick Alert

Writing, modifying, editing, changing, adding to, and subtracting from content are important steps in writing a good resume. For this reason, I suggest that you write yours on a computer if you can, where you can make changes quickly.

Edit, edit, and edit again. Every word has to count in your resume, so keep editing until it is right. This may require you to make multiple passes and to change your resume many times. But, if you did as I suggested and have created a simple but acceptable resume, fretting over your "better" resume shouldn't delay your job search one bit. Right?

Get Someone Else to Review Your Resume for Errors

After you have finished writing your resume, ask someone with good spelling and grammar skills to review it once again. It is simply amazing how efforts crepe into the most carefully edit resume (like the ones in this very sentence).

More Tips to Improve Your Resume's Design

Just as some people aren't good at resume writing, others are not good at design. Many resumes use simple designs, and this is acceptable for most situations. But you can do other things to improve your resume's appearance, and I will cover some basics in this section.

Quick Tip

When looking at the sample resumes in Section Three, note how some have a better appearance than others. Some have rules and bullets; others do not. Some include lots of white space, while others are quite crowded. Compromises are made in most resumes, but some clearly look better than others. Note the resumes whose appearance you like and try to incorporate those design principles into your own resume.

What to Do If You Don't Have the Best Computer Equipment or Design Experience

No problem. As I mentioned earlier, many people can help you with word processing and design. Just go out and have it done by a professional resume writer. At the beginning of this chapter, I provided referral services where you can find others to do your word processing and design work.

Quick Alert

If you are not familiar with how to use a computer and its related software, now is not the time to learn. You can waste lots of time trying to use a computer to do simple tasks such as laying out a resume or printing a letter. If computers are new to you, let someone else create your resume on his or her computer system. Once you have your resume, you might have someone show you how to use the computer for tasks like correspondence. But avoid the fancy stuff. Trust me on this.

Increase Readability with Some Simple Design Principles

People who design advertising know what makes something easy or hard to read—and they work very hard to make things easy. Here are some things they have found to improve readability. You can apply these same principles in writing your resume.

- Short sentences and short words are better than long ones.
- Short paragraphs are easier to read than long ones.
- Narrow columns are easier to read than wide ones.
- Put important information on the top and to the left, since people scan materials from left to right and top to bottom.
- Using plenty of white space increases the readability of the text that remains. And it looks better.
- Don't use too many (more than two) type styles on the same page.
- Use underlining, bold type, and bullets to emphasize and separate text—but use them sparingly.

Avoid "Packing" Your Resume with Small Print

Sometimes it's hard to avoid including lots of detail, but doing so can make your resume appear crowded and hard to read. In many cases, crowded resumes can be shortened with good editing, which allows for considerably more white space.

Use Two Pages at the Most

One page is often enough if you are disciplined in your editing, but two uncrowded pages are far better than one crowded one. Those with considerable experience or high levels of responsibility often require a two-page resume, but very, very few justify more than two.

Quick Tip

If you end up with one-and-a-half pages of resume, add content or white space until it fills the whole two pages. It just looks better.

Use Type Fonts Sparingly

Just because you have many fonts on your computer does not mean you have to use them all on your resume. Doing so creates a cluttered, hard-to-read look and is a sure sign of someone without design skills. Good resume design requires relatively few easy-to-read fonts in limited sizes. Look at the sample resumes in Section Three—few use more than one or two type fonts and most use bold and different font sizes sparingly.

Consider Graphics

I included some sample resumes in Section Three that use graphic elements to make them more interesting (see pages 205, 231, and 239). Although resumes with extensive graphic design elements were not my focus for this book (this is a "quick" resume book), some resumes clearly benefit from this. Good graphic design is more important for those in creative jobs such as advertising, art, and desktop publishing. One book that emphasizes resumes with great graphic designs, papers, shapes, and other features is titled *The Edge Resume & Job Search Strategy* by Bill Corbin and Shelbi Wright (JIST Publishing).

Edit Again for Appearance

Just as your resume requires editing, you should be prepared to review and make additional changes to your resume's design. After you have written the content just as you want it, you will probably need to make additional editing and design changes so that everything looks right.

Quick Tip

If someone else will help you with the design of your resume, show or e-mail this person copies of resumes you like as design examples. Be open to suggestions, but be willing to assert your taste regarding your resume's final appearance.

Select Top-Quality Paper

Don't use cheap copy machine paper. After all your work, you should use only top-quality paper. Most print shops are used to doing resumes and will have paper selections. The better-quality papers often contain a percentage of cotton or other fibers. I prefer an off-white or light cream color, because it gives a professional, clean appearance. Pastel colors such as gray and light blue are also acceptable, but avoid bright colors such as pink, green, or red.

Get Matching Stationery and Envelopes

Envelopes made of the same paper as your resume present a professional look. Select an envelope of the same paper type and color at the time you choose your resume paper. You should also get some blank sheets of this same paper for your cover letters and other job search correspondence. In some cases, you may also be able to obtain matching thank-you-note envelopes and paper.

Good-Quality Photocopies and Laser Printer Copies Are Fine

Many photocopy machines now create excellent images, and these can be used to reproduce your resume—as long as you use high-grade paper. Check out the copy quality first. Most laser printers also create good-quality images and can be used to make multiple resume copies.

How Many Copies to Make

If you print your resume on your own printer, print enough to have extras on hand at all times. You just never know. If you are photocopying your resume, make about 25 to 50 copies at any one time. You might want to make changes after you "field test" your resume, so don't make too many copies up front. If you are having the resume offset printed, the big cost is getting the job on the press; additional copies done at the same time are often quite inexpensive.

The best use of your resume is to get it into circulation early and often—so have enough so that you don't feel like you need to "save" them. Plan on giving multiple copies to friends, relatives, and acquaintances and sending out lots prior to and after interviews.

Section Three

A Stupendous Collection of Professionally Written and Designed Resumes

The resumes in the two chapters of this section were written by professional resume writers. As a result, they present a wonderful variety of writing and design styles and techniques. Each was written with great care and skill to present a real (but fictionalized) person in the best way possible. I want to thank all the writers who submitted resumes. There were so many good ones that I could have filled a 1,000-page book!

How to Use the Sample Resumes in This Section

There is no one right way to do a resume. Each person has unique information to present, and each resume can look and feel different. Often there are good reasons for this. For example, some occupations (such as accounting or law) have more formal traditions, so those resumes typically are more formal. Someone looking for a job in graphic design or marketing might have a more colorful, graphic, and nontraditional resume.

There are many reasons to use different writing and design styles, and the resumes in this section show wide variety in all their elements. There are samples of chronological resumes in Chapter 10 and samples of skills-based, combination, and creative resumes in Chapter 11. There are resumes for all sorts of people looking for all sorts of jobs. Some resumes include interesting graphic elements and others are quite plain.

This variety will give you ideas for writing and creating your own resume. I hope that it will also give you permission to experiment and use whatever style best suits you.

If You Need Help Writing Your Resume

If you need help writing your resume—or with career planning or job search advice—I recommend you use a writer whose work is included in this book. Each resume shows its writer's name at the bottom, and all contact information appears in Appendix B. Most writers will help you even if you don't live in the same area. Many of them provide long-distance services using the phone and e-mail.

You should also know that people need no credentials to be listed in the Yellow Pages under "Resume Service," so beware of picking a resume writer that way. All resume writers whose work appears in this book, on the other hand, do have the proper credentials. They are members of the Professional Association of Résumé Writers & Career Coaches, the National Résumé Writers' Association, the Professional Resume Writing and Research Association, and/or the Career Masters Institute. Many have earned special certifications granted by these associations. That is a big deal because they must pass a rigorous competency test and adhere to a code of ethics. The Web addresses of these associations are in Appendix B. The Web sites provide listings of other members in addition to the members who contributed to this book. If you need help with career counseling, job seeking, or resume writing, I recommend you use someone who is a member of one of these associations.

Chapter 10

Sample Chronological Resumes

I have organized the resumes into clusters so that you can easily find ones that relate to your background or job objective. Here are the job categories covered in this chapter:

One obvious way to use the samples is to turn to the section that seems most compatible with your career goals. Doing so will allow you to see how others with similar experience or seeking similar jobs have handled their resumes. But I also encourage you to look at all the samples for formats, presentation styles, and content ideas to use in your resume. For example, some resumes have superior graphic design elements that may inspire you, even though your job objective lies in a different area.

The handwritten comments on the resumes point out features, provide information on the person behind the resume, or give other details. This unique approach will give you insights into the strategies used by the professional writers who created these resumes.

Writer's comments: Client had been downsized and lacked confidence in her ability to find new employment at her age. This chronological resume focused on more recent experiences and eliminated prior employment spanning 25 years in a variety of occupations. She was offered a great position in her field within 30 days at a salary increase.

Karen J. Miller

780 Blueberry Hill
Newburg, New York 00000
(555) 555-5555

Profile

Experienced professional in the development and documentation of procedures for product/system enhancements to meet business requirements. Recognized by senior management and promoted to increasingly responsible positions based on performance results, technical expertise and team work. Proficient in managing multiple priorities and projects within tight deadlines. Strong analytical, detail/follow-through and problem-solving skills. Well-versed in various computer software programs.

Professional Employment

CARRIER INSURANCE COMPANY, New Rochelle, New York — 1986-XXXX

Business Consultant — 1988-XXXX

Developed and documented procedures for products, systems and enhancements for the policy change and amendment tracking functions. Analyzed and recommended changes to product/business specifications. Provided timely technical support to managers, employees, and field personnel in the resolution of system and other problems. Key role on numerous product and system enhancement projects. Developed expertise in Traditional and Interest Sensitive products and administration systems.

- Designed and presented training programs to managers and change analysts on new/existing products, procedures and administration systems.
- Authored/updated 3 comprehensive procedural manuals, each one created with unique format and features to improve readability.
- Initiated and wrote bulletin to communicate new information and updates on policy changes; contributed to, and edited, product guides.
- Collaborated on implementation team for new processing system in a model office environment. Created test cases, tracked problems and resolutions, prepared documentation, and trained end users.
- Recognized by management for resolving over 90% of problem cases on specific project.
- Tracked and evaluated time service, resulting in recommendation and implementation of procedural/ system changes which ensured consistency in meeting objectives.

Summarizes years of experience into brief statement to keep resume to one page

Technical Analyst — 1987-1988

Processed financial and nonfinancial system changes for Universal Life policies. Analyzed cases and policies for system processing. Calculated and balanced annual policy statements for exception cases.

- Contributed substantially to the elimination of large inventory of backlog cases.
- Trained staff in processing system changes and objectives of new process to customer service areas.
- Coauthored several sections of 150-page procedural manual.

Customer Service Representative — 1986-1987

No details needed for old job, since more recent experiences were more important

Education

B.S. (Accounting)
New York State University, New Paltz, New York

Submitted by Louise Garver

This resume was winner of the 1998 PARW Convention Best Résumé Contest—Finance Category.

Writer's comments: Unemployed for nearly a year, my client had a resume that presented a sketchy employment history. He had mailed over 1,000 resumes with no response. This format showcased his achievements in three areas. He immediately began interviewing and is now happily employed as CFO for a large company.

RAYMOND MONROE

12 Main Street

New York, New York 00000

(555) 555-5555

SENIOR FINANCE EXECUTIVE

Finance & Accounting Management … Banking & Cash Management … Budgeting
Insurance & Risk Management … Tax & Regulatory Compliance … Information Systems

Senior-level executive with extensive finance, administration and public accounting experience in diverse industries including retail/wholesale distribution, financial services and manufacturing. Proven ability to improve operations, impact business growth and maximize profits through achievements in finance management, cost reductions, internal controls, and productivity/efficiency improvements. Strong qualifications in general management, business planning, systems technology design and implementation, and staff development/leadership.

PROFESSIONAL EXPERIENCE

<u>**SOUTHINGTON COMPANY**</u> • New York, New York • 1991-XXXX
Treasurer/Senior Controller • 1993-XXXX
Corporate Controller • 1991-1993

Chief financial officer appointed to treasurer and Executive Committee member directing $500M international consumer products company. Accountable for strategic planning, development and leadership of entire finance function as well as day-to-day operations management of company's largest domestic division. Recruited, developed and managed team of finance professionals, managers and support staff.

(1) ***Operations Achievements***

Uses numbers to reinforce his results

- **Instrumental in improving operating profits from less than $400K to over $4M, equity from $8.6M to $13.6M and assets from $29.7M to $44.4M.**
- **Boosted market penetration by 27% which increased gross sales 32% through acquisition of 25 operating units as key member of due diligence team.**
- **Initiated strategies to redeploy company resources, resulting in 54% increase in gross margin by partial withdrawal from high-risk/low-margin product lines.**
- **Directed annual plan review process and strengthened accountability by partnering with senior-level department and district managers in all business units.**

Organizes results into three major groups

(2) ***Financial Achievements***

- **Cut receivable write-offs $440K by developing credit policies, instituting aggressive collection strategies and establishing constructive dialogue with delinquent accounts.**
- **Negotiated and structured financing agreements, resulting in basis point reductions, easing/more favorable covenant restrictions and simplification of borrowing process.**
- **Saved over $2M through self-insurance strategy and an estimated $200K annually by positioning company to qualify to self-insure future workers' compensation claims.**
- **Designed executive and management reporting systems and tailored financial and operating reporting system to meet requirements of 100+ business units.**

RAYMOND MONROE • **(555) 555-5555** • **Page 2**

Southington Company continued…

Note how every statement is results-oriented

(3) ***Technology Achievements***

- **Turned around organization-wide resistance toward automation and streamlined procedures that significantly improved efficiency while reducing costs.**
- **Championed installation of leading-edge systems technology resolving long-standing profit measurement problems and created infrastructure to support corporate growth.**
- **Implemented automated cash management system in over 100 business unit locations and reduced daily idle cash by 50% ($750K).**
- **Recognized critical need and upgraded automated systems to track long-term assets which had increased from $28M to $48.8M in 5 years.**

HAMDEN COMPANY • New York, New York • 1987-1991
Chief Financial Officer

Recruited for 3-year executive assignment to assume key role in building solid management infrastructure and positioning $15M company for its profitable sale in 1991. Directed general accounting, cash management, financial and tax reporting, banking relations, credit and collections, data processing, employee benefits, and administration. Managed and developed staff.

- **Converted company to small business corporation saving $450K in taxes over 3-year period.**
- **Realized $195K in accumulated tax savings through strategies adopting LIFO inventory method, minimizing taxes on a continual basis.**
- **Secured 25% of company's major client base (50% of total sales volume) by leading design, installation and administration of computer-based EDI program.**
- **Reduced collection period from 3 weeks to 5 days by initiating new policies and procedures.**

MADISON COMPANY • New York, New York • 1981-1987
Partner

Jointly acquired and managed public accounting firm serving privately held companies (up to $200M in revenues) in wholesale distribution, financial services and manufacturing industries. Concurrent responsibility for practice administration and providing accounting, business and MIS consulting services to corporate clients.

EDUCATION

B.S. in Accounting
New York University • New York, New York

Certified Public Accountant - New York

Submitted by Louise Garver

This job seeker got two call-backs within one hour of faxing this resume to employers!

COLE A. THOMES

8 Thornton Way Chicago, Illinois 60626 773-545-5555 cthomes@lsl.net

PROFESSIONAL GOAL & PROFILE

Financial Services—Training & Instruction

- Financial services experience of 20+ years in highly competitive markets. Areas of expertise:
  - Training / Instructing
  - Investment / Retirement Planning
  - Disability Income Replacement
  - Motivation of Sales Team / Agents
  - Sales / Marketing
  - Long-Term Care / Life Insurance / Annuities
- Valued by clients and colleagues for integrity, professionalism, and product knowledge.
- Effective in guiding others in investment vehicles, options, and choices to support desired goals.
- Readily earn the trust and confidence of others with "either / or" sales closing approach.
- Self-motivated and passionate in helping people feel good about where they invest their money.

EXPERIENCE

Major Market Investors, Inc.—Investment Strategist, Chicago, IL, 2001–Present

- Recruited by principals of this property casualty and group benefits agency to expand market growth.
- Developed strong business relationships with existing clientele, specializing in retirement and pension plans, predominantly in the transportation industry.
- Trusted by clients for the ability to "manage money well in a down market."

Lots of results

Investors Services, Inc.—Senior Investment Specialist, Chicago, IL, 1993–2001

- Took agency from 49th place ranking (of 57) to rank of #3 within a two-year timeframe.
- Received numerous "Top Sales Achievement" awards for variable annuities and mutual funds.
- Trained, educated, and motivated agents and sales representatives.
- Accountable for compliance with NASD and Securities rules and regulations.

Financials, Inc.—Securities Manager, Memphis, TN, 1988–1993

- Established solid client and agent relationships based on confidence and consistency in helping others generate additional income. Served on the National Board of Financial Advisors for four-year term.
- Trained, educated, and motivated agents in sales / marketing of investment products.
- Named "Securities Manager of the Year" four consecutive years.
- Contributed to the #1 Agency ranking for Investment Sales four consecutive years.
- Recognized and appreciated by agents for exemplary performance in investment sales field.

LBlythe Group, PC—Stockbroker Account Executive, Chicago, IL, 1986–1988

- Built a strong client following through face-to-face contacts. Marketed and sold a complete line of financial products and services to individuals known from prior business endeavors.

Thomes, Inc.—President, Chicago, IL, 1974–1986

- Founder and developer of a highly successful record retail chain called Rock 4Ever. Promoted music venues throughout the country hosting big-name feature attractions. Recruited by PlayIt Studios, Detroit, for collaboration with artists / producers / engineers on musical direction of new songs.

EDUCATION & INTERESTS

Vanderbilt University, Nashville, Tennessee, 1974

- **Bachelor of Business Administration** with Finance Emphasis—Music Minor

NASD Series 7 & 63; Health & Life Insurance Licenses; Certified Instructor in Power Sales Training

- Interests: stock market, baseball, golf, music, and family activities

Submitted by Billie Ruth Sucher

Writer's comments: This client wanted a job at once, in the middle of the Christmas holidays! Therefore, we targeted organizations that had no advertised openings. She was hired, sight unseen, by the state of Texas.

CONFIDENTIAL

CATHY M. TURNER
214 Maple Forrest Drive ⌖ Montgomery, Alabama 36109 ⌖ [334] 555-5555

Value to Burns & McDonnell: As an **environmental specialist**, design, direct and execute studies with findings and recommendations you and your clients can stand behind.

→ An example of a resume targeted to a specific employer

Capabilities you can use now:

- **Expertise** to produce solid results in minimum time
- **Dedication** to steadily increase my value to your clients
- **Calmness** to delivery quality analyses despite pressure

An unconventional but effective approach

Work history with selected examples of success:

- **Environmental Scientist**, Terran Sciences, Montgomery, Alabama, XX – Present

  Terran Sciences is a 22-year old environmental and geotechnical consulting firm with 80 employees in four offices serving private and public sector clients in Alabama and Florida.

Results→

- Quickly pulled together seven data bases we needed to serve our clients. *Payoffs:* Got 10 MB of data in two weeks – and **persuaded providers to waive $500** in fees.
- Inherited nine Phase I studies which had made no progress for two months. *Payoffs:* With no experience in Phase I studies, **did all nine in 90 days**, many *before* the deadline. Lender's environmental scientist said: **"Great job."** Multi-million dollar loans moved forward quickly.
- Pointed out a major flaw in claimant's action against one of our clients – after two of our larger competitors missed it. *Payoffs:* Reduced the impact of claimant's $54M suit.

- **Environmental Scientist**, Alabama Department of Environmental Management Montgomery, Alabama, XX – XX

  ADEM is the agency that issues every environmental permit in the state. Its annual budget exceeds $32.9M

Results→

- Found and corrected shortfalls in toxicity testing. *Payoffs:* Agency **now meeting EPA guidelines. Extended toxicity testing** to lowest level of the food chain. My **QA protocols sharpen impact of** chronic and acute **pollution.**
- Helped convert 22 years of paper records scattered over four agencies into data base that produces pinpoint results fast. *Payoffs:* What took **six months now done in minutes**. Health Department now assesses risk in water statewide with greater accuracy.
- Added new biological information to water quality assessment. *Payoffs*: Supervisor with 17 years experience said: **"Best assessment we've ever produced."**
- Persuaded hostile decision makers to abandon $3M environmental "fix" that would not work. *Payoffs:* **Problem solved**. Edible fish **population returned to health.**
- Set up Alabama's algal assay program from scratch in just 90 days.

CONFIDENTIAL

(continued)

CONFIDENTIAL
Cathy Turner **Environmental Specialist** [334] 555-5555

Examples of success (continued):

- **Aquatic Biologist,** Wildlife International, Limited
  Montgomery, Alabama, XX – XX
  This national leader provides the research results chemical producers rely upon to meet EPA guidelines. Up to 200 people employed nationwide.

Results

  - Helped complete research that traced pesticide levels in aquatic macroinvertebrates and fish. Measured water quality levels. ***Payoffs:*** Helped set instructions guiding consumers to apply pesticides and herbicides safely.

- **Cooperative Education Student Aide**, Alabama Department of Environmental Management, Montgomery, Alabama, XX – XX

  - Mastered skills in laboratory toxicity testing protocols, maintaining vertebrate test species, collecting and identifying aquatic macroinvertebrates.

Education:

- B.S., **Biology and Environmental Science**, Auburn University at Montgomery, **Dean's List,** XX – *Working up to 40 hours a week while carrying up to 20 credit hours.*

Training:

- Algal Assay Techniques and Culture Procedures, XX
- Toxicity Identification Evaluation, XX
- Water Quality Based Permitting, Enforcement, & Toxicity Reduction Evaluations, XX
- Compliance Monitoring, XX
- Aquatic Toxicity Course for Evaluating Applications for Permits Under the National Pollutant Discharge Elimination System, XX
- Culture and Toxicity Testing Techniques of *Ceriodaphnia dubia,* XX

Computer literacy:

- **Expert:** Sanitas (statistical analysis package), Windows 3.x, Windows 95, Excel, Word 6
- **Proficient:** LogDraft 3.0, MS Works, Harvard Graphics, NetScape Navigator, Internet search tools and FTP
- **Working knowledge:** Surfer (plat producing program), Lotus 1-2-3, Symphony, WP+

More specific things she can do

Submitted by Don Orlando

2 CONFIDENTIAL

Good overview of her many skills, including many skill words

GRACE CHELMAN

55 Walkill Road
Key West, FL 00000
(444) 444-4444

FOOD TECHNOLOGIST

Dairy Foods / Food Microbiology / R&D / Beverages & Sweeteners

Strong project manager with effective partnering skills and proven ability to conceive and present innovative approaches to clients. Expert in formulating flavor combinations and taking new products/line extensions from bench to marketing. Combines extensive lab experience with thorough understanding of ingredient functionality to drive forward new products and advance the development process. Experienced in bakery, culinary, nutrition, focus group tests, and supervising first runs. Extensive qualifications in:

- **Quality Assurance**
- **Prototype Development**
- **Product Development**
- **Sensory Evaluation**
- **Client Presentations**
- **Nutritional Labeling**
- **Product Formulations**
- **Data Collection/Analysis**
- **Shelf-Life Testing**

Technically proficient with detailed documentation on all product formulas, tests, and results. Exceptional verbal and written communication skills. Sharp presentation, negotiation, and team building abilities.

CAREER HISTORY:

ABC INDUSTRIES, INC., *Tampa, FL* **xxxx to Present**

R&D Manager

Lead the complete R&D function for this family-owned company. Custom-create flavor systems, develop new beverages, prepare manufacturer's formulations, provide per unit pricing and formulate nutritional fact panels to regional, national, and Fortune 500 companies. Management accountability includes direct supervision of chemist, lab assistant, account representative and clerk. Serve as a liaison and resource person from initial sales presentation, through feasibility and development to first-run supervision.

- Maintain a high prototype approval rating and fast accurate turnaround time through extensive technical knowledge, broad experience, and complete understanding of ingredient compatibility.
- Increased client base and profits by enhancing services (ie: providing nutritional fact panels), utilizing effective fact-finding & interview techniques, and streamlining the development process.
- Directed the selection, conversion and implementation of laboratory instrumentation and manufacturing equipment which significantly upgraded production capabilities.
- Invited to collaborate on critical business decisions due to unique insight into client goals & objectives,understanding of market trends, and knowledge of government regulations.
- Successfully interact with clients, marketing, and technology groups to bring projects to fruition.
- Consistently find new and creative ways to enhance existing products and identify/develop value-added products. Successfully developed and introduced a chocolate malt-based beverage.
- Initiated the development of a clerical position which redirected professional staff to specific project requirements, improved operating efficiency, and strengthened administrative functions.
- Established numerous industry contacts and built effective working relationships by maintaining a competitive market presence, contributing to professional associations, and continuing education.

Emphasis on results

(continued)

(continued)

GRACE CHELMAN - Page Two

CAREER HISTORY con't:

ABC FOODS, INC., *Miami, FL* **February to August, xxxx**

Product & Process Specialist - R&D Department

Dealt with quality control, compositional standards, sensory evaluation and the biotechnology of dairy cultures. Worked with textural food ingredients, new products, product formulations and process.

- Gained extensive experience in cultured dairy products including sour cream, yogurt, cottage cheese, ice cream - soft serve to hard pack, zero fat to decadent full fat.
- Prepared cost-saving formulations on a pilot plant scale.
- Experimented with various bacteriological cultures and line extensions.

THE ABC FOOD NETWORK, *Manta, FL* **xxxx to xxxx**

Lab Technician

Handled overall project management and hands-on product development from bench to production. Worked with sensory evaluation and the composition and properties including chemical, physical, and biological changes in food constituents as a result of preparation, processing and storage.

- Integral member in directing a pharmaceutical ingredient supplier's entrance into the food industry.
- Worked extensively on projects for a market leader in weight loss reduction products.
- Requested to exclusively work with two food ingredient suppliers.

ABC UNIVERSITY FOOD SCIENCE DEPARTMENT, *Orlando, FL* **xxxx to xxxx**

Dairy Microbiology Technician

Assigned to a State Cooperative Extension project conducting ongoing stability testing for fluid milk in dairy plants.

- Evaluated and documented processes, equipment and plant design, and sanitation.
- Verified product quality over shelf life.
- Tested and evaluated to ensure that good manufacturing procedures were successful.
- Compiled results and reported findings to representatives for the individual dairy plants.

PROFESSIONAL DEVELOPMENT:

Education	• **A.A.S. in Dairy & Food Sciences** - UCLA State Technology Center
Continuing Education	• **Basic Food Science** - Cornell University • **Food Science, Food Science Seminar, Food Microbiology** - Rutgers University
Computer	• MS Word, Excel, Internet
Associations	• Institute of Food Technologists

Submitted by Kristen Mroz Coleman

Attractive layout and concise but strong content.

Mary D. Douglas
28 Brahms Road
Silver Spring, MD 20904
301-555-5555

ADULT NURSE PRACTITIONER

Accomplished professional with extensive nursing experience and a commitment to quality patient care. Built successful career in a variety of healthcare settings including private medical practice, nursing homes, hospitals, and homecare.

Nursing style: Combine professionalism and compassion to provide exceptional medical and emotional care. Communicate exceptionally well with doctors, colleagues, and patient families.

Special expertise: Gained extensive experience dealing with long-term care and end-of-life issues, including providing support and counseling to family members and patients.

OK to put this section → early in the resume because it's relevant to this job seeker's profession.

EDUCATION, LICENSURE & CERTIFICATION

RN, CRNP, Maryland State: License #NP05555

Adult Nurse Practitioner Certificate, American Nurses Credentialing Center: #555555-21

Master of Science, University of Maryland at Baltimore, Baltimore MD

Bachelor of Science in Nursing, cum laude, Columbia College, New York, NY

PROFESSIONAL EXPERIENCE

TRUECARE, Elkridge, MD 1998–Present
Nurse Practitioner
Truecare is a leading provider of care and care coordination to elderly, vulnerable, and chronically ill individuals living on their own, in community-based settings, or in nursing homes.

Currently oversee total care for 100 long-term-care patients in three nursing homes. Collaborate with physicians and nursing home staff, troubleshoot problems, order diagnostic tests, oversee treatment, and counsel family members.

- Take a compassionate and proactive approach to patients' care, working with the families to ensure that patients are able to remain in the facility whenever possible.
- Received three performance awards for excellence in care and teamwork.
- Consistently achieved the lowest hospitalization rate of all 45 nurse practitioners as a result of collaborative approach and close involvement in patient well-being.

BRANDON PHEBES, M.D., P.A., Baltimore, MD 1997–1998
Nurse Practitioner

Assisted doctor with 25–30 patients per day in this busy office, conducting comprehensive physical assessments of patients and determining when to involve the doctor.

- Established medical diagnoses, ordered and evaluated diagnostic tests, and referred certain cases to the physician.
- Prescribed/ regulated medications and oversaw patient therapy, including emotional support and regular follow-up.
- Worked with patients on preventive health measures and helped them create action plans to carry out prescribed treatments or health regimens.

Submitted by Louise Fletcher

(continued)

(continued)

Mary D. Douglas
– Page 2 –

PROFESSIONAL EXPERIENCE (CONTINUED)

MONTGOMERY GENERAL HOSPITAL, Olney, MD 1990–1997
Staff Nurse

- Planned and managed total care for 10–12 acutely ill med-surg patients; conducted diagnostic assessments; ordered and interpreted tests; and administered medication.
- Provided support and encouragement to patients in carrying out prescribed medical regimen.
- Advised patients on prognosis and treatment possibilities.
- Prioritized, delegated, and managed other personnel in delivering patient care.
- Gained thorough understanding of all areas of the hospital and provided "floating" support in areas that needed additional assistance.

ACE PROFESSIONAL STAFFING SERVICE, Rockville, MD 1988–1990
Staff Nurse

Good way to summarize older experience and keep the resume to two pages.

EARLY CAREER:

Held various nursing positions, including 2 years as a Staff Nurse at Massachusetts General Hospital, 2 years at Greater Southeast Community Hospital, and experience as a Public Health Nurse and Home Health Nurse. Full details available on request.

AFFILIATIONS, HONORS, AND AWARDS

Member, Nurse Practitioner Association of Maryland

Maryland Gubernatorial Scholarship, 1997

Montgomery General Hospital Scholarship, 1996

ONGOING PROFESSIONAL DEVELOPMENT

Ongoing professional development includes regular attendance at conferences, training seminars, and lecture programs, including

- Legal Aspects Facing the Nurse Practitioner in Long-Term Care—Baltimore, MD (2004)
- Primary Care of the Older Adult Conference—Hyannis, MA (2003)
- Living with Grief: Loss Later in Life—Hospice Foundation of America, Washington, DC (2003)
- Ethical Considerations and Controversies—Suburban Hospital, Bethesda, MD (2003)
- Ophthalmology for the Medical Practitioner—Johns Hopkins, Baltimore, MD (2002)
- The 27th Annual Current Topics in Geriatrics—Johns Hopkins, Baltimore, MD (2002)
- The 18th Annual National Nurse Practitioner Symposium—Baltimore, MD (2001)

Clean layout — easy to read

Nancy Jennings

4211 Mesa Verde Drive
Costa Mesa, CA 92626

Home: 949-274-0254
njennings@cox.net

REGISTERED NURSE / CERTIFIED DIABETES EDUCATOR

"Committed to Providing the Highest-Quality Patient Care" ← Effective to include a "mission statement"

Dedicated, competent Registered Nurse with extensive experience in Diabetes, Home Health Nursing, Oncology, Medical/Surgical, Orthopedic, and Telemetry fields. Certified Diabetes Educator who consistently strives to improve the quality of care for all assigned patients. Minimize stress by providing comfort and compassion with an awareness and sensitivity of patients' needs. Take-charge provider and advocate for patients in medical centers and home settings. Utilize excellent communication skills to present diabetes educational seminars in medical facilities and communities.

SUMMARY OF QUALIFICATIONS

- Diabetes specialist skilled in care of Type 1 and Type 2 diabetes clients (ages 15 to 102).
- Adept in ascertaining individualized diabetes and blood-sugar-meter supplies.
- Nutritional management and counseling.
- Analysis of laboratory results, head-to-toe assessments, and patient history.
- Obtain realistic goals with clients' choices and decisions.
- Assess and treat cardiovascular status.
- Proficient with insulin pump maintenance and use of resources.
- Knowledgeable in Medicare and Medi-Cal criteria, as well as Board and Care regulations.
- Competent with Windows-based McKesson HBOC system program and use of PowerPoint.
- Utilize CADD pump, chemotherapy, Port-a-cath, and other intravenous-line care.
- Substantial experience with patients on a one-on-one basis.
- Design personalized plans for patients based on individual needs.
- Coordinate all required services for patients' families.
- Work closely and collaborate with an interdisciplinary team.
- Coordinate with community resources to provide health services and medical equipment to patients.

PROFESSIONAL EXPERIENCE

Memorial Medical Center, Costa Mesa, CA — 1998–Present

Memorial Heart Institute and Wellness Center—Diabetes Clinic
Diabetes Self-Management Training Program—ADA recognized
Certified Diabetes Nurse Educator / Advisory Board Member

- Instruct diabetes clients in an outpatient setting in groups of 10 or less.
- Direct diabetes teaching and promotion of self-management, including assessing diabetes clients physically and psychosocially to determine appropriateness of care.
- Provide nursing measures as delineated in care plan and directed by continual evaluation.
- Recommend appropriate diet, activity, and medical regime.
- Liaison between physician and client in promoting diabetic wellness.
- Perform a multitude of skilled nursing interventions, including venipuncture, diabetic management, and all types of wound care. Special-needs clients seen one-on-one.
- Case-manage a variety of patients of all ages, especially geriatric patients.
- Troubleshoot and problem-solve difficult cases for physicians.

Submitted by Pearl White

(continued)

(continued)

Nancy Jennings **Resume—Page 2**

PROFESSIONAL EXPERIENCE
(Continued)

Coordinated Home Care, Costa Mesa, CA 1993–Present
Certified Diabetes Nurse Educator (1998–Present)
Diabetes Nurse (1995–1998)

- Care management of diabetic patients from start of care to discharge.
- Establish a comprehensive care plan with patient, family, and other disciplines ensuring continuity of care.
- Supervise and instruct client and care providers in the disease process and treatment plan.
- Overseer and trainer of diabetes sub-specialty team.
- Subject matter expert in infection control for JCAHO preparation.
- Participate in marketing opportunities.
- Attend and participate in team and quality improvement meetings and various leadership conferences.
- Take part in after-hour triaging and scheduled patient visits.

Oncology Nurse (1993–1995)

- Organized, implemented, and instructed individual client care according to diagnosis and needs of client and family.

Home Health Services, Santa Ana, CA 1990–1993
Registered Nurse (1990–1993)
Scheduling Coordinator (1992–1993)

- Supervised and coordinated daily staff schedules.
- Led team conferences and staff meetings.
- Maintained liaison with agency disciplines and other business associates.

Evaluation Nurse (1991–1992)

- Admitted all new clients.
- Incorporated and reviewed treatment plans for quality and comprehensiveness.

Field Nurse (1990–1991)

- Established quality home care for all clients and families by assessment, problem identification, utilizing appropriate disciplines, and care planning.

LICENSES and CERTIFICATIONS

- Registered Nurses—State of California, 1988–Present
- Certified Diabetes Educator, American Association of Diabetes Educators, 1998–Present

PROFESSIONAL AFFILIATIONS

- Orange County Association of Diabetes Educators
- American Diabetes Association
- American Association of Diabetes Educators

Writer's comments: Mary's work history was choppy but with lots of pertinent volunteer work while raising young children. Nutrition was one area of her expertise, so we decided to call her a nutrition counselor rather than an independent distributor for a multilevel marketing company. By combining two volunteer positions into one listing as a Volunteer Community Health Worker, her history looks a lot less choppy.

Mary B. Friendly

444 Laughing Eagle Place
Raleigh, NC 22222
(919) 333-3333

Community-oriented professional with 9 years' experience in Child Development, Day Care, Nutrition, and Pre-Natal Programs.

- Consistent record of commitment, compassion and good judgment at both the provider and administrative levels.
- Highly organized and effective at managing multiple tasks for time-critical projects. Skilled at planning, coordinating, training and monitoring programs.
- Exceptional communication, interpersonal, and conflict resolution skills. Proven ability to develop trusting relationships within diverse populations.

HEALTHY LIFE CORPORATION, Raleigh NC and Redwood City, CA
Nutrition Counselor XXXX-Present

Design and set up nutritional programs for adults and children. Make group presentations.

- Coordinating with Community Women's Center, organized walking club in conjunction with weight loss program.

YMCA OF REDWOOD CITY, Redwood City, CA
Child Care Coordinator XXXX

Oversaw 6 child care facilities with 450 children. Handled administrative functions related to new employee intake and employee records.

- Visited sites, monitored activities, trained Site Directors, and worked with families to meet needs of both children and parents.

PRENATAL SERVICES, Redwood City, CA
BERKELEY JUNIOR LEAGUE, Berkeley, CA
Volunteer Community Health Worker XXXX-XXXX

Previous experience is carefully presented to reinforce her job objective

- Served as a resource for Black Infant Health Project teaching prenatal care to high-risk pregnant teens. Worked on special project to encourage fathers to participate in families.
- Managed caseload of 6 pregnant teenagers and served as birthing coach.

CHILD CARE COORDINATING COUNCIL, Burlingame, CA
Nutrition Department XXXX-XXXX

Monitored 50 home day care facilities to ensure nutrition and health standards.

Licensed Day Care Provider, Burlingame, CA XXXX-XXXX

Worked with State and County agencies to assist welfare and special-needs families.

UNIVERSITY CHILDREN'S CENTER, University Town, CA
Preschool Teacher XXXX-XXXX

Taught classes of approximately 20 preschoolers.

EDUCATION

Certificate, Child Development, Community College, Redwood City, CA
Sign Language, Ohlone College, Fremont, CA

Submitted by Sydney J. Reuben

Juanita Santiago 488 Kennedy Parkway, Linden, NJ 00000 ⌘ (555) 555-5555

⌘ Seeking position in guest services with an Atlantic City casino.

↳ A very specific objective helps her target her search

Carefully selected content supports her current objective

Profile

- *Transferrable background and skills in dealing with the public gained through previous work as a flight attendant and a fine dining server.*
- *Display a friendly and enthusiastic interpersonal manner with individuals and groups; successful in putting all types of people at ease. Fluent in Spanish.*
- *Thrive in an exciting, multi-tasking environment with daily challenges.*
- *Extremely service oriented and resourceful, with ability to assess needs, provide appropriate solutions, and follow-through to satisfaction of clients.*

Related Experience

BICOASTAL AIRLINES *XXXX–Present*
Newark International Airport, Newark, NJ

Flight Attendant

- *Fly approximately 80 hours a month, which includes regularly scheduled routes and on-call assignments.*
- *Serve as liaison between cabin and cockpit crews to convey important information.*
- *Alleviate the concerns of first-time flyers and attend to children traveling alone.*
- *Received numerous customer service awards for quick identification and response to passengers' needs.*

Writer's comments: The client had moved to Atlantic City and wanted to make a career move to the gaming industry. I highlighted her previous customer service experience to support her current objective.

MAPLE CREST COUNTRY CLUB *XXXX–XXXX*
Maple Crest, NJ

Server

- *Started as back runner, and shortly thereafter was given exposure to front-of-house operations involving banquet serving, cocktails, and ala carte service for dining room accommodating 150.*
- *Took initiative to learn all aspects of dining service, such as knowledge of ingredients in special menu items, methods of preparation, and accommodations available for special dietary needs.*
- *Entered customer food orders on Basic Four computer system, providing faster service.*

Education & Training

- *Courses in Hospitality Management at Jersey City State College* *XXXX*
- *Bicoastal Airlines Flight Attendant Training Program (four weeks)* *XXXX*
  FAA-approved intensive program at Bicoastal base station in Los Angeles, which included technical and operational instruction, customer service orientation, passenger safety and security, swift food and beverage serving procedures, personal grooming and poise.

Submitted by Melanie Noonan

A clean, simple format with an emphasis on skills and results

CHARLES A. ZIMMER
73 Fourth Street • Sea Plains, New Jersey xxxxx
(xxx) xxx-xxxx

CORPORATE TRAVEL SUPERVISOR

A knowledgeable travel professional with excellent negotiation skills and the ability to significantly reduce company expenditures. A dedicated individual with a commitment to excellence and customer service. Technical knowledge includes PC equipment, Lotus 1-2-3 software, Internet and Sabre System application.

PROFESSIONAL EXPERIENCE:

TOYS "R" US — New York, New York
Travel Coordinator — *xxxx - Present*

- Oversee daily functions pertaining to the Travel Department including supervision of five in-house agents.
- Troubleshoot and resolve inquiries pertaining to policy and agency errors.
- Negotiate air travel, car rentals, ground transportation contracts.
- Audit all PNRs for policy compliance.
- Prepare and present management reports to senior level management.
- Serve as a liaison between on-site and both Toys "R" Us and Kids "R" Us employees.
- Reconcile monthly bills, authorize reservations and randomly audit expense reports for accuracy.
- Coordinate Vice President level special requests.

Selected Accomplishments: ✓ Emphasizes results

- ***Saved the company $160,000 in xxxx and over $140,000 in xxxx.***
- ***Implemented a Corporate Card Program.***
- ***Negotiated policies which reduced ticket prices by an average of $100 and significantly reduced hotel expenditures.***
- ***Designed improved Standard Operating Procedures for travel expense reports to enhance tracking methods.***
- ***Instrumental in activating specific training for counselors.***

NEW RIDGE TRAVEL — New Ridge, NJ
On-Site Supervisor — *xxxx - xxxx*

- Directly supervised three travel agents on-site at Toys "R" Us.
- Accountable for coordinating travel reservations, resolving problems and developing staff.

PACK & GO TRAVEL — Hackensack, NJ
Assistant Manager — *xxxx - xxxx*

- Oversaw agency operations including training and development of staff.
- Finalized accounts to ensure client satisfaction.
- Reviewed financial matters and performed bookkeeping functions.

ABC TRAVEL — Clifton, NJ
Travel Counselor — *xxxx - xxxx*

- Accountable for instituting travel arrangements and handling reservations for outside sales manager.

EDUCATION:

A.A. in Travel & Tourism, Johnson & Wales • Providence, RI

PROFESSIONAL AFFILIATION:

New Jersey Travel Association

Submitted by Alesia Benedict

CRAIG LAWRENCE

15-15 55th Road, Apt. 5 • Staten Island, NY 55555
(555) 555-1515 • Cellular: (555) 555-1111 • E-mail: cl15@xxx.com

Detailed and effective opening

CONCIERGE • HALLMAN • DOORMAN

Perfect Security Background / Bondable / New York State Driver's License

Highly motivated and dedicated professional with over 10 years of experience as a concierge and doorman. Provide courteous and efficient service to tenants and guests. Demonstrated record of exceptional reliability and perfect attendance. Resourceful and knowledgeable about travel and entertainment services in the New York metropolitan area. Strong interpersonal skills and positive work ethic; keep a neat, clean, and professional appearance. Excellent common sense, judgment, and decision-making abilities. Computer literate in Windows 98, Internet programs, and Microsoft Works.

PROFESSIONAL EXPERIENCE

Impressive statements

PARK HOUSE REALTY COMPANY – New York, NY
Concierge, 19XX to 19XX

- Served as concierge at 555 East 32nd Street, a prestigious co-op apartment building housing celebrities, high-ranking dignitaries, and top corporate executives.
- Took over management responsibilities of superintendent in his absence.
- Directly supervised team of lobby workers and doormen. Trained new staff members.
- Earned a reputation for going above and beyond concierge responsibilities to ensure satisfaction of residents and visitors.
- Regarded by tenants, guests, managers, board members, and colleagues as the consummate professional, committed to providing impeccable service.
- Maintained the highest emphasis on safety and security at all times; monitored traffic and deliveries in and out of building.
- Handled telephone communications; reserved cars, limousines, and taxis.

ABC REAL ESTATE COMPANY – New York, NY
Doorman, 19XX to 19XX

- Provided doorman services at 222 West 92nd Street, a luxury residential building with 400 apartments and 1,000 residents.
- Greeted tenants and guests in a friendly and courteous manner; provided tenants with a clean and safe environment.
- Hailed taxis and assisted with luggage and packages as needed.
- Monitored the building's arrivals and departures.

ACTION CAR, INC. – New York, NY
Owner / Operator, 19XX to 19XX

- Provided limousine services on order of 25 calls per day.

NYC TAXI – New York, NY
Owner / Operator, 19XX to 19XX

Writer's comments: This job seeker secured a concierge position with a prestigious hotel. The employer was impressed by the professionalism portrayed by the candidate's resume and interview.

EDUCATION

ABC MECHANICAL ENGINEERING COLLEGE – London, England
Mechanical engineering courses, 19XX to 19XX

Submitted by Kim Isaacs

Writer's comments: The graphic tells you that this trim resume is about food—the serving or preparation of it—before you have a chance to read one word.

François J. Boudreau

88 Harbor Place
Rock Cove, ME 00000

(207) 555-5555

Objective:

Assistant or Sous Chef

Good design, lots of white space, and few but well-chosen words make this an effective resume

Summary of Qualifications:

- Associate's Degree in Culinary Arts with training in American and International Cuisines
- Restaurant experience has included broiler, grill, sauté, fryer, expo, breakfast and salads
- Able to handle a multitude of tasks at once, meeting deadlines under pressure
- Demonstrates ability to respond with speed and accuracy in a highly productive setting
- Works cooperatively and harmoniously with coworkers and supervisors
- Dedicated to quality in service and product

Experience:

Broiler/Prep Cook — Jacques Restaurant, West Cove, Maine (9/94 to Present)
200-seat Four Diamond restaurant featuring an extensive menu of French and American cuisine

Fry Cook — The Lobster Net, Port Hancock, Maine (1992-94)
Indoor and outdoor dining, specializing in fresh lobsters and seafood; take-out and banquet service

Fry/Prep Cook — The Weathervane, Rocky Coast, Maine (1991)
Traditional New England seafood served in a casual setting

Education:

Associate's Degree in Culinary Arts – Newbury College, Brookline, Massachusetts (1992)
Curriculum and Training included:

- Soup, Stock and Sauces
- Breads and Rolls
- Desserts
- Classical Bakeshop
- American Cuisine
- International Cuisine
- Yarde Manger
- Sanitation and Dining Room

Submitted by Becky J. Davis

ROGER P. BARNES
196 East Goldwater Road
Tempe, Arizona 85858
(555) 555-5555

SUMMARY: *Skilled Hospitality Manager with exceptional customer focus and organizational skills. Successful track-record identifying niche market, defining lounge/club concept, and implementing operating plan. Experienced in controlling costs, booking entertainment, and fostering repeat business with corporate clientele.*

PROFESSIONAL EXPERIENCE:

Jan. 1997 - Present **Manager, Time Square Lounge;** City, State.
Accountable for day-to-day operations and overall management of night club grossing $50,000 monthly.

- Book live music and DJ's to play Salsa, Mérengue, and Hip Hop.
- Plan and implement advertising and promotion for musical acts.
- Control inventory and purchase all liquor.
- Negotiate purchase agreements with suppliers; control pour costs.
- Supervise 27 employees, including security staff.
- Account for daily receipts, prepare bank deposits, and administer payables.

Lists diverse responsibilities in a space-efficient format

Major Accomplishment:
Increased gross revenues by over 400%. Redefined club concept from Top 40 to Salsa/Hip Hop, successfully appealing to under-served niche market. Booked musical acts and designed promotional campaign to tout club's new focus.

Aug. 1995 - July 1996 **Bartender, Mesa Mountain Ranch;** City, State.
Serviced lounge seating 150, plus 15 wait staff serving adjacent pool area.

- Developed rapport with customers and fostered cordial atmosphere.
- Up-sold patrons on food items, increasing overall revenue.
- Established corporate contacts that led to repeat business.
- Significantly reduced pour costs through negotiation with suppliers.

July 1993 - Aug. 1995 **Bar Manager, Marriott Hotel;** City, State.
Managed lounge seating 500 and grossing $60,000 monthly.

- Hired, scheduled, and supervised bartenders and wait staff.
- Controlled inventory and pour costs.
- Booked corporate parties.
- Developed special promotions; implemented promotional campaigns.

Major Accomplishments:
Increased bar gross revenues by up to 700%. Improved food revenues in lounge from virtually zero to $2,500 per week.

Introduced cable TV, pool table, and other amenities to enhance atmosphere. Developed repeat business with corporate clientele.

Received numerous Honored Guest Awards for outstanding customer service.

An important section to show his results

1990 - 1993 **Waiter / Bartender, High Falls Grill;** City, State.
Served lunch and Happy Hour customers. Booked live entertainment and implemented promotions.

1987 - 1989 **Room Service Supervisor / Waiter, Posh Resort;** City, State.
Participated in the set-up and launch of Room Service at this golf resort in suburban City, State.

- Hired, trained, and supervised Room Service staff.
- Received bartender training.

EDUCATION:

1993 **A.A.S., Marketing;** City Community College; City, State.
DWI / TIPS Training

Submitted by Arnold G. Boldt

E-MAIL ADDRESS: xxxxxxxx@hotmail.com

DARRELL C. BRIGGS

Writer's comments: Client was 5555 Oak Woods Court ~ Tampa, Florida 33600 ~ (000) 000-0000
undecided on a career path and never completed a four-year degree program.

INFORMATION TECHNOLOGY SPECIALIST

Delivering Technological Solutions to Improve Operational Productivity and Efficiency

Because he seems to have found his niche in the IT field, I focused on only the relevant information for his current job target.

SUMMARY OF QUALIFICATIONS

Motivated, IT Specialist offering dynamic experience in the design, development, and delivery of results-oriented solutions to meet the emerging technological needs of diverse business environments and customer-driven initiatives. Self-directed facilitator, well-versed in areas such as ***systems engineering, client/server architecture, programming analysis, optimizing network performance, and customizing hardware/software applications***. Equal strengths in problem solving, troubleshooting, and organizational/time management. Hard working, quick learner with keen analytical ability and initiative. Record of peak performance and exceeding corporate expectations.

TECHNICAL SKILLS

Operating Systems	Windows 95 & 98 ~ NT Workstation ~ NT Server ~ DOS
Software Programs	Microsoft Office Suite 95 & 97 ~ Word ~ Excel ~ Access ~ PowerPoint ~ System 4 ~ T3
Applications	PC Tech ~ Hardware/Software Troubleshooting ~ Performance Monitoring ~ Hardware Installation Software Configurations ~ Peripheral Equipment Testing/Maintenance
Languages	BASIC ~ FORTRAN ~ COBOL ~ PASCAL ~ "C" ~ ADA
Networks	Ethernet ~ Token Ring ~ LAN ~ WAN
Internet	Explorer ~ Netscape Browsers ~ Outlook ~ Exchange
Utility Programs	PC Tools ~ Norton Utilities ~ System Commander

White space makes this resume easier to read

EDUCATION / PROFESSIONAL TRAINING

Important, so these are put toward top of resume

BAY AREA COMMUNITY COLLEGE - Tampa, FL
A. A. - Computer Science (19XX) *(Self-financed 100% of college education)*

Implication: hard worker

Microsoft Certified Professional – ID #1133563
- ***MCP Systems Engineer***
- ***MCP Internet***

LDT Customer Service Certifications
- ***LDT Gold Service***
- ***Signature Service***

PROFESSIONAL EXPERIENCE

AAA COMPUTER TECHNOLOGY GROUP - Tampa, FL ***(Temp-Perm Professional Staffing Agency)*** **12/XX - Present**
Technical Support Specialist/ Help Desk Technician

Assigned to GTE-ES Department; charged with manning the Help Desk and facilitating a diverse scope of technical services to support client/server functions. Instrumental role in troubleshooting and orchestrating connectivity of System 4, T3 Project involving the rollout of an innovative real estate software program. Conduct instructional training classes for real estate professionals on software applications.

COMPUTER CONSULTANTS - Tampa, FL ***(Professional Staffing Agency)*** **9/XX - 11/XX**
Computer Technician/Consultant

Fulfilled 90-day contract with Intermedia Communications. Services provided included building and imaging computers, establishing LAN infrastructure, troubleshooting, and supporting IT Department.

LD TELECOMMNICATIONS - Pinellas Park, FL **1/XX -8/XX**
Level I & II Help Desk/Technical Support

High-level performance led to progressive duties as Level II technician; monitored call escalations and resolutions. Notable success working on projects involving NEC and Hewlett Packard. Developed and implemented guidelines for successive training of Level I Techs.

- **Achieved two Club Awards - outstanding performance and exceeding corporate goals; ranked in top 5% at that facility**
- **Recipient of Spotlight Award - recognition for exceeding work objectives not aligned with project goals**

EMERGING TEK CORPORATION - Tampa, FL ***(part-time)*** **19XX - 19XX**
Independent Consultant

Built, repaired, and performed troubleshooting/testing activities on computer systems and peripheral equipment.

Submitted by Diane McGoldrick

JOHN DOE
823 7th Avenue
Nicetown, Minnesota 55555

555 555 5555

Writer's comments: This resume helped John get a job that tripled his pay within a year. He used this resume on the Internet, and its many keywords helped him get many "hits" from employers.

JOB TARGET: QA/QC * Customer Engineer * R&D

QUALIFICATIONS SUMMARY

Consultant-Level Dasd Specialist
Certified AA/400 Professional System Administrator
Certified AA/400 Professional System Operator

Very strong analytical and organizational skills. Supervisory experience. Skilled documenting, writing and communicating. Learn new skills quickly and enjoy challenge. Serve as positive and professional example to others. Work easily under pressure. Productive worker willing to go above and beyond (43% OT rate). Medical background, with training in CPR, safety and hazardous materials. Prior Level I military security clearance.

AREAS OF SPECIALIZED TRAINING / EXPERTISE

The many keywords are to help get selected in Internet searches by employers

AA/400 and RR/6000 server manufacturing ... AA/400 base hardware service training ... AA/400 security ... MagStar 3494 tape library ... 3590 Mag tape subsystems ... backup and recovery management ... Raid ... mirroring ... Dasd and system restoration management ... Dasd migration ... hardware product training 5XX, 6XX models ... clustering / high availability ... single level storage ... process management ... basic system operation and administration (including advanced system operator) ... storage management networking ... PCI ... SCSI ... microchannel ... SMP ... ISA ... Sun and UNIX mainframes ... Power PC overview ... PC and Macintosh ... HP3070.

VM ... client / server computing ... Web technology ... creating applications for Java ... overview of Domino ... Novell 4.1 ... LAN ... Token Ring and Ethernet Topologies ... Internet / Intranet ... Netscape ... Microsoft Explorer ... E-mail ... Windows — NT Server 4.0, 95 and 3.1 ... OS/2 Warp ... Lotus Notes ... software customization and installation migration ... BASIC.

ISO 9000 ... JIT manufacturing ... installation, setups, builds, debugging, testing, analysis, repairs and system / hardware modifications ... pre-load software ... integrated circuits and circuit design ... numeric control ... plotting systems ... Scorpion testing ... Duluth, MFS, AIX, and HTX testing and tools ... oscilloscopes ... box sort tests ... defect logs ... soldering ... blueprints and schematics ... calibration and adjustments ... QA/QC and quality improvement ... continuous flow manufacturing ... voice communications ... fiber optics ... sonar / radar.

ADMINISTRATIVE, BUSINESS and MISCELLANEOUS SKILLS

Supervisory and training of manufacturing personnel and operators ... writing of training documents and procedures ... troubleshooting, problem resolution and decision making ... team building and participation ... leadership qualities ... liaison and communication with engineers and manufacturing personnel regarding test and quality problems ... revenue generation ... customer satisfaction ... repair and preventive maintenance.

Transferable skills

John Doe
Page Two

TECHNICAL EXPERIENCE

Shows promotions

BIG CORPORATION, NICETOWN MN
* Customer Engineer, 19XX to present
* Technician, 19XX to 19XX
* Production Specialist, 19XX to 19XX
* Electronic Technician (Electronic Card, Assembly and Test), 19XX to 19XX

Assist in post sale maintenance for customers of IBM equipment. Serve in capacity of customer technical interface for hardware support and delivery of operational services, including post sale support for hardware. Service activities include system assurance, installation, team account management, problem determination, discontinuance and relocation of BIG systems. Exercise problem determination and problem solving to restore customer hardware and software integrity.

Worked closely with manufacturing, R&D, engineering and production control teams in the server divisions. Provided feedback to other technicians on the floor. Served as Quality Advocate and perform QA/QC, very complex testing and analysis, assembly, rework, debugging, repairs, and reliability tests. Performed precision adjustments and setups of sensitive equipment, with attention to component variances and close tolerances. Compiled detailed logs of functional failures, defects, and repairs for management review. Repaired and maintained test equipment. Installed and tested profile programs.

Achievements: Assisted in piloting the Bird S70 (first server to integrate AA/400 and RR/6000 technology), wrote test policies and procedures, and prepped machine for lab code. Earned two leadership team awards. Recognized for contributions and suggestions which led to cost savings, increased quality, and operational efficiency. Instrumental in improving first pass yields and implementing new test procedures, resulting in 30-40% improvement rate. Piloted new process for pre-box sort test which eliminated basic failures on planar boards and other components.

Certifications for RR/6000 builds, test, and repair: all stations, models R24 / 30 / 40 / 50 * two stations, models 770 / 771 * 7006 / 7009 * ICT and BST tests * Carolina products

Good use of related military experience

U.S. NAVY, San Diego and Long Beach CA
Interior Communications Systems Electrician, 19XX to 19XX

Organizational and intermediate maintenance / installation of navigational equipment, radar, sonar, fiber optics, ships control systems, gyrocompasses, plotting systems, phones, TVs, alarm systems and switches. Served as **Section Leader** and received commendation from commanding officer. Earned **National Defense Medal**.

EDUCATION
Associate Degree in Electronics * Interior Communications School at Service School Command

Additional relevant course work and classes: propulsion alarm and indicating system maintenance * MK NC-2 MOD 2/2A plotting system maintenance * fiber optics * problem solving and decision making * "Train the Trainer" and "Communicate With Confidence" * firefighter training and LPN nursing courses * MK numeric control plotting systems maintenance

Important to include

Submitted by Beverley Drake

Writer's comment: Client wanted to transition from a project leader to an engineering management position, as well as change industries from defense to the commercial sector. Although he had progressed to a leadership role, he did not have the formal title of manager. This resume minimizes lack of an engineering degree and downplays his defense industry background.

TIMOTHY HANKS

45 Main Street • City, State 13468 • (555) 555-5555 • XXX@aol.com

He received 4 interviews out of 6 applications and 3 job offers.

ENGINEERING & PROJECT MANAGEMENT

Experienced engineering professional with a successful career leading the design and development of sophisticated products for diverse industries/markets. Analytical, technical, supervisory and engineering expertise combines with achievements in cost reductions, quality improvement and project management. Strengths:

- **Extensive qualifications in training and supervision of engineering personnel, resource management, project planning and documentation.**
- **Proficient in all aspects of electro-mechanical design from requirements definition and analysis through conceptual design, drawings and customer presentations.**
- **Effective customer, vendor and inter-departmental liaison with outstanding troubleshooting, problem solving, relationship management and negotiation skills.**
- **Thoroughly versed in commercial and MIL specifications, CAD and other applications; DOD secret clearance.**

PROFESSIONAL EXPERIENCE & ACCOMPLISHMENTS

THOMPSON CORPORATION, Hamden, Massachusetts (1987-Present)
Project Leader
Advanced Mechanical Designer

Promoted to oversee design and development of multi-million dollar electro-mechanical and mechanical projects. Create conceptual and detail designs, delivering presentations in senior management and customer design reviews. Recruit, train and lead engineering and drafting teams. Establish and maintain all documentation standards. Source, select and negotiate with vendors.

Good use of numbers to quantify results

- **Selected as project engineer to spearhead $35 million program, delivered ahead of schedule and well within budget.**
- **Led project team in concept development and design of new product line generating $20 million in annual sales.**
- **Saved $1.2 million in annual production costs through implementation of continuous improvement initiatives.**
- **Discovered and rectified critical design flaw, preventing costly, catastrophic system failure of product.**
- **Created and instituted CAD standards and trained engineering staff company-wide.**
- **Instrumental in engineering department's efforts in achievement of ISO 9001 certification.**

PIERSON CORPORATION, Fullerton, California (1985-1987)
Senior Engineering Designer

Developed and designed electro-mechanical consoles for multi-billion dollar global corporation. Trained and delegated project assignments to technical staff.

- **Selected as 1 of 3 top designers in division to lead project team in development of high-priority product line.**
- **Developed design methods for CAD system, incorporated in division-wide staff training.**

TIMOTHY HANKS • (555) 222-1111 • Page 2

JOHNSON CORPORATION, Anaheim, California (1983-1985)
Associate Engineer

Coordinated design, development and manufacturing of precision dental instruments for $10 million industry leader. Tested and evaluated all new products. Supervised drafting and toolmaking staff.

Results

- **Developed new instrument at half the cost of previous models without compromising quality standards.**
- **Redesigned x-ray machine with expanded application capabilities which generated $500,000 in sales.**

MORELAND COMPANY, Fullerton, California (1980-1983)
Mechanical Designer

Designed mechanical assemblies, tooling and molded plastic parts for $100 million international manufacturer of latches and fasteners.

Results

- **Contributed to diversification of product line and boosted sales by developing new fasteners for electrical assemblies.**
- **Designed tooling which expanded production capacity by 25% while reducing costs 10%.**

COMPUTER CAPABILITIES

ProEngineer
AutoCAD
Computervision Personal Designer
MicroStation Modeler
Windows NT and 98
Microsoft Office Suite

All of this, plus his experience, offsets his lack of a four-year degree.

EDUCATION

FULLERTON COLLEGE, Fullerton, California
Associate of Arts

Additional Training:

ANSI Y14.5M - 1982 ... ASME Y14.5M - 1994
MicroStation Modeler ... AutoCAD
TQM/Continuous Improvement
Project Management ... Team Building

AFFILIATIONS

American Society of Mechanical Engineers

Submitted by Louise Garver

Writer's comments: Client had been unsuccessful in generating interviews from his outdated resume that was nothing but an employment list. This aggressive resume focused on the depth of his expertise and credentials. He secured a new position earning 35% more.

NORMAN LATHROP

450 Spencer Road • San Jose, California 00000 • (555) 555-5555 • XXXX@aol.com

Strong, specific content

INFORMATION SYSTEMS CONSULTANT

An experienced information systems professional, Certified Disaster Recovery Planner (CDRP) and Certified Business Continuity Planner (MBCI) serving a diverse client base in finance and banking, health care, telecommunications, insurance, gas, chemicals, publishing, and government. Project management qualifications combine with demonstrated ability to develop and implement technical solutions to meet critical business needs. Outstanding leadership and interpersonal skills resulting in effective working relationships and top performance among staff. An excellent communicator between technical and business units who can translate complex data into easily understood terms.

AREAS of EXPERTISE

Keywords for electronic resume

Information Systems Integrity • Business Impact Analysis • Systems Applications
Disaster Recovery Planning & Auditing • Technical Support & Training • Regulatory Compliance
Business Continuity Planning • Information Protection Analysis • Technical Documentation

PROFESSIONAL EXPERIENCE

DEP SOLUTIONS • San Jose, California 1996-XXXX
Information Systems Consultant

Recruited to manage development, implementation and enhancement of business resumption and computer disaster recovery programs for corporate clients in finance/banking, health care, publishing, insurance, gas/chemicals, telecommunications, and government. ~~Achieved~~ distinction as first recipient of company's recognition award for outstanding performance. Key Projects:

- **Developed and implemented business recovery program with 5 platforms, data center and complex network at financial services organization with 32 business units at 6 regional sites.**
- **Created business recovery plans with 2-year maintenance program for 2 major customer service centers supporting client company and its operations globally.**
- **Designed voice systems disaster recovery plans and models for corporate headquarters/field locations of major telecommunications corporation.**

"Key Projects" allows him to focus on what he can do

APEX SYSTEMS • San Jose, California 1993-1996
Manager of Planning Services *1995-1996*

Planned, developed and managed all disaster and business recovery projects for entire company. Functioned as information systems security administrator controlling user identification creation and distribution as well as menu creation and distribution access. ~~Researched~~, planned and provided technical support for work flow and document management projects. Key Projects:

- **Performed risk assessment, analyzed business impact and led crisis management team in the development of data and business recovery plan.**
- **Instrumental in saving $7 million annually through coordination and transition to an in-house claims data processing system.**
- **Collaborated on the design and implementation of mainframe-based system completed in just 15 months.**
- **Analyzed work flow procedures and downtime costs for utilization management and provided recommendations to maximize future growth potential.**

NORMAN LATHROP • (555) 555-5555 • Page 2

Manager of Special Projects *1994-1995*

Managed all phases of MIS project planning, development, implementation, and management. Represented MIS Department to all business units and with subcontractors. Initiated and wrote procedures to automate MIS request system increasing efficiency, accountability and control. **Key Projects:**

- **Strengthened confidence and productivity level of 100+ nontechnical staff through training in microcomputers and software applications.**
- **Created new system to organize and categorize 350 internal/external reports for a state contract.**
- **Provided technical solutions to expedite completion of Medicare contract; company was awarded contract out of 450 respondents nationwide.**

Manager of Enrollment Services *1993-1994*

Reorganized and supervised staff in the daily operations of department. Reviewed, developed and implemented new policies and procedures. Involved in the development of system enhancements and participated in the design and implementation of a new automated membership system.

- **Significantly improved productivity through outstanding team-building and leadership skills.**
- **Increased applications processing 25% in just one month by redesigning work flow procedures.**
- **Introduced successful cross-training program turning around employee morale and performance.**

RYAN-LANCE CORPORATION • San Jose, California 1992-1993
Systems Analyst

Important information for this job!

EDUCATIONAL BACKGROUND

B.S. (Computer Science) New York University, New York, New York

Additional Training

Windows 3.1 Maintenance • Hewlett Packard Product Support • NEC Product Marketing
UNIX & 3b2 • Epson Computers & Printers • Development of Disaster Recovery Strategies
AutoCAD • Compaq • Novell Netware Engineer • IBM Business Partner • Apple Products
Emerging Technologies: Voice/Data Telecommunications (ATM, SONET & Frame Relay) - Bell Atlantic
Disaster Recovery Institute Training Program

COMPUTER CAPABILITIES

Hardware: IBM 9672 • IBM 9221 • HP 3000-III • AT&T 3b2 • Compaq Systempro
Apple Macintosh • HP Vectra • Epson • various PC platforms

Software: Netware • Lotus 1-2-3 • dBASE III • WordPerfect • Microsoft Windows, Word, Access, Project & Excel • Harvard Graphics • Paradox • Quattro Pro • FoxPro • Ami Pro • CorelDRAW • AutoCAD

Languages: COBOL • SPL • Pascal • C

ASSOCIATIONS

Disaster Recovery Institute • Business Continuity Institute • Survive!, U.S.A.
Information Systems Audit & Control Association

Submitted by Louise Garver

Writer's comments: The resume emphasizes on-the-job results for a highly technical candidate with a short work history.

THEODORE BUCHMANN
555 Pinewood Avenue, Apt. B00, New Rochelle, NY 00000
Home: (000) 000-0000 **E-mail: theodoreb@product.net** **Work: (000) 000-0000**

INFORMATION TECHNOLOGY / NETWORK MANAGEMENT

- **LAN/WAN Technologies**
- **Client/Server Architecture**
- **Applications Development**
- **Internet/Intranet Design**

Highly qualified manager offers extensive background in developing computer networks for multisite organization.... Instrumental in improving communications and expanding corporate capabilities through automation.... Guided management team in long-range planning and system implementation.

CAREER EXPERIENCE

FREIGHT MOVERS, INC., New York, NY xxxx-Present

MIS Manager

Manage computer system operations for this international freight forwarder/consolidator and customs broker with ten offices in North America. Supervise technical staff of four in addition to outside consultants. Maintain a networked system of seven LANs and a WAN, troubleshooting problems and providing user support on daily basis. Promoted from Systems Administrator based on performance.

Accomplishments

Shows a wide range of tasks and a results-orientation

- Led company in setting up fully networked computer system, including user support procedures and training programs.
- Designed and implemented current Frame Relay WAN, including a PPP dial-up solution.
- Set up e-mail function for all employees in US and South America. Reduced communications overhead by approximately 40%.
- Headed up design team that developed company's client server Logistics Tracking System. Significantly improved freight tracking, allowing company to bid on larger jobs.
- Standardized and upgraded software in all offices. Achieved more efficient maintenance as well as improved data exchange.
- Secured savings of $250,000 annually from long distance carrier by negotiating contract based on combined usage of all offices as one account.

NATIONAL POWER, Hamburg, Germany xxxx-xxxx

Application Developer

Developed UNIX-based application for the remote control of power plants and substations for second largest power supply company in Germany.

- Responsible for testing and implementing program on-site and at main control.

PREVIOUS EXPERIENCE includes position of Technical Coordinator for major project sponsored by UNICEF, which rebuilt Kurdish Hospitals destroyed by Iraqi Army after Gulf War.

EDUCATION/LANGUAGES

EE Degree, Hamburg Technical College, Hamburg, Germany
Fluent in German / Basic French

The specifics here are important

TECHNICAL

Operating Systems
Windows NT 4.0
Workstation Windows 95 & 3.1

Networking
Windows NT Server 4.0
Novell NetWare 2.2,3.12, 4.11

Software
MS-SQL Server 6.5 / MS-IIS 3.0
ARCserve (NT & NetWare)
PowerPoint / Word / Excel / Access / Act

Hardware
Workstations / Servers / Notebooks / Tape
Libraries / RAID storage system
Hubs / Bridges / Routers (Cisco)

Submitted by Vivian Belen

David Arnold

491 Chestnut Lane • Needham, MA 02492 • (781) 555–5555 • dave01@xyz.com

IT Manager

Writer's comments: The client had advanced in a management position with minimal education. The resume needed to highlight his expertise.

Profile

Proactive and results-oriented IT Manager with over 20 years of experience overseeing technical projects from design through implementation. Skilled business analyst and problem solver, able to improve efficiency of operations and complete projects on time and within budget. Comprehensive knowledge of wide array of hardware and software, combined with outstanding managerial skills. Proven ability to communicate effectively with both technical and non-technical personnel, from end-users to senior management. Experience with client/server systems, Y2K programming, and relational databases. Solid planning skills, with ability to manage and distribute workloads, prioritize needs, and establish and attain realistic schedules.

Technical Skills

Databases: HP Turbo Image, Oracle 7.X, IBM IMS, MS Access, VSAM, CTree
Developer Tools: ETW, Brio, Crystal, HP300 View, Qedit, Suprtool
Hardware: HP3000, HP 9000 client/server, IBM Mainframes, IBM PC's, Macintosh, RS6000
Languages: COBOL, Windows API, Powerhouse, SQL, Cognos, JCL, Visual Basic, Basic
Operating Systems: MPEXL, UNIX, Windows NT, Windows 95, Wang VS, IBM OS/VS2
Third Party Applications: DSS, Data Warehouse, Excel, MS Word, PowerPoint, BSA Order Management System, MCBA Suite of Order Management packages, Ask MANMAN

Experience

ACE TECHNOLOGY, Burlington, MA xxxx–present

Project Leader–Direct Marketing Division (xxxx–present)
Manage the implementation and support of a direct marketing client/server call center running on UNIX, MPEIX, and NT platforms. Hire and supervise 5-10 analysts, programmers, and consultants working on multiple projects. Consult with end-users and vendors to analyze requirements and maintain smooth operation of systems. Coordinate unit, system, stress, and regression testing. Oversee budget of $500,000.

Systems Analyst–Direct Marketing Division (xxxx–xxxx)
Designed, programmed, and provided ongoing support for BSA order management software. Coordinated upgrades and testing of system. Designed customized programs in consultation with end-users. Performed programming as needed from design to implementation.

Key Accomplishments

- Directed entire Y2K conversion effort: assessment of all equipment, scheduling of conversions of hardware and software, testing, and final implementation.
- Reduced warehouse-processing time by 40% by designing and implementing an enhanced shipping document.
- Coordinated and supported the conversion of 200 users to an upgraded and newly installed computer system.
- Trained and supported users, team members and partnership companies.
- Initiated expanded technical coverage for call center to maintain maximum efficiency of order processing during peak season.
- Fostered teamwork and high morale while meeting the requirements of senior management.
- Led or participated in improvement teams that enhanced automated commission processing and reduced unnecessary customer service call volume.

(continued)

(continued)

David Arnold **Page 2**

Experience (continued)

TECHDATA, Waltham, MA xxxx–xxxx

IS Manager of Development (xxxx–xxxx)

- Hired and managed up to 20 programmers and analysts to implement customized software enhancements for customers.
- Collaborated with sales representatives who marketed specialized manufacturing, financial, and order management software.
- Consulted with clients to determine customer requirements and explain technical capabilities; designed, tested, and implemented customized components.
- Trained clients to use software.

Software Consultant (xxxx–xxxx)

- Assisted in analysis and programming as a consultant on a wide range of hardware platforms, including IBM mainframes, HP, and WANG.
- Serviced wide array of small and large companies, including Westinghouse, Commercial Union, NECCO, Codex (Motorola), and New York Life Insurance.

CAMBRIDGE CREDIT, INC., Cambridge, MA xxxx–xxxx

Programmer Analyst

- Supported credit union financial package.
- Participated in installation and training for new credit union.

JOHNSON MARKETING, Boston, MA xxxx–xxxx

Programmer (xxxx–xxxx)

Computer Operator (xxxx–xxxx)

- Wrote programs in COBOL to support order processing fulfillment software.

Education

Two years of study toward B.S. in Computer Science at Boston College, with additional coursework at Boston University.

Ongoing Professional Development:

Certification in Oracle, SQL, ETW, Project Management.

Submitted by Wendy Gelberg

SHELLY DOE
2333 W. Addison, #A1
Oak Hill, IL 60689
Home: (773) 567-8910 Mobile: (312) 345-6789
shellydoe@hotmail.com

SUMMARY *Good, concise summary.*

Network and Senior Systems Engineer with extensive and diverse experience in network LAN/WAN data communications equipment infrastructure engineering, as well as systems engineering. Experience includes installing, configuring, troubleshooting, and supporting routers, switches, hubs, servers, and network operating systems. Solid knowledge and experience working with both networks and systems.

TECHNICAL SKILLS *— Tech skills are relevant enough to this job seeker's objective to be placed this early in the resume.*

Network Protocols:	TCP/IP, IPX/SPX, FTP, TFTP, X.25, RIP, IGRP, HSRP, VTP, STP, PPP, ISDN
Topologies:	Ethernet and Token Ring
Hardware:	3Com, HP, and Bay Hubs; Cisco Catalyst 2900XL and 5500 Series Switches and 2500, 3640, 1720 and 700 Series Routers
Network Tools and System Management:	Sniffer Protocol Analyzer, Cable Tracer, Openview, Compaq's Insight Manager Cisco IOS 11.3–12.2; MS Windows 2000, NT 4.0, and 3.51 Server, XP and 2000 Professional, 98, 95, 3.1, and 3.11; DOS 3.x–6.x; Novell NetWare 2.x–5.x
Operating Systems:	Cisco IOS 11.3–12.2; MS Windows 2000, NT 4.0, and 3.51 Server
Applications:	MS Internet Information Server 3.0 and 4.0; SQL Server 6.5; Exchange
Business Applications:	MS Office 2000, 97, and 95; Lotus SmartSuite and Freelance; Visio

PROFESSIONAL EXPERIENCE

PEBOTT SYSTEMS, Chicago, IL **1999 to Present**

Senior Systems Engineer with BTT Global Asset Management (2000 to Present)

Manage more than 100 Compaq servers with Microsoft BackOffice products in the Chicago and New York data centers. Design, purchase, and configure new HP/Compaq ProLiant platform servers, and Microsoft Windows 2000 Advanced Server and NT 4.0 Server products with IIS, MS SQL 6.5 and 2000, WINS, and DNS. Maintain, upgrade, and troubleshoot all related servers and products. *Opening paragraph of each job entry gives overview of the role.*

- Co-administer and support North American MS Exchange 5.5 servers.
- Co-design and implement global Windows 2000 production/test environment, including the migration of current production environment in Chicago and New York City to Win2K Active Directory. Co-design global DNS and WINS structures.
- Plan and implement physical server moves to brand new data center in downtown Chicago, including specification, implementation, and support of EMC Clarion SAN storage solution; implementation of NetIQ's AppManager and Security Manager server performance and security monitoring tools.

Bullets highlight key achievements

Inet Engineer with PBB Karson (1999 to 2000)

Managed Inet Engineering department computer lab, including management server hardware and software. Developed and implemented departmental intranet website focusing on the engineering of an automated document publishing and submission process, and the development of COM DLLs, MS Transaction Server packages, and VB6 IIS Applications to accommodate department informational needs.

- Engineered, troubleshot, and documented IIS solution; tested and administered Windows 2000 Developer's Pilot, including troubleshooting of Windows 2000 RC1/RC2 on 250 workstations and 6 servers.

Systems Engineer with PBB Brinson (1999 to 1999)

Managed Compaq hardware and Microsoft BackOffice products. Designed, purchased, configured, and installed Compaq ProLiant platform servers, and Microsoft Windows NT 4.0 Server and NT 4.0 Terminal Server products with IIS 4.0, MS SQL 6.5, and MS SQL 7.0, WINS, and DNS. Maintained, upgraded, and troubleshot all related servers and products.

Submitted by Hal Flantzer

(continued)

(continued)

Shelly Doe, Page 2

MIDNIGHT COWGIRL MANAGEMENT COMPANY, Ft. Worth, TX **1997 to 1999**
Senior Server and Network Administrator
Administered National Windows NT 4.0/Exchange Server 5.5 for four boot manufacturing companies with more than 1,000 end users. Designed, implemented, and managed 47 Windows NT/BackOffice Servers, including 17 SAP R/3 systems with Oracle for NT 7.3.3 database. Sized and configured servers used in migration from IBM mainframe to SAP R/3 AFS business and SAP R/3 HR systems. Administered Windows NT network. Administered and maintained Microsoft Exchange 5.5 server, including Microsoft Outlook 97/98 electronic forms creation and distribution. Performed miscellaneous Microsoft Visual Basic programming. Managed WINS and DNS servers.

- Co-created and implemented desktop software standards.

NFL OFFICE PRODUCTS INTERNATIONAL, Chicago, IL, and Arlington, TX **1995 to 1997**
Client Network Specialist, National Systems Division (1996 to 1997)
Administered National Windows NT 4.0/Exchange Server 4.0 with more than 2,300 users. Installed and configured new servers. Co-designed, implemented, and supported national MS Exchange servers and infrastructure. Maintained Corporate Internet Firewall network, as well as email connectivity problem identification and resolution. Performed troubleshooting for 40+ sites nationwide. Performed second- and third-line support for regional LAN administrators.

- Designed, implemented, and supported a national domain structure, including a migration plan and security design.
- Co-designed national desktop software and hardware standards.

LAN Administrator, Great Lakes Region (1996)
Regional Windows NT 3.51/4.0 network administrator. Installed and configured all new servers (hardware and software) in 7 locations, as well as for connectivity across WAN utilizing TCP/IP. Designed and configured RAID systems. Coordinated WAN troubleshooting with provider. Designed and implemented regional domain structure and security. Maintained router and concentrator. Performed troubleshooting for connectivity problems both locally and between sites.

Help Desk Analyst, Chicago Division (1995)
Identified first-time problems and found solutions. Supported all internal and external customers, and provided all desktop-level support, including the installation of all new PCs and printers, as well as support for legacy terminal-based UNIX system. Also provided support for the Windows NT network administrator, including user creation and deletion, directory and share-level security control, printer creation, program installation, and all TCP/IP address assignments. Maintained router and concentrator, including installation of users and redirection from Sun terminal servers to PC network concentrators, and performed troubleshooting on connection problems both locally and between sites.

CERTIFICATIONS

Microsoft Certified Systems Engineer

Microsoft Windows NT Server 3.51
Microsoft Windows NT Workstation 3.51
Microsoft Windows 95
Microsoft Systems Management Server 1.1
Microsoft Exchange 5.5
Microsoft Networking

EDUCATION

BFA, Art History, **Pennsyltucky State University,** Pennsyltucky, Ohio

Writer's comments: Heddi needed to explain her limited experience while simultaneously emphasizing her strengths.

HEDDI A. MACKENZIE

2222 Avila Drive
Fayetteville, NC 24000
(000) 000-0000

PROFILE

Former "trailing military spouse" who is an ***aggressive, self-starter*** experienced in areas such as general management, customer service, staff supervision, shipping/receiving, and computerized inventory control systems. ***Excellent performance record*** reflecting successive advancement to positions of increased responsibilities. ***Quick learner, easily trained;*** willing to accept challenging responsibilities and follow through with directives. Demonstrated strengths in prioritizing, organizing and handling multiple tasks efficiently and accurately. ***Very conscientious***, reliable and hard working; able to work effectively as a group leader or independently. Proficient in motivating others to achieve common goals. Personable and outgoing with ***strong "people" skills***. Familiar with Windows 95 Inventory Control System.

Notable performance record as a U.S. Army community housing volunteer in El Paso, Texas; organizing stay-at-home Moms to support in-home day care services for military families stationed in Italy; and upholding routine home management duties.

EMPLOYMENT HISTORY

Because of frequent moves, her work experience was weak but shows what she could do.

The Food Mart - Fayetteville, NC **19XX - 19XX**
Assistant Manager
Cashier/Clerk

After three months promoted to Assistant Manager. Accountable for overseeing routine store operations, daily reconciliation and audit of receivables, preparing bank deposits, handling large amounts of cash, training new employees, and supervising five employees. Utilized Windows 95 inventory control tracking system to monitor merchandise activity. Position required solid customer service skills, team-oriented attitude, and problem-solving ability.

Uses many skill words

Clothier Boutique - Tampa, FL **19XX - 19XX**
Assistant Manager, Shipping & Receiving Department
Sales Associate

Initially hired as Retail Sales Associate and advanced to Assistant Manager within two months. Handled ticketing, shipping/receiving, stock distribution, and updating/tracking inventory.

VOLUNTEER EXPERIENCE

A good thing to include here

Mayor, Off-Base Military Family Housing Community - El Paso, TX **19XX - 19XX**
Hand-selected to serve as Mayor of U.S. Army housing community. Worked with the Commanding Officer to co-chair Town Meetings and resolve community issues pertaining to the civilian family residents. Supervised eight Block Captains and wrote community newsletters. Interacted with neighborhood residents, solicited suggestions for common area improvements and recreational activities, and addressed complaints/recommendations pertaining to safety issues and well-being of children and community residents.

- **Successful in eight-month pursuit of gaining approval for a new community playground.**
- **Awarded plaque for Outstanding Citizenship & Achievement**

EDUCATION & TRAINING

Graduated with honors from dual enrollment programs
Elizabethtown Area High School - Elizabethtown, PA
Diploma

Mt. Joy Vocational Technical School - Mt. Joy, PA
Cosmetology Diploma

Management Training The Food Mart - Fayetteville, NC

Submitted by Diane McGoldrick

Uses small but readable type to fit on one page, rather than two

SAM D. FINCH

27-A Burton Road
Raleigh, NC 55555

(000) 000-0000

Objective: To manage painting operations for an auto body shop needing to increase efficiency and profitability in this area without jeopardizing quality.

Strengths & Skills:

Emphasizes skills needed to support a higher-paying management job →

- Extensive knowledge of urethane paint systems, including computerized mixing to produce customized colors.
- Expertise in precise color matching and blending in exact quantities needed to avoid waste.
- Good working knowledge of all modern techniques and equipment including downdraft spray booths, filters, lights, and oil or gas fired burners.
- Able to establish beneficial relationships with jobbers and regional suppliers of Sikkens, Spies-Hecker, Glasurit, DuPont and PPG paint lines to support shops' needs quickly and efficiently.
- Perform all painting operations neatly and in strict compliance with all safety and environmental standards.
- Self-motivated and productive in a heavy volume environment.
- Passed all drug testing and bonding requirements.

Related Experience:

1994 - Present — **Auto Body Painter** — Triangle Buick & Mazda, Clayton, NC (Body shop sales of $1 million in 1994)
- Work alone at night on a commission basis, producing an average of 100-140 paint/labor billable hours a week.
- Entrusted with full responsibility for physical building security at end of shift.

1992 - 1994 — **Auto Body Painting Subcontractor** (self-employed)
- Classic Auto Restoration, Cary, NC
- George's Auto Body, Durham, NC
- Wilson Collision Works, Raleigh, NC

1989 - 1990 — **Auto Body Painter** — Square Deal Toyota, Roxbury, NJ

1986 - 1989 — **Auto Body Painter** advancing to **Lead Painter** — Olafsen Auto Restoration, Dover, NJ

Other Employment:

1991 — **Over-the-Road Truck Driver** (self-employed)

1986 — **Administrative Assistant** — Commercial Mortgage Co., Pequannock, NJ

Military Experience:

1986 - 1990 — **United Stated Navy** — Active duty at San Diego Naval Amphibious Base, Coronado, CA
- STG "A" Service School — Received training in surface sonar (submarine tracking), explosive ordnance disposal and marine mammal systems.
- Assigned to hazardous material control unit with responsibility for the proper storage of caustic and corrosive materials and coordination of Material Safety Data Sheets (MSDS).

Education:

1994 — PPG Paint School — Refinish Training Course

1985 - 1986 — County College of Morris, Randolph, NJ — Math and business courses.

1984 — Morris County Vo-Tech, Adult Night School — Auto Body Repair course with on-the-job training at Olafsen Auto Restoration.

Additional Credentials:

- ASE Certified — Recertified in 1994.
- Class "A" Commercial Driver's License with hazardous materials endorsement.

Submitted by Melanie Noonan

Writer's comments: This previously self-employed contractor had dreamed of working for the Disney Co. In the cover letter, we emphasized skills that would be valuable to the company's construction department. Sometimes it is impressive to just include experience in list form, as I did under "Areas of Expertise"

Use of lines and two columns create a good visual layout

James R. Dickerson

1436 Clark Street
Charles City, Iowa 55616
515-555-2344 *or* 515-555-8762 (pager)

Profile

- Licensed builder/remodeler since 19xx
- Over seventeen years of experience in building, remodeling, maintenance and repair
- Self-motivated; ability to lead and motivate others
- Good verbal and listening skills; skilled in maintaining open lines of communication with owners
- Finely tuned troubleshooting skills

Areas of Expertise

Uses few but carefully selected words to allow for lots of white space

New construction:
- Homes
- Additions
- Garages
- Restaurants

Remodeling:
- Bathrooms
- Kitchens
- Dilapidated homes
- Fire restoration

Technical Skills:
- Framing
- Siding
- Roofing
- Concrete
- Windows
- Dry wall
- Formica
- Tile
- Detail/Trim

Experience

DICKERSON CONSTRUCTION • Charles City, IA xxxx-Present
Founder and Owner
- Perform new construction and remodeling projects.
- Collaborate with building/home owners to ensure satisfaction.
- Ensure adherence to appropriate federal, state and local regulations; interact with inspectors during inspections.
- Order and schedule delivery of materials.
- Act as crew chief; oversee and schedule subcontractors.

MASTERPIECE HOMES • Mason City, IA xxxx-xxxx
Electrician and **Plumber**

Military Experience

UNITED STATES ARMY xxxx-xxxx
Spec 4
- Trained as electrician.
- Honorably discharged.

Education

CHARLES CITY HIGH SCHOOL • Charles City, IA xxxx
Graduated

References

Available on request.

Submitted by Janet L. Beckstrom

Writer's comments: Frank's experience, safety record, and strong qualifications should open up opportunities despite the fact that he is not affiliated with a trade union.

Frank Taglione

▪ 203 Stonypoint Drive, Lewiston, ME 00000 ▪
(555) 555-5555

Pipefitter/Plumber skilled in mechanical and electrical installations

Many job-related skills are listed throughout, plus some very important adaptive skills

- Experience with pipes constructed of carbon steel, stainless steel, copper, alloys and galvanized metal, plastic lined pipe, and prefabricated piping assemblies, as well as all related fittings and joining compounds.
- Five years of practice in different industrial settings, ranging from a water treatment plant to a pharmaceutical testing lab.
- Own specialized hand tools to measure, cut, bend and thread pipe to precise specifications.
- Excellent safety record for operation of forklift, hydraulic jack, arc welding equipment and acetylene torch.
- Able to read piping assembly drawings and wiring schematics with understanding of system operations.
- Can identify such problems as pipe assemblies constructed of the wrong material or with incorrect dimensions.

▪ Employment ▪

19XX–Present — HYDROPURE SYSTEMS, INC.
Pipefitter/Plumber — Lewiston, ME

- Fabricate, assemble and install the interior and exterior piping of large water treatment units.
  — Plan material layout — Assemble prefabricated piping in accordance with engineering drawings — Size and build threaded piping systems, including rigid electrical conduits to motor-operated valves — Make and install steel pipe supports — Hydro-test the finished units.
- Commended by management with regard to excellence in attitude, attendance, productivity, and the ability to learn new tasks.

19XX—19XX — ADVANCED INDUSTRIAL MAINTENANCE
Pipefitter/Plumber — Portland, ME

- Assignments through this job shop have included running water lines for new installations in laboratories and manufacturing operations at AllCan Plastics, Warnesco, and Ultran Corporations.
- Kept plumbing in good working order at these facilities.

19XX–Present, Weekends — GUIDO TAGLIONE, PLUMBING CONTRACTOR
Plumber — Auburn, ME

- Assist brother with installation and service of residential plumbing fixtures, piping, boilers and hot water heaters. Mainly called upon to measure and cut pipe and to form either sweat soldered or threaded connections.

▪ Training ▪

Journeyman Pipefitter Certificate — 19XX — STATE OF MAINE DEPARTMENT OF EDUCATION

- Completed four-year apprenticeship and course in the plumbing and pipefitting trades at Auburn Technical and Vocational High School.
- Currently enrolled in state-sponsored asbestos removal training course.

Submitted by Melanie Noonan

Writer's comments: This resume is much improved over the original, with a solid summary, check marks for the strong experience sections, and other changes. Karen got a head librarian job.

Karen A. Librarian

000 Any Street • Anywhere, Michigan 00000 • (000) 000-0000

Summary of Qualifications

Over 10 years of Librarian experience with 8 years at the supervisory level, maintaining a positive working environment. Possess excellent verbal and written communications skills and significant knowledge in reference materials. Conscientious and detail-oriented with ability to plan, organize, and direct library services and programs. Substantial computer experience, including Internet support.

Strong opening

Professional Experience

Any Public Library – Anywhere, Michigan ***XXXX – Present***

Assistant to the Director

- ✓ Supervise, instruct, and schedule 11 staff members, including entire faculty in director's absence
- ✓ Automation Project Manager in regards to interlibrary loans, book status, and budgeting
- ✓ Administer reference and reader advisory services to patrons, provide outreach services to senior center, and schedule various meetings
- ✓ Lead adult book discussions including book selections and conduct library tours
- ✓ Assisted in library expansion, design, and construction (XXXX-XXXX)

Another Public Library – Anywhere, Michigan ***XXXX – XXXX***

Assistant to the Director, (XXXX – XXXX)

- ✓ Supervised, instructed, and scheduled 9 staff members
- ✓ Maintained microfiche and microfilm storage
- ✓ Handled bookkeeping responsibilities and routine operations of the library

An effective, space-efficient format

Children's and Young Adult Librarian, (XXXX – XXXX)

- ✓ Selected books, periodicals, and nonprint material for collection development
- ✓ Planned and implemented "Story Time" programs for preschool students, summer reading programs for grade school students, and "Computer Pix" for young adults
- ✓ Updated reference and library materials to exhibit most current information

Another Branch Library – Anywhere, California ***XXXX – XXXX***

Reference Librarian (Temporary)

- ✓ Examined ordered resources for collection development
- ✓ Assisted coworkers and patrons in microfiche operation and computer usage
- ✓ Handled book reservations and answered reference inquiries

Computer Experience

- ✓ Microsoft Word, Excel, and PowerPoint
- ✓ Michigan Occupational Information Systems (MOIS)
- ✓ Data Research Associates (DRA), Intelligent Catalog-Bibliofile, TDD, Magnifiers, RLIN, CLSI, OCLC, GEAC, ERIC Data Base, and Info Track – Magazine Index

Education

Texas Woman's University – Denton, Texas

- Master of Library Science, XXXX • Bachelor of Library Science, XXXX

Submitted by Maria E. Hebda

Writer's comments: Lizzy was an extremely talented technical writer for a world-known computer company. But all her experience was in her most recent position for that company. So I separated her two positions by job title but did not list years in each position. Finally, rather than detract from recent accomplishments, pertinent accomplishments from previous jobs were bulleted under Previous Employment.

Lizzy B. Wright

8888 Calla Lily Lane
Mountain View, CA 99999
lbwright@batnet.com
(650) 999-9999

TECHNICAL WRITER — Highly Skilled, Technically Savvy, Energetic

A clean, disciplined format appropriate for a technical writer

- Award-winning writer and editor of highly technical documentation (print and online) for Silicon Valley giant. Documents include: manuals, guides, articles for trade journals, PR, proposals, course development, employee bulletins, technical reports.
- Strong communication, training and interviewing skills. Translate "engineer-ese" into users' language with a clear and accurate writing style.
- Excellent cross-organizational skills and teamwork. Work closely with engineers, editors, other departments and team members.
- History of learning applications with exceptional speed and handling multiple projects, from outline to finished product, within extremely tight schedules.

Systems:	UNIX, Windows, Macintosh, VMS, Solaris, OpenWindows, All-in-One, Netware
Applications:	Framemaker, Framemaker+ SGML, Interleaf, MS Office, MS Project, PhotoShop, Illustrator, Lotus 1-2-3, Sun's workstation tools, Filemaker Pro
Web Skills:	HTML, graphics design and layout, information mapping, content development

MAJOR SILICON PLAYER, INC., Computerville, CA XXXX-Present

Technical Writer II

Promoted from Technical Writer I to Sustaining Project Lead, Illustration Project Lead and Technical Writer II within a year. Produce documentation for online and print at all testing stages.

- Maintain document sets and all revisions for 4 mid-range servers and wrote section of Well-Known Hardware Platform Notes.
- Currently developing document set (hardware and software) for next generation of servers.
- > Won *Touchstone Award* for Hardware Reference Category (one of three contributors) presented by Northern California Chapter of STC.

Global Project Coordinator

Developed/maintained documentation and communications for 3 worldwide projects. Organized international team meetings and coordinated projects, including budget and metrics tracking.

- Designed award-winning intranet web site. Served as web master and content developer for 50-page site containing Global Travel Policy (for 14 countries) and monthly Employee Newsletter.
- Designed user surveys, compiled information from hundreds of responses, and wrote 30-40 page recommendation reports used by Engineering in designing online tools.

PREVIOUS EMPLOYMENT

- Edited journal articles, wrote news releases and speeches, coordinated press relations for various contract positions, XXXX-XXXX.
- Fully computerized busy six-doctor practice using Alpha4 database system, Medical Center of Northeast, XXXX-XXXX.
- Developed information database used in health care reform initiatives, Regional Coalition for National Health Care, XXXX.

EDUCATION Related training

BA, Sociology (Vocal Performance), Oberlin College and Conservatory, Oberlin, OH
Premed Certificate Program, University of Massachusetts, Boston, MA
Information Architecture; Advanced Technical Communications, UC Berkeley Extension
C Programming, Foothill College, Los Altos, Hills, CA
Languages: Conversational Spanish, French, Italian

Submitted by Sydney J. Reuben

RUBY TUESDAY

55 E. Michigan Street ▪ High Falls, MI 00000 ▪ (555) 555-5555

Special papers can improve appearance

PROFESSIONAL PROFILE

Hard Rock . . . . Classic Rock . . . . Alternative . . . . Dance

A high-energy, creative, and outgoing disc jockey with a professional attitude and diverse experience within the radio industry. Possesses an effective combination of technical, managerial & communication abilities along with excellent team skills and a sincere enthusiasm for music. Recognized for developing strong networks, dedication to station objectives, and skills in adjusting to the rapidly changing needs of the highly competitive radio business. Areas of special emphasis include:

- **On-Air Broadcasting**
- **Control Board Operations**
- **Computer Utilization**
- **Training/Supervision**
- **Production**
- **Programming/Contests**
- **Remote Broadcasts**
- **Guest Interviews**
- **Special Event Planning**

Excellent intro with lots of skills included

INDUSTRY EXPERIENCE

Emphasizes results

Asst. Program Director / Music Director - WPLI FM / ABC AM, *Adult & CHR* **xxxx to Present**

Scope of responsibility includes board operation for weekly baseball games, coordination of special events, securing guests, and programming the Smartcaster computer.

- Developed a successful program "80's at 8". President of Warner Brothers Records heard show and called station to praise the segment and performance.
- Improved station ratings and increased advertising sponsors.
- Significantly increased the amount of promotional product received from record companies.
- Involved with organizing "Cool Bash" which featured Cool Artist & attracted x people.
- Named "DJ of the Week" in *Network Magazine*.

Assistant Manager - Cool Music Shop, Saratoga, NY **xxxx to Present**

Perform all retail functions including: inventory control, vendor relations, customer service, display merchandising, and cash management. Observe/anticipate music trends for profitable purchasing.

- Updated image of the store and successively improved gross sales for each of the past 8 years.

Disc Jockey, Overnight Full-Time - WLPJ Rock 101, *Classic Rock* **xxxx to xxxx**

- Earned on-air spot within 2-weeks of being hired.
- Recognized for prompt follow-through and greatly improving the station's sound.
- Praised for conscientious work ethic, confident delivery, and excellent voice skills.

Disc Jockey, Overnight/Weekends Part-Time - WBV/K-Rock, *HardRock / Alternative* **xxxx to xxxx**

- Earned spot as #1 part-timer and given weekend assignment.
- Selected to be the first DJ on-the-air when the station entered the market.
- Successfully conducted an unscheduled interview with Bad Band member Mike Howley.
- Brought weekend show to #1 during its time slot.

Engineer/Disc Jockey, Weekends - WCJC-AM, *Big Band / Oldies* **xxxx to xxxx**

- Worked as an engineer for the Radio Show (a political talk show) and the church service.
- Produced and ran the Ukranian, Italian, and Polish shows.

Submitted by Kristin Mroz Coleman

EDUCATION

Arlington High School, Poughkeepsie, NY, xxxx

WILLIAM T. JOHNSON

35 Sunderland Drive
Shrewsbury, NJ 07702

E-mail: wtjohnson@compuserv.com

Home: (732) 530-5592
Mobile: (732) 530-6632

PLANT / OPERATIONS / GENERAL MANAGEMENT EXECUTIVE

Multi-site manufacturing plant/general management career building and leading high-growth, transition, and start-up operations in domestic and international environments with annual revenues of up to $680 million.

Expertise: Organizational Development • Productivity & Cost Reduction Improvements • Supply Chain Management • Acquisitions & Divestitures • IPOs • Plant Rationalizations • Safety Performance • Customer Relations • Change Agent

CORE COMPETENCIES

Manufacturing Leadership—Strong P&L track record with functional management experience in all disciplines of manufacturing operations • Developing and managing operating budgets • Spearheading restructuring and rationalization of plants and contracted distribution facilities • Initiating lean manufacturing processes, utilizing SMED principles • Establishing performance metrics and supply-chain management teams.

Continuous Improvement & Training—Designing and instituting leadership-enhancement training program for all key plant management • Instituting Total Quality System (TQS) process in domestic plants to promote the business culture of continuous improvement and leading the ISO 9001 certification process.

New Product Development—Initiating plant-based "New Product Development Think Tank" that developed 130 new products for marketing review, resulting in the successful launch of 5 new products in 2000.

Engineering Management—Oversight of corporate machine design and development teams • Developing 3-year operating plan • Directing the design, fabrication, and installation of several proprietary machines • Creating project cost tracking systems and introducing ROI accountability.

PROFESSIONAL EXPERIENCE

BEACON INDUSTRIES, INC., New York, NY (1994–Present)
Record of continuous promotions to executive-level position in manufacturing and operations management despite periods of transition/acquisition at a $680 million Fortune 500 international manufacturing company. Career highlights include

Vice President of Manufacturing (1997–Present)

Senior Operating Executive responsible for the performance of 7 manufacturing/distribution facilities for a company that experienced rapid growth from 4 plants generating $350 million in annual revenues to 14 manufacturing facilities with revenues of $680 million. Charged with driving the organization to become a low-cost producer. Established performance indicators, operating goals, realignment initiatives, productivity improvements, and cost-reduction programs that consistently improved product output, product quality, and customer satisfaction.

Accomplishments:

- Selected to lead corporate team in developing and driving forward cost-reduction initiatives that will result in $21 million saved over the next 3 years through capital infusion, process automation, and additional rationalizations.
- Saved $13 million annually by reducing fixed spending 11% and variable overhead spending 18% through effective utilization of operating resources and cost-improvement initiatives.
- Cut Workers' Compensation costs 40% ($750,000 annually) by implementing effective health and safety plans, employee training, management accountability, and equipment safeguarding. Led company to achieve recognition as "Best in Industry" regarding OSHA frequency and Lost Workday Incident rates.
- Reduced waste generation 31%, saving $1 million in material usage by optimizing manufacturing processes as well as instituting controls and accountability.
- Enhanced customer service satisfaction 3% annually during past year (measured by order fill and on-time delivery percentage) through supply-chain management initiatives, inventory control, and flexible manufacturing practices.
- Trimmed manufacturing and shipping-related credits to customers from 1.04% to .5% of total sales in 1999, representing annual $1.8 million reduction.
- Decreased total inventories 43% from 1997 base through combination of supply-chain management, purchasing, master scheduling, and global utilization initiatives.
- Rationalized 3 manufacturing plants and 6 distribution facilities, saving $6 million over 3 years.

Submitted by Louise Garver

WILLIAM T. JOHNSON • Page 2

General Manager, Northeast (1994–1997)

Assumed full P&L responsibility of 2 manufacturing facilities and a $20 million annual operating budget. Directly supervised facility managers and indirectly 250 employees in a multi-line, multicultural manufacturing environment. Planned and realigned organizational structure and operations to position company for high growth as a result of acquiring a major account, 2 new product lines, and 800 additional SKUs.

Accomplishments:

- Reduced operating costs by $4.5 million through consolidation of 2 distribution locations without adverse impact on customer service.
- Accomplished the start-up of 2 new manufacturing operations, which encompassed a plant closing and the integration of acquired equipment into existing production lines for 2 new product lines without interruption to customer service; achieved 2 months ahead of target and $400,000 below budget.
- Increased operating performance by 15% while reducing labor costs by $540,000.
- Reduced frequency and severity of accidents by 50% in 3 years, contributing to a Workers' Compensation and cost avoidance reduction of $1 million.
- Decreased operating waste by 2% for an annual cost savings of $800,000 in 2 manufacturing facilities.
- Negotiated turnkey contracts for 2 distribution warehouses to meet expanded volume requirements.
- Maintained general management and administrative cost (GMA) at a flat rate as sales grew by 25% annually over 3 years.

ROMELARD CORPORATION, Detroit, MI (1984–1994)
Division Manufacturing Director (1990–1994)

Fast-track advancement in engineering, manufacturing, and operations management to division-level position. Retained by new corporate owners and promoted in 1994 based on consistent contributions to revenue growth, profit improvements, and cost reductions. Scope of responsibility encompassed P&L for 3 manufacturing facilities and a distribution center with 500 employees in production, quality, distribution, inventory control, and maintenance.

Accomplishments:

- Delivered strong and sustainable operating gains: increased customer fill rate by 18%; improved operating performance by 20%; reduced operating waste by 15%; and reduced inventory by $6 million.
- Justified, sourced, and directed the installation of $10 million of automated plant equipment.
- Implemented and managed a centralized master scheduling for all manufacturing facilities.
- Reduced annual Workers' Compensation costs by $600,000.
- Created Customer Satisfaction Initiative program to identify areas of concern and implemented recommendations, significantly improving customer satisfaction.

Prior Positions with Romelard Corporation: Manufacturing Manager (1987–1990); Plant Manager (1986–1987); Engineering Manager (1984–1986).

EDUCATION & PROFESSIONAL DEVELOPMENT

Bachelor of Science in Manufacturing Engineering
Syracuse University, Syracuse, NY

Continuing professional development programs in
Executive Management, Leadership, and Finance

Writer's Comments: This manufacturing executive had been in the same industry his entire career. His industry was declining and this resume helped him land a position at the Sr. VP level in another industry by focusing on his core competencies and outstanding achievements.

Writer's comments: No education, overworked and underpaid in a dying industry (independent bookseller), Gloria was a real go-getter with impressive accomplishments that I highlighted with bullets and numbers. The summary stresses her customer service and general management abilities because she did not know to which industry she was going to switch.

Gloria Gaughetter

999 Perky Street
Beautiful Vista, CA 99999
(666) 666-6666

Highly-motivated Customer Service / Operations Manager with strong commitment to achieving company goals.

Key adaptive and transferable skills

- Hands-on manager who leads by example and develops well-trained, motivated staff.
- Excellent communication, interpersonal, and customer service skills.
- History of successfully managing multiple operations within tight deadlines, making sound decisions, and meeting and/or surpassing sales objectives.
- 10 years of experience within the Book Industry. Areas of experience and/or expertise include:

Purchasing	**Customer Service**
Staffing	**Shipping & Receiving**
Scheduling	**Inventory Control**
Organizing	**Budget Management**

← Positions she can handle

Manager, MOUNTAIN BOOKS, Beautiful Vista, CA XXXX-Present

Direct operations, with P&L responsibility, for one of the few independent booksellers to achieve increased revenues in recent years.

Good use of numbers to emphasize her skills

- Purchase approximately 90,000 book titles plus a full line of accessories from 600 different vendors.
- Hire, train, and maintain high level of motivation for staff of 30.
- Broke $2 million sales barrier in first year as Manager by gearing products for a largely high tech, business-oriented clientele and emphasizing customer service.
- Increased net profit by 11% through controlling cost of goods and staff turnover.

Buyer, MOUNTAIN BOOKS, Sicily, CA XXXX-XXXX

- Ensured optimal product supply and selection for highly academic clientele.
- In addition to purchasing, supervised staff of 35-40.

Shift Manager, MOUNTAIN RECORDS, Sicily, CA XXXX-XXXX

Based on reliability and results, was rapidly promoted to supervise shift employees.

COMPUTER SKILLS

Windows 98, MS Word, proprietary Inventory Control system, Internet

PROFESSIONAL AFFILIATIONS

Member, Northern California Independent Booksellers Association (NCIBA)

Submitted by Sydney J. Reuben

Writer's comments: Although he doesn't have a degree, the Summary of Qualifications positioned Bill for the next level, which was reinforced by his responsibilities and accomplishments. With this resume, he was able to compete effectively and landed a management-level position.

WILLIAM T. HUNTINGTON
23 Sumner Drive
New York, New York 00000
(555) 777-8888

SUMMARY of QUALIFICATIONS

An experienced professional with a progressive career in aircraft maintenance management, customer service and sales support. Extensive technical expertise in all major aircraft product lines, providing sales/technical support to Fortune 50 customers. Flawless record for the coordination of top quality maintenance services within budget while consistently ensuring customer satisfaction. Key Strengths:

Maintenance Operations • Project Management • Budgeting/Costing • Negotiations
Staff Training & Leadership • Customer Service • Client Relationship Management

Emphasis is on most recent job in management with earlier positions at bottom

PROFESSIONAL EMPLOYMENT

AIRCRAFT COMPANY • New York, New York (1985-XXXX)
Rapid advancement through series of progressively responsible positions in recognition of leadership capabilities, performance and technical expertise. Career highlights include:
***Maintenance Supervisor** (1991-XXXX)*

Selected for newly created position to manage all aspects of maintenance operations and provide technical expertise to aircraft sales department. Plan, schedule and oversee all maintenance services/refurbishing, coordinating with company's 10 service centers to ensure top quality performance and on-time customer delivery. Build and maintain strong customer relations, maximizing service satisfaction. Hire, train, develop and manage maintenance staff.

- **Thoroughly examine condition of aircrafts for resale at customer sites worldwide; prepare specification sheet and develop maintenance projection with budgetary requirements.**
- **Coordinate all pre-purchase inspection details for each trade, thoroughly reviewing all maintenance records and effectively negotiating costs with aircraft owners, customers and prospective customers.**
- **Oversee all global import and export activities for aircraft, involving preparation of complex documentation and interaction with FAA and government representatives worldwide.**
- **Promoted from Lead Technician (1990-1991), "A" Technician (1987-1990) and "B" Technician (1985-1987).**

EDUCATION

All details support his objective

Certificate - Aeronautical Maintenance Technology
Technical School, City, State

Additional Training:

All Challenger Maintenance Training courses including:
CL600, CL601, CL601-3A/3R, CL 604, Canadair Challenger Blueprint Reading
Garrett Auxiliary Power Unit Line Maintenance, Customer Awareness and Support
Computer Applications: MS Windows 95, Excel and Word

Licensed FAA Airframe and Powerplant Technician

Submitted by Louise Garver

Michele Gibson

842 N. Main ▪ Menasha, Wisconsin 54952 ▪ (414) 784-8752

Packed with details, this resume's design and short statements keep it readable and effective.

Licensed Cosmetologist, State of Wisconsin

Summary of Attributes

- Enthusiastic professional with outstanding customer relation skills; upbeat, friendly, and genuinely care about providing satisfactory service.
- Strong sales techniques; consistently increase volume through additional product purchases.
- Carefully listen to clients to correctly address their needs/desires.
- Good business management aptitude; knowledgeable in all aspects of salon operation.
- Excellent technical skills evidenced through extemely loyal clientele and high referral rate.

Experience

The Ultimate Salon, Appleton, Wisconsin
Independent Hair Stylist/Make-Up Artist 1994-Present

- Provide full range of services including precision hair cuts, permanent waving, color, and styling.
- Conduct one-on-one make-up consultations, providing hands-on instruction, individualized color selection, and written guidelines.
- Manage all aspects of business including inventory control, bookkeeping, price determination, and marketing.

Accomplishments:

- Conceptualized and publish a quarterly client newsletter which contributed to an increase in client base, as well as product sales.
- Specialize in creating unique images for bridal clients incorporating various ornamentations into hair styles.
- Researched and introduced a private label make-up line.

These statements reinforce Michele's strong business skills

A New You Salon, Menasha, Wisconsin
Hair Stylist/Make-Up Artist 1991-1994

- Performed hair stylist duties including cuts, styles, color, and permanent waves. Functioned as an apprentice, 1991-1993.
- Lead Make-Up Artist for special occasions and one-on-one demonstrations.

Accomplishments:

- Achieved retail sales of 31% compared to national average of 15%, 1993.
- Orchestrated salon-wide Cut-A-Thon to benefit United Cerebral Palsy, including public relations, donation solicitation, and raffle organization. Tripled donations over previous year.
- Coordinated complimentary seminar to educate clients on new hair trends, products, and the benefits of various salon services.

Education

Northeast Wisconsin Technical College, Green Bay, Wisconsin 1993
Certificate of Completion; Cosmetology Training (included 400 hours of classroom instruction and 3,600 hours of on-the-floor supervised training)

Industry Involvement

Redken Symposium, Las Vegas, Nevada, January 1996
Redken Regional Seminar, Schaumburg, Illinois, 1994

- Assisted national and regional platform artists.

Aerial Hair Show, Stevens Point, Wisconsin, 1994

- Applied stage and runway make-up for models.

Submitted by Kathy Keshemberg

A very clean, open format on one page. Good use of white space. Note how she is not limiting herself to one industry.

VIRGINIA S. GANT

1234 Lake Circle ♦ Burlingame, California 94222 ♦ vgant@gte.net
(415) 222-1222

QUALIFICATIONS

PROFIT-CONSCIOUS SALES MANAGER with proven success in building and motivating high-growth sales organizations. Equally competent in direct sales, including national/key account management. Career highlights:

Emphasis is on results

- **Sales Management** — Recruited, developed, and coached national distributor sales organization that more than doubled sales volume for six consecutive years. Led market expansion from local to national distribution, positioning company as the industry leader in recreational water treatment solutions.
- **Marketing** — Researched and identified target markets, selected channels of distribution, determined pricing structure, and developed packaging for new products. Successfully introduced new items that gained #1 market share in less than one year.
- **Technical Sales** — Strong technical background in sales of chemical products for recreational and industrial water uses. Led research and development functions for new treatment systems including label development, regulatory compliance, and market support. Excellent relationships with federal and state EPA officials.

PROFESSIONAL EXPERIENCE

CRAY COMPANY, BURLINGAME, CALIFORNIA — [date]–[date]

VICE PRESIDENT, MARKETING & SALES

Led this small, privately held company with sales in one western state through successful expansion into the national marketplace. Given complete autonomy for profit center reengineering and market alignment for the Recreational Chemical Division. Established and directed manufacturer's rep sales force. Established relationships with and serviced key national accounts. Directed advertising, merchandising, and account management strategies.

Accomplishments

A very effective visual

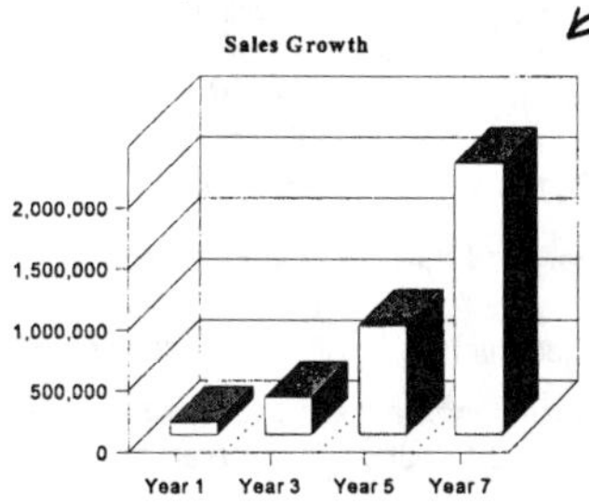

Emphasis is on results

- Recognized market opportunities and initiated expansion to build strong national market presence, achieving revenue growth of $100,000 in 1st year sales to more than $2 million in [date].
- Launched new products and line extension (R&D, EPA approval, pricing, market planning, sales presentations), capturing leading market share in less than six months.
- Secured new business with national accounts such as Wal★Mart (10 states), Home Depot, and Orchard Supply Hardware, negotiating prime retail space and capturing maximum distribution in accounts.
- Built number and quality of accounts from 100 to over 1,300.
- Maintained lucrative profit margins (7-8% over industry average) throughout rapid growth stage.
- Consulted clients such as The Disney Company and Caesar's Palace regarding above-ground water treatment.

STORE MANAGER, K&M COMPANY, BURLINGAME, CALIFORNIA — [date]–[date]

EDUCATION, AFFILIATIONS

Tom Hopkins Sales Seminar ... technical seminars on water treatment chemistry sponsored by Buckman Laboratories ... ongoing self-initiated study. Member, Association of Water Treaters and community service club.

♦ ♦ ♦

Submitted by Susan Britton Whitcomb
Résumé Magic

Writer's comments: Resume focuses on technology knowledge because job seeker wants to leave the finance industry. Sales accomplishments are highlighted throughout.

MARYANNE WALKER

maryanne.walker@somewhere.com

Home: (333) 555-2222
Cellular: (777) 555-3333

15 West 52nd Street, Apt. 3K
Brooklyn, New York 55555

Presents many adaptive and transferable skills

SALES PROFESSIONAL

SOFTWARE / INFORMATION TECHNOLOGY / FINANCE

- Top-producing sales expert with 10 years of experience maximizing sales, driving revenue growth, and developing new business within highly competitive markets.
- Unique combination of knowledge of retail sales and information technology; expertise in providing technical and systems support. Computer literate – knowledge of Word, Excel, Outlook, and Windows NT/98.
- Establish genuine rapport and build solid relationships with prospects and clients. Utilize comprehensive product knowledge, familiarity with diverse cultures and personalities, and enthusiastic personality to quickly map out client needs and recommend appropriate solutions. Earn clients' trust by consistently proving that their needs are paramount.
- Confident, articulate, and professional speaking abilities. Team leader and team player.
- Combine patience, determination, and persistence to troubleshoot client issues and ensure their satisfaction.

PROFESSIONAL EXPERIENCE

Careful wording emphasizes skills needed for new job objective

MAJOR INVESTMENT COMPANY – New York, New York — 19XX to present

Financial Representative / Technology Specialist, 19XX to present

Promoted to highly visible position with multi-billion dollar Wall Street Investment Division based on ability to prospect, negotiate and close deals, and forecast and track business activities. Serve high-net-worth clients, including CEOs of Fortune 500 companies. Build relationships and drive business through new account, portfolio review, and MAPS prospecting. Provide information on brokerage services, including stock trades, mutual funds, estate planning, life insurance, fixed income securities, and variable annuities. Develop asset allocation strategies to maximize investor return while minimizing risk. Achievements include:

- Established relations with institutional clients for the first time on a large scale; successfully landed ABC Company account, resulting in over $200 million in additional assets. Act as main contact person for account.
- By providing excellent service and follow-up, generate a high number of referrals and repeat business.
- Regularly featured in New York / New Jersey sales highlights publication for outstanding sales achievements.
- Ranked in top third of peer group, which includes 145 representatives.
- Regarded as in-house systems expert; provide hardware and software troubleshooting for LAN-based system.

Mutual Fund Sales Representative, 19XX to 19XX

Sold mutual funds using Major Investment Company's proprietary sales profiling techniques. Provided clients with trade, account information, and account maintenance services. Achievements include:

- Consistently met and exceeded sales expectations while maintaining a high level of customer satisfaction.
- Ranked 12 out of 260 (September 19XX), 31st in nation for accounts YTD, and 28th in conversions.

ABC MEDICAL SUPPLY – Brooklyn, New York — 19XX to 19XX

Sales Representative

Sold medical supplies to doctors and health care facilities; built solid customer base.

EDUCATION & LICENSURE

UNIVERSITY OF TAMPA – Tampa, Florida

Bachelor of Arts – History, 19XX

- Dean's List • Founded and led Debate Team – qualified for state finals, 19XX • Semester abroad in Rome

Licensure: Series 7, Series 6, Series 63, New York State Life

Submitted by Kim Isaacs

Writer's comments: Sharon acquired technical expertise on the job and achieved a high level of success in a short period selling in a competitive industry. Since her promotion within the company is clear and her consistent achievements are quantified, a traditional chronological format is appropriate.

Sharon Lebovsky

83 Oak Street • Newton, MA 02459 • 617-555-5555 • lebovsky@telecom.com

Summary

Hard working, self-motivated, high achieving sales professional with eight years experience in the telecommunications industry, including work with key/hybrid systems and high-end PBX systems. Recognized for excellent ability to build and maintain relationships through long and short sales cycles. Quick learner, with outstanding presentation skills. Strong commitment to customer service.

Work History

TELECOMMUNICATIONS COMPANY, Newton, MA xxxx–present

National telecommunications company with 50 offices across the United States and annual sales volume of $120 million. Primary market is small to medium size companies.

National Account Executive (xxxx–present)

Emphasizes skills and results

- Promoted to National Accounts Executive, reporting to Vice President National Accounts on the East Coast, in recognition of outstanding performance as Account Executive.
- Achieved sales volume of $1.1 million, with above average gross profit margin of $308,000.
- Sell Mitel, Northern Telecom, and Nitsuko hardware along with long distance services, video conferencing, and voice mail technology, targeting New England-based national accounts with multiple sites.
- Develop long-term relationships by prospecting senior management at corporate offices, determining client needs, demonstrating product, and providing ongoing management of all accounts as single point of contact for service and support.
- Coordinate and facilitate installations on a nationwide basis.

Account Executive (xxxx–xxxx)

- Doubled sales volume within two years after introduction into the industry.
- Exceeded sales quota by 31% (19xx), 22% (19xx), and 20% (19xx), achieving top ten rank among sales reps nationwide.
- Awarded Achievers Club (120% of quota), 19xx, 19xx, 19xx.
- Achieved President's Circle (top account representative in North America), 19xx.
- Received National Leasing Gold Star, 19xx, 19xx, 19xx.
- Developed and implemented client satisfaction survey.
- Introduced new proposal standard for use by sales force.
- Generated sales to local companies through telemarketing, prospecting, and networking.
- Perform product demonstrations, design proposals, and service client problems.

Education

B.S., Business Administration, Marketing xxxx

Bentley College, Waltham, MA

Ongoing training includes Burton Sales Training Program (19xx) on consultative sales, and training in Mitel and Northern Telecom systems.

Computer Skills

Microsoft Windows '95, Microsoft Word, Excel, Powerpoint, Internet.

Submitted by Wendy Gelberg

Writer's comments: I revised Ryan's lackluster resume into one that showcased his accomplishments.

RYAN J. HILTON
123 Main Street, Anytown, USA 00001
Voice (XXX) XXX-XXXX ▪ Cell (XXX) XXX-XXXX ▪ Fax (XXX) XXX-XXXX ▪ E-Mail: rjhilton@isp.com

DIRECTOR OF SALES

Fueled Sales and Profitability, Developed New Distribution Channels, Delivered Critical Marketing and Product Launch Decisions, and Led Companies Through Dynamic Growth and Expansion

➤ Competitive-spirited, profit-driven executive sales professional offering an outstanding track record of results maneuvering companies through periods of explosive growth and territory expansion.

➤ Contributed expertise in strategic planning, operations management, sales and sales support, profit and loss, revenue enhancement, customer needs analysis, cost containment, and team building.

➤ Advanced ahead of peers to tackle positions of significant challenge and responsibility, delivering proven results across broad disciplines. Consistently recognized as a top-performer.

➤ Confident leader and motivator with excellent success recruiting and training top sales talent. Articulate communicator with demonstrated competencies in customer relationship management.

➤ Exceptional record in devising strategies that deliver immediately profitable results and revitalize stagnant or declining operations and revenues.

PROFESSIONAL EXPERIENCE

COMPANY A, Anytown, USA — **19XX-Present**

Director of Sales

Direct day-to-day sales operations and a team of 30 account representatives in the sales of plastics products to 9 groups covering the Midwest, South, and West Coast territories. Supervise a total account base of more than 125 active customers, who contribute $20 million in annual sales revenues. Oversee profit and loss forecasting, reporting, and analysis. Spearhead multi-million dollar retail programs, buy backs, and related marketing and sales campaigns.

- Boosted sales 35% from 19XX to 19XX, with key increases generated from clients including Client A (130%), Client B (164%), and Client C (120%).
- Placed product line in Client D and Client E for first-year yields of $1.6 million and $1 million respectively.
- Developed a 26-piece food storage set that will generate an estimate $2 million in 19XX alone.
- Increased gross margin the first year in 4 out of 5 categories.
- Raised gross margin an average 15% in 2 categories at 2 key accounts in 19XX.
- Placed product in 3 new channels of distribution: hardware (Client F), fabric (Client G and Client H), and government (Client I).

Uses numbers to support results!

COMPANY B, Anytown, USA — **19XX-19XX**

Sales Representative

Managed Anytown-area accounts for 15 distinctly different product lines, contributing over $3 million in sales revenue each year. Prospected customers through cold calls, sales presentations, and primarily by delivering exceptional customer service and follow-up to existing clients, who referred more than 40% of new business.

- Named Salesman of the Year in 19XX by Company A, in 19XX for Client C, and in 19XX for Client J.

COMPANY C, Anytown, USA — **19XX-19XX**

Flight Instructor / Corporate Pilot

Gave instruction and hands-on flight training to an average class size of 35 students per month.

- Maintained a 95% pass rate for all students.
- First graduate to be asked to serve as an instructor; named Instructor of the Year in 19XX.

EDUCATION

Bachelor of Science – Business Administration / Aviation Management
Samovar University, Anytown, USA

COMPUTER SKILLS

MS Word, MS Excel, MS PowerPoint

Submitted by E. Rene' Hart

Chapter 11

Sample Skills-Based, Combination, and Creative Resumes

Just like in Chapter 10, the resumes in this chapter are organized around various functional roles, but be sure to browse all the samples for ideas, not just the ones that relate to your targeted job.

Writer's comments: Mary's positive personality was an asset for the reception job she sought, so I contacted people who knew her work and included their comments.

"Mary takes the extra steps to assist her callers . . . she cares to make a difference."
—James Dunn, Chevrolet Representative

"She is polite and helpful, and has a wonderful personality . . . I would rate her a '10'!"
—Robert Maxwell, New Car Customer

"The sound of Mary's voice can turn around anyone's bad mood. She can really perk you up."
—Susan Anthony, Car Conversions

"Mary goes beyond just answering the telephone. She holds herself accountable for the calls she processes."
—Gil Baker, Manufacturers Representative

MARY F. JOHNSON
12440 Miller Road
Clio, MI 48420
810-555-3299

PROFILE

Presents key adaptive skills

- Extensive successful experience dealing with the public.
- Possess many traits of an effective communicator:
  - Professional presence
  - Warm, friendly demeanor
  - Outgoing personality
  - Sincerity
  - Patience
  - Diplomacy
  - Instinct
  - Composure
- Front-line team player who presents a positive company image; committed to delivering top-quality service to all customers.
- Self-confident and level-headed; ability to remain poised even in demanding situations.
- Keen ability to recognize voices and remember names.
- Skilled in intuitively assessing and relating to customers' moods and preferences while adapting to their diverse personalities.

HIGHLIGHTS OF EXPERIENCE

Her key job-related skills

- Single-handedly answer 25 phone lines and route calls (average volume: 100 per hour) to 30+ salespeople and departments.
- Manually track calls to generate informal statistical reports.
- Monitor disposition of calls to ensure satisfactory completion.
- Greet customers as they enter showroom.
- Provide support to sales staff as requested.
- Participated in the research process for new telephone system.
- Founded and operated dessert catering service; handled all aspects of business including marketing, purchasing, production, and delivery.

EMPLOYMENT HISTORY

A simple list works well here, since it shows a good work listing

NIXON CHEVROLET-GEO • Pontiac, MI — xxxx-xxxx
Receptionist

ARMOUR SUPPLIES • Flint, MI — xxxx-xxxx
Receptionist

MID-MICHIGAN MOTORS • St. Johns, MI — xxxx-xxxx
Receptionist

MARY'S COOKIES • Lansing, MI — xxxx-xxxx
Owner/Founder

Excellent references available on request

Submitted by Janet L. Beckstrom

CHARLES CONKLIN

■ 55 RIVER RUN LANE, SMITHTOWN, NY 11922
■ 516-555-5555

CAREER PROFILE

Notice his emphasis on results

High-energy, cross-functional background as resourceful fast-track insurance claims specialist with an outstanding record of success in winning settlements and reducing claims payouts to acceptable and just amounts. Investigate, negotiate, and settle complex claims, from beginning stages up to trial, for Property Casualty Corp. and HTP Claims Services, Inc.

AREAS OF EXPERTISE

ADMINISTRATION

organized and effective performance in high-pressure environments

presentation development and delivery

claims investigation with meticulous documentation

heavy phones / switchboard

skilled customer care

word processing and spreadsheet development (type 60 words per minute)

Microsoft Office, Internet, and Intranet proficiency

A very effective presentation

INSURANCE CLAIMS

commercial and personal lines liability

general liability, auto, homeowners, and products liability

property damage and bodily injury claims

injury exposure values

claimant, attorney, and litigation representation

complex arbitration and mediation negotiation

settlement and target value range setting

medical and liability evaluation

HIGHLIGHTS

Good use of numbers to specifically reinforce results

- Handle case load of up to 230 pending commercial and personal lines claims. Establish contact within 24 hours, maintain impeccable documentation, and determine value of case based on liability / injury. Decide claim values up to $50,000. Negotiate / settle cases in mediation, arbitration, or litigation. Productive in judge's chambers, courtroom, or at mediation table.
- Delivered a $15,000 savings to Property Casualty Corp. by obtaining a defense verdict on a case that a judge suggested firm "buy out" for $15,000. Communicated with attorneys, evaluated liability / facts and determined feasibility for trial. Case went to trial and firm paid nothing but legal costs.
- Saved HTP $40,000 on complex $100,000 second-degree burn claim by determining case's suitability for mediation, and meeting with judge and plaintiff's attorneys. Case was settled for a fair $60,000 without incurring major legal costs for HTP.
- Promoted onto the HTP fast-track after only one year; became the youngest adjuster in company history. Track record of positive mediation, arbitration, and litigation outcomes is equal to or better than that of more senior professionals.
- Possess outstanding administrative / organizational skills, superior presentation and negotiation abilities, a passion for excellence, and a contagious enthusiasm. Work well in independent or team environments. Tenacious, with the stamina needed to function in high-pressure environments.

EMPLOYMENT

PROPERTY CASUALTY CORP., HICKSVILLE, NY — 1998 to present
Claims Representative, Investigative Unit

HTP CLAIMS SERVICES, INC, FARMINGDALE, NY — 1994 to 1998
Claims Specialist (1997 to 1998)
Fast-track Representative (1995 to 1997)
Claims Assistant (1994 to 1995)

EDUCATION AND PROFESSIONAL DEVELOPMENT

Good to include!

A.A.S. in Business, Insurance and Real Estate, Suffolk Community College, Selden, NY
Anticipated completion, Fall 1999. Maintaining a 3.5 GPA while working full-time.

New York University University: Two-day Negotiation Seminar

Industry Courses: Commercial General Liability, Claims Statements, Property Casualty Principles, Litigation Guidelines, Medical Terminology and Treatment, How to Handle Cases to Avoid Litigation, Accurate Reserving

Since he does not yet have a degree, it's good to include continuing education activities

Submitted by Deborah Wile Dib

Writer's comments: For an older worker who does not plan on retiring, this resume hides her age and emphasizes her computer skills, productivity, and flexibility.

Mary O'Reilly

593 Maple Avenue • Brighton, MA 02135 • (617) 555-5555

OVERVIEW

Most of the words here portray a very capable and results-driven person

Hard-working and conscientious secretary with a broad range of experience in legal and corporate settings. Solid background maintaining the smooth flow of work in a busy office. Able to meet tight deadlines in fast-paced environment. Combination of strong administrative ability and excellent oral, written, and electronic communication skills. Team player with outstanding work ethic. Computer proficient. Eager to take on new challenges and learn new skills.

SECRETARIAL SKILLS

- 70+ wpm typing speed
- tape transcription
- telephone answering / screening
- statistical typing
- scheduling
- Corel / WordPerfect
- Microsoft Word / Excel
- editing

CAREER HIGHLIGHTS

Note the emphasis on high performance

- Edited, typed, and transcribed correspondence, legal documents, reports, proposals, and financial statements in various office settings, accurately and on time.
- Prioritized work flow to meet tight deadlines in busy departments.
- Rotated among different departments, filling in for secretaries who are on vacation or out sick; adapted to different formats, time constraints, work styles, and areas of specialization while keeping work flow on schedule.
- Answered and screened phone calls and scheduled appointments for up to 14 people.
- Set up and maintained filing systems to expedite tracking of documents.
- Performed overflow work to maintain work production timetables.
- Learned and used software upgrades, applying more sophisticated features to increase work efficiency.
- Interacted effectively with people at all levels of the organization as well as with the general public.

EXPERIENCE

Covers just the past 13 years, to help de-emphasize her age

LAW FIRM OF ANDERSON, THORNTON, SOCOLOVE & DOE, Boston, MA — xxxx-Present
Floater Secretary (xxxx-Present)
Overflow Secretary (xxxx-xxxx)
Word Processor/Lead Operator (xxxx-xxxx)
Word Processor (part-time) (xxxx-xxxx)

ERNST & YOUNG, Boston, MA — xxxx-xxxx
Word Processor (part-time)

LAW OFFICES OF SMITH, JONES, JOHNSON & ANDREWS, Boston, MA — xxxx-xxxx
Word Processor (part-time)

POLAROID CORPORATION, Cambridge, MA — xxxx-xxxx
Secretary, Marketing Department (xxxx-xxxx)
Secretary, Financial Planning Department (xxxx-xxxx)

EDUCATION

No dates are included

Coursework, University of Massachusetts, Boston, MA
Training in WordPerfect, E-mail

Submitted by Wendy Gelberg

Writer's comments: I revised this resume from a simple "just the facts" format to one that reflects his talents. The graphic and quote are perfect for the elementary grades.

The two-column format and use of white space present an attractive, orderly image

RANDY BEZ

123 E. Kids Circle
Fresno, CA 93711

(209) 234-2342

PROFESSION

Elementary Educator, Grades 2-5—highlights of 16-year career with Fresno Unified include the following:

- Three years' experience as Mentor Teacher.
- Experience as Master Teacher for CSUF Option IV Program.
- Strengths in science and math; effective classroom management skills; excellent rapport with multicultural, LEP, special needs, and at-risk students.

EDUCATION, CREDENTIAL

Language Development Specialist Certificate
Multiple Subject Credential—California State University, Fresno
B.A., Education/Biology Minor—University of Texas, Austin

PROFESSIONAL EXPERIENCE

He lists four jobs then presents content for all of them—an effective way to handle this

FRESNO UNIFIED SCHOOL DISTRICT [date]–Present

Teacher, 3/4 Combination—High Elementary (date-Present)
Literacy Summer School Teacher—Stars School (date)
Certificated Math Tutor—Ariana Elementary (date–date)
Summer School Teacher—Middleton School (date)

- Create an engaging, positive learning environment featuring integrated curriculum, hands-on lessons, computer applications, and use of portfolios to document students' growth and talents.
- Structure whole group, small group, and individual instruction to accommodate different academic levels and learning styles.
- Apply cooperative learning and cross-age tutoring to increase learning, self-esteem, and cross-cultural understanding.
- Employ C-SIN and AIMS in science and math to develop critical thinking skills and improve overall comprehension.
- Utilize SDAIE, Natural Approach, Language Experience Approach, and TPR to overcome language barriers.
- Selected by principal to develop special programs, such as Margaret Smith's MTA, TRIBES conflict resolution, and DBAE.
- Wrote and received community partnership minigrant "Walk Through California."

The graphic and quote add considerable visual impact

One hundred years from now it will not matter what my bank account was, the sort of house I lived in, or the kind of car I drove but the world may be different because I was important in the life of a child.
—Anonymous

CONTINUING EDUCATION—Received training in and implemented the following:

Multi-Sensory Teaching Approach	Tribes
C-SIN (CA Science Implementation Network)	True Colors
Lee Canter's Assertive Discipline	FUSD Math Camp
Lee Canter's Beyond Assertive Discipline	Santillana
DBAE (Discipline-Based Art Education)	Cooperative Learning
Portfolio Assessment	Peer Coaching
Conducting Staff In-services	SDAIE
Parent Partnerships	Early Literacy

Submitted by Susan Britton Whitcomb
Résumé Magic

Writer's comments: Client wanted to change careers from insurance underwriting to corporate training and development. A functional format emphasizes her training experiences while minimizing insurance background. Client was offered two training positions.

Melinda Anderson

578 Northridge Road ▪ City, State 77777 ▪ (555) 777-2234

Profile

Creative professional experienced in designing and conducting training and development programs/materials to develop employee performance. Recognized for dynamic presentation style in training marketing, sales, customer service, and field office personnel. Adept in managing multiple projects from initial planning through successful implementation. Strengths in motivating, coaching and leading teams to achieve business objectives. Proficient in desktop publishing, word processing and other applications. Well-versed in insurance industry products and services.

Professional Accomplishments

This approach emphasizes skills she wants to use in a new career.

Program Development & Training

- Designed and presented workshops on change management, customer service, time management, and goal setting that enhanced employee development and productivity.
- Conducted needs analysis, designed and coordinated cross-training for 50-member department.
- Initiated training procedures which streamlined processes and increased efficiency 30%.
- Created and presented seminars to educate consumers on financial planning products/services.

Project Management/Team Leadership

- Recruited, developed and managed staff of 25 professionals, leading team to exceed productivity objectives and improve customer service.
- Key contributor on cross-functional teams and selected to lead major projects which enhanced interdepartmental communications, streamlined operations and improved work flow.
- Cut costs 15% and increased efficiency 20% by initiating and instituting new procedures department-wide.

Customer Relations/Communications

- Developed training manuals and marketing support materials for entire region. Authored articles for monthly field office newsletters.
- Formalized and documented departmental policies and procedures. Built positive relationships with corporate, regional and field personnel through ongoing communications.
- Consistently commended for exceptional customer relations skills and ability to resolve problems and enhance service satisfaction.

Professional Employment

Less emphasis here, on a career field she wants to leave

INSURANCE COMPANY • City, State	1985-Present
Regional Team Leader/Underwriter	1990-Present
Lead Underwriter	1987-1990
Underwriter	1985-1987

Education

B.S. (Education) • State University • City, State

Additional Training:
Train-the-Trainer … Powerful Presentation Skills
Creating Seminars … Sales Training

Submitted by Louise Garver

Writer's comments: Client wanted to design and implement sales training in a corporate environment. I created a functional resume that emphasized his program design, training, and presentation skills. I listed his Navy positions without description to avoid distracting readers from the client's objective.

Fredrick Smith

678 Willow Lane • City, State • (555) 555-5555

CAREER OBJECTIVE

Sales training position for a technical products company seeking a motivating individual with excellent presentation and leadership skills. Fredrick quickly found a position he wanted!

ACCOMPLISHMENTS

Military experience presented in skills and business language

Program Design/Training

- Designed and conducted numerous training programs for 500+ employees and supervisory personnel, resulting in highly skilled, knowledgeable teams.
- Presented experiential workshops on operational procedures and related technical information, personnel policies, new program requirements on security and safety issues, and other topics.
- Researched and implemented several new programs on security, safety and occupational health, telecommunications system and other topics which were introduced organization-wide.

Operations & Maintenance/Technical

- Directed day-to-day operations and equipment maintenance/repair functions in several departments.
- Demonstrated technical knowledge in telecommunications, electronic/electrical systems and equipment, nuclear power and strategic weapons.
- Supervised the operation and maintenance of a nuclear submarine power plant.

Management/Leadership

- Created two new departments, which included staffing, development of all policies/procedures and training subsequently instituted organization-wide.
- Supervised, developed and evaluated performance of up to 45 technical, maintenance, and administrative support staffs. Recognized for ability to motivate and build cohesive teams.
- Experienced in planning, implementing and managing large-scale projects which were completed ahead of schedule and consistently received outstanding evaluations.
- Orchestrated and supervised 3 shifts of 70 employees in the flawless installation and testing of more than $1 billion in sensitive technical equipment.

PROFESSIONAL EXPERIENCE

UNITED STATES NAVY (1982-XXXX)
Department Head (1991-XXXX)
Engineering Assistant/Division Supervisor (1989-1991)
Department Head (1986-1988)
Operations Assistant/Division Supervisor (1983-1986)

MANUFACTURING COMPANY, City, State (1981-1982)
Production Control Staff

EDUCATIONAL BACKGROUND

B.A. (Chemistry) College, City, State, 1982
Naval Nuclear Power School, City, State, 1989
Naval Nuclear Prototype, City, State, 1989
Naval Submarine School, City, State, 1987

Submitted by Louise Garver

Writer's comments: This client held two long-term substitute teaching positions. This resume needed to minimize the short-lived assignments and emphasize her potential to be a dynamite teacher in a classroom of her own. The first page focuses on skills and achievements, so the reader gets a big dose of what this teacher can do before ever seeing the dates on page 2.

Priscilla Dailey

69 Spruce Street
Boston, MA 02131

(617) 555–5555
pdailey@teacher.net

TEACHER, PreK–3

Energetic, enthusiastic teacher with unyielding commitment to educating children. Proven ability to foster trusting, cooperative environment that enables children to reach their full potential. Skilled in the design of challenging, enriching, and innovative activities that address the diverse interests and needs of students. Experience in multicultural and inclusion classrooms. Recognized for excellent interpersonal, organizational, and classroom management skills. Active member of school community. Master's Degree in Early Childhood Education.

"...a very effective teacher...a creative, organized, and energetic person who motivates students with exciting and interesting learning activities."
J. Franklin Thomas, Principal
Russell P. Williams School, Boston, MA

An excellent addition!

This approach allows her to emphasize strengths better than a chronological format

SELECTED ACHIEVEMENTS

- Developed theme-based units that tie together different subject areas to reinforce learning of key concepts.
- Introduced a "peace table" strategy to assist students with conflict resolution and encouraged students to take responsibility for behaviors and their consequences.
- Tailored curriculum to engage students to learn most effectively by applying the concept of "multiple intelligences."
- Encouraged literacy with the creation of an author's corner for writing and reading activities.
- Engaged in school-wide activities: directed spring variety show; volunteered to chaperone week-long overnight trip for older students; participated in Home School Association that focused on long-range fiscal planning needs of school.
- Implemented Wellesley Social Competency Curriculum to teach students appropriate social and interpersonal skills.
- Participated in Core Evaluations and design and implementation of IEPs; adapted curriculum to accommodate a wide variety of special needs.
- Selected mid-year to take charge of unfocused classes in transition following teacher's departure; successfully managed behavior problems and directed children's energy toward new learning activities.
- Participated in scoring the Early Childhood writing samples for the Massachusetts Teachers Test.

Priscilla Dailey **Page 2**

Makes the most of her experience

TEACHING EXPERIENCE

Kindergarten Teacher – St. Catherine's School, Roslindale, MA 11/xx–6/xx
Taught full-day class of 20 kindergartners from multicultural backgrounds in private, parochial school. Developed and implemented curriculum in all subject areas, assessed student development, and made recommendations to implement services from outside sources, when necessary. Served as Faculty Representative to Home/School Association.

Kindergarten Teacher – Williams School, Roxbury, MA 1/xx–6/xx
Hired to take charge of full-day kindergarten class during teacher's extended absence. Established order and planned and taught lessons in all subject areas. Maintained ongoing communication with students' families.

Grade 2 Teacher (Clinical Practicum) – Curley School, Hyde Park, MA 9/xx–12/xx
Taught an inclusive, multicultural second grade classroom. Prepared lessons in reading, language arts, math, science, and social studies, using whole group and small group activities and tailoring curriculum to meet individual needs. Implemented objectives identified in IEP's.

Grade 1 Teacher (Provisional Practicum) – Fayerweather School, Cambridge, MA 1/xx–5/xx
Planned and implemented curriculum for reading, language arts, math, social studies, and science for students of varying abilities in multicultural setting.

Substitute Teacher – Boston and Lynn Public Schools xxxx–xxxx

RELATED EXPERIENCE

Licensed Daycare Provider – Priscilla Dailey Child Care, Boston, MA xxxx–xxxx
Community Trainer – Catholic Family and Children's Services, Boston, MA xxxx–xxxx
Residential House Manager – Cambridge Children's Services, Cambridge, MA xxxx–xxxx

EDUCATION / CERTIFICATION

MS, Early Childhood Education, Lesley College, Cambridge, MA xxxx
BA, Political Science, Boston University, Boston, MA xxxx

Certification: Standard, Early Childhood Education (PreK-3)

Submitted by Wendy Gelberg

Writer's comments: A creative format for a drama teacher. Testimonials showcase her excellent reputation with school administrators.

ANDI SIMMONS

Theatre & Speech Instructor

56 Preston Street, #14 • Brooklyn, NY 11111 • (555) 222-5555 • andisimmons@aol.com

PROFILE Every word works

Award-winning **theatre & speech instructor** with 10 years of teaching, directing, and choreographing experience at the high school and college level. Teaching certifications in New York, Florida, New Jersey, and California.

Intense educator, with the ability to motivate students to appreciate the arts and achieve their potential. Organized, goal-oriented director with a proven ability to create high-caliber theatrical events. Directorial skills have enabled students to enhance their performances and win numerous awards. Actively involved in educational committees and associations.

EDUCATION A good way to communicate competence without bragging →

Graduate of New York University (New York, NY) with a Master of Arts in Theatre, 19XX. Completed additional graduate studies at Brooklyn College of the Arts.

Bachelor of Arts in Speech and Theater, University of New York, 19XX.

Honors: Recognized for Best Children's Theatre, Applebee College, 19XX; Best Musical Theatre, ABC College, 19XX; Outstanding Direction in One-Act Plays, New York State Center for the Arts, 19XX to 19XX.

PROFESSIONAL EXPERIENCE This well-designed, one-page format presents an experienced teacher in a most effective way

ABC HIGH SCHOOL - Brooklyn, NY
Drama Teacher / Director, Sept. 19XX to present

- Chairperson of the Visual and Performing Arts Department.
- Teach 4 drama classes and direct 2 mainstage productions each year.
- Won Best Director for 3 consecutive years for one-act competition.
- International Thespian Club and Drama Club director.
- Piloted "Appreciation of the Arts" class, accepted by Brooklyn College.
- Nominated by students for Who's Who in Professional Women.

UNIVERSITY OF NEW YORK - New York, NY
Guest Director / Teacher, Jan. 19XX to Apr. 19XX

- Directed college students in children's theatre tour of Albany.

ABC HIGH SCHOOL - New York, NY
Director / Substitute Teacher, Sept. 19XX to Dec. 19XX

Very compact format but presents essential information

PRODUCTION HIGHLIGHTS

Once Upon a Shoe...Beyond Therapy...The Natural Look...Chicago... West Side Story...Grease...A Tribute to Dr. Seuss...Jabberwock...Cheaper by the Dozen...The Good Doctor...Voices from the High School...Story Theatre...Guys and Dolls...Bye Bye Birdie...Hold Me...And They Dance Real Slow...Working...The Velveteen Rabbit...Cabaret...The Outsiders... Godspell...Charlotte's Web...Little Shop of Horrors...Fools...

RAVE REVIEWS

"...extraordinary in her ability to direct, choreograph and produce outstanding drama performances by her students..."

— Brett Robles
Superintendent, New York School District 15

"I can readily attest to her accomplishments in the classroom; and to the high regard with which she is held by our students, her faculty peers and administrative colleagues..."

— Neil Harris
Principal, ABC High School

"...She developed an excellent rapport with our students, turning a diverse group of kids into a cohesive ensemble. She asked them to stretch their abilities and under her tutelage, they rose to the occasion..."

— Craig Simms
Assistant Principal, ABC High School

"...Andi is an outstanding teacher, director, play producer and innovator, but the quality that I value most is her true concern for the welfare of her students..."

— Brenda Mondi
Board of Trustees, Manhattan School District 15

"...As a director and choreographer, she is professionally demanding and expects the best from her cast and crew. Under her direction, ABC School produces serious drama, children's theater, full-scale musicals and ensemble productions..."

— Carlo Corrao
Assistant Principal, ABC School

Submitted by Kim Isaacs

Very attractive resume with excellent layout and content.

PENELOPE TAYLOR

526 East Street ❖ White Plains, NY 10601
Home: 914-555-5555 ❖ Fax 914-555-5555

SPECIAL EDUCATION TEACHER

Highly motivated, certified educator in elementary and special education. Multicultural background enhances sensitivity and helps create a nurturing environment focusing on individual emotional and academic needs through use of innovative kinesthetic and tactile modes.

Effective use of an endorsement. →

"Ms. Taylor's use of space and her positive interactions with her pupils create a learning atmosphere that encourages students to attempt difficult tasks and to persevere when they encounter difficulty."

— Patricia Parker, Ed.D., Administrator, Westchester County Public Schools

QUALIFICATIONS

- ❒ Student Motivation
- ❒ Team Teaching
- ❒ IEP Development
- ❒ Curriculum Development
- ❒ Visual Cues, Technology & Gross Motor Activities User
- ❒ Functional Behavior Assessment
- ❒ Fluent in Spanish, English, and French
- ❒ Whole Group Learning
- ❒ Interactive Learning
- ❒ Cross Department Integration
- ❒ Cultural Sensitivity
- ❒ Kinesthetic and Tactile Teaching
- ❒ Cultural Sensitivity
- ❒ Improving Reading and Math Skills

CERTIFICATIONS

New York State Certificate of Qualification, Special Education, K–12
New York State Certificate of Qualification, Elementary Education, K–6

TEACHING EXPERIENCE

COLLEGE GARDENS ELEMENTARY SCHOOL, New York, NY 2000–Present
Resource Specialist ~ Public education institution with 1,480 students.

Good achievement statements.

- ❒ Spearheaded successful completion of annual reviews, meeting federal deadlines.
- ❒ Helped emotionally troubled students refocus energy and improve classroom behavior.
- ❒ Established student government association leading to increase in student volunteerism.
- ❒ Devised successful restrictive learning environment utilizing assistive technology and augmentative communications for mentally challenged students.
- ❒ Chosen as one of four educators to pilot inclusion model instruction.
- ❒ Improved student phonetic skills through "Touch Phonics," a multisensory program.
- ❒ Implemented and increased student reading comprehension skills through "Soar to Success" program.
- ❒ Co-piloted "Learning Community" program based on *Explosive/Non-Compliant Student* by Dr. Ross W. Green.
- ❒ Administered information reading inventory program used to place students in appropriate groups.
- ❒ Recommended additional resources for special-needs students.

Submitted by Patricia Traina-Duckers

(continued)

(continued)

PENELOPE TAYLOR

Page ❖ 2

TEACHING EXPERIENCE ~ CONTINUED

CHRISTOPHER COLUMBUS ELEMENTARY SCHOOL ~ Pleasantville, NY 1997–1998
Teaching Assistant ~ Worked with kindergarten and first-grade students in self-contained classes.

- ❒ Reinforced language skills through use of class activity photographs.
- ❒ Used poetry and prose to teach sequence, initial sounds, and rhyming patterns.
- ❒ Integrated art and music to develop auditory and visual discrimination.
- ❒ Utilized different manipulatives to teach addition, money sense, and patterning.
- ❒ Engaged students in taste-testing activities to develop classification skills.
- ❒ Helped teach study of animals, crops, and farm equipment by assisting children with creation of farm community mural.

ALEXANDER HAMILTON PREPARATORY SCHOOL ~ Pleasantville, NY 1997
Head Teacher ~ Educated children at the pre-K level.

- ❒ Introduced number recognition and concepts via creation of individual numbered books.
- ❒ Taught letter recognition using weekly themes.
- ❒ Prepared IEPs for special-needs children.
- ❒ Assessed all students through narrative report cards and parent conferences.
- ❒ Introduced cultural awareness by teaching simple phrases in various foreign languages.

SHORT HILLS ELEMENTARY SCHOOL ~ Springfield, NJ 1996
Student Teacher ~ Instructed third-grade students in self-contained classes.

- ❒ Used kinesthetic and movement activities to teach language skills.
- ❒ Incorporated music and art to facilitate sound-symbol connection and increase attention span.
- ❒ Integrated computer use to develop reading readiness and reasoning skills.
- ❒ Designed "Nursery Rhymes" unit focusing on sound repetition and word patterns.
- ❒ Established an interest center where students sequenced and illustrated rhyming books.
- ❒ Helped students recognize math patterns and geometric shapes by using art activities.

ADDITIONAL EXPERIENCE

TARGET EVALUATIONS, INC. ~ Brooklyn, NY 1998–2002
Bilingual Education Evaluator

- ❒ Administered *Woodcock-Johnson Tests of Achievement* and the *Woodcock-Munoz Language Survey* to ESL students, and the *Brigance Diagnostic Inventory of Basic Skills*.
- ❒ Evaluated each student's scores and presented recommendations to parents/guardians.
- ❒ Scored tests to determine age and grade equivalency and wrote comprehensive reports.

EDUCATION

Master of Science, Special Education
State University of New York at Stony Brook

Bachelor of Arts, Social Sciences Interdisciplinary
(Minor in Child and Family Studies)
State University of New York at Stony Brook

Writer's comments: The goal was to show Ms. Solent as a competent, problem-solving biologist—even though she had never worked in that field. I did it by documenting her class work in terms an employer would be drawn to.

Ann Marie Solent

5355 Nora Road ○ Montgomery, Alabama 36100 ○ ✆[334] 555-5555

WHAT I BRING TO **EARTHTECH**: As an entry-level **water pollution biologist**, help complete the well done environmental studies needed to support your mission.

EDUCATION AND PROFESSIONAL DEVELOPMENT:

- Bachelor of **Biological Sciences**, major **Environmental Science**, Auburn University, **GPA 3.19, Dean's List**, Dec XX – *Earned taking up to 20 credit hours and working up to 40 hours a week.*
  - Carried nearly double the biology class hours required for my major.
  - Found and fixed variable that was skewing data supporting study of symbiotic protection strategies in anemones. ***Results:*** New control group provided reliable baseline.
  - Corrected stubborn problem that had produced strong, but unexpected, results in study of scent tracking ability in lizards. ***Results:*** By eliminating environmental factor I had isolated, study produced results we were looking for.
  - Documented unlooked for relationship between sea urchins and arthropods. ***Results:*** Published biologist accepted my paper without change. Asked to present results in class.
  - Pursuing Corps of Engineers Wetland Delineation Certification

Statements support her as hardworking, thorough, and competent

COMPUTER LITERACY:

- Proficient: MiniTab (statistical analysis package)
- Working knowledge: Windows 95, Internet search tools

PUBLICATIONS:

Strike-induced Chemosensory Searching in the Colobrid Snakes *Elaphe g. guttata* and *Thamnophis siralis*, with Fred S. Falby, Ph.D., and Susan J. Winters, Ph.D., Ethology, Vol. 89, pp 19 – 28, XX

WORK HISTORY:

- **Helped with study design, field work and reporting results:**
  - Dr. William E. Cooper, Jr., Professor of Biology, Auburn University, Jul XX, Dec XX
  - Dr. William Brooks, Professor of Biology, Auburn University, Dec XX, Dec XX
- **Produced topographical survey maps** and **served as survey crewmember**
  - NorTrans, Inc. Montgomery, Alabama, Jul XX – Jan XX
  - Jacob Marley & Associates, Mobile, Alabama, Summers of XX and XX
- Worked my way through school in positions in sales, retail management, equipment repair

Submitted by Don Orlando

STEWART E. MARTIN

Post Office Box 258
Arlington, Texas 55555
555.555.5555

Writer's comments: This resume uses lines to help focus the reader. Bulleted items mix achievements and functions. Stewart was hired after just two rounds of interviews.

PROFESSIONAL OVERVIEW

PROFILE **FINANCE EXECUTIVE**

- Top-performing finance professional with a strong background in senior-level finance management. Record for improving processes and systems through analysis, problem resolution, and benchmarking activities.

STRENGTHS

- Proficient in knowledge of and adherence to GASB pronouncements.
- Areas of expertise include:
  - financial analysis and planning
  - budgeting and cost reduction
  - revenue compliance/enhancement programs
  - risk management
  - contracts and procurement
  - performance improvement
  - debt management
  - municipal investments
- Strong personnel and document management, supervisory, verbal, and written communication skills.

RESULTS

A very good thing to emphasize

- Initiated sales tax compliance program resulting in $3 - 400,000 additional revenue to the city.
- Developed Finance Department manual detailing procedural operations, job descriptions, and task delineations.
- Established 1st detailed inventory of city owned assets, including discovering resources unknown to city officials.
- Restructured city budget process from annual spending plan to 5-year financial long-range projection program.
- Implemented a citywide Financial Operations Guide detailing the procedural operation of the city's accounting services.
- Created a citywide Personnel Operations Guide establishing a user friendly reference to the city's personnel and accident reporting procedures.

QUALIFICATIONS SUMMARY

Key job-related skills

- Effectively plans projects, assesses tasks involved, makes manpower assignments, and provides scheduling, and training.
- Able to teach, train and motivate with a "team player" attitude.
- Utilizes solid organizational, work and time management skills.
- Performs effectively both as an autonomous, self-motivated individual and as an active member of a decision making team.
- Strong interpersonal skills are evident in the ability to interface with individuals at all levels of an organization; excellent customer service skills.
- Supervisory/management experience including hiring, termination process, performing staff evaluations, prioritizing assignments and determining productivity benchmark.

EXPERIENCE

CITY OF ARLINGTON — Arlington, Texas

FINANCE DIRECTOR/TREASURER, 19XX to current

Use of bullets allows for an effective presentation of past jobs

- Multi-functional position encompassing the full range of accounting skills and office management of financial operations.
- Computer/MIS Network Administrator for city's MIS system.
- Manage and direct Personnel and Safety for all city departments.
- Prepares financial statements; budget comparisons; audits overruns; determines course of action in problem resolution.

EXPERIENCE - *continued* ◂ *Page two* ▸

SHERMAN COUNTY GOVERNMENT Fort Worth, Texas

ASSISTANT DIRECTOR - AHCCCS Program, 19XX to 19XX

- Review and assess applications to determine statutory compliance for enrollment in Arizona's indigent health care program.

The bullet approach allows him to select items that best support his objective without being redundant

LOVELACE MEDICAL CENTER Houston, Texas

BUSINESS MANAGER, 19XX to 19XX

- Management of two satellite multispecialty physician groups with responsibilities encompassing:
  - communication and coordination liaison with corporate headquarters.
  - directing accounting/control systems, accounts receivables, budgeting.
  - organizing, planning, and directing activities of 40 employees.
  - marketing and community relations.

CHICKASAW NATION, Oklahoma, 19XX to 19XX:

Chickasaw Nation Family Planning Corp. Window Rock, Oklahoma
Chickasaw Nation Health Foundation Granado, Oklahoma
Native Americans for Community Action Shawnee, Oklahoma

FINANCE DIRECTOR

- Developed and enhanced financial systems for 3 Native American programs.
- Trained a qualified Native American as replacement, in pursuit of Native American self-determination.

CITY OF SHAWNEE Shawnee, Oklahoma

INTERNAL AUDITOR, 19XX to 19XX

- Conducted audits of accounts and records in municipal departments and private enterprises to determine compliance with established principles, agreements, procedures, and contracts.

EDUCATION

BENTLEY COLLEGE **BACHELOR OF SCIENCE** - Accounting, 19XX Tulsa, Oklahoma

PROFESSIONAL DEVELOPMENT

Emphasis on training tends to offset lack of a master's degree

WOODWARD COLLEGE, 19XX to current Arlington, Texas

Computer Science: MS-DOS, Windows, Lotus1-2-3, Word processing software, Internet knowledgeable

GOVERNMENT FINANCE OFFICERS ASSOCIATION, 19XX to current Dallas, Texas

Distinguished Budget Presentation Awards Program
Advanced Governmental Accounting
Intermediate Governmental Accounting

MICROPROFESSIONALS, 19XX to current Dallas, Texas

Novell Netware 4.1x - NetWare Administrator
Novell Network 2.2

NATIONAL SEMINARS GROUP, 19XX Shawnee Mission, Kansas

Troubleshooting and Maintaining PCs

PROFESSIONAL AFFILIATIONS

Government Finance Officers Association
Texas Finance Association
Municipal Treasurer's Association

Submitted by Patricia S. Cash

STEWART E. MARTIN Post Office Box 258 ◂▸ Arlington, Texas 55555 555.555.5555

Writer's comments: This recent graduate's experience was limited. Using a functional format, her non-related employment history was minimized while her education, certifications, and clinical training were stressed. She was offered a position on the spot.

MARY ANN BURROWS
123 Randolph Street
City, State 99999
(555) 555-5555

CERTIFIED MEDICAL ASSISTANT

Health care professional with solid qualifications in clinical medical assisting, including performing basic laboratory procedures, assisting with medical/emergency procedures and taking medical histories. Thorough and accurate in completion of insurance forms and patient documentation. Demonstrate a sensitive, caring approach to patient care along with the ability to work cooperatively with all members of the health care team. Excellent interpersonal, organizational, problem solving and communication skills. Computer proficient.

All of this supports what she can do, not her chronological work history

EDUCATIONAL BACKGROUND

Certificate - Medical Assistant Program, Clinical Specialty
Westchester Community College, Valhalla, New York (1997)

Certifications:

Registered Medical Assistant, 1997 (#567834) - American Registry of Medical Assistants
Phlebotomy Technician • EKG Technician • CPR Certified
Level III Collection Services Technician • Psychemedics Sample Collection

CLINICAL and MEDICAL OFFICE SKILLS

Skin/Venipuncture ... Specimen Collections (Urinalysis, Hematology & Psychemedics)
Medical Histories ... Lab Procedures ... Vital Signs ... EKGs ... Emergency Treatment
Assisting with Physical Examinations ... Medical Terminology ... Biohazardous Materials Disposal

ACCOMPLISHMENTS

- Conducted examinations involving complete patient medical histories, blood pressure readings, urine and blood sample collections, and drug screening for company serving the insurance industry. Frequently assigned to handle difficult clients and recaptured key accounts by ensuring timely service.
- Provided ongoing care to private, elderly patients. Took vital signs, administered medications and supplemental nourishment through IV therapy, and assisted patients with activities of daily living.
- Performed emergency services rotations at Memorial Hospital, assisting medical team in providing treatment at accidents and other emergency situations.
- Taught several courses in Medical Assistant Training Program at Health Education Centers, including anatomy, physiology, medical assisting, EKG, phlebotomy, and medical laboratory testing.

PROFESSIONAL EMPLOYMENT

Paramedical Insurance Examiner • INSURANCE SERVICES, INC., White Plains, New York • 1996-1997
Instructor - Medical Assisting • HEALTH EDUCATION CENTERS, White Plains, New York • 1994-1996

PRIOR EXPERIENCE

Office Manager • SCOPE COMMUNICATIONS, White Plains, New York • 1993-1994
Customer Service Representative • BOWEN CORPORATION, White Plains, New York • 1991-1993

Submitted by Louise Garver

Rochelle Simonson, RN, BSN, CGRN

10 Cloudell Road
Levittown, NY 11756
(516) 555-5555

The first page presents an image of a very competent, skilled applicant. Her strong credentials on page 2 simply reinforce this.

Statements from others allow you to communicate things you might not say about yourself but that can be very important to employers.

"...Rochelle has always been a very competent person who remains calm in the face of adversity...Her abilities have grown as her responsibilities have grown. She is always pleasant and I would recommend her highly for any position that she is qualified for..."

Garth N. Green, MD
Medical Director
Mid-Suffolk Hospital

"... You are doing an excellent job of caring for the patients entrusted to your care...it is not only the excellent care, but caring manner, compassion and understanding..."

Letter of Commendation
Delia Topping, RN, MA
Vice-president
Nursing Administration

Professional Profile

- Fourteen years experience as nurse and nurse manager in hospital and out-patient settings. Currently employed as assistant head nurse in 14 patient Endoscopy Unit. Certified in Gastroenterology. Licensed in New York State and Florida.
- Recognized for initiative, self-direction and ability to accurately perform multiple tasks. Cool-headed and effective under pressure. Interact well with all levels of staff. Deeply committed to exceptional and compassionate patient care.

Summary of Qualifications

Organized into groups to support her job objective of management

Nursing Management and Administration

- Designed Endoscopy Unit functions; run continuous quality improvement analysis and evaluation. Supervise and schedule 4 to 5 part-time nurses, full-time endoscopy technician and full-time nurses aide. Order all unit supplies and equipment
- As OR director for outpatient cosmetic surgery practice, handled all opening procedures for new practice: set-up operating room and instrumentation; developed policys and procedures; ordered supplies and equipment.

Patient Care and Communication

- Perform all diagnostic and therapeutic endoscopic procedures for up to 14 endoscopy patients a day, working directly with patients and physcians. Experienced in-patient and out-patient OR nurse. Adept at preparing patients for ambulatory surgery; able to do all IVs, meds etc. in one hour for up to 18 pre-surgical patients.
- Treat patients with respect and compassion, using a sense of humor to promote relaxation. Explain all procedures to allay fears and increase comfort levels. Establish a genuine rapport with patients and families. Act as liason between family, patients, and doctors; often consulted for opinion by physcians.

Staff Training and Development

- Train entire endoscopy team and precept new staff members. Directly involved in staff development and evaluation. Give classes on IV insertion
- Developed Endoscopy orientation and competency manuals and exams. Aided in creation of hospital policies for endoscopy unit that are now part of policy and procedure manual.

(continued)

(continued)

Rochelle Simonson, RN, BSN, CGRN

page two

Comments from "customers" are very convincing when used as they are here

↓

"...I wish to make a point as to the excellent nursing staff, in particular, Rochelle S., who carefully went about her work using her notable abilities to work with all the patients in her care while devoting that special attention to each one as an individual..."

Letter of Commendation
Lyndon Smythe
Patient

"...writing to tell you of the excellent care I received...Rochelle made a follow-up phone call, during which she made a most constructive suggestion...needless to say, I am pleased with the overall regard for the patient..."

Letter of Commendation
Lauren T. Macalister
Patient

Licensure and Certification

- RN: New York State License # 375453-1
- RN: Florida License # 2650712
- Gastroenterology Certification
- IV Therapy Certification
- EKG Certification
- BCLS Certification

Education

B.S. in Nursing
State University of New York at Stony Brook 1984

A.A.S. in Surgical Technology
Nassau Community College, Garden City, NY 1971

Continuing Education

- Conscious Sedation: Nursing Perspectives and Responsibilities
- Clinical Controversies in Conscious Sedation
- AIDS: Legal & Ethical Considerations
- You're in Charge! Now, Create Order Out of Chaos
- The Aging of the Brain, The Aging of the Mind
- Fred Pryor Seminars: How to Supervise People

Career Development

Mid-Suffolk Hospital, Bethpage, NY	**1989 to present**
Assistant Head Nurse	1995 to present
Endoscopy Staff Nurse	1991 to 1995
OR Nurse	1989 to 1991
Cosmetic Surgery Accents, Plainview NY	**1988 to 1989**
OR Director	
North Shore University Hospital, Manhasset, NY	**1986 to 1988**
OR Nurse	
Acting Head Nurse—Ambulatory and Endoscopy	
New York Hospital, New York, NY	**1974 to 1977**
OR Technician	
Terrace Heights Hospital, Jamaica, NY	**1971 to 1974**
OR Technician	

Professional Affiliations

- SGNA Society of Gastroenterology Nurses and Associates
- New York State Nurses Association

Submitted by Deborah Wile Dib

Writer's comments: This resume was written to help Daniel obtain a senior internship at a respected health care facility. It was a highly competitive process. He got the internship!

DANIEL J. WOODMAN

PO Box XXXX • Asheville, NC 28800 • (828) 555-0000

. . . Seeking an Internship position in healthcare facility

Beginner's Experience in . . .

Patient Education (Elderly to Children) • Dietary Analysis and Education • Fitness Evaluation
Physical Therapy • Wound Care Management • Orthopedic & Cardiac Rehabilitation • Patient Services
Record Management • Exercise Prescription

- Computer friendly: E-mail, Excel, Lotus 1-2-3, MacWrite, MacDraw, WordPerfect, Nutritional Assessment programs, Wellsource-Health Check Plus, General Well Being Scale/Stress Software Program, Health Age Software Program, YMCA Fitness Analyst, Health Risk Appraisal.
- Use and maintenance of health machines: Monark stationary bicycle, free weights, blood pressure cuff, pulse oximeter machine, CPM machines, EKG, treadmill, whirlpool.
- Evaluation & testing: % body fat, blood pressure, flexibility screening, strength and endurance testing, VO_2 Max testing.
- Gregarious, with public speaking, counseling and coaching skills; good listener and motivator. Goal-oriented, well organized, excellent management of time and priorities; planning abilities.
- Familiar with medical terminology; some German.

B.S., Health Promotions, expected 19xx
Appalachian State University, Boone, NC
• Chancellor's List ~ Dean's List ~ Honor Society
• Brotherhood Chairman and member of Judicial Board, Alpha Tau Omega:
set up company retreats and social functions, coordinate intramural sports program
• Pay 100% of college expenses

Certifications:
American Cancer Society Smoking Cessation Facilitator
American Red Cross CPR & First Responder

HIGHLIGHTS OF EXPERIENCE

CMI Fitness Center Volunteer • Forsyth Hospital, Winston-Salem, NC • 19xx-19xx
Assisted in setting up and implementing diabetes education classes. Fitness evaluation (% body fat, blood pressure, flexibility screening, strength and endurance testing, VO_2 Max testing); oriented employees to cardio-fitness machines and free weights. Assisted in establishing appropriate exercise programs.

Physical Therapist Technician • St. Joseph's Hospital, Asheville, NC • May 19xx-August 19xx
Assisted orthopedic patients with treatment (e.g., exercise, walking, CPM machines); cleaned and maintained PT equipment; maintained inventory and ordered equipment and supplies. Recorded patient progress notes (in computer) and ensured physicians and nurses were informed of patient condition. Pre-op and post-op patient education.

PTT Wound Care • St. Joseph's Hospital, Asheville, NC • May 19xx-August 19xx
Prepped patients for whirlpool therapy; removed bandages, assisted them in and out of whirlpool. Cleaned whirlpools and woundcare carts. Transported woundcare utensils to and from sterile processing, stocked inventory, scheduled appointments using computer.

Watauga Cardiac Rehab Volunteer • Appalachian State, Boone, NC • Spring 19xx
Monitored (primarily elderly) patient blood pressure and pulse rate, walked with them, kept them company by simply talking with them, motivating them to work harder so they would recover quickly and totally. Set up and calibrated stationery bikes and treadmills.

Submitted by Dayna Feist

LENOIR P. JENNSON, *MSN, APRN-BC*

White space here in the letterhead makes this resume look uncrowded.

9876 Arena Way
Apex, North Carolina 27539
(919) 555-5555
lpj@speedworks.com

FAMILY NURSE PRACTITIONER / PHYSICIAN EXTENDER
~ Multi-Year ICU-CCU Nursing Experience ~

PROFESSIONAL CREDENTIALS

Advanced Practice Registered Nurse—Board Certified
Family Nurse Practitioner, North Carolina State Board of Nursing
License: (Pending)

Registered Nurse
North Carolina State Board of Nursing
License: (000009)

Registered Nurse
Virginia State Board of Nursing
License: (0000098)

ACLS-Certified & BLS-Certified
American Heart Association
Renewal Date: 9/2002 & 8/2002

SKILLS SUMMARY

Quality Health Care Provider/ICU-CCU	***Communication Skills/Patient Instruction***
Nursing Staff Supervision/Training	***Analytically Focused/Excellent Research Skills***
Medical Equipment/Application Knowledge	***Multi-System Interrelatedness***
Patient Health Education/Training on Disease States	***Advanced Decision Making Skills***
Total Patient Care	***Flexible/Adaptable/Energetic***
Pharmaceutical Product Knowledge	***Team Player/Build Team Dynamics***
OSHA/JCAOH Standards/Regulation Knowledge	***Lab Support/Venipuncture/Specimen Preparation***

SUMMARY OF QUALIFICATIONS Highlights three key areas of strength.

- *Multi-year ICU-CCU nursing experience including responsibilities for the training and supervision of other nursing professionals. Self-motivated, clinically strong, and capable of meeting a variety of health issues independently.*
- *Consistently provide quality care and ensure that proper education is given for the promotion of health and the maintenance of disease states. Able to successfully interact and communicate with individuals and families to acquire and maintain a high-quality care level in various health states.*
- *Identify conditions that require more advanced medical intervention and make the proper referral to a primary physician or specialist. Participate in the education of families and patients; formulate and implement formal and informal educational programs. Exposed to the intricacies of multi-system interrelatedness and the necessity of assimilating and analyzing data in laboratory values. Offer astute and critical observations and an ability to make careful medical decisions.*

PROFESSIONAL EXPERIENCE

CLEVELAND FAMILY HEALTH, Garner, NC
Family Nurse Practitioner, RN, FNP, 2002–Present
- Responsibilities encompass a broad spectrum of health care clients. Health services include school physicals, wellness visits, immunizations, GERD, diabetes type 2, anxiety, depression, bipolar disorder, and onychomycosos.

Submitted by John O'Connor

LENOIR P. JENNSON, *MSN, APRN-BC*
Page 2

PROFESSIONAL EXPERIENCE, cont.

SOUTHSIDE REGIONAL MEDICAL CENTER, SCHOOL OF NURSING, Petersburg, VA
Classroom & Clinical Instructor (1993–1996)

SOUTHSIDE REGIONAL MEDICAL CENTER, Petersburg, VA
Cardiac & Intensive Care Staff Registered Nurse (1986–1992)

EDUCATION

NORFOLK STATE UNIVERSITY, Norfolk, VA
Master of Science in Nursing, December 2001
Family Nurse Practitioner Program
- ***Sigma Theta Tau—National Nursing Honor Society, Epsilon Chi Chapter***
- ***Helen Petra—Kura Award Nominee for Excellence in Nursing***

UNIVERSITY OF NORTH CAROLINA, Chapel Hill, NC
Bachelor of Science in Nursing, May 1986

PROFESSIONAL MEMBERSHIPS
- American Academy of Nurse Practitioners
- Virginia Council of Nurse Practitioners
- Virginia Nurses Association
- Sigma Theta Tau

FNP TRAINING & ROTATIONS

Specifics of training and experience provided for those who want a greater level of detail.

VILLAGE MEDICAL CENTER, Midlothian, VA
Preceptor: Kara Foster-Weiss, RN, MSN, FNP
- Gained experience in and exposure to a variety of acute and chronic illnesses, including cardiovascular disease, hypertension, hypercholesterolemia, diabetes type 2, GERD, anxiety, depression, HIV, musculoskeletal injuries, domestic abuse, dermatological injuries and disorders, hormonal imbalances, wellness visits, gynecological exams, allergic rhinitis, otitis media, and many others.
- Worked with and educated families to promote health care and quality disease maintenance.

SUTHERLAND FAMILY PRACTICE, INC., Sutherland, VA
Preceptor: Mildred Spiers, RN, FNP
- Responsibilities encompassed a broad spectrum of health care clients ranging from pediatrics to geriatrics. Gained an appreciation for and understanding of the entire family, its interrelationships, and its dynamics. Care was modified to meet specific needs of the family unit. Health services included school physicals, wellness visits, immunizations, GERD, diabetes type 2, anxiety, depression, bipolar disorder, onychomycosos, and others.

PRIMARY CARE ASSOCIATES—VCU / MCU
Preceptor: Elaine Ferrary, RN, MSN, ANP
- An in-hospital, outpatient clinic for indigent adults with chronic illnesses, typically multi-systems. Along with hypertension, cardiovascular disease, type 2 diabetes mellitus, GERD, renal impairment, hypercholesterolemia, and peripheral vascular involvement, there were accompanying substance-abuse issues and psychological disturbances that figured into the management and care of these individuals.

WOMEN'S HEALTH CLINIC, Petersburg, VA
Preceptor: Barbara Klein, RN, MSN, WHNP
- Health care focus was primarily on the assessment, diagnosis, and treatment of sexually transmitted diseases. Additionally, provided information and intervention for pregnancy prevention.

References Available upon Request

LISA A. MILLS, RT-M, LRT
414 St. John Place
Rochester, New York 14623
585-765-4321
millsla@anymail.com

Eye-catching taglines help the reader get a quick glimpse of her expertise.

RADIOLOGIC TECHNOLOGIST / MAMMOGRAPHY TECHNOLOGIST
Health Care ♦ Teaching ♦ Consulting / Private Industry

Accomplished health care professional with track record of acquiring and applying leading-edge technologies and procedures in clinical settings. Outstanding patient rapport and exceptional patient satisfaction. Superb teamwork skills, plus strong organizational/administrative capabilities. Excellent project management skills, encompassing sourcing and purchasing capital equipment and supplies, collaborating with engineers on facilities construction issues, and developing written procedures for new clinical techniques.

PROFESSIONAL EXPERIENCE

ROCHESTER GENERAL HOSPITAL; Rochester, New York (1985–Present)
Mammography / Radiologic Technician—Women's Health Center **1998–Present**

- See up to 30 mammogram patients daily.
- Assist physicians with various procedures, including stereotactic procedures and breast biopsies.
- Educate patients about procedures, and train co-workers in new procedures.
- Ensure that quality standards, including Mammography Quality Standards Act (MQSA) inspection requirements are maintained.

Key Accomplishments: ← Good highlighting of accomplishments.

Chosen to serve on team that pioneered Women's Health Center at Rochester General Hospital, with specific accountability for set-up and launch of Mammography Department.

- Conferred with clinical engineers and medical physicists on the physical layout of the department.
- Ensured facilities met federal and state regulations for quality standards and environmental issues.
- Sourced and evaluated equipment and supplies; made purchase recommendations to decision-makers.
- Wrote manuals and policies for mammography, breast biopsies, and other related procedures.

Played a key role in introducing stereotactic breast biopsy procedures to the department.

- Evaluated equipment and reviewed facilities needs for this new technology.
- Established sterile processes and set up surgical procedures.
- Collaborated with other hospital departments to ensure that all clinical requirements were met.
- Coordinated administrative procedures with outpatient registration and nursing staff to facilitate processing of patients and proper charting/documentation.

Radiologic Technologist **1985–1998**
Performed general radiography tests and procedures.

- Utilized portable radiography equipment and performed operating-room procedures.
- Conducted gastro-intestinal (GI) tract and vascular tests.
- Performed mammography tests until joining Women's Health Center in 1998.
- Maintained positive and productive rapport with emergency, nursing, and operating-room departments.

Key Accomplishment:

Pioneered introduction of mammography to RGH in 1986. Acquired specialized training, instructed colleagues in newly learned techniques, and ensured that strict quality standards were maintained. Functioned as in-house mammography specialist, leading to participation in set-up of Women's Health Center.

Submitted by Arnold Boldt

Lisa A. Mills **Résumé—Page Two**

Note how this experience is separate so as to not distract from the core, relevant experience on Page One.

ADDITIONAL EXPERIENCE

FINGER LAKES COMMUNITY COLLEGE; Canandaigua, New York
Adjunct Instructor **1986–Present**
Train and mentor college students majoring in Radiologic Technology.

- Follow three to four students during extensive clinical rotations.
- Provide hands-on training on various equipment and procedures.
- Conduct competency tests to establish students' speed and accuracy in performing tests.

EAST ROCHESTER UNION FREE SCHOOL DISTRICT; Rochester, New York
Mentor **1989–1990**
Introduced middle-school students to radiography as a potential career choice. Allowed students to observe day-to-day activities and responded to questions about radiography.

EDUCATION

FINGER LAKES COMMUNITY COLLEGE; Canandaigua, New York
Associate of Applied Science, Radiologic Technology **1984**
GPA: 3.75; Honors Graduate

Associate of Applied Science, Secretarial Science (Medical) **1982**
GPA: 3.5

PROFESSIONAL DEVELOPMENT

SLOAN-KETTERING CANCER INSTITUTE; New York, New York
Breast Radiology, Chemotherapy & Radiation Therapy, Stereotactic Positioning (one-day program)

Numerous additional continuing-education programs and professional conferences.

TECHNICAL PROFICIENCIES

Fisher Stereotactic Table; LoRad Mammography techniques; GE and Phillips Radiology equipment.

Windows, Microsoft Office, online patient information systems.

LICENSURE

American Registry of Radiologic Technologists (1984–Present)
American Registry of Radiologic Technologists—Mammography (1991–Present)
NYS Department of Health—Diagnostic Radiology (1984–Present)

References Provided on Request

Optional line but OK to include here as there is plenty of space.

Writer's comments: This client had the unique opportunity to open and manage a restaurant in a foreign country. Now she was back in the U.S. and ready to work in the food and beverage industry, especially in a position that would capitalize on her international experience.

Melinda E. Pelon

1759 Miller Way | Hudson, OH 44116 | 330-555-1468

Strong statements of competence as a manager

Profile

- Significant experience in food and beverage industry in diverse—including international—settings.
- Surprised skeptics by opening and successfully operating two food service properties . . . doubly challenging being a woman *and* an entrepreneur in a foreign country.
- A hands-on leader with expertise in building cooperative teams who enjoy their jobs.
- Innate understanding of what customers want, with ability to adapt and utilize that knowledge.
- Bilingual in English and Italian; conversational knowledge of Spanish and Portuguese.

Highlights of Experience

Good list of specific things she can do

MANAGEMENT

- Managed all aspects of business operations including budgeting, cost control, payroll and accounting functions.
- Monitored and purchased inventory, ensuring sufficient levels to accommodate demands; ordered perishables to maximize freshness and minimize waste.
- Built reputation and recognition of facilities through a variety of marketing efforts.
- Recruited, trained and motivated staff of chef, cooks, front house staff, servers, and bartenders.
- Auditioned and selected musicians to provide live entertainment.
- Delivered personal attention to customers to ensure high level of satisfaction, to generate repeat clientele, and to encourage word of mouth referrals.
- Collaborated with vendors to plan and implement promotions and special events.

BUSINESS START-UP

- Conceptualized and launched successful restaurant frequented by locals and tourists alike.
- Supervised all aspects of property preparation (renovation, selection of equipment, furnishings, decorating) from empty building to efficient, profit-producing operation.
- Developed and opened coffee house-concept property in neighboring community.
- Envisioned and implemented specific decor; searched for and identified local artist to create unique designs for facilities.
- Operated banquet facility (850 capacity) from separate kitchen simultaneously with restaurant.
- Collaborated with chef to create menus and develop dishes.

Professional Experience

HOMETOWN BAR • Hudson, Ohio
Neighborhood lounge catering to long-time clientele.
Manager xxxx-Present
Bartender xxxx-xxxx

OLIVE BASKET & BANQUET HALL • Milan, Italy
Unique and intimate atmosphere, specializing in Italian and American cuisine.
Founder/Owner xxxx-xxxx

Education

OHIO STATE UNIVERSITY • Columbus, OH
Proficiency in English *(certified to teach English abroad)* xxxx

COE COLLEGE • Akron, OH
Associate Degree - Marketing/Advertising xxxx

QUALITY TRAVEL SCHOOL • Cleveland, Ohio
Certified Travel Agent xxxx

References available on request

Submitted by Janet L. Beckstrom

One page is the right length for this recent grad's resume.

ROSA HERNANDEZ

3246 Schroeder Avenue • Grand Island, NE 68803 • 308-381-2284 • hernandezr@hotmail.com

TECHNICAL SUPPORT / PROGRAMMER

Even-keeled manner, deal with highly stressful situations calmly, focusing on successful resolution of problems. Demonstrated record of achieving goals as a team leader. Proven technical abilities in

- **Languages**—C++, COBOL, HTML, and Visual Basic.
- **Applications**—Microsoft Office Suite (Word, Excel, PowerPoint, Access, Outlook, and Project).
- **Hardware**—CD/DVD drives, network cards, memory, and hard drives.
- **Operating Systems**—Windows 95, 98, ME, 2000, and XP; Mac OS.
- **Telecommunications**—Router configuration. Network card, router, and modem installation.

EDUCATION

B.S. in Computer Information Systems 2004
Minor in **Telecommunications Management,** GPA 3.48/4.0
University of Nebraska at Lincoln

- Received the **Outstanding Graduate Award** from the Information Systems Department.
- Placed on Dean's List—5 semesters.

Note the effective challenge-result format.

This job seeker has no formal relevant work experience, so class projects are emphasized.

IT / TEAMWORK PROJECTS

CHALLENGE Develop a clinical and marketing database for an optometrist.
RESULT Led team by training others on software design. Motivated team members to produce highly functional, easy-to-use database tracking patient and exam data.

CHALLENGE Provide technical assistance to co-workers during downtime in shift.
RESULT Trained co-workers on software including Microsoft Office Suite and Internet browsers. Maintained office efficiency by answering questions promptly.

CHALLENGE Lead group preparing multiple reports documenting networks at businesses utilizing telecommunication services.
RESULT Analyzed areas for improvement and scheduled duties accordingly. Mentored team to meet 100% of deadlines by submitting accurate, detailed reports.

EMPLOYMENT

Accounts Receivable Clerk 2002–present
St. Francis Medical Center, Grand Island, NE

- Received customer service recognition for assisting co-workers by developing cooperative, team-oriented working relationships with them.

Cashier 1998–2002
La Consentida Grocery, Grand Island, NE

- Managed customer requests with tact and attention to prompt customer service.

Submitted by Michelle Fleig-Palmer

Writer's comments: This young man was targeting Physical Education as a major and switched to Computer Technology. This resume ties together his technical skills, education, and experience with his targeted objective. By my enhancing the text box, it added some uniqueness to the resume.

JOSEPH G. BUSH

8880 St. Lucia Court, #3 ❖ Tampa, Florida 33600 ❖ (000) 000-0000
E-mail: xxxxxx75@hotmail.com

Computer Technician

Pursuing part-time employment to supplement college expenses. Targeting a business environment emphasizing hands-on, technical, computer experience. Offer solid customer service, problem solving, and troubleshooting skills.

SUMMARY OF QUALIFICATIONS

Includes key adaptive skills up front

- Three years technical experience combined with solid work history throughout high school and college.
- Multi-task oriented, effective working independently or as part of a team; efficient in following through with directives.
- Quick learner with keen analytical ability and initiative; adept in grasping new material. Self-taught in various computer applications and functions.
- Excellent "people" skills; routinely interact with diverse customer levels to provide computer training and assistance.
- Hardworking and conscientious, willing ***"to go the extra mile to get the job done."***

TECHNICAL SKILLS

A clear, effective format

Systems:	DOS, Windows 3.1, Windows 95; familiar with Mac OS
Software:	MS Word & Works, MS Office, MS Money
Utility Programs:	Norton Utilities, Norton Antivirus, Mactest Pro
Applications:	Troubleshooting, installing and configuring hardware — memory, processors, expansion cards, hard drives, and removable storage devices; familiar with monitors, printers and other peripherals
Internet:	Browser, Search Engines, E-mail

EDUCATION

This resume won Best Resume Contest – Student Category – at the 1998 PARW Convention

COUNTY COMMUNITY COLLEGE - Tampa, FL (19XX-Present)
Pursing A.A. - Computer Technology (Graduation expected 12/XX)

AREA COMMUNITY COLLEGE - Fort Myers, FL (19XX-19XX)
Accredited Studies in Computer Technology

SANTA BARBARA CITY COLLEGE - Santa Barbara, CA (19XX-19XX)
Accredited General Studies

RELEVANT EXPERIENCE

***Computer Technician,* BCD Computers** - Tampa, FL **19XX - 19XX**
Actively involved in building customized computers. Accountable for maintenance/repairs and providing technical support.

***Computer Technician,* MicroAge Computer Center** - Fort Myers, FL **19XX - 19XX**
Conducted installation of memory, expansion cards, drives, processors and software. Diagnosed and corrected hardware and software problems and performed testing/debugging processes. Advised customers on repairs, upgrades and configurations.

***Computer Technician,* Computer Link, Inc.** - Santa Barbara, CA **19XX - 19XX**
Implemented troubleshooting measures to detect hardware and software problems. Assisted in training customers to work in a windows environment utilizing different applications.

Submitted by Diane McGoldrick

Writer's comments: This client was finishing computer programming school and had no work experience in the field. After listing the topics covered in the course, I summarized her employment experience, specifying that she earned promotions quickly. This Mary Beth Kurzak would be attractive to any employer.

Mary Beth Kurzak

2188 Huron River Drive • Ann Arbor, MI 48104 • 734-555-4912

Profile

- ➤ Strong educational preparation with practical applications in computer/internet programming.
- ➤ Highly motivated to excel in new career.
- ➤ A fast learner, as evidenced by success in accelerated training program.
- ➤ Self-directed, independent worker with proven ability to meet deadlines and work under pressure.
- ➤ Maintain team perspective with ability to build positive working relationships and foster open communication.

Education/Training

ADVANCED TECHNOLOGY CENTER • Dearborn, MI — xxxx-Present
Pursuing Certification in **Internet/Information Technology** — *Anticipated completion:* Aug. xxxx
An accelerated program focusing on computer and internet programming.
Highlights of Training:

- Networking Concepts	- Client Server	- UNIX
- Programming Concepts	- Visual Basic	- IIS
- Programming in Java/Java Script	- C/C++	- VB/ASP
- Web Authoring Using HTML	- Oracle	- CGI
- Photoshop	- DHTML, XML	- Perl

Important to include specific things learned

Highlights of Experience and Abilities

Experiences selected to support job objective

Customer Service
- ➤ Determined member eligibility and verified policy benefits.
- ➤ Responded to customer questions; interpreted and explained complex insurance concepts.
- ➤ Collaborated with health care providers regarding billing and claim procedures.

Leadership
- ➤ Creatively supervised 30 employees, many of whom were significantly older.
- ➤ Motivated employees and improved working conditions, resulting in greater camaraderie.
- ➤ Trained coworkers in various technical and nontechnical processes.

Analytical/Troubleshooting
- ➤ Investigated and resolved computer system errors.
- ➤ Researched discrepancies in claims and identified appropriate actions.
- ➤ Compiled and analyzed claims statistics.

Administrative Support and Accounting
- ➤ Managed and processed medical, mental health and substance abuse claims.
- ➤ Oversaw accounts receivable; reconciled receipts and prepared bank deposits.
- ➤ Coordinated 50+ line switchboard; routed calls as appropriate.

Employment History

MEDICAL SERVICES PLUS [Contracted by Health Solutions - Southfield, MI] — xxxx-xxxx
Promoted within eight months of hire.
Claims Supervisor / Claims Adjudicator

HANSEN AGENCY OF MICHIGAN • Ann Arbor, MI — xxxx-xxxx
Earned two promotions in one year.
Claims Adjudicator / Accounting Clerk / Receptionist

FORD WILLOW RUN TRANSMISSION PLANT • Ypsilanti, MI — Summer xxxx
Temporary Production Worker

PEARL HARBOR MEMORIAL MUSEUM • Pearl Harbor, HI — xxxx-xxxx
Assistant Crew Manager

References available on request

Submitted by Janet L. Beckstrom

An effective format with all key summary data on Page One and details on Page Two.

GORDON STRAW

straw@netzero.net

3731 Honeysuckle Hill Bellingham, Washington 98225-2006 (360) 731-5704

SOFTWARE ENGINEERING MANAGER / DEVELOPMENT LEAD

Software Creation, Maintenance, Enhancement / Internet & Intranet Technologies
AS-400 and Mainframe Access / Architectures / Conversion and Migration
Turnaround, High-Growth, and Multinational Operations

Exceptionally well-qualified senior software engineer and manager with sophisticated programming skills and a sincere passion for resolving complex problems and business challenges through technical innovation. Extensive experience in developing / supporting company-wide systems within a PC-to-host environment. Proven ability to work with a wide range of departments and levels of management, providing training and technical assistance.

Outstanding analysis, programming, and debugging capabilities. Ability to work autonomously and as a team player, with demonstrated strengths in leadership and mentoring situations. Excel at motivating one group to communicate with another. Set and drive clear priorities. Easily adaptable to change, with an eagerness toward learning and expanding abilities. Extensive international travel as well as throughout the U.S. Core strengths in

- Project Management
- Product Quality Assurance
- Product Conception, Design & Development
- Custom Software Engineering
- Troubleshooting and Customer Support
- General Business Management

Energetic and decisive business leader able to merge disparate technologies and personnel into team-centered business units. Expert in the design, development, and delivery of cost-effective, high-performance technology solutions to meet challenging business demands and drive performance. Extensive qualifications in all facets of project lifecycle development from initial feasibility analysis and conceptual design through documentation, implementation, user training, and enhancement **without any down time for customer.** Excellent organizational, leadership, team building, and project management qualifications. Successful in intense and demanding environments experiencing rapid change through internal growth, acquisition, and revitalization.

TECHNICAL SKILLS

Development Platforms Technologies	MFC Java DLL	ActiveX Windows APIs COM
Development IDEs	Visual Studio HomeSite	Visual Café Dreamweaver
Languages	C / C++ Java Pascal	Visual Basic JavaScript Prolog
Internet Technologies	IIS HTML	Browsers Software Deployment
Software	**Created RUMBA** MS Project	MS Office Suite PVCS
Operating Systems	MS Windows (Western, Eastern European, Japanese—DBCS) DOS IBM AS/400	OS/2

Alternating use of paragraphs, bullet points, and the skills table makes this long summary readable.

Submitted by Myriam-Rose Kahn

GORDON STRAW – Page 2

PROFESSIONAL EXPERIENCE

Data Resources—Pecopee, WA 1991–Present

Advanced through a series of increasingly responsible management positions based on consistent contributions to innovations, as well as revenue and profit improvement.

Software Engineering Manager (2000–Present)
Senior Software Engineer (1999–2000)

Manage engineering team on RUMBA Management Server, RUMBA Web-to-Host, and RUMBA Developer Edition. Conceptualized, designed, and implemented the development of Java RUMBA 3812 IBM AS/400 print emulator. Design major enhancements to existing products. Formulate and implement quality assurance policies, procedures, and methodologies. Interact with project stakeholders, office site managers, and senior technical support engineers. Provide clear information by authoring automated reports dealing with customer-support issues and new product development, which are published on website.

Lead a staff of 18. Conduct monthly and annual performance reviews for 5 staff members. Interview, train, motivate, and mentor new software developers.

Earned professional reputation for exceptionally solid, high-quality, and supportable software products through stringent oversight of specifications, code version control, code reuse, documentation, and testing. Incrementally improved on efficiencies and communications of numerous development groups. Transitioned engineering and management of RUMBA to engineering facilities in Ottawa, Canada, and Haifa, Israel.

Senior Software Developer (Dublin, Ireland—1997–1999)

Spearheaded this department, which dealt specifically with software maintenance for European markets. Performed engineering and QA duties; supported product maintenance. Recruited and trained development staff for Dublin. Coordinated programming in collaboration with translations—software localization for British English, French, Spanish, Italian, German, Polish, Czech, and Greek, among others.

Software Development Manager (1995–1997)

Supervised AS/400 Win32 development team. Invented, designed, and integrated new features utilizing special talent for analyzing customer requirements and envisioning new enhanced marketable products to meet needs.

Senior Software Developer (1994–1995)—Migrated 3812 emulator to OS/2 and Windows 95/NT.
Software Developer (1991–1993)

Conceptualized, designed, and implemented the development of Java RUMBA 3812 IBM AS/400 print emulator for Windows 3.x, DBCS-enabled 3812.

Prior to 1991

Software Developer, Boston Yacht Design, Victoria, B.C., Canada
Designed and implemented new software for naval architecture.
Programmer, Independent Contractor, Vancouver, B.C., Canada
Designed and implemented new expert system scheduling software.

Good example of including relevant volunteer work.

COMMUNITY AFFILIATION

Board Member, Technology Committee, Everett School, Pecopee, WA (2000–Present)
Serve as **Technical Lead, Sole Technology Advisor, LAN and PC Administrator, Teacher Trainer** (Microsoft software). Challenged to take a few standalone non-networked PCs and build a lab from the ground up with 17 networked PCs connected to the Internet. Laptop technology and domain server soon to be added.

EDUCATION

Bachelor of Science, Computer Science, Mt. St. Helen's University, WA
Scientific Computer Applications and Technology Diploma, Trano College
North Vancouver, B.C., Canada
The Dale Carnegie Course / Numerous seminars in management and training.

Writer's comments: A career mom who did an admirable job of raising three children (I speak from experience) used a functional format to sum up years of volunteer work. Her only paid experience was as a secretary over 20 years ago. Yet skills in planning, administration, and office operations landed her a job managing business affairs for an agriculture company.

Marlene Britton

(555) 555-5555

target

Business Office Administration and Support

qualifications

Accounting . . . Business Office . . . Clerical

- Performed full-charge bookkeeping functions for family partnership—accounts payable, accounts receivable, payroll, payroll tax returns, and working papers for CPA preparation of federal and state returns (volunteer bookkeeper, 5 years).
- Provided secretarial support for Burroughs Corporation sales office—typed correspondence and reports, transcribed dictation, maintained files (secretary, 2 years).
- Developed and maintained a system to track invitations (1,000+), reservations, ticket sales, and deposits for annual fund-raising event (reservations chair, 5 years).

Does not mention that this was 20+ years ago

A pure skills format presents unpaid work as real work, which it is

Leadership . . . Community Service

- Elected president of nonprofit guild benefiting a regional children's hospital. Directed 30-member organization in planning dinner-dance attended by 600-1,000 each year. Asked to return and serve another term as president to help revitalize organization when on the verge of disbanding—membership grew and participation increased by year's end.
- Served as adult advisor to nonprofit girls' organization. Supported girls, ages 13 to 18, in conducting monthly meetings, developing public speaking skills, and planning community service projects. Recruited and worked with adult advisory board.
- Regularly supported junior high and high school bands in practice sessions and state-wide competitions. Helped arrange fund-raisers that generated finances to send 100-member marching band to Europe for two-week tour.
- Counted on as a reliable committee member and volunteer for numerous church, school, and community service projects. Assist wherever needed (program planning, record keeping, letter writing, needlepoint and sewing projects, baking, and more).

education, computer skills

- Recent workshops in Internet navigation and research, Microsoft applications, and specialized agricultural accounting and production software. Keyboard skills: 65 w.p.m.
- College courses in accounting, business office operations, and secretarial science at Fresno State College, Fresno, California.

r é s u m é

111 North Washoe Avenue • Great Little Town, CA 91111

Submitted by Susan Britton Whitcomb (from Résume' Magic)

This one page resume uses several techniques to present his experience effectively in few words. The informal type font helps separate it from the "usual."

JOHN DOE **823 7th Avenue, Nicetown, Minnesota 55555 • 555-555-5555**

MACHINIST
Specialization in Wire Electrical Discharge Machining

One and one half years experience working in Wire EDM using Mitsubishi machines and programming Espirit CNCs. Certified in Safety and Wild Fire Training. Two years high school Spanish.

Lists key adaptive and transferable skills →

Hard working, reliable team player with favorable attendance record. Able to work under pressure and with tight deadlines. Effective at prioritizing and decision making regarding part schedules and due dates. Strong sense of responsibility and maturity. Easily able to adapt to changing work environment or industry trends.

Friendly and easy to get along with. Sense of humor and positive communication skills.

EDUCATION

Rochester Community and Technical College, Minnesota
- Diploma in Machine Tool Technology, 19XX
- Other courses: math, psychology, sociology, health

TECHNICAL AND TECHNOLOGY SKILLS

A very efficient way to present job-related skills →

- Read Blueprints and Schematics
- CAD
- Electrical Discharge Machines
- CNC Milling Machine
- Wire EDM
- Drip Torches
- PC with Windows 95/98
- Internet and Search Engines
- Netscape
- Lathes
- Grinders and Sanders
- Sheet Metal Cutters
- Sheet Metal Brakes
- Paint Spray Guns
- Sand Blasters
- Chain Saws
- ATVs
- Forklifts

WORK HISTORY

Less detail needed here, since it is included elsewhere

HEAD MACHINIST, Smith's Shop, Nicetown MN
Load programs and perform machine setups. Run and inspect parts, comparing to blueprints. Operate CAD programs. 19XX TO present

MECHANIC'S HELPER, City of Rochester, MN Summers 19XX, 19XX, 19XX

WORKER FOR MINNESOTA DEPARTMENT OF CONSERVATION CORP.
Department of Natural Resources 19XX

Submitted by Beverley Drake

Writer's comments: Because Ozzie had a back injury, he could no longer lift heavy items. I concentrated on abilities that don't require physical exertion.

Ozzie Chambers

Lot 16-B, Stardust Trailer Park, Tupelo, MS 00000 (555) 555-5555

A large mail order company hired him for alternating tasks of taking phone orders and performing pick/pack and shipping operations.

Job Desired

To perform a variety of warehousing functions in a distribution center or catalog order business.

Experience

Order Fulfillment

- Quickly and accurately picked numerically coded stock from thousands of items in many different categories. Used bar code scanners to automatically deduct items from inventory.

Shipping

- Prepared various types of goods for shipment including delicate instruments.
- Selected packing methods, materials, containers and labeling best suited to assure safe transit. Had a 100% record of damage-free deliveries.
- Operated lift truck to stage shipments according to destination for most efficient loading.

Emphasis on these skills allows him more flexibility for non-lifting jobs

Receiving/Expediting

- Unpacked incoming shipments, checking that material received agreed with packing slip specifications and quantities.
- Rejected damaged goods and arranged for their return to vendor.
- Transferred incoming goods to proper storage area or department within same day of its arrival to avoid backlogs.
- Picked up urgently needed material from local suppliers.

Data Entry/ Inventory Control

- Used computer to enter incoming material and track status of inventory.
- Accessed/retrieved information on computer regarding whereabouts of shipments transferred between stores.
- Informed management of backorders and low stock conditions.
- Conducted physical counts on a regular basis, transcribing numerical data accurately to eliminate necessity of recounts.

Retail Sales

- Acquired selling skills in part-time business as a flea market vendor.
- Obtained quality stock at closeouts and auctions, negotiating for best deals.
- Attracted customers by carrying a variety of popular merchandise such as compact discs, audio and videotapes, automotive parts, and baseball cards. Influenced purchasing decisions because of product knowledge.
- Displayed goods so that they were easily visible and accessible to shoppers.
- Set pricing which moved slow selling merchandise and brought the highest profit margin in a competitive environment.

Personal Strengths

- Cooperative team player, adaptable and willing to help wherever needed.
- Take all responsibilities seriously, with outstanding record of completing assignments correctly the first time.
- Enjoy working with people, solving problems, sharing knowledge, and learning new job skills.

Employment

Stock Handler *Grand Prix Wholesale Automotive, Tupelo, MS* *19XX-19XX*
Worked at distribution center supplying 25 Grand Prix stores with car and truck parts as well as aftermarket accessories and stereo equipment.

Self-Employed Flea Market Vendor *19XX-Present*
Operate business on weekends, usually at car shows or fairgrounds.

Submitted by Melanie Noonan

Writer's comments: This recent graduate had no relevant work experience but plenty of talent. The resume presents his degree and major as the prominent information. It includes a detailed subcategory of Skill Areas, with bolded headings supported by a summary of accomplishments in each area. This presents him as a versatile, capable prospective employee.

Jason Bryant Morgan
3 Elm Street
Weston, MA 02493
(781) 555-5555

Qualifications

Includes key adaptive and transferable skill words

Hard-working and accomplished broadcasting major with excellent interpersonal, research, and oral/written communication skills. Solid record of academic performance, resulting in Dean's scholarship. Proven ability to work under time pressure and meet tight deadlines. Recognized for ability to think independently and solve problems. High standards of accuracy along with excellent attention to detail.

Education

B.S. **Boston University** May xxxx
Boston, MA
Major: Broadcast Journalism
Minor: History
GPA: 3.26 (Dean's list, Dean's scholarship)
One semester junior year spent at Boston University's London campus.

Activities:

- DJ and News Reporter at campus radio stations.
- Producer/Host of weekly campus TV sports wrap-up program.
- Intern at WXXX, Channel 1, Boston

Special Project/Community Service:

- Researched and wrote 12-page promotional handbook designed to increase clientele of London's Children's Society, England.

Skill Areas:

Organizes experience into key areas

- **Communication** - Created and presented accurate and thorough reports of news and sports events under deadlines, developed promotional materials, and wrote advertising/marketing copy.
- **Information Management/Research** - Gathered reliable information through interviews, library investigation, and Internet research.
- **Interpersonal** - Collaborated with others to produce and develop radio/TV broadcasts and prepare reports.
- **Computer** - Developed proficiency in Microsoft Word for IBM and Macintosh and in various customized software programs.

Work History

Assistant (work-study) - DataCom, Boston, MA xxxx-xxxx
Accounts Payable Data Clerk - Boston Edison, Boston, MA Summer xxxx
Vendor - Creative Baskets, Framingham, MA Summer xxxx
Lab Assistant, Blood Lab - Newton-Wellesley Hospital, Newton, MA Summer xxxx
Cashier - various retail businesses, Greater Boston, MA xxxx-xxxx

Submitted by Wendy Gelberg

Heather Schumacher

Good graphic design and strong skills language

Key adaptive skills →

A creative thinker and tenacious achiever.
Always accomplish goals, persevering with wit and energy.
Learn and contribute quickly.

Writer
Designer
Graphic Artist

◆

Seeking Entry Level Position in Creative Field

◆

New York Institute of Technology Graduate

◆

Currently Pursuing 90 Credit Degree in Graphic Design

◆

Focus on Excellence, Imagination, Impact

◆

↑ Interesting format and statements

Highlights

Proficient writer and designer with experience in the production of CD covers, menus, advertisements, video sleeves, book covers, package designs, coupons, flyers, brochures, pamphlets, business cards, and logo designs. Currently enrolled in 90 credit degree program for graphic design. Hold Bachelor of Science from New York Institute of Technology.

Excited about the future of graphics and committed to continuous learning of new programs, methods, and technology. Have toured 15 different Long Island media, publication, and graphics companies to obtain a comprehensive and useful overview of these industries. Companies include Newsday, Contemporary Color and Graphics, Erin Edwards, A&B Graphics, and Brooks Lithograph.

Make competent decisions on the fly, keep a cool head in any situation, produce with vigor and fun. Have been described as creative...imaginative...a student of social satire with a quirky sense of humor...a hard worker who always gives extra effort...patient...concerned...responsible on many levels...one who takes initiative...balanced and broad...articulate...motivated...original.

Believe that the creative process, in team or independent environments, creates an impact that supports client or corporate goals, energizes through personal satisfaction, and makes a time clock meaningless.

Technology Expertise

- ◆ Proficient in PC and Mac environments.
- ◆ Experienced user of Adobe Photoshop, Adobe Illustrator, and Quark Xpress.
- ◆ Knowledgeable in the use of MS Word, WordPerfect, and the Internet.
- ◆ Trained in computer graphics, typography, drawing, animation, multimedia, and electronic page design.

Education

Graphic Design Associate Degree in Applied Sciences (in progress)
Berkley College, Bethpage, NY, expected completion, January, 2000
90 credit program of intensive training in graphics, typography, drawing, animation, computer graphics, multimedia, and related courses. Achieved President's List for academic excellence.

Bachelor of Science in Communication Arts
New York Institute of Technology, 1998
Concentrations in Writing and Graphic Design. Transferred to New York Institute of Technology with an A.A. in Liberal Arts that included courses in Animation with the Macintosh, Electronic Page Design, 2D Design, Creative Writing, and Oral Communications.

Course in Adobe Illustrator 7.0
Suffolk BOCES, 1999

Employment

Larson Reynolds Fulfillment, Melville, NY, 1991 to present
Materials Handler and Trainer
Record of increasing accountability leading to current responsibility for shipping of high-security products. Work in hectic area under accuracy and deadline pressures. Have learned to think on feet and constantly re-prioritize to maintain pace and accuracy. Train and mentor new employees.

43 Larchwood Drive, Rocky Point, NY 11933 ◆ 516.555-5555 ◆ hschum@mindspring.com

Submitted by Deborah Wile Dib

Writer's comments: Skip has limited broadcasting experience, so the challenge was to demonstrate his potential for success. The resume emphasizes Skip's production and on-air experience, stressing high-quality production, audience appeal and broad knowledge of many kinds of music. The graphic and fonts gave the resume the desired funky look.

Daniel "Skip" Norton

44 Buckingham Road • Allston, MA 02132 • (617) 555–5555

Summary

Over 5 years in broadcasting, including production, engineering, and on-air experience. Knowledge of extensive variety of music with appeal to broad range of listeners. Expertise in state-of-the art technology, including 24-track recording and digital editing. Ability to work well under pressure. Commitment to high standards of quality.

Related Experience

WZZX 92.9 FM Boston, MA xxxx–present

Host, Producer, Engineer of six-hour weekly show called Daydream. Freeform format consisting of music from station's playlist and from extensive personal library and combining alternative and popular material.

- Expanded audience size by encouraging and increasing listener feedback.
- Successfully modified format to appeal to broader audience.
- Serve as substitute host for other shows, as needed.
- Maintain consistent, high standards of production by reviewing program tapes and responding to listener feedback.
- Introduce and feature new local artists.
- Produce promotional spots.

A very clean format with good use of white space

Boston Audio, Allston, MA xxxx–present

Producer, Manager of my own project studio.

- Archive rare and odd records.
- Record material for promotions, including sound effects and music.
- Produce and record local artists for demos and release material.

Other Experience

Head Barista, Coffee Brewers, Newton, MA xxxx–present

Assistant Manager, Coffee Specialties, Needham, MA xxxx–xxxx

Education

Full Sail Center for the Recording Arts, Winter Park, FL xxxx

Associate's Degree in Audio Engineering

Submitted by Wendy Gelberg

A creative person with management skills and lots of experience uses good design and careful wording to make a good impression.

Marc Aigner

14 Sundale Place ★ Scarsdale, NY 10583 ★ (914) 555-0000

Feature Films ★ Theatre ★ Television ★ Shorts ★ Video ★ Documentaries

Creative Profile

Good visual design and impact

Highly creative **production manager** and **independent filmmaker** with more than 15 years of diversified industry experience. Well-regarded, warm and energetic **teacher** who readily shares technical expertise and passion for filmmaking. Outstanding management, communication and collaborative skills that help get the job done. Effective troubleshooter whose strengths include ***producing, directing, writing*** and ***editing***. Expertise in ***camerawork*** and ***direction of photography***.

Career Highlights

★ **Management** Emphasizes results

Manage university Film Production Office and Facilities, including sound stage, film, video, computer-editing, mixing and transfer rooms and equipment.

- Spearheaded and managed a turnaround operation for university film department. Improved viability and quality of production/post-production film equipment by determining complex repair needs and establishing controls.
- Served as catalyst for increased productivity among faculty and students for on-time project completion of independent films.
- Creatively used budget allocations for staffing needs and facilities upgrades.

"... particular strengths are commitment, energy, knowledge of cameras and concern for students."
—Tom Gunning, Author, "D.W. Griffith and the Origins of American Narrative Film."

★ **Independent Filmmaking** A very compact way to present this

Collaborated in the making of numerous feature, television, short and documentary films.

- Director of Photography/Producer: "European and Poetic," 90 min. Stefano Mario Baratti, Director.
- Writer/Producer/Director: "Gypsy Cab," 16mm, 30 min., in color. Original project filmed on location in The Bronx, depicting an immigrant man's struggle to adapt to a new life. Screened at area film festival.
- Cameraman: "Vinal," 16mm, 30 min., in color. Director, Marissa Benedetto.
- Assistant Director: "The Suitors," 35mm, 90 min. Director, G. Ebrahimian.
- Cameraman: "Bone White," 16mm, 60 min., in color.
- Director of Photography: "Vanitas," 16mm, 60 min., in black and white. Stefano Mario Baratti, Director.
- Production/Camera Assistant: Ebra Films. Several documentary projects for BBC, French and Italian Television.

" Mr. Aigner has many of the same admirable personal values that former Film Chair Avakian possessed" ... "he is patient and willing to help in problem-solving, and takes a personal interest in student projects."
—Richard Dawson, NYU colleague.

★ **Instruction** More skills and results

Hire and supervise work/study students, offering group and one-on-one instruction. Support film faculty in organizing film festivals and outside screenings.

- Designed and taught course *Production Workshop* focusing on proper operation of cameras, lighting, sound, editing, mixing and transfer equipment.
- Simplified instructional methodology and improved student morale by completely rewiring sound-mixing studio, creating universal access to sophisticated controls.

Marc Aigner
Page Two

Employment History	1990–present	**Film Production Manager** and **Instructional Support**, Film Department, New York University, New York, NY.
	1988–1989	**Cameraman.** WVVA-TV (NBC affiliate), Bluefield, West Virginia.
	1982–1988	**Independent Filmmaker.** Ebra Films, New York, NY.

Education

New York University, New York, NY:
Bachelor of Fine Arts in Film Production, 1985.
Additional coursework in engineering.

Special Talents

Languages:
Trilingual—Fluency in written and spoken English/French; spoken Italian.

Technical:
- Adept in using all 16mm and 35mm film equipment, and applying latest technology such as DVD.
- Use specialized software such as *Movie Magic* and *Final Draft*.

Related Professional Activities

Participated in several film productions that appeared at the:
Sundance Film Festival, 1997 (Winner—First Prize).
Empire State Exhibition Film Festival, 1995.
Cannes Film Festival, 1988.

More accomplishments

Submitted by Phyllis B. Shabad

EXPERTISE

Commercial Artist
Graphic Artist

Résumé

J a n e l l a L a r r i c a

1234 North Adelaide
Monterey, CA 94444
(408) 444-4444

Graphic Art Skills

- ◆ Display Advertising
- ◆ Coupon Pages
- ◆ Promotional Material
- ◆ Logos
- ◆ Business Cards
- ◆ Letterhead
- ◆ Specialty Display Ads (back covers, inside covers)

Commercial Art Skills

- ◆ Illustration
- ◆ Redraw

Computer Skills

- ◆ PageMaker
- ◆ QuarkXpress
- ◆ Freehand
- ◆ PhotoShop (basic skills)

Professional Experience

Graphic Artist

ABC Publishing (6/94–Present)
XYZ Directory Co. (12/90–6/94)

(In-house production of telephone directories for California and Colorado)

Develop ads, coupons, and specialty pages using advanced computer software skills. Accountable for paging and layout of directories. Experience includes computerized color separation of ads and coupon pages.

- Generate high-volume production, creating 18-20 quality display ads daily.
- Worked effectively with clients to determine target markets and product features and benefits.
- Served on multidisciplinary team and collaborated with management, sales associates, accounting, and support staff.

Graphic Artist

L&M Signs (9/88–11/90)

Rendered scale drawings of signs. Performed layout and paste-up. Produced PMTs and halftones.

Professional Experience
(continued)

Graphic Artist

Screen Play *The Agency* (6/86–9/88)

Charged with full accountability for complete production of T-shirt designs from layout to finished artwork. Assisted Art Director with layout and paste-up of newspaper advertisements and brochures.

Education

Bachelor of Arts degree (1986)
Major: Industrial Arts/Design
California State University, San Jose

Associate of Arts degree (1983)
Bayview City College

Interests

Movie buff
Roller-blading
Avid reader (mysteries and suspense!)

References

Portfolio and references available on request.

While this info is rarely necessary, it is acceptable here since the client is an actor. →

G. MATHEW COLLINS

When in transition, this is a good way to make sure employers can contact you.

Height	5'11"
Weight	160
Hair	Red
Eyes	Blue

Present:
123 W. 35th
New York, NY 10019
(212) 555-5555
collins@ny.net

←

Permanent:
4321 Bridger Rd
Evansville, IN 47710
(812) 555-5555
collins@in.com

TRAINING

BFA-Musical Theatre
University of Concord College—Conservatory of Music

Acting: Diane Kvapil, Alan Arkin, Jeff Corey, Meisner Technique
Voice: Mary Henderson, Phillip Ewart
Vocal Coaching: Terry LaBolt, Phil Kern, Jeff Saver
Dance: James Truitte – Modern, Diane Lala - Jazz

PROFESSIONAL THEATRE

• Evita	Che	New Monterey Theatre, New Monterey, MA
• Man of La Mancha	Don Quixote	Long Winter Nights, Concord, OH
• Forum	Marcus Lycus	HSN
• Gail Warnings	Joseph	Cape Park/Columbia Playhouse
• Pirates of Penzance	Samuel	Southwest Montana Opera

UNIVERSITY MUSICAL THEATRE

• Company	Bobby	University of Concord College Conservatory of Music
• Chess	American	UC, CCM
• Carousel	Jigger	UC, CCM
• Working	Mason, Gas Man, Hippie, Executive	UC, CCM
• Kiss Me Kate	Harrison Howell	UC, CCM
• Two Gents of Verona	Eglamour	UC, CCM
• Candide	Voltaire, Pengloss, Governor	Indiana University

UNIVERSITY THEATRE

• Crucible	Governor Danforth	UC, CCM
• One for the Road	Nicolas	UC, CCM
• Zoo Story	Jerry	ISU
• Romeo and Juliet	Mercutio	ISU

An unusual format but an effective way to present a lot of info.

Special Skills: Guitar • Football and Baseball • Historian • Cabaret • Studio Vocalist

Submitted by Teresa Collins + Erica Hanson

LORRAINE A. LARSON

22 Meadow Lane, St. Louis, MO
(555) 222-1111

Writer's comments: Functional format enabled client to easily transition from account executive in financial services to special events management. The format highlights her experience in volunteer positions with minimal focus on financial services.

PROFILE SUMMARY

Conferences · Fund-raising · Trade Shows · Meeting Planning · Cultural Programs

Creative professional with expertise in all aspects of successful event/program planning, development and management. Excel in managing multiple projects concurrently with strong detail, problem solving and follow-through capabilities. Demonstrated ability to recruit, motivate and build cohesive teams that achieve results. Sourced vendors, negotiated contracts and managed budgets. Superb written communications, interpersonal and presentation skills.

SELECTED ACCOMPLISHMENTS

Lorraine applied for a Special Events Manager position at an art museum and was immediately hired.

Special Events Management:

Format allows volunteer activities to have value equal to paid work experience

Planned and coordinated conferences, meetings and events for companies, professional associations, arts/cultural, and other organizations. Developed program content and administered budgets. Arranged all on-site logistics, including transportation, accommodations, meals, guest speakers and entertainers, and audiovisual support. Coordinated participation and represented companies at industry trade shows. Recognized for creating and planning some of the most successful events ever held state-wide.

- **Created cultural events for an arts organization that boosted membership enrollment.**
- **Organized 5 well-attended conferences for 2 national professional associations.**
- **Designed successful community educational campaigns promoting safety awareness.**

Results

Fund-raising & Public Relations:

Created, planned and managed all aspects of several major fundraising campaigns resulting in a significant increase in contributions raised for each function over prior years. Recruited volunteers and developed corporate sponsorships. Generated extensive media coverage through effective promotional and public relations strategies. Created newsletters distributed to employees, customers and others.

- **Co-chaired capital fund campaign raising $3.5 million for new facility.**
- **Coordinated 3 auctions raising over $140,000 for an educational institution.**
- **Initiated successful publication generating $25,000 to finance community programs.**

Results

Sales & Marketing:

Selected by management to spearhead opening of regional office, including all logistics, staff relocation and business development efforts. Designed and implemented creative sales and marketing strategies to capitalize on consumer trends and penetrate new market. Coordinated and conducted sales training.

- **Developed and managed 17 key accounts generating $10 million annually.**
- **Recognized for managing top revenue-generating program company-wide.**
- **Consistently exceeded sales forecast and led region to rank #1 out of 15 offices in profitability nationwide.**

Results

Submitted by Louise Garver

(continued)

(continued)

Page 2

LORRAINE A. LARSON

(555) 222-1111

EVENTS MANAGEMENT EXPERIENCE

Special Events/Conference/Program Coordinator: 1983-Present

Mostly volunteer

AREA ARTS COUNCIL • St. Louis, Missouri

UNITED COMMUNITY • St. Louis, Missouri

SAFETY COUNCIL • St. Louis, Missouri

BOTANICAL GARDENS • St. Louis, Missouri

NATIONAL ASSOCIATION OF INSURANCE WOMEN • St. Louis, Missouri

INSURANCE COUNCIL OF ST. LOUIS • St. Louis, Missouri

PROFESSIONAL EMPLOYMENT

MARCON FINANCIAL SERVICES COMPANY • St. Louis, Missouri 1988-Present
Regional Manager
Account Executive

SENTINEL BANK • St. Louis, Missouri 1985-1988
Financial Underwriter

ROBERTS INSURANCE COMPANY • Springfield, Illinois 1980-1985
Claims Analyst
Senior Processor
Health Claim Processor

EDUCATION

SPRINGFIELD COLLEGE • Springfield, Massachusetts
B.A. in Business Administration • 1980

Writer's comment: Client had wonderful work history with one employer, but no formal education beyond high school. He knew he had marketable skills but needed help expressing them. We focused on his wide-ranging experience as well as demonstrating how he had worked his way up. I got a note from him within a month that he had "gotten a good job."

James P. Miller

1254 Crestview Drive • Swartz Creek, MI 48473 • 810-555-1299

Highlights of Experience

— 14+ years in land development and construction management —

Organizes experience into three categories of importance to employers

(1) RESIDENTIAL CONSTRUCTION MANAGEMENT

- ➤ Supervised all aspects of construction: land development and groundbreaking through occupancy (total 150+ homes, average 15 simultaneously in progress).
- ➤ Utilized strong organizational skills and experience to perform critical path scheduling.
- ➤ Hired and directed subcontractors; monitored work for quality and safety issues.
- ➤ Ordered lumber and construction supplies; negotiated with vendors for lowest costs and just-in-time delivery service; approved accounts payable.
- ➤ Monitored costs and progress to ensure project completion within budget and deadlines.
- ➤ Facilitated communication between subcontractors, employees and management.
- ➤ Collaborated with home owners and architects regarding requests for deviations to plans.
- ➤ Represented company in interaction with building inspectors.

(2) LAND DEVELOPMENT

- ➤ Oversaw and participated in comprehensive land development and landscaping; hired and supervised direct-employ crews.
- ➤ Readied land above and below ground for electrical, water and sanitary/storm sewer services; prepared surfaces for concrete flat work and asphalt for roads.
- ➤ Operated back hoe, excavator, dozer, scraper, loader and dump truck.

(3) PROPERTY MANAGEMENT

- ➤ Managed 100+ lots/units.
- ➤ Acted as liaison with residents/owners regarding lot maintenance issues.
- ➤ Performed landscaping, lawn and street maintenance.

Employment History

His experience is above, so he only needs the facts here

JOHNSON DEVELOPMENT - MAPLE VILLAGE COURT - MILL CREEK CENTER - BAY VIEW ESTATES • Bay City, MI xxxx-xxxx
Condominium and mobile home developments under single ownership; two-time recipient of Bay City Parade of Homes awards
Superintendent - Bay View Estates (xxxx-xxxx)
Assistant Superintendent - Bay View Estates (xxxx-xxxx)
Manager - Mill Creek Center (xxxx-xxxx)
Heavy Equipment Operator - Maple Village Court (xxxx-xxxx & xxxx-xxxx)
Co-op Student & Lawn Maintenance Worker - Johnson Development (xxxx-xxxx)

Shows his promotions

Training & Education

DELTA COLLEGE • University Center, MI
Builders License course leading to earning
State of Michigan Builders License xxxx

SWARTZ CREEK HIGH SCHOOL • Swartz Creek, MI
Diploma xxxx

References available on request

Submitted by Janet L. Beckstrom

A compact, one-page format

BRUCE A. HAYLET
45 Old Tappan Avenue • Maywood, New Jersey xxxxx • **(xxx) xxx-xxxx**

Job objective is flexible

MANUFACTURING PROFESSIONAL
MATERIAL MANAGEMENT • INVENTORY MANAGEMENT • MIS MANAGEMENT

Proven ability to define critical problem areas/weaknesses and institute improved processes for maximum efficiency. Excel in driving productivity and profits while streamlining procedures. Build staff to peak levels of performance, instituting a team-approach. Computer proficiency includes the Internet, Windows and Microsoft Suite.

States what he can do, not what he wants

DEMONSTRATED STRENGTHS:

Material Flow Management · *MRP Systems* · *Inventory Control*
Process Re-Engineering · *New Process Development* · *Materials Management*
Information Processing · *Data Management*

SELECTED ACHIEVEMENTS:

Includes numbers to stress results

- **Consistent record of leading and developing departments from initial start-up phase to successful operations. Requested by senior management to establish and guide the Customer Service, Inventory Control and MIS departments.**
- **Spearheaded the implementation of ABC Codes for stock items and instituted daily cycle counting: increased productivity while reducing staffing expenses and improved accuracy from 62% to 96%.**
- **Slashed pick-per-line time from 7 minutes to 3 minutes.**
- **Streamlined the time needed in recording physical inventory from 5 days to 3 days, substantially improving productivity and profitability.**
- **Implemented a forecast policy which analyzed sales history and predicted future sales trends, and pioneered an MRP policy: combined policies were instrumental in slashing product delivery lead times from 120 days to 5 days and in driving annual sales from $12 million to $52 million.**
- **Replaced telephone system from a 32 line in-house MYTEL PBX system to a 250 line, full feature NYNEX Centrex Intellipath system with ISDN and voicemail.**

PROFESSIONAL EXPERIENCE:

NATIONAL DYNAMICS - Orange, New York **xxxx - Present**

MIS MANAGER (xxxx-Present)
High profile position reporting directly to the Vice President of Finance and Chief Operating Officer. Accountable for the development and maintenance of operational procedures for information processing. Recruit, motivate and lead a staff of programmers, network administrators and network technicians. Assess needs to develop new information processing systems and improve program design. Successfully interface with corporate MIS Department in co-aligning strategies and achieving goals. Develop and submit bids. Implement and manage complex telecommunication systems.

MATERIAL CONTROL MANAGER (xxxx-xxxx)
Reporting to the Director of Operations, managed daily operations including shipping, receiving, warehouse and inventory control. Led and managed a staff of 22 employees. Identified and resolved critical problem areas to ensure efficiency and timely project completion. Increased department competency of all material handling personnel through strategic staff re-engineering. Served as a liaison with department heads to ensure efficiency, timely completion and increased productivity.

A good way to present two jobs with one employer

EDUCATIONAL BACKGROUND:

S.U.N.Y. • Plattsburg, New York • Psychology Major

Advanced Training and Development:
Inventory Management • APICS

No degree, but his experience offsets this

Submitted by Alesia Benedict

Gary F. Bigelow

256 Meredith Drive • Garden City, MI 48135 • (248) 555-3401

Profile

- ❒ Ability to make decisions under pressure and to excel in high stress, just-in-time environment.
- ❒ A strong leader who earns respect of colleagues and subordinates.
- ❒ Excellent rapport with union employees and officials.
- ❒ Broad background and experience contributes to versatility.
- ❒ Diligent and detail-oriented.

A clean format with many items to emphasize his competence as a supervisor — a higher-paying position

Highlights of Experience

Management/Supervision

- ❒ Dispatch and supervise up to 150 drivers providing just-in-time delivery service between component manufacturing plants and Chrysler assembly plants.
- ❒ Evaluate and establish or revise routes; set-up route bidding system.
- ❒ Provide on-site liaison with Chrysler plant management and staff.
- ❒ Interact with UAW-represented drivers and union officials.
- ❒ Monitor driver logs and track driver hours; process daily, weekly and monthly reports.
- ❒ Conduct new employee orientation; act as resource person for operational questions.

Operations/Logistics

- ❒ Continually analyze operations and identify measures to reduce delay and overhead costs, thereby increasing efficiency and cost savings.
- ❒ Communicate with drivers and track truck locations utilizing Qual-Comm automated system.
- ❒ Contact plant officials and when unexpected delays occur; identify and propose remedies.
- ❒ Constantly monitor production status; adjust loading and delivery schedules as needed.
- ❒ Enter and retrieve data from computerized Quality Management System (QMS).

Employment History

Dispatcher/Supervisor — xxxx-Present
RYDER TRUCKS OF MICHIGAN • Livonia, MI

Meat Cutter — xxxx-xxxx
CLIO IGA • Clio, MI

Fire Sprinkler Technician — xxxx-xxxx
MAST SERVICES • Miami, FL

This simple list shows stability of work history

Over-the-Road and Short Haul Truck Driver — xxxx-xxxx
HOMESTEAD TRUCKING • Iowa City, IA
YELLOW FREIGHT • Madison, IA
RAPID XPRESS • Orlando, FL
PENSKE TRUCK LINES • Parma, OH

Training & Certifications

Commercial Drivers License - Class A Endorsement

Logistical Planned Maintenance Workshop, Quality Management System (QMS), Lock Out Energy Control Course, Interaction Management Program
CHRYSLER CORPORATION, HOMESTEAD TRUCKING, AND YELLOW FREIGHT

Truck Driving Course • DELTA COLLEGE

Retail Meat Cutting & Store Management • WASHTENAW COMMUNITY COLLEGE

Most support his job objective

References available on request

Submitted by Janet L. Beckstrom

Writer's comments: This client had spent most of his life working on his family dairy farm. When the farm was sold, he needed to find a job. Since few farm jobs are in the area, he wanted to step into a supervision or sales capacity. He was hired as an admissions representative for a local college.

Jonathon P. Ford

4384 Country Road 10
Midland, MI 48642
517-555-3922

Profile

Over 11 years of hands-on management experience based on foundation of Bachelor's degree in Business. Committed to the highest level of excellence through achievement. A respected manager who leads by example. Excellent decision-making and problem-solving skills developed while meeting the challenges of constantly fluctuating agricultural business environment.

Highlights of Experience

Accurately presents skills so they could apply in many jobs

Management

- Negotiate contracts for purchasing and selling dairy and niche products.
- Manage inventories of perishable feed, breeding, and other supplies to achieve maximum cost effectiveness.
- Market niche product to buyers in the United States and 17 countries.
- Thoroughly research scientific information regarding procedures which create niche product for greater understanding and to knowledgeably plan results.
- Contribute to developing and monitoring budgets.
- Developed and implemented advertising program.

Operations

- Oversee 7 day/week operations on 3,500 acre farmstead.
- Ensure adherence with appropriate health and safety regulations; inspect facilities for cleanliness and equipment for optimum operation; perform maintenance as needed.
- Collaborate with veterinary specialists to conduct procedures resulting in marketable niche products.
- Monitor general health of livestock; identify situations requiring additional expertise.

Supervision

- Hire, train, supervise, motivate, and evaluate permanent and seasonal employees.
- Demonstrate and practice safe work procedures to ensure accident-free environment.
- Develop policies and procedures for all jobs.

Highlights of Achievements

- Refined and specialized the focus of the business resulting in entry into new, niche product market.
- Developed and implemented innovative labor-saving and quality-improving process preparation technique.
- Achieved **2nd Highest Quality** (19xx) and **4th Highest Quality** (19xx) rating out of 38,000 herds across the nation through selective breeding and thorough knowledge of bloodlines.
- Oversaw breeding and development of more than 10 All-American and All-Canadian nominated animals.

Professional Experience

Manager/Co-Owner xxxx-Present
MIDLAND DAIRY/APPLEWOOD BREEDERS • Midland, MI
Dairy farm producing 35,000 pounds of milk per day from up to 700 head of cattle; specialize in developing and marketing embryos from award-winning livestock. Named Michigan Quality Farm of the Year for two consecutive years.

Education

Bachelor of Arts - Business xxxx
CENTRAL MICHIGAN UNIVERSITY • Mt. Pleasant, MI

- Served as football team Captain (2 years).

Submitted by Janet L. Beckstrom

An unusual and eye-catching format that indicates she is creative in getting attention — an asset for her job objective.

ACCOUNT COORDINATOR

During my tenure with Harrington Associates, I worked as an Assistant Account Executive on the Hardee's fast food account.
Am familiar with the Indianapolis market and its competitors.

SKILLS ACQUIRED

Analytical Reports – Overseeing Projects – Verbal Communication Skills – Putting Forth Best Effort *at All Times*

PROMOTION COORDINATOR

Handle promotions in their entirety. Most recent promotion was for Hardee's and Conner Prairie. Responsibilities included producing promotional support items for in-store distribution.

SKILLS ACQUIRED

Team Member – Quick Learner – Coordinator – Able to Meet Deadlines – Creativity – Professional Attitude

Note that no employment dates are included, nor are educational specifics. She can, of course, explain those in an interview.

MARGO S. BERNS
Executive Account Assistant

Addie Advertising, Inc.

Lots of skills mentioned

CLIENT AND SERVICE ORIENTED

Experience in the service industry.
Assertive personality that allows me to deal with clients and franchisees in a professional manner.
Able to think quickly and prioritize needs from corporate to client level.
Educational background in Business/Marketing.

SKILLS ACQUIRED

High Energy Level – Ability to Speak in Front of Crowds – Listening Skills – Able to Analyze Client Needs – Negotiating Techniques

FLEXIBLE AND DEDICATED

Take responsibility for getting the job done completely and efficiently. Can work well on all levels – from budgetary needs, product knowledge, demographics, to planning marketing objectives for future quarters.
Computer skills include Macintosh, PC, Microsoft Word, WordPerfect, Internet, email.

SKILLS ACQUIRED

Managerial Skills – Being Persistent and Not Giving Up! – Public Relations – Never-Ending Search for Knowledge and Information

Submitted by Gayle Bernstein

Writer's comments: The client had many years of experience but no formal education past high school. He wanted to leave his long-term employer and take another grocery store position or go into sales for a food broker.

John P. Finley

2311 McKinley Road • Port Huron, Michigan 48689 • 810-555-0988

Bulleted format is an effective way to present this information

Profile

- Respected manager with 15+ years of experience in grocery industry.
- Expertise in developing and retaining employees; demonstrated ability to turn around poor-performing workers.
- Comprehensive knowledge of retail —particularly meat department—operations, products, and trends.
- Eager to utilize extensive experience and hands-on knowledge to meet challenges in new setting.

Highlights of Experience

Organizes skills and experience into three key areas

MANAGEMENT

- Manage day-to-day operations of meat department in the chain's highest volume store.
- Independently negotiate special purchase prices with vendors.
- Selected by administrators to manage meat departments in other stores during the respective managers' absences.
- Build rapport with customers by being visible and approachable.
- Maintain departmental gross profit margins of 21-24%, approximately 1 1/2-2% higher than meat departments in other stores within chain.

OPERATIONS

- Creatively merchandise cases and institute in-store specials to generate interest in high profit or slow moving products.
- Plan and implement periodic department resets.
- Generate orders; maintain appropriate levels of inventory to adequately cover projected sales and ensure timely turnover of perishable products.
- Conduct routine inventories to a high degree of accuracy.
- Process special orders; advise customers on product usage.
- Review and confirm accuracy of invoices before submitting for payment.

Includes many strong statements to reinforce competence and results

HUMAN RESOURCES

- Recruit, hire, train, and supervise trade employees.
- Utilize intuition and experience to identify and hire top quality, productive workers.
- Motivate employees to achieve and maintain high standards of sanitation, product handling, and customer service.
- Monitor payroll budget and prepare employee schedules.

Employment History

FRIENDLY'S MARKET • Tuscola, Michigan — xxxx-Present

Meat Department Manager
Meat Cutter
Apprentice Meat Cutter

Shows promotions

UNITED STATES MARINE CORPS — xxxx-xxxx

Sergeant (Rank E5) - Honorably discharged

Education

Completed **Leadership** and other relevant courses through the U.S. Marine Corp.

JOHNSON HIGH SCHOOL • Clio, Michigan

Diploma

Submitted by Janet L. Beckstrom

Good design elements make this attractive and easy to read in spite of small type font

Key words organized into important clusters

Angela Ocipoff

(516) 555-5555
64 Cologne Avenue, Apt. B1 • Malverne, NY 55555

Special Skills

Event Production and Marketing

themes
budgets
advertising
collateral materials
event coordination
local partnerships
media participation

Mall/Tenant Communications

program coordination
event promotion
mall shows
advertising tie-ins
vendor ad budgets
sales surveys
consumer profiles
one-on-one interface

Mall Service Management

concierge service
customer assistance
complaint resolution
certificate promotions
operations budgets
staff administration

Experienced Marketing and Promotion Professional

High-energy background in all aspects of retail center marketing and promotion with Marketing Property Investors, a leader in major shopping center and commercial real estate ownership, operation and management.

Summary of Qualifications

All skills and accomplishments

- Blend creative and administrative abilities to achieve bottom-line results.
- Excellent rapport with management, vendors, media and agencies.
- Tenacious and resourceful; will always find a way to get project done.
- Team with agencies to edit and design event ads and collateral materials.
- Smithaven Mall newsletter editor and contributor.
- Management and budgetary oversight for staff of twelve.
- Frequent presenter at board of director and mall tenant meetings.
- Experienced with MS Word, WordPerfect, Lotus 123 and Pagemaker.

Career Highlights

- Produced charity event that helped Seaview Mall continue to develop a strong community presence. Solicited merchant donations, radio coverage, local politicians and community group involvement. Wrote press releases, determined and placed advertising. Event was well attended and received great press.
- Administered production of Seaview Mall's Summer Sidewalk Sale and developed free "Rainy Day Kids" craft center and Summer Concert Series. Advertised throughout thriving summer beach communities, arranged aerial banner pulls, developed radio/newspaper campaign, solicited for tenant participation.
- Planned new customer service kiosk and implemented concierge type customer service at Smithaven. Hired, budgeted and managed staff of twelve. Offered gift certificates, mall information, complaint resolution and special services. Commended by customers for problem resolution.
- Managed all pre-production and production of Seaview Mall's for-profit Women's Health Show. Wrote contracts, obtained permits, planned and placed ads, handled tenant interface.
- Directly involved in planning and production of Smithaven Mall's grand re-opening party with $750,000 budget. Managed administration and follow-up of corporate guest list. Personally distilled numerous press releases into concise brochure profiling new up-scale shops.

(continued)

(continued)

Angela Ocipoff

page two

Each statement supports her job objective

Employment

MARKETING PROPERTY INVESTORS (Fallbrook Operations), New York, NY — 1995 to present

Acting Marketing Director, Seaview Mall, NJ (6/97 to present)

- Conceive, develop and coordinate numerous profit and non-profit special events and mall shows.
- Determine event/show content, solicit media participation, plan and produce advertising and collateral materials.
- Formulate advertising budgets, administer payroll and oversee lease required advertising program.

Marketing Specialist, Smithaven Mall, NY (4/96 to 6/97)

- Developed customer service kiosk and concierge service concepts. Hired, budgeted, scheduled and managed staff of twelve. Reconciled $2.5 million sales accounts.
- Participated in special event planning and implementation logistics. Aided in advertising production and campaigns. Edited advertorials, worked with media for print, television and radio advertising.
- Conducted sales and marketing surveys of customers and tenants to determine shopping patterns, demographics and advertising benefits.

Specialty Leasing Assistant, MPI, New York, NY (1/96 to 4/96)

- Evaluated perspective tenants for kiosk/cart leasing for 20+ nationwide shopping centers. Controlled paperwork; determined product suitability.

Marketing Assistant, Sparksville Center Mall, PA (6/95 to 1/96)

- Created and set-up special programs. Aided fashion coordinator in planning shows and soliciting tenant participation/donations. Implemented surveys for advertising and event follow-up; analyzed and presented results.

Education

B. A. in English Literature, Hofstra University, Uniondale, NY

- Attended on academic/tennis scholarship
- Achieved Most Valuable Player award
- Won Collegiate Tennis Number One Doubles Championship

Personal Interests and Volunteer Activities

- Accomplished tennis player and national lifetime member of USTA.
- Taught for two years at USTA Tennis Center at Flushing Meadow.
- Experienced traveler. Studied in Venice. Toured France and England.
- Lived for one month in Kenya to help construct church library.
- Volunteered in patient recovery area of North Shore University Hospital.

Submitted by Deborah Wile Dib

Writer's comments: This format effectively presents the professional skills of a recent college graduate for an entry-level position in sales. The client was successful in reaching his objective.

JAMES WESTBROOK

3075 West Street
City, State 77777
(555) 555-5555
XXXX@aol.com

CAREER FOCUS: Marketing / Sales / Account Relations

STRENGTHS and SKILLS:

- Highly creative, self-motivated professional with marketing, sales and customer relations experience.
- Ability to conceptualize and generate new ideas, analyze problems and develop effective solutions.
- A dependable team player who relates well and works cooperatively with diverse personalities.
- Fast learner with demonstrated initiative and dedication to the achievement of organizational goals.
- Focus on providing exceptional service resulting in customer satisfaction and repeat business.
- Computer capabilities include Windows 95, Microsoft Office Suite, Publisher, and Lotus 1-2-3.

The emphasis on skills and accomplishments allows him to emphasize strengths

EDUCATION:

B.S. in Marketing • UNIVERSITY • City, State • 1996

Courses included:

Marketing Principles ... **Marketing Research** ... **Consumer Behavior**
Advertising Principles ... **Advertising Campaigns** ... **Sales Management**

ACCOMPLISHMENTS:

Marketing & Research

- Organized and launched successful direct mail marketing campaign for new product.
- Created an advertising campaign for Levi jeans from concept development through copywriting for a college advertising project.
- Earned top grade for designing comprehensive business, marketing and sales plan as well as management structure for a college marketing project.
- Researched and compiled target database of 100 clients representing diverse industries.

Sales & Promotions

- Consistently achieved high sales volume for a sporting equipment retail business.
- Recognized by management for sales performance, surpassing productivity levels of full-time associates store-wide.
- Promoted and sold products at Fenway Park for the Red Sox, earning more than $5000 in commissions and tips to contribute to college expenses.

Customer Relations & Service

- Addressed customer inquiries, serving as an informational resource and referring calls to appropriate staff for technical support.
- Commended by management and customers for ability to build trust and confidence, resulting in repeat business and increased sales.

EXPERIENCE:

Carpenter's Assistant • NBP, INC., Weymouth, Massachusetts • 1996-Present
Sales Associate • NATIONAL SHOES, Kingston, Massachusetts • 1995-1996
Marketing Intern • COMPUTER SOLUTIONS, Boston, Massachusetts • 1994
Sales Associate • BROWN & STEVENS, INC., Boston, MA • 1991-1994

Submitted by Louise Garver

Rebecca T. Fowler

2517 Pickwick Place ❖ Mt. Morris, MI 48458 ❖ 810-555-3541

This format allows her to organize skills from all prior jobs into key groupings.

HIGHLIGHTS OF EXPERIENCE

GENERAL SECURITY

- ❖ Responded to emergency calls for assistance.
- ❖ Performed patient watch; assisted medical staff with restraining patients as requested.
- ❖ Ensured security for and transported funds throughout the state; certified to carry and use weapon.
- ❖ Interacted with law enforcement officials and client representatives.
- ❖ Patrolled medical facility, parking lots, plants, warehouses, offices, and shipping areas.
- ❖ Checked identification and belongings of employees and visitors including international guests.
- ❖ Verified integrity of incoming and outgoing shipments.
- ❖ Tactfully responded to problems with difficult employees, patients and visitors.
- ❖ Maintained activity logs and generated reports utilizing computer system.
- ❖ Monitored alarm system and video surveillance equipment; checked for malfunctions.
- ❖ Enforced rules and regulations established by client companies; performed special assignments.

INVESTIGATION

- ❖ Conducted investigations; prepared incident and accident reports for employer and clients.
- ❖ Reviewed surveillance tapes; gathered evidence as part of investigations.
- ❖ Trained to work in non-uniformed investigation unit; identified shoplifters, collaborated with police to develop cases; testified in court.
- ❖ Assisted management in hiring process by conducting background checks.
- ❖ Collaborated with police detectives to act as decoy during investigations.

ADVOCACY

- ❖ Investigated reports of child abuse and neglect.
- ❖ Recommended alternative living arrangements such as foster care.
- ❖ Represented children in court; interacted with police, lawyers, and court officials.
- ❖ Made referrals to appropriate social service agencies.
- ❖ Conducted home visits; monitored visits between children and their families by court order.
- ❖ Ensured well being of patients such as terminally ill, mentally incompetent, suicidal, elderly.

RELEVANT EXPERIENCE

PINKERTON SECURITY SERVICES • Detroit, MI — xxxx-Present
Sergeant/Supervisor - *Assigned to Community Medical Center*
Security Guard

BRINKS TRUCKS • Southfield, MI — xxxx
Armored Courier and Guard

NATIONWIDE SERVICES. • Detroit, MI [assigned to accounts in Saginaw, MI] — xxxx-xxxx
Security Guard - *Assigned to Fenton Manufacturing* and *PepsiCo Bottling Plant*

QUALITY HEALTH PERSONNEL • Flint, MI — xxxx-xxxx
Patient Monitor – *Assigned Community Medical Center*

CONSORTIUM ON CHILD ABUSE AND NEGLECT (C/CAN) • Saginaw, MI — xxxx-xxxx
Volunteer

CITY OF SAGINAW POLICE DEPARTMENT • Saginaw, MI — xxxx
Student Intern

EDUCATION

DELTA COLLEGE • Flint, MI
Associate Degree in Applied Science - Criminal Justice — xxxx

CERTIFICATIONS & SPECIALIZED TRAINING

• CPR • First Aid • 2nd degree Green Belt in Karate

Submitted by Janet L. Beckstrom

"...[Aurora] has performed all assigned duties in a competent and efficient fashion. Her confession rate is the highest in the Polygraph Section." M.C. Kohn, Commanding Officer

EXPERTISE

Law Enforcement
▪ ▪ ▪
PDD Examinations
▪ ▪ ▪
Linguistics Analysis
▪ ▪ ▪
Forensic Hypnosis
▪ ▪ ▪
Negotiation / Interrogation
▪ ▪ ▪
Public / Media Relations
▪ ▪ ▪
Investigator Training
▪ ▪ ▪
Multiple Agency Support
▪ ▪ ▪
Public Speaking
▪ ▪ ▪
Critical Report Writing
▪ ▪ ▪
Investigative Research and Analysis
▪ ▪ ▪
Regulatory and Legal Compliance
▪ ▪ ▪
Criminal Law
▪ ▪ ▪
Public Safety
▪ ▪ ▪
Restraint Methods
▪ ▪ ▪
Stress Management

Aurora Cortes

547 Springfield Rd. ▪ St. James, NY 11780 ▪ acortes@aol.com ▪ (631) 382-2425

TARGET: CORPORATE SECURITY

Clear objective and solid content in summary.

Outstanding criminalist with 21-year progressive career in law enforcement. Ten years of superior performance as investigator / polygraph examiner utilizing extensive knowledge of interrogation techniques, polygraph questioning strategies, forensic psychophysiology and hypnosis, and linguistic analysis to determine integrity of criminal suspects and witnesses. Exemplary success rate eliciting felony crime confessions from suspects involved in arson, fraud, robbery, and sexual deviancy, to name a few. Ability to screen applicants for misrepresentation. BA in Criminal Justice.

CAREER PROGRESSION

WINSTON COUNTY POLICE DEPARTMENT, Yaphank, NY — 1983–Present

Detective / Polygraph Examiner (1990–Present)

Conduct interrogations and polygraph testing for arrested suspects and witnesses. Assess the credibility of written statements through linguistic analysis. Interview and screen law enforcement candidates to ensure upstanding backgrounds using similar techniques. Teach In-service Detective Investigator School regarding polygraph examination procedures, interrogation techniques, and stress management to classes of 50 students. Assist in-house task forces, i.e., Drug Task Force and Armed Robbery Task Force in breaking difficult cases. Requested as polygraph expert by U.S. Customs Department in high-profile crimes.

- Utilize polygraph examination questions and techniques to elicit confessions to felony crimes.
- Screen all police candidates to verify information supplied on applications.
- Examine written statements by suspects and witnesses to determine credibility; exceptional confession rate in the history of Suffolk County during tenure as Polygraph Examiner.
- Acumen for using recollection techniques and forensic hypnosis to coax additional crime scene information from witnesses.

Public Information Officer (1988–1990)

Improved Suffolk County Police Department's reputation by increasing public and community awareness through positive news stories, press releases, and press conference representation. Reported to police commissioner.

- Forged strong police-community relations through sustainable cohesive relationships with business, community, civic, and religious leaders, as well as with the media.
- Taught stress management and alcohol awareness to police officers; increased police department participation in and sponsorship of wide variety of community volunteer programs for win/win outcomes.

Highway / Police Patrol Officer (1985–1988)

Provided public safety by maintaining order, responding to emergencies, protecting people and property, enforcing motor vehicle and criminal laws, and promoting good community relations. Identified, pursued, and arrested suspects and perpetrators of criminal acts. Investigated accidents to determine causes and extenuating circumstances. Issued citations. Performed breathalyzer tests. Recorded and reported facts.

PROFESSIONAL CERTIFICATIONS & AFFILIATIONS

New York State Certified Police Instructor, Municipal Police Training Council

Member, American Polygraph Association (APA), Chattanooga, TN

EDUCATION AND TRAINING

BA in Criminal Justice, C.W. Post, Brookville, NY

Training: Department of Defense, Polygraph Institute, Ft. Jackson, SC

PDD (Psychological Detection of Deception) Polygraph Examiner
PDD (Psychological Detection of Deception) Examinations Involving Sexual Disorders
Credibility Assessment through Linguistic Analysis

Submitted by Linda Matias

Writer's comments: Richard had a breadth of experience and know-how which I highlighted by bulleting the security systems he's familiar with in the summary and later emphasizing his colorful accomplishments.

Richard London

7777 Tumbling Creek Road
Union City, CA 99999
(666) 666-6666
rlondon@yahoo.com

This approach allows him to emphasize skills from throughout his entire career.

Self-motivated Corporate Security Consultant with 10 years' experience providing design, selection, operation and monitoring of commercial security programs at a multi-site international corporation.

- Multi-level Building Access Control
- Fire and Intrusion Systems
- Contract Guard Service
- CCTV Systems
- Proprietary Control Room Operations
- Executive Home Alarm Program

Thorough knowledge of security equipment and extensive network of vendors and service providers. Regularly attend trade shows to keep current on latest technology.

Effective inter-disciplinary team member with excellent communication skills. Serve as Security Representative on project teams for new or modified facilities. Interface well at all levels with associates, law enforcement and government agencies, and other security companies.

Track record of consistent top-level performance:

> Recognized by Regional Manager as Top Performer worldwide.
> Selected for special assignment in Bogata, Columbia.
> Received numerous police commendations for solving difficult crimes.

BLACKWELL INDUSTRIES, San Jose, CA XXXX-Present
Security Consultant

Emphasis here is on his most recent and relevant experience

Develop strategies, programs, and procedures to protect company personnel and safeguard corporate facilities and assets throughout Western Region.

- Design and implement security systems for new facilities in Northern California, Oregon, Washington, and Canada. Modify/update systems for older buildings.
- Develop procedures for workplace preparedness. Train and oversee facilities' personnel in proper execution of security procedures.
- Manage disaster/emergency situations for security, scene control, logistics and liaison work with police. Conduct investigations for both internal and external crimes.
- Plan and ensure security arrangements are in place for executive travel.
- For Bogata project, met with military and embassy officials to assess risk, obtained permits, and designed system that secured a 3-square-block compound, including housing, work and recreation areas for up to 600 employees during year-long project.

SAFE-RITE INSURANCE COMPANY, San Mateo, CA XXXX-XXXX
Investigator

CITY OF ROLLING HILLS, Rolling Hills, CA XXXX-XXXX
Detective/Police Officer

Investigated and solved wide range of difficult cases.

- Commended for creative problem-solving, thoroughness, and productivity.

EDUCATION: B. A. Political Science, San Francisco State University
Computer Skills: Windows 95 and Office 97 (MS Word, Excel)

Submitted by Sydney J. Reuben

Excellent example of a combination resume with achievements noted on the first page as Career Highlights.

JANET BERENDS

5678 North Avenue • Los Angeles, CA 92009 • 619.222.9874 (H) • jberends@hotmail.com

INVESTIGATOR / FRAUD & LOSS MINIMIZATION SPECIALIST

Credit Card/Check Fraud ♦ Loss Aversion ♦ Fund Protection & Recovery ♦ Problem Resolution

15-year veteran within the banking & finance industry.

QUALIFICATIONS PROFILE

High performance, results-focused professional with exceptional insight and experience into the investigation of credit card / check fraud and implementing initiatives to minimize loss while optimizing the recovery and protection of funds for bank and clientele. Possess extensive experience and outstanding accomplishments within the banking and finance industry delivering customer service excellence to drive revenues, market growth, and overall bottom-line performance. Comprehensive insight into and full compliance with Code of Banking Practice, Privacy Act, and Discrimination and Harassment; sound knowledge of banking products, policies, and procedures.

- Investigation & Arbitration Excellence
- Loss & Fraud Minimization
- Procedural Design & Execution
- Research & Analytical Excellence
- Credit Card Fraud Prevention
- Guideline & Protocol Compliance

Computer Expertise: CAPS, Control D, CICS, Vision, Microsoft Office Suite

Good summary format makes the readers job easy.

QUALIFICATIONS & TRAINING

Code of Banking Practice ♦ Privacy Act ♦ Discrimination & Harassment ♦ Introduction to Legal Aspects of Banking ♦ Consumer Affairs & Trade Practices

Bachelor's Degree in Law ♦ NORTHEASTERN UNIVERSITY, Massachusetts

SELECTED CAREER HIGHLIGHTS

Circumvented Ombudsman/media involvement and averted losses through incisive investigative, negotiation, and arbitration competencies, and insight into distinguishing genuine from fraudulent claims, while executing strategic initiatives to secure successful outcomes without incident.

- Isolated and impeded numerous inaccurate claims for compensation against credit cards, merchant customers, and the bank by unscrupulous and often re-offending parties; investigated and interfaced with various departments/organizations to ascertain accurate occurrences; and executed strategic resolutions with full compliance to set guidelines and protocols.
- Prevented cashing of stolen checks; optimized bank's profile with large corporate client.
- Five years of experience within Fraud & Forgeries Department in a banking environment; gained exceptional understanding into operational methodologies/protocols and the establishment and maintenance of profiles for suspicious customers and account transactions.

Developed key alliances with law enforcement authorities, local community representatives, and cross-functional internal/external banking departments to facilitate achievement of goals and objectives in the prevention of fraudulent activities.

- Interfaced with local crime prevention groups in the establishment and coordination of fraud profiles on suspicious entities, patterns, and behavior, with meticulous input into comprehensive database; remained abreast of fraud activity trends.
- Provided pertinent credit card and other information to police to facilitate investigations and subsequent arrest of fraudulent credit card suspects.
- Collaborated with law enforcement authorities to ascertain and document associated crime statistics, which enhanced and optimized crime prevention within the local community.

Continued...

Submitted by Annemarie Cross

(continued)

(continued)

JANET BERENDS — Page 2

Problem-solved and defused numerous customer complaints and concerns without incident, executing strategic customer relationship management techniques to secure client satisfaction, retention, and repeat business, while upholding the bank's reputation and professional profile.

- Arbitrated diverse cases, minimizing loss/claims through tactical investigation, sound judgment, and ability to devise and implement mutually acceptable solutions; renowned for expertise in resolving issues fairly; often called upon by clients to mediate and offer advice concerning arising banking issues.
- Researched, advised, and arranged suitable banking products for customers unaware of best options to suit their needs; established rapport, trust, and recognition for banking product knowledge and expertise.
- Placated displeased client after they discovered double insurance premiums were deducted from their account over a two-year period; investigated and implemented corrective actions that successfully appeased and prevented customer from taking further action.

PROFESSIONAL EXPERIENCE

U.S. BANKING CORPORATION — 1991–Present

National Customer Liaison Officer (1995–Present)

Restore relationships with disgruntled customers over products/services or unresolved long-term issues to circumvent Ombudsman involvement. Establish and maintain strategic alliances with cross-functional departments to facilitate speedy resolution of client complaints. Maintain scrupulous records and detailed accounts of customer contact, conversations, and reactions to impede possible future claims alleging improper handling of concerns. Minimize and reduce risks for customers and the bank through remaining current with credit risk procedures in order to identify trends in fraudulent activity and subsequently expedite necessary steps.

- Achieved stringent weekly targets of finalizing 24 cases requiring outstanding research, analysis, and resolution competencies to achieve realistic win-win outcomes, thus circumventing potential costly legal action.
- Frequently awarded *Certificates of Recognition* for exceeding 100% of targets.
- Distinguished from peers by receiving the majority of formal customer compliments for going "above and beyond" the call of duty.
- Entrusted by management to present induction training programs to new recruits due to extensive retail banking and credit card knowledge. Coaching encompassed standard protocols, role expectations, and methods to balance the art of customer service with diplomatic conflict resolution.

Customer Service Officer, Head Office Contact Center (1991–1995)

Fast-track appointment to Acting Team Leader role; supervising, training, and mentoring 30 staff to maximize team performance within a complex, high-pressure customer service environment.

- Recognized for outstanding performances, possessing a record of achievement that remains unbeaten to present day for exceeding call targets and selling most banking products.
- Enhanced and revitalized call center staff performance through provision of on-the-job training in product sales and customer needs analysis; crafted scripts of suggested responses to "brick walls" or rejection. Created environment that encouraged staff's continual knowledge growth.
- Pioneered comprehensive list of "dos and don'ts" to standardize telephone protocols, improve workflow, and drive revenues and market growth.

UNITED BANKERS NOMINEES — 1988–1990

Data-Entry Operator—Settlements Department

Meticulous data entry into computerized mainframe system under pressure for rapid delivery output to achieve time-critical deadlines.

- Instrumental in capturing significant reduction in error rates, with virtual elimination of re-keying labor and overtime costs, through strategic monitoring of entries for anomalies.

Career Highlights section gets employers interested; now the Professional Experience section fills in the work history details.

Section Four

Quick Cover Letters, Thank-You Notes, JIST Cards®, and Other Job Search Correspondence

During an active job search, you will probably send out a variety of correspondence in either paper or electronic form. Resumes are typically sent with a cover letter or cover e-mail. But there are several other useful written communications that most resume books overlook.

Thank-you notes, for example, can make a big difference if used well. And JIST Cards, an innovative mini-resume format that I developed, are a powerful new job search tool. These and related forms of written communication are the focus of the two chapters in this section.

Chapters in This Section

Chapter 12: The 15-Minute Cover Letter, Plus Tips on How and When to Use It

Provides specific information on creating and using cover letters. You typically send a resume with a separate letter or e-mail that "covers" the resume. This letter often provides details that may not be included in the resume. As with resumes, a big mistake with cover letters is to use them as part of a passive job search campaign. This is when you send out lots of unsolicited resumes in either paper or electronic form. It is important to remember that cover letters are best used *after* you have made personal contact with a potential employer (by phone, e-mail, or in person) rather than as a replacement for direct contact. This chapter presents the basics of how to write cover letters that are appropriate for most situations and gives specific examples.

Chapter 13: Two of the Most Effective Job Search Tools—Thank-You Notes and JIST Cards®, Plus Other Job Search Correspondence

Discusses other important but often-overlooked job search correspondence, including thank-you notes and JIST Cards. Thank-you notes and e-mails do make a difference. If used well, they can help you be remembered positively following interviews and in many other situations throughout your job search. Believe it or not, that can make a big difference in getting or not getting job offers. This chapter also covers JIST Cards, as well as a variety of other job search correspondence including letters of reference and follow-up letters and e-mails.

Chapter 12

The 15-Minute Cover Letter, Plus Tips on How and When to Use It

This chapter provides advice on writing cover letters and includes various samples. I've tried to keep this basic, with an emphasis on letters that are sent after you have made some sort of personal contact with an employer. That's because letters—just like resumes—won't get you a job offer. Interviews do.

Writing a simple cover letter is pretty simple. Once you know how it's done, you should be able to write one in about 15 minutes or so.

It is not appropriate to send a resume to someone without explaining why. Whether you're mailing, faxing, or e-mailing your resume, it is important to provide a letter along with your resume—a cover letter (or cover message, in the case of e-mailing). Even when you post your resume in an online database (also known as a resume bank), the Web site where you're posting often has a place where you can upload or paste a cover letter. (You can learn more about Internet job searching in Chapter 15.) Depending on the circumstances, the letter would explain your situation and would ask the recipient for some specific action, consideration, or response.

Entire books discuss the art of writing cover letters. Some authors go into great detail on how to construct "powerful" cover letters. Some suggest that a cover letter can replace a resume by providing information specifically targeted to the person receiving it. While these ideas have merit, my objective here is to give you a simple, quick review of cover letter basics that will meet most needs.

Quick Tip

While most people think of a resume as one in printed form and a cover letter as a traditional letter on paper, I trust you will understand that these things can also be sent as e-mail or an attachment.

Only Two Groups of People Will Receive Your Cover Letters

If you think about it, you will send a resume and cover letter to only two groups of people:

- People you know.
- People you don't know.

While I realize this sounds overly simple, it's true. And this observation makes it easier to understand how to structure your letters to each group. Before I show you some useful and effective cover letter samples for both groups, let's first review some basics regarding writing cover letters in general.

Quick Reference

While many situations require writing a formal letter, a simple note will do in many instances (for example, when you know the person you are writing to). Chapter 13 gives additional information on writing informal notes.

Seven Quick Tips for Writing a Superior Cover Letter in 15 Minutes

No matter who you are writing to, virtually every good cover letter should follow these guidelines:

1. Write to Someone in Particular

Never send a cover letter "To whom it may concern" or use some other impersonal opening. We all get enough junk mail, and if you don't send your letter to someone by name, it will be treated like junk mail.

2. Make Absolutely No Errors

One way to offend people quickly is to misspell their names or use incorrect titles. If you have any question, call and verify the correct spelling of the name and other details before you send the letter. Also, review your letters carefully to be sure they contain no typographical, grammatical, or other errors.

3. Personalize Your Content

I've never been impressed by form letters, and you should not use them. Those computer-generated letters that automatically insert a name (merge mailings) never fool anyone, and I find cover letters done in this way offensive. While some resume and cover letter books recommend that you send out lots of these "broadcast letters" to people you don't know, you will most likely find that doing so wastes time and money. Small, targeted mailings or e-mailings to a carefully selected group of prospective employers can be effective if you tailor your cover letter to each recipient, but large mass mailings are a waste of time.

4. Present a Good Appearance

> If you can't personalize your letter in some way, don't send it.

Your contacts with prospective employers should always be professional, so buy good quality stationery and matching envelopes for times when you'll be mailing or hand-delivering a letter and resume. Use papers and envelopes that match or complement your resume paper. The standard 8½ × 11 paper size is typically used, but you can also use the smaller Monarch-size paper with matching envelopes. For colors, I recommend white, ivory, or light beige that matches your resume paper.

Quick Alert

Cover letters are almost never handwritten anymore; employers expect them to be word processed and produced with excellent print quality. So don't send a handwritten cover letter!

Use a standard letter format that complements your resume type and format. Most word-processing software provides templates or "wizards" to automate your letter's format and design. I used such templates to create the formats for the sample letters in this chapter. And don't forget the envelope! It should be typed and printed carefully, without abbreviations or errors.

5. Provide a Friendly Opening

Begin your letter with a reminder of any prior contacts and the reason for your correspondence now. The examples later in this chapter will give you some ideas on how to handle this.

6. Target Your Skills and Experiences

To do this well, you must know something about the organization or person with whom you are dealing. Present any relevant background you have that may be of particular interest to the person to whom you are writing.

7. Close with an Action Statement

Don't close your letter without clearly identifying what you will do next. I do not recommend that you leave it up to the employer to contact you, since that doesn't guarantee a response. Close on a positive note and let the employer know you desire further contact.

Quick Reference

Using a few simple techniques, it is possible to make the acquaintance of all sorts of people. That's why I say that it wastes time and money to send your resume or cover letter to strangers—it is relatively easy to make direct contact. Chapter 14 provides details on how to make contact with people you don't know.

Writing Cover Letters to People You Know

It is always best if you know the person to whom you are writing. As I have said elsewhere, any written correspondence is less effective than personal contact, so the ideal circumstance is to send a resume and cover letter after having spoken with the person directly.

For example, it is far more effective to first call someone who has advertised a job in the paper than to simply send a letter and resume. You can come to know people through the Yellow Pages, personal referrals, and other ways. You might not have known them yesterday, but you can get to know them today.

So, for the purposes of teaching you good job search principles, I'll assume you have made some sort of personal contact before sending your resume. Within this assumption are hundreds of variations, but I will review the most common situations and let you adapt them to your own circumstances.

The Four Types of Cover Letters to People You Know

When sending cover letters to people you know, you will be in one of four basic situations described here. Each situation requires a different approach. I'll provide sample cover letters for each situation later in this chapter.

1. **An interview is scheduled, and a specific job opening may interest you.** In this case, you have already arranged an interview for a job opening that interests you, and the cover letter should provide details of your experience that relate to the specific job.

2. **An interview is scheduled, but no specific job is available.** In Chapter 14, I will explain in more detail why this situation is such a good one for you to set up. In essence, this is a letter you will send for an exploratory interview to negotiate an appointment with an employer who does not have a specific opening for you now but who might in the future. This is fertile ground for finding job leads where no one else may be looking.

3. **After an interview takes place.** Many people overlook the importance of sending a letter after an interview. This is a time to say that you want the job (if that is the case, your letter should say so) and to add any details on why you think you can do the job well.

4. **No interview is scheduled yet.** There are situations where you just can't arrange an interview before you send a resume and cover letter. For example, you may be trying to see a person whose name was given to you by a friend, but that person is on vacation. In these cases, sending a good cover letter and resume make any later contacts more effective.

The four types of cover letters illustrate an approach that can be used in getting interviews, which is the real task in the job search. Look at the samples for each type of cover letter and see how, in most cases, they assume that personal contact has been made before the resume was sent.

Sample Cover Letters to People You Know

The following are sample cover letters for the four situations. Note that they use different formats and styles to show you the range of styles that are appropriate. Each addresses a different situation, and each incorporates all of the cover letter writing guidelines from the preceding section of this chapter.

I hope that these samples give you ideas on writing your own cover letters. Once you get the hang of it, you should be able to write a simple cover letter in about 15 minutes. Just keep in mind that the best cover letter is one that follows you having set up an interview. Anything else is just second best, at best.

Figure 12-1: Sample cover letter, pre-interview, for a specific job opening.

Comments: This writer called first and arranged an interview, which is the best approach. Note how this new graduate included a specific example of how he saved money for a business by changing its procedures. Though it is not clear from the letter, his experience with lots of people was gained by working as a waiter. Note also how he included skills such as "hard worker" and "deadline pressure" that I reviewed in Chapter 5.

Richard Swanson
113 South Meridian
Greenwich, Connecticut 11721

March 10, XXXX

Mr. William Hines
New England Power and Light Company
604 Waterway Boulevard
Parien, Connecticut 11716

Dear Mr. Hines:

I am following up on the brief chat we had today by phone. After getting the details on the position you have open, I am certain that it is the kind of job I have been looking for. A copy of my resume is enclosed providing more details of my background. I hope you have a chance to review it before we meet next week.

My special interest has long been in the large-volume order processing systems that your organization has developed so well. While in school, I researched the flow of order processing work for a large corporation as part of a class assignment. With some simple and inexpensive procedural changes I recommended, check-processing time was reduced by an average of three days. For the number of checks and dollars involved, this one change resulted in an estimated increase in interest revenues of over $35,000 per year.

While I have recently graduated from business school, I have considerable experience for a person of my age. I have worked in a variety of jobs dealing with large numbers of people and deadline pressures. My studies have also been far more "hands-on" and practical than those of most schools, so I have a good working knowledge of current business systems and procedures. This includes a good understanding of various computer spreadsheet and applications programs, the use of automation, and experience with cutting costs and increasing profits. I am also a hard worker and realize I will need to apply myself to get established in my career.

I am most interested in the position you have available and am excited about the potential it offers. I look forward to seeing you next week. If you need to reach me before then, you can call me at (973) 299–3643 or email me at rswanson@msn.net.

Sincerely,

Richard Swanson

Figure 12-2: Sample cover letter, pre-interview, no specific job opening.

Comments: This letter indicates that the writer first called and set up an interview as the result of someone else's tip. The writer explains why she is moving to the city and asks for help in making contacts there. While no job opening exists here, she is wise in assuming that there might be one in the future. Even if this is not the case, she asks the employer to think of others who might have a position for someone with her skills. Assuming that the interview goes well and the employer gives her names of others to call, she can then follow up with them.

ANNE MARIE ROAD

February 20, XXXX

Ms. Francine Cook
Park-Halsey Corporation
5413 Armstrong Drive
Minneapolis, Minnesota 56317

Dear Ms. Cook:

When Steve Marks suggested I call you, I had no idea you would be so helpful. I've already followed up with several of the suggestions you made and am now looking forward to meeting with you next Tuesday. The resume I've enclosed is to give you a better sense of my qualifications. Perhaps it will help you think of other organizations that may be interested in my background.

The resume does not say why I've moved to Minneapolis and you may find that of interest. My spouse and I visited the city several years ago and thought it a good place to live. He has obtained a very good position here and, based on that, we decided it was time to commit ourselves to a move.

As you can see from my work experience, I tend to stay on and move up in jobs, so I now want to research the job opportunities here more carefully before making a commitment. Your help in this task is greatly appreciated.

Feel free to contact me at (834) 264-3720 if you have any questions; otherwise, I look forward to meeting with you next Tuesday.

Sincerely,

Anne Marie Road

616 KINGS WAY ROAD
MINNEAPOLIS, MINNESOTA 54312
(834) 264-3720

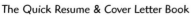

Figure 12-3: Sample cover letter, after an interview.

Comments: This letter shows how you might follow up after an informational interview and make a pitch for solving a problem—even when no job formally exists. In this example, the writer suggests that she can use her skills to solve a specific problem she uncovered during her conversation with the employer. Although it never occurs to many job seekers to set up an interview where there appears to be no job opening, jobs are created as a result of such interviews.

Sandra A. Zaremba

115 South Hawthorn Drive
Dunwoody, Georgia 21599

April 10, XXXX

Ms. Christine Massey
Import Distributors, Inc.
417 East Main Street
Atlanta, Georgia 21649

Dear Ms. Massey:

I know you have a busy schedule so I was pleasantly surprised when you arranged a time for me to see you. While you don't have a position open now, your organization is just the sort of place I would like to work. As we discussed, I like to be busy with a variety of duties and the active pace I saw at your company is what I seek.

Your ideas on increasing business sound creative. I've thought about the customer service problem and would like to discuss a possible solution. It would involve the use of a simple system of color-coded files that would prioritize correspondence to give older requests priority status. The handling of complaints could also be speeded up through the use of simple form letters similar to those you mentioned. I have some thoughts on how this might be done too, and I will work out a draft of procedures and sample letters if you are interested. It can be done on the computers your staff already uses and would not require any additional cost to implement.

Whether or not you have a position for me in the future, I appreciate the time you have given me. An extra copy of my resume is enclosed for your files—or to pass on to someone else.

Let me know if you want to discuss the ideas I presented earlier in this letter. I can be reached at any time on my cell phone at (942) 267-1103. I will call you next week, as you suggested, to keep you informed of my progress.

Sincerely,

Sandra A. Zaremba

Figure 12-4: Sample cover letter, no interview is scheduled.

Comments: This letter explains why the person is looking for a job as well as presents additional information that would not normally be included in a resume. Note that the writer obtained the employer's name from the membership list of a professional organization, one excellent source of job leads. Also note that the writer stated that he would call again to arrange an appointment. Although this letter might turn off some employers, many others would be impressed with his assertiveness and willing to see him. The JIST Card mentioned in this letter can be found in Chapter 13.

8661 Bay Drive
Tempe, Arizona 27317
827-994-2765

Justin Moore

January 5, XXXX

Ms. Doris Michaelmann
Michaelmann Clothing
8661 Parkway Boulevard
Phoenix, Arizona 27312

Dear Ms. Michaelmann:

As you may know, I phoned you several times over the past week while you were in meetings. I hope that you received the messages. Since I did not want to delay contacting you, I decided to write. I got your name from the American Retail Clothing Association membership list. I am a member of this group and wanted to contact local members to ask their help in locating a suitable position. I realize that you probably don't have an available position for someone with my skills, but I ask you to do two things on my behalf.

First, I ask that you consider seeing me at your convenience within the next few weeks. Though you may not have a position available for me, you may be able to assist me in other ways. And, of course, I would appreciate any consideration for future openings. Second, you may know of others who have job openings now or might possibly have them in the future.

While I realize that this is an unusual request and that you are quite busy, I do plan on staying in the retail clothing business in this area for some time and would appreciate any assistance you can give me in my search for a new job.

My resume is attached for your information along with a "JIST Card" that summarizes my background. As you probably know, Allied Tailoring has closed and I stayed on to shut things down in an orderly way. Despite their regrettable business failure, I was one of those responsible for Allied's enormous sales increases over the past decade and have substantial experience to bring to any growing retail clothing concern, such as I hear yours is.

I will contact you next week and arrange a time that is good for us both. Please feel free to contact me at any time regarding this matter. You can reach me on my beeper by calling 827-994-2765 and entering your phone number or leaving a voice message.

Sincerely,

Justin Moore

Writing Cover Letters to People You Don't Know

If it is not practical to directly contact a prospective employer by phone or some other method, it is acceptable to send a resume and cover letter. This approach makes sense in some situations, such as if you are moving to a distant location or responding to a blind ad offering only a post office box number.

The approach of sending out "To Whom It May Concern" letters by the basketful has been discussed elsewhere in this book. I do not recommend it.

Sending an unsolicited resume can make sense in some situations, and there are ways to modify this "shotgun" approach to be more effective. For example, try to find something you have in common with the person you are contacting. By mentioning this link, your letter then becomes a very personal request for assistance. Look at the two letters that follow for ideas.

Quick Reminder

These letters were formatted using templates from popular word-processing programs and then printed on good paper using a laser printer. Using templates takes away the worry of how your cover letters look. You can concentrate on making your letters sound great! Another benefit is that you will spend less time working on your correspondence and more time getting interviews.

Figure 12-5: Response to a want ad.

Comments: This letter does a good job of outlining the candidate's credentials as relevant to the position advertised. The bullet points give the reader a quick overview of his qualifications. Then more detail is provided in case the reader cares to know more before turning to the resume. (Letter submitted by Myriam-Rose Kohn.)

GORDON STRAW

straw@netzero.net

3731 Honeysuckle Hill — Bellingham, Washington 98225-2006 — (360) 731-5704

September 30, 2005

Illusion Software, Inc.
Seattle, Washington

Reference ID: 2051-3
Project Manager

Throughout my Project Management career, I have provided the strategic and tactical leadership to accelerate revenue and earnings gains for high-growth, technology-based corporations. Highlights include the following:

- More than 15 years of top-flight project management experience with leading high-technology corporations.
- Extensive project management and business development in the U.S. and Europe.
- Strong technical qualifications and experience with mainframe, mid- to high-range technologies, global information networks, numerous operating systems, and virtually all leading software packages.
- Created the RUMBA Developer and Web-to-Host Editions.

I am direct and decisive in my leadership style, yet flexible in responding to constantly changing markets, economies, and competitors. I set and drive clear priorities and can work autonomously as well as part of a team. I built and led U.S. and multinational teams responsible for product development, marketing, sales, technical support, internal MIS, human resources, and administration. I possess outstanding qualifications in all facets of the project lifecycle development from initial feasibility analysis and conceptual design through documentation, implementation, user training, and enhancement; my projects have always been completed on time (even while meeting tight deadlines) and within budget.

With a unique blend of MIS and general management experience, I have positioned each technology organization as a key partner to the operating management team, responding to their specific needs and recommending proactive systems solutions. Most recently, I transitioned my experience into non-profits, providing them with competitive technologies to drive performance improvement.

Currently, I am exploring new professional challenges and opportunities. The enclosed resume shows I meet most of your requirements for this position; therefore, I would welcome a personal interview to explore your needs for a strong and decisive project manager.

Thank you for your consideration.

Sincerely,

Gordon Straw

Enclosure

Figure 12-6: Unsolicited resume sent to obtain an interview.

Comments: This is an example of a person conducting a long-distance job search using names obtained from a professional association, which is a good strategy. This letter also explains why he is leaving his old job and includes positive information regarding his references and skills that would not normally be found in a resume. John asks for an interview even though there may not be any jobs open now, and also asks for names of others to contact.

July 10, XXXX

Mr. Paul Resley
Operations Manager
Rollem Trucking Co.
I-70 Freeway Drive
Kansas City, Missouri 78401

Mr. Resley:

I obtained your name from the membership directory of the Affiliated Trucking Association. I have been a member for over 10 years, and I am very active in the Southeast Region. The reason I am writing is to ask for your help. The firm I had been employed with has been bought by a larger corporation. The operations here have been disbanded, leaving me unemployed.

While I like where I live, I know that finding a position at the level of responsibility I seek may require a move. As a center of the transportation business, your city is one I have targeted for special attention. A copy of my resume is enclosed for your use. I'd like you to review it and consider where a person with my background would get a good reception in Kansas City. Perhaps you could think of a specific person for me to contact?

I have specialized in fast-growing organizations or ones that have experienced rapid change. My particular strength is in bringing things under control, then increasing profits. While my resume does not state this, I have excellent references from my former employer and would have stayed if a similar position existed at its new location.

As a member of the association, I hoped that you would provide some special attention to my request for assistance. I plan on coming to Kansas City on a job-hunting trip within the next six weeks. Prior to my trip I will call you for advice on who I might contact for interviews. Even if they have no jobs open for me now, perhaps they will know of someone else who does.

My enclosed resume lists my phone number and other contact information should you want to reach me before I call you. Thanks in advance for your help on this.

Sincerely,

John B. Goode
Treasurer, Southeast Region
Affiliated Trucking Association

John B. Goode

312 Smokie Way Nashville, Tennessee 31201

Additional Sample Cover Letters

I've included some additional cover letters that address a variety of situations. While the formats are not fancy, they are acceptable and quick.

Figure 12-7: No interview is scheduled.

947 Cherry Street
Middleville, Ohio 01234

October 22, XXXX

Mr. Alfred E. Newman, President
Alnew Consolidated Stores, Inc.
1 Newman Place
New City, OK 03000

Dear Mr. Newman:

I am interested in the position of national sales director, which you recently advertised in the *Retail Sales and Marketing* newsletter.

I am very familiar with your company's innovative marketing techniques as well as your enlightened policy in promoting and selling environmentally sound merchandise nationwide. I have been active for some time now in environmental protection projects, both as a representative of my current employer and on my own. I recently successfully introduced a new line of kitchen products that exceeds federal standards, is environmentally safe, and is selling well.

The enclosed resume outlines my experience and skills in both sales and marketing in the retail field. I would like to meet with you to discuss how my skills would benefit Alnew Consolidated Stores. I will contact you soon to request an interview for current or future positions and may be reached at (513) 987-6543.

Thank you for your time and consideration.

Sincerely,

Robin Redding

Figure 12-8: Pre-interview, no specific job opening.

Lisa Marie Farkel

3321 Haverford Road
Baldwin, North Carolina 12294

Email: lfarkel@dotcom.net
Phone: 400-541-0877
FAX: 400-541-0988

March 15, XXXX

Mr. Howard Duty
WXLC TV
10212 North Oxford Avenue
Halstead, South Carolina 12456

Dear Mr. Duty:

Thank you for agreeing to meet with me at 3 p.m. on March 23rd to talk about job opportunities for broadcast technicians. Although I understand that you have no openings right now, I'm enclosing my resume to give you some information about my training and background.

You will see that I have worked on both up-to-date and as well as older equipment. Working part time for a small station, I've learned to monitor, adjust, and repair a variety of equipment including both the newer automated and computerized items as well as the older ones. Keeping a mix of older and newer equipment working smoothly has required me to learn many things and has been an invaluable experience. At Halstead Junior College, I have become the person to call if the new, state-of-the-art audio and video equipment does not perform as it should.

I look forward to graduating and devoting all my time and energy to my career. Your help is greatly appreciated, particularly your invitation to spend more time observing field operations during your live election coverage.

Sincerely,

Lisa Marie Farkel

P.S. I found your Web site and was *very* impressed that you did most of the work on it. You may be interested to know that I have created a Web site for our college TV station. If you have time, you can find it at halstead.edu/WNCSTV —I'd like your feedback!

Enclosure: resume

Figure 12-9: No interview is scheduled.

JANE MAEYERS
123 Alexandria Drive
Alexandria, Louisiana 71409
(318) 443-0101

October 23, XXXX

Attention: Ms. Brenda Barnes
Coordinator of Student Activities
Screening Committee
Coldgate University
Campus Box 7
Emporia, Kansas 66801

RE: Position as Coordinator of Student
Activities Organization & Special Events,
or related position

Dear Screening Committee:

I have planned, developed, supervised, taught, and successfully completed numerous tasks assigned to me in my 10 years of experience as a recreation specialist. Now I'm ready to apply the same expertise and principles of hard work in starting a productive and challenging career as Coordinator of Student Activities Organization & Special Events, or related position, with your organization. Because this position matches my interests, qualifications, work, and education experience, I can be a productive and valuable director from day one.

The resume enclosed also outlines all the details of my career background as a recreation specialist. With these credentials and my belief in quality hard work, I will make a significant contribution to Coldgate University.

I am looking forward to working with your organization and would appreciate the opportunity to discuss employment opportunities with you soon.

Please inform by letter or call (318) 443-0101 to arrange a time when we can meet at your convenience. I can also be contacted via email at jmaey@alexu.edu.net. Thank you for your time and consideration.

Sincerely,

Jane Maeyers

Figure 12-10: No interview is scheduled.

ROBERT P. BARNES, CBCP
Certified Business Continuity Professional

1434 Madison Boulevard
Orlando, FL 38917
Residence: 954-555-1212
Mobile: 954-555-1212
RobertPBarnes@earthlink.net

April 8, 2005

Samuel Ryan, CIO
Global Financial Services, Inc.
495 Central Avenue
Orlando, FL 38917

Dear Mr. Ryan:

Development of a comprehensive, state-of-the-industry business-continuity program is critical to a company's ability to achieve its core mission. Employee safety, shareholder value, corporate reputation, revenues and profits, data integrity, and IT systems—these are some of the corporate interests that an effective business continuity program is designed to protect. My expertise is the ability to deliver, within a complex multinational organization, innovative business-continuity plans that are integrated with overall corporate strategy and aligned with corporate goals.

In my work as Business Recovery Manager at Morgan Summers Financial Services, I established just such a program. My groundbreaking thinking and writing promotes business-continuity planning as a strategic, business-driven process in which IT plays a supporting role. My contributions helped ensure that the company would mitigate risk, survive potential disruptions, and recover in a timely manner. Achievements included the following:

— Developed and executed business-continuity plans for an organization with $176 billion in assets under management, 40 business units, 800 employees, and 19 different IT systems running 200 applications.

— Promoted my visionary concept of the role of business-continuity planning throughout the organization and achieved buy-in for plan initiatives from 40 business units (including 6 IT business units) and 2 disaster-recovery vendors.

— Implemented a multifaceted employee-awareness program to help ensure that employees knew how to implement plans in the event of a business disruption.

I came up through the ranks as an IT professional and earned both my M.B.A. degree and my Bachelor's degree in Business Computer Information Systems. As an experienced BCP manager who is a Certified Business Continuity Professional, I am well credentialed for assuming a leadership position in business-continuity planning.

Please contact me if you are interested in my demonstrated ability to help a company mitigate risk and protect critical assets. I look forward to an opportunity to speak with you in person about your business requirements and will call you next week to set a mutually convenient time. Thank you.

Sincerely,

Robert P. Barnes

Enclosure

Submitted by Jean Cummings.

Figure 12-11: Pre-interview, for a specific job opening.

1768 South Carrollton Street
Nashville, Tennessee 96050
May 26, XXXX

Ms. Karen Miller
Office Manager
Lendon, Lendon, and Sears
Suite 101, Landmark Building
Summit, New Jersey 11736

Dear Ms. Miller:

Enclosed is a copy of my resume that describes my work experience as a legal assistant. I hope this information will be helpful as background for our interview next Monday at 4 p.m.

I appreciate your taking time to describe your requirements so fully. This sounds like a position that could develop into a satisfying career. And my training in accounting—along with experience using a variety of computer programs—seems to match your needs.

Lendon, Lendon, and Sears is a highly respected name in New Jersey. I am excited about this opportunity and I look forward to meeting with you.

Sincerely,

Richard Wittenberg

Figure 12-12: No interview is scheduled.

ALBAROSA BARTON
12603 SOUTH 33RD STREET
OMAHA, NEBRASKA 68123
PHONE (402) 292-9052
FAX (402) 393-0099
EMAIL ALBAROSA@OFCORPS.COM

March 30, XXXX

YALE BUSINESS SERVICES
Alexander Bell, Director of Human Resources
1005 Denver Street, Suite 1
Bellevue, Nebraska 68005-4145

Dear Mr. Bell:

I am enclosing a copy of my resume for your consideration and would like to call your attention to the skills and achievements in my background that are most relevant.

I am an achiever, with four years of experience as a highly successful administrator. I've always set high standards and consistently achieved my goals. I've served in the United States Air Force since February 1998 as an Administrative Specialist/Assistant. I acquired my training through the excellent programs the Air Force provides. I am highly motivated and would be a dynamic administrator for whatever company I represent.

I am confident in my administrative abilities and have already proven myself in the areas of office administration and customer relations.

I look forward to hearing from you soon and having the opportunity to discuss your needs and plans.

Cordially,

ALBAROSA BARTON

Figure 12-13: No interview is scheduled.

4550 Parrier Street
Espinosa, California 44478

September 11, XXXX

Mr. Craig Schmidt
District Manager
Desert Chicken Shops
Post Office Box 6230
Los Angeles, California 98865

Dear Mr. Schmidt:

My resume (enclosed) outlines my four years of successful experience as a fast food manager with a nationwide network of restaurants. I graduated from a Restaurant Management curriculum at Harman University with a 3.75 GPA in 1998.

I have been impressed with the rapid growth and exceptional quality of product and service for which Desert Chicken has become well known. This is the kind of organization I hope to work for now.

My experience includes positions as cook, night manager, assistant manager, and manager for my current employer.

I will call your office in a few days to see if we might schedule a convenient time to meet and discuss some areas of mutual interest.

Thanks very much for your consideration.

Sincerely,

Douglas Parker

Enclosure

Figure 12-14: No interview is scheduled.

Patricia R. Coleman

584 Glascott Avenue ❖ Bloomfield Hills, MI 48323 ❖ 248-555-9146

October 19, 2005

Starboard Cruise Services
Attention: Human Resources
8052 N.W. 14th Street
Miami, FL 33126

Dear Recruiter:

Outgoing. Personable. Upbeat. Customer service–focused. Professional appearance. Youthful. Hardworking. Dynamic.

Aren't these just a few of the traits you look for in applicants for shipboard positions? If so, I hope you will review my credentials. I am extremely excited about this opportunity to apply for a position in a guest service capacity. My resume highlighting my extensive background in sales and customer service is enclosed.

I have been interacting with customers since I was 10 years old and began helping out in my parents' store. The work ethic I grew up with is now engrained in me. As you can see from my resume, the breadth of my experience includes customer service, retail store operations and management. You will find that one of my greatest assets is the level of customer service I provide, not to mention my strong performance in sales. Additionally, I believe my personal attributes meet your expectations for crew members (I am single, 5'5", 120 lbs. and turn 21 this month).

I am confident my background is a great match for your reputation in the cruise industry, and I am ready to meet the high customer care standards which you set. I will call next week to make an appointment to see you and share my enthusiasm for this position. Thank you for your time and consideration.

Sincerely,

Patricia R. Coleman

Enclosure

Submitted by Janet Beckstrom.

Figure 12-15: No interview is scheduled.

JASON R. GOODSON

1843 Lake Johanna Blvd. Roseville, MN 55112 651-555-6633

August 31, 2005

Mr. Robert McCarthy, Director of Personnel
Roseville Area Schools
1251 W. County Road B2
Roseville, MN 55113

Dear Mr. McCarthy:

Thank you for this opportunity to formally express my interest in the Athletic Director position. I appreciated Bill Murphy's suggestion that I apply, especially because Bill is familiar with my abilities through our collaboration on Roseville's football coaching staff last fall. I understand you have my resume on file.

My qualifications for this position closely match those listed in your posting:

Desired Qualifications	*My Qualifications*
☐ M.A. in Education or School Administration	☒ M.A. in Secondary Administration from U-M.
☐ Minimum 5 years teaching experience	☒ Almost 10 years as classroom teacher.
☐ Outstanding leadership and personal qualifications	☒ Spearheaded drive for state-of-the-art health & fitness facility and monitored its construction. Developed and presented motivational program on interpersonal skills to high school students, families, and educators.
☐ Successful coaching experience at varsity level	☒ 9 years as varsity football coach. Led team to State Semifinals. Received Tri-State Athletic League Coaches award as second-year coach.
☐ Excellence in organizational skills and problem-solving strategies	☒ Effectively balance roles as teacher, coach, and parent. Evaluated and implemented strategies to turn around poor-performing team to reach its first 7-consecutive-win season in 27 years.
☐ Mental/physical ability and stamina	☒ Actively participate in personal health and fitness plan to ensure peak performance.

Throughout my career as an educator and coach, I have recognized the importance of my position as a role model and motivator for students. But I also relate well to parents and humbly state that I have an excellent reputation among game officials and coaching peers within Ramsey County.

I welcome the chance to speak with the Selection Committee about this position so that I can elaborate on my enthusiasm and commitment to Roseville Area Schools. I will call next week to set up an interview. Thank you again for this opportunity.

Sincerely,

Jason R. Goodson

Submitted by Janet Beckstrom.

Figure 12-16: Response to an ad.

JILL LAFLEUR
2101 Sweet Meadow Drive, Tampa, Florida 33624
813-687-6415 • Jlafleur@aol.com

RE: PHARMACEUTICAL SALES REPRESENTATIVE POSITION

July 1, 2005

careers@pharmaceuticalrecruit.com
ATTN: Pharmaceutical Recruiters
4020 Green Mount Crossing Drive
Suite 330
Fairview Heights, IL 62269

Dear Hiring Professional:

In response to your search for an entry-level pharmaceutical sales representative, I am ready to start my career!

I have several years of experience in health care and am used to working with doctors and nurses in a busy, hectic hospital setting. I recently earned my bachelor's degree in Biology and am looking to combine my academic knowledge and love of learning with my interest in health care and my goal of becoming an outstanding pharmaceutical sales rep.

Here is how I meet/exceed your needs listed in the job posting:

- *Diverse, dynamic professional:* I've held a variety of jobs in and out of the health care field, coupled with a degree in Psychology.
- *Verifiable record of achievement:* My 5-year employment at St. Joseph's Women's Hospital and my excellent and respected standing as an employee show my ability to stick with a job, be reliable, and be goal oriented.
- *Level-headed, competitive, assertive, self-motivated, one who works well independently, computer literate, and possesses a high energy level:* People who have worked with me will state I am all these things. In fact, my positions as a Patient Care Technician and Certified Nursing Assistant have demanded these exact qualities.
- *Call on physicians, hospitals, pharmacies, and other caregivers:* I currently work in a fast-paced medical-care setting, where relationships have to be built and maintained. I use my relationship-building and persuasive skills daily with medical professionals and patients.
- *Able to comply with legal and regulatory requirements governing the sale and promotion of the company's pharmaceutical products:* Working in a hospital requires knowledge of and compliance with many different legal and bureaucratic policies and procedures. I am used to navigating myriad important requirements.

My resume provides further details of my accomplishments. I look forward to discussing a new career opportunity with you. If I don't hear from you, I will contact you next week to arrange a meeting to discuss your company's needs in greater detail.

Sincerely,

Jill LaFleur

Enclosure

Submitted by Gail Frank.

Figure 12-17: Career changer.

LISA ANN CRAMMER

3550 Sunglow Drive • Oroville, CA 96221 • 533-226-5896

March 23, 2005

Wendy Templeton, Human Resources Director
Northern California Regional Hospital
2801 Evergreen Way
Oroville, CA 96221

Dear Ms. Templeton:

After recently completing billing, coding, and medical terminology courses through the Meditec Support Services Training Program, I am currently exploring medical coding, billing, and records opportunities where I can utilize my strengths in program development, organization, and researching. After reviewing your company website, I have decided to contact you about possible job openings within your organization.

Two things really stood out and impressed me about your company. The first is your dedication to fostering positive relationships with both your patients and employees. Coming from a background in special education, I have always believed this to be the most essential goal for creating an environment where individuals can flourish and reach their fullest potential. The second thing that impressed me was your mission to provide personal and attentive care to every patient and his or her family. It is important for me to work for a company where patients' personal needs and well-being take top priority.

As you will see from my enclosed resume, I have completed my medical coding and billing training in the top tenth percentile of all students who have ever gone through the Meditec program. I am very detail oriented with strong research and analytical skills. As a resource specialist I utilized these skills on a daily basis. Through the detailed analysis of student work and test scores, I was able to create personalized learning experiences for learning-disabled students, which allowed them to learn important skills by maximizing their own unique learning capabilities.

These strengths will also be important for me to utilize in the medical support services area. As a medical support services employee, I will be committed to paying thorough attention to the details of my job, as I fully understand the importance of carefully examining all data when dealing with personal and confidential medical records and insurance forms. The ability to analyze data and extract the most specific and important information from coding references and other materials can greatly affect reimbursement payments and can have a significant influence upon compliance issues as well.

Should you have a need for someone with my qualifications and experience, please contact me at 533-226-5896. I look forward to hearing from you and will follow up next week by phone. Thank you for your time.

Sincerely,

Lisa Ann Crammer

Enclosure

Submitted by Carla Barnett.

Chapter 13

Two of the Most Effective Job Search Tools—Thank-You Notes and JIST Cards®, Plus Other Job Search Correspondence

Much of the information in this chapter is often overlooked in resume books. That is too bad, since in my experience thank-you notes are a very effective job search tool. So are JIST Cards. Other related correspondence can also play an important part in a quick, successful job search.

So give attention to this chapter's tips and tools. It is short but important.

The Importance of Thank-You Notes

While resumes and cover letters get the attention, thank-you notes often get results. That's right. Sending thank-you notes makes both good manners and good job search sense. When used properly, thank-you notes can help you create a positive impression with employers that more formal correspondence often can't.

So, in just a few pages, here are the basics of writing and using thank-you notes.

Three Times When You Should Definitely Send Thank-You Notes—and Why

Thank-you notes have a more intimate and friendly social tradition than formal and manipulative business correspondence. I think that is one reason they work so well—people respond to those who show good manners and say thank you. Here are some situations when you should use them, along with some sample notes.

1. Before an Interview

In some situations, you can send a less formal note before an interview, usually by e-mail unless the interview is scheduled for a fairly distant future date. For example, you can simply thank someone for being willing to see you. Depending on the situation, enclosing a resume could be a bit inappropriate. Remember, this is supposed to be sincere thanks for help and not an assertive business situation. This also serves as a way to confirm the date and time of the scheduled interview and as a gentle reminder to the recipient that you will be showing up at that time.

QUICK TIP

Enclose a JIST Card with your thank-you notes. You can find JIST Card samples later in this chapter and in Chapter 3. JIST Cards fit well into a note-sized envelope, and they provide key information an employer can use to contact you. JIST Cards also list key skills and other credentials that will help you create a good impression. And the employer might forward the card to someone who might have a job opening for you.

Figure 13-1: Sample thank-you note 1, before an interview.

April 5, 20XX

Ms. Kijek,

Thanks so much for your willingness to see me next Wednesday at 9 a.m.

I know that I am one of many who are interested in working with your organization, but I'm confident that you'll find my qualifications are a good fit for the role. I've enclosed a JIST Card that presents the basics of my skills for this job and will bring my resume to the interview.

I appreciate the opportunity to meet you and learn more about the position. Please call me if you have any questions at all.

Sincerely,

Bruce Vernon

2. After an Interview

One of the best times to send a thank-you note is right after an interview. Here are several reasons why:

- Doing so creates a positive impression. The employer will assume you have good follow-up skills—to say nothing of good manners.
- It creates yet another opportunity for you to remain in the employer's consciousness at an important time.
- It gives you a chance to get in the last word. You get to include a subtle reminder of why you're the best candidate for the job and can even address any concerns that might have come up during the interview.
- Should they have buried, passed along, or otherwise lost your resume and previous correspondence, a thank-you note and corresponding JIST Card provide one more chance for employers to find your number and call you.

For these reasons, I suggest you send a thank-you note right after the interview and certainly within 24 hours. The following is an example of such a note.

Figure 13-2: Sample thank-you note 2, after an interview.

August 11, 20XX

Dear Mr. O'Beel,

Thank you for the opportunity to interview for the position available in your production department. I want you to know that this is the sort of job I have been looking for and I am enthusiastic about the possibility of working for you.

Now that we have spoken, I know that I have both the experience and skills to fit nicely into your organization and to be productive quickly. The process improvements I implemented at Logistics, Inc., increased their productivity 34%, and I'm confident that I could do the same for you.

Thanks again for the interview; I enjoyed the visit.

Sara Smith

Quick Tip

Send a thank-you note by e-mail or mail as soon as possible after an interview or meeting. This is when you are freshest in the mind of the person who receives it and are most likely to make a good impression.

3. Whenever Anyone Helps You in Your Job Search

Send a thank-you note to anyone who helps you during your job search. This includes those who give you referrals, people who provide advice, or simply those who are supportive during your search. I suggest you routinely enclose one or more JIST Cards in these notes because recipients can give them to others who may be in a better position to help you.

Figure 13-3: Sample thank-you note 3, to someone who helped in a job search.

October 31, 20XX
2234 Riverbed Ave.
Philadelphia, PA 17963

Ms. Helen A. Colcord
Henderson and Associates, Inc.
1801 Washington Blvd., Suite 1201
Philadelphia, PA 17963

Dear Ms. Colcord,

Thank you for sharing your time with me so generously yesterday. I really appreciated talking to you about your career field.

The information you shared with me increased my desire to work in such an area. Your advice has already proven helpful—I have an appointment to meet with Robert Hopper on Friday.

In case you think of someone else who might need a person like me, I'm enclosing another resume and JIST Card.

Sincerely,

Debbie Childs

Eight Quick Tips for Writing Thank-You Notes

Here are some brief tips to help you write your thank-you notes.

1. Decide Whether E-mail or Snail Mail Makes More Sense

Consider the timing involved and the formality of the person and organization you're sending it to. If you need to get a letter out quickly because it has to arrive before an interview that's coming up soon, or if it's a thank-you note after an interview and you know the employer will be making a decision soon, e-mail is your best bet. Use regular mail if there's no rush and if you sense that the other person would appreciate the formality of a business letter printed on nice paper and received in the mail.

2. Use Quality Paper and Envelopes

For mailed thank-you notes, use good-quality notepaper with matching envelopes. Most stationery and office-supply stores have thank-you note cards and envelopes in a variety of styles. Select a note that is simple and professional—avoid cute graphics and sayings. A blank card or simple "Thank You" on the front will do. For a professional look, match your resume and thank-you note papers by getting them at the same time. I suggest off-white and buff colors.

3. Handwritten or Typed Is Acceptable

Traditionally, thank-you notes were handwritten, but most are typed these days. If your handwriting is good, it is perfectly acceptable to write them, and can be a nice touch. If not, they can be word-processed.

4. Use a Formal Salutation

Do not make your thank-you notes appear too formal.

Unless you know the person you are thanking, don't use a first name unless you've already met the person you're writing and he or she has asked you to use first names, or if you're writing to someone in a young, hip environment. Instead, use "Dear Ms. Smith" or "Ms. Smith," rather than the less formal "Dear Pam." Include the date.

5. Keep the Note Informal and Friendly

Keep your note short and friendly. Remember, the note is a thank you for what someone else did, not a hard-sell pitch for what you want. Make sure, though, that in a thank-you note after an interview you give a subtle, gentle reminder of your skills or other qualifications that are relevant to the job. This lets the thank-you note serve as not only an expression of appreciation but a chance to get the last word on why you should be hired. The more savvy members of your competition will be doing this, so you had better do it, too.

Also, make sure your thank-you note does not sound like a form letter. Put some time and effort into it to tailor it to the recipient and the situation.

As appropriate, be specific about when you will next contact the person. If you plan to meet soon, still send a note saying that you look forward to the meeting and say thank you for the appointment. And make sure that you include something to remind the employer of who you are and how to reach you, since your name alone may not be enough to be remembered.

6. Sign It

Sign your first and last name. Avoid initials and make your signature legible (unless you're being hired for your creative talents, in which case a wacky-looking, illegible signature could be a plus!).

7. Send It Right Away

Write and send your note or e-mail no later than 24 hours after you make your contact. Ideally, you should write it immediately after the contact, while the details are fresh in your mind.

8. Enclose a JIST Card

Depending on the situation, a JIST Card is often the ideal enclosure to include with a printed thank-you note. It's small, soft sell, and provides your contact information, should the employer wish to reach you. It is both a reminder of you, should any jobs open up, and a tool to pass along to someone else (see the next section of this chapter for details on writing JIST Cards). Make sure your thank-you notes and envelopes are big enough to enclose an unfolded JIST Card.

More Sample Thank-You Notes

Following are a few more samples of thank-you notes and letters. They cover a variety of situations and will give you ideas on how to structure your own correspondence. Notice that they are all short, are friendly, and typically mention that the writer will follow up in the future—a key element of a successful job search campaign.

Also note that several of these candidates are following up on interviews where no specific job opening exists yet. As I've mentioned elsewhere in this book, getting interviews before a job opening exists is a very smart thing to do.

> Always send a note or e-mail after an interview, even if things did not go well. It can't hurt.

The sample notes that follow were provided by David Swanson, a cover letter expert and speaker, and are used with permission.

Figure 13-4: Sample thank-you note.

April 22, 20XX

Dear Mr. Nelson,

Thank you so much for seeing me while I was in town last week. I am grateful for your kindness, the interview, and all the information you gave me.

I will call you once again in a few weeks to see if any openings have developed in your marketing research department's planned expansion.

Appreciatively,

Phil Simons

Voicemail: (633) 299-3034

Email: psimons@email.cmm

Figure 13-5: Sample thank-you note.

September 17, 20XX

Mr. Bill Kenner
Sales Manager
WRTV
Rochester, MN 87236

Dear Mr. Kenner:

Thank you very much for the interview and the market information you gave me yesterday. I was most impressed with the city, your station, and with everyone I met.

As you requested, I am enclosing a resume and have requested that my former manager call you on Tuesday, the 27th, at 10 a.m.

Working at WRTV with you and your team would be both interesting and exciting for me. I look forward to your reply and the possibility of helping you set new records next year.

Sincerely,

Anne Bently
1434 River Dr.
Polo, WA 99656
Pager: (545) 555-0032

Figure 13-6: Sample thank-you note.

October 14, 20XX

Dear Bill,

I really appreciate your recommending me to Alan Stevens at Wexler Cadillac. We met yesterday for almost an hour and we're having lunch again on Friday. If this develops into a job offer, as you think it may, I will be most grateful.

Enclosed is a reference letter by my summer employer. I thought you might find this helpful.

You're a good friend, and I appreciate your thinking of me.

Sincerely,

Dave

Figure 13-7: Sample thank-you note.

July 26, 20XX

Dear Ms. Bailey,

Thank you for the interview for the auditor's job last week.

I appreciate the information you gave me and the opportunity to interview with John Petero. He asked me for a transcript, which I am forwarding today.

Working in my field of finance in a respected firm such as Barry Productions appeals to me greatly. I appreciate your consideration and look forward to hearing from you.

Sincerely,

Dan Rehling
Cell phone: 404-991-3443

JIST Cards®—A Mini-Resume and a Powerful Job Search Tool

JIST Cards are a job search tool that gets results. They have been mentioned several times throughout this book. I've included a few samples in other chapters, but they are helpful enough to justify a bit more space here.

I developed JIST Cards many years ago, almost by accident, as a tool to help job seekers. I was surprised by the positive employer reaction they received back then, so paid attention and developed them further. Over the years, I have seen them in every imaginable format, and forms of JIST Cards are now being used on the Internet, in personal video interviews, and in other electronic media.

How Did JIST Cards Get Their Name?

In case you were wondering, the word "JIST" is an acronym originally created for a self-directed job search program I developed years ago. It stands for "Job Information & Seeking Training." The word JIST was later trademarked and has been used for many years now in various forms (including JIST Publishing) to identify self-directed job search, career, and other materials.

Think of a JIST Card as a Very Small Resume

A JIST Card is carefully constructed to contain all the essential information most employers want to know in a very short format. It typically uses a 3 × 5–inch card format, but has been designed into many other sizes and formats, such as a folded business card, or included in e-mail.

Your JIST Cards can be as simple as handwritten or created with graphics and on special papers or electronic formats. You should create a JIST Card in addition to a resume, since a JIST Card is used in a different way.

JIST Cards Get Results

What matters is what JIST Cards accomplish—they get results. In my surveys of employers, more than 90 percent of JIST Cards form a positive impression of the writer within 30 seconds. More amazing is that about 80 percent of employers say they would be willing to interview the person behind the JIST Card, even if they did not have a job opening now. I know of no other job search technique that has this effect. And to have this effect in about 30 seconds is simply, well, amazing.

Quick Tip

JIST Cards are harder to write than they look, so carefully review the examples and use the content of your resume as a starting point for content. Once you have your own JIST Card, put hundreds of them in circulation. JIST Cards work, but only if you get them to the people in your network.

How You Can Use JIST Cards

You can use a JIST Card in many ways, including the following:

- Attach one to your resume or application
- Enclose one in a thank-you note
- Give them to your friends, relatives, and other contacts—so they can give them to other people
- Send them out to everyone who graduated from your school or who is a member of your professional association
- Put them on car windshields
- Post them on the supermarket bulletin board
- Send them in electronic form as an e-mail

I'm not kidding about finding JIST Cards on windshields or bulletin boards. I've seen them used in these ways and hear about more ways people are using them all the time.

JIST Card Paper and Format Tips

JIST Cards are most often used in paper formats. Many office-supply stores have perforated light card stock sheets that you can run through your computer printer. These will then tear apart into 3 × 5–inch cards. Many word-processing programs have templates that allow you to format a 3 × 5–inch card size. You can also use regular size paper, print several cards on a sheet, and cut it to the size you need. Print shops can also photocopy or print them in the size you need. Get a few hundred at a time. They are cheap, and the objective is to get lots of them in circulation.

Sample JIST Cards

The following sample JIST Cards use a plain format, but you can make them as fancy as you want. So be creative. Look over the examples to see how they are constructed. Some are for entry-level jobs and some are for more advanced ones. The content of the samples, and of your own JIST Card, can be adapted for use as e-mail attachments, as part of an online or other portfolio, and other formats. So be creative and adapt the idea to best fit your own situation.

Figure 13-8: Sample JIST Card for an office worker.

Sandy Nolan

Position: General Office/Clerical

Message: (512) 232-9213

More than two years of work experience plus one year of training in office practices. Type 55 wpm, trained in word processing, post general ledger, have good interpersonal skills, and get along with most people. Can meet deadlines and handle pressure well.

Willing to work any hours.

Organized, honest, reliable, and hardworking.

Figure 13-9: Sample JIST Card for a systems analyst.

Joyce Hua

Home: (214) 173-1659
Message: (214) 274-1436
Email: jhua@yahoo.com

Position: Programming/Systems Analyst

More than 10 years of combined education and experience in data processing and related fields. Competent programming in Visual Basic, C, C++, FORTRAN, and Java, and database management. Extensive PC network applications experience. Have supervised a staff as large as seven on special projects and have a record of meeting deadlines. Operations background in management, sales, and accounting.

Desire career-oriented position, will relocate.

Dedicated, self-starter, creative problem solver.

Figure 13-10: Sample JIST Card for a chemist.

Paul Thomas

Home: (301) 681-3922
Message: (301) 681-6966
Cell phone: (301) 927-9856

Position: Research Chemist, Research Management in a small-to-medium-sized company

Ph.D. in biochemistry plus more than 15 years of work experience. Developed and patented various processes with current commercial applications worth many millions of dollars. Experienced with all phases of lab work with an emphasis on chromatography, isolation, and purification of organic and biochemical compounds. Specialize in practical pharmaceutical and agricultural applications of chemical research. Have teaching, supervision, and project management experience.

Married more than 15 years, stable work history, results and task oriented, ambitious, and willing to relocate.

Figure 13-11: Sample JIST Card for an electronics installer.

Richard Straightarrow

Home: (602) 253-9678
Message: (602) 257-6643
E-mail: RSS@email.cmm

Objective: Electronics installation, maintenance, and sales

Four years of work experience plus a two-year A.S. degree in Electronics Engineering Technology. Managed a $360,000/year business while going to school full time, with grades in the top 25%. Familiar with all major electronic diagnostic and repair equipment. Hands-on experience with medical, consumer, communication, and industrial electronics equipment and applications. Good problem-solving and communication skills. Customer service oriented.

Willing to do what it takes to get the job done.

Self motivated, dependable, learn quickly.

Figure 13-12: Sample JIST Card for a warehouse manager.

Juanita Rodriguez

Message: (639) 361-1754
Email: jrodriguez@email.cmm

Position: Warehouse Management

Six years of experience plus two years of formal business course work. Have supervised a staff as large as 16 people and warehousing operations covering over two acres and valued at more than $14,000,000. Automated inventory operations resulting in a 30% increase in turnover and estimated annual savings more than $250,000. Working knowledge of accounting, computer systems, time and motion studies, and advanced inventory management systems.

Will work any hours.

Responsible, hardworking, and can solve problems.

Figure 13-13: Sample JIST Card for a hotel manager.

Deborah Levy

Home: (213) 432-8064
Pager: (212) 876-9487

Position: Hotel Management Professional

Four years of experience in sales, catering, and accounting in a 300-room hotel. Associate degree in Hotel Management plus one year with the Boileau Culinary Institute. Doubled revenues from meetings and conferences. Increased dining room and bar revenues by 44%. Have been commended for improving staff productivity and courtesy. I approach my work with industry, imagination, and creative problem-solving skills.

Enthusiastic, well-organized, and detail-oriented.

Figure 13-14: Sample JIST Card for a manager.

Jonathan Michael

Cell phone: (614) 788-2434
E-mail: jonn@pike.org

Objective: Management

More than 7 years of management experience plus a B.S. degree in business. Managed budgets as large as $10 million. Experienced in cost control and reduction, cutting more than 20% of overhead while business increased more than 30%. Good organizer and problem solver. Excellent communication skills.

Prefer responsible position in a medium-to-large business.

Cope well with deadline pressure, seek challenge, flexible.

Other Job Search Correspondence

Besides thank-you notes and JIST Cards, you can send a variety of other items to people during your job search. Following are brief comments about some of these items.

Follow-Up Letters After an Interview

After an interview, you might wish to send follow-up correspondence to solve a problem the employer mentioned or to present a proposal. The preceding section showed examples of letters and notes that were sent following an interview. You can easily adapt the content for use in follow-up e-mails.

In some instances, a longer or more detailed letter would be appropriate. The objective would be to provide additional information or to present a proposal. The sample letter from Sandra A. Zaremba in Chapter 12 is an example of a follow-up letter that suggests a specific proposal.

In some cases, you could submit a much more comprehensive proposal that would essentially justify your job. If a job opening is available, you can submit an outline of what you would do if hired. If no job is available, you can submit a proposal for creating a job and state what you would do to make it pay off.

In writing such a proposal, it is essential that you be specific in telling an employer what you would do and what results these actions would bring. For example, if you propose to increase sales, how would you do it and how much might sales increase? Tell the employer what you could accomplish, and he or she may just create a new position for you. It happens this way more often than you probably realize.

Enclosures and E-mail Attachments

In some cases, you may want to include items along with the correspondence, such as a writing sample. This can be appropriate, although I advise against sending too much material unless the employer requests it. Never send originals unless you are willing to lose them. Assume, in all cases, that what you send will not be returned to you.

Self-Sticking Notes

You have surely used those little notes that stick to papers, walls, and other things. There's a size usually called "flags" that are smaller and narrower than most of the square stick-on notes you probably use. Some even have an arrow design on them. These can be useful when calling attention to specific points on attachments or to provide additional details.

Quick Alert

Use one or two self-sticking notes at the most. Avoid making your correspondence look like a patchwork quilt.

List of References

Once employers begin to get serious, they may want to contact your references as part of their final screening process. To make this easier for them, I suggest that you prepare a list of people to contact. This list should include the complete name, title, organization, address, phone number and e-mail address for each reference. You should include information about how each person knows you. For example, indicate that Ms. Rivera was your immediate supervisor for two years.

Be sure to inform those on your list that they might be contacted and asked to provide references. In some cases, you should take the time to prepare them by sending information on the types of jobs you now seek, a current resume, a JIST Card, and other details.

Quick Tip

If you have any question whether a person will provide you with a positive reference, discuss this in advance so you know what the individual is likely to say about you. If it is not positive, consider dropping this person from your list.

Letters of Reference

Many organizations fear lawsuits as the result of giving out negative information regarding an ex-employee. For this reason, it can often be difficult for an employer to get any meaningful information about you over the phone. I recommend you request previous employers and other references to write a letter or e-mail that you can submit to others when asked.

If the letters are positive, the advantages should be clear. Even if the letter is negative, at least you now know that there is a problem with this reference. Depending on the situation, you might contact this previous employer and negotiate what he or she will say.

Unsolicited Letters Requesting an Interview or Other Assistance

Once more, I want to discourage you from sending out unsolicited letters or e-mail as a primary job search technique. Even though many resume books recommend sending out lots of unsolicited resumes, the evidence is overwhelming that this method does not work for most people. Doing the same thing on the Internet often results in the same outcome. The rare exception is if your skills are very much in demand.

I do think that sending a letter or e-mail to people with whom you share a common bond, such as alumni or members of a professional group, can be reasonably effective. This is particularly so if you are looking for a job in another city or region and you send a letter or e-mail asking someone to help you by providing names of contacts. Several of the sample cover letters in Chapter 12 provide examples of this very technique and it can work, particularly if you follow up by phone and e-mail.

Section Five

GETTING A GOOD JOB IN LESS TIME

This could be the most important section in this book. It consists of two chapters focused on finding a good job quickly. It gives you all the tools you will need to conduct a quick and effective job search. Remember that a resume alone can't get you a job. That's why I'm providing this extra information—so that your job search will be as short as possible and that you will find the right job for you.

Chapters in This Section

Chapter 14: Seven Steps to Getting a Good Job in Less Time

Chapter 14 covers the major tools you need to explore career options and to conduct an effective job search. The techniques it presents have been proven to reduce the time it takes to find a job and are widely used by job search programs throughout North America.

Chapter 15: Quick Tips for Using the Internet in Your Job Search

Chapter 15 focuses on using the Internet as a powerful tool in your search, but using it wisely.

Chapter 14

Seven Steps to Getting a Good Job in Less Time

This chapter is based on *The Quick Job Search,* which was originally published as a separate booklet. I wrote the booklet in response to a question I asked myself: "If time were short, what would be the most important things I would tell someone about career planning and job search?" And the answer is, if I had just a few hours, I would explain the points in *The Quick Job Search.* The content provides a very nice outline for a brief career planning and job search workshop and has been used many times in just that way.

This chapter is designed to provide you with an overview of career planning and job seeking skills. It illustrates quick but helpful techniques that you can use to shorten the time it takes to get a job.

You should have jumped to this chapter after finishing one of the basic resumes I suggested in Section One. I hope that is the case, because a resume's value is in what it will help you accomplish—which is getting a good job.

The Quick Job Search: Career Planning and Job Search Advice

While a resume is a tool to help you get a job, few resume books provide good advice on job seeking. In fact, most resume books give bad advice. For example, they often tell you to send out lots of resumes and get them into the stacks on employers' desks. Then, if your resume (or cover letter) is good enough, employers will pick it out of the pile and ask you in for an interview.

This advice is old fashioned and downright harmful. It puts you at the mercy of some employer whose mindset is to screen people out. It encourages you to be passive and wait for employers to call you. And, worst of all, it assumes that the job search is limited to talking to employers who have job openings now and excludes all those who do not—but who might soon.

Quick Reference

If you are planning your career or need to know more about finding a job, I strongly encourage you to learn more. A book that I wrote titled *The Very Quick Job Search,* also published by JIST, covers the techniques in this section in much greater depth and provides other information as well. It is available through most bookstores and libraries.

> If you follow the suggestions here, you can cut the time it takes to find a job by quite a bit.

So I think the traditional advice on resumes and job seeking is (to put it kindly) not good. You can use techniques that are far more effective than the traditional ones. I've been working on this for more than 25 years now, and the best job search techniques are based on common sense. They encourage you to be clear about what you want and then to go out and actively look for it. It takes some nerve, but people who use the techniques presented in this section have proven that they do work. The techniques help you find better jobs in less time. And that is what job search should be all about, isn't it?

I want to make two points that apply to the Internet as well as to other job search methods:

1. It is unwise to rely on just one or two job search methods.
2. It is essential that you take an active rather than a passive approach in your job search.

Avoid the Temptation to Just Scan This Material—Do the Activities

I know that you will resist doing the activities included here. But trust me, completing them is worthwhile. Those who do them will have a better sense of what they are good at, what they want to do, and how to go about doing it. They are likely to get more interviews and to present themselves better in those interviews. Is this worth giving up a night of TV? Yes, I think so.

Interestingly, you will—after reading this section and doing its activities—have spent more time planning your career than most people. You will know far more than the average job seeker about how to go about finding a job. While you may want to know more, I hope that this is enough to get you started.

While this book will teach you techniques to find a better job in less time, job seeking requires you to act, not just learn. So consider what you can do to put the techniques to work for you. Do the activities. Create a daily plan. Get more interviews. Today, not tomorrow. You see, the sooner and harder you get to work on your job search, the shorter it is likely to be.

Changing Jobs and Careers Is Often Healthy

Most of us were told from an early age that each career move must be up, involving more money, responsibility, and prestige. However, research indicates that people change careers for many other reasons as well.

In a survey conducted by the Gallup Organization for the National Occupational Information Coordinating Committee, 44 percent of the working adults surveyed expected to be in a different job within three years. Yet only 41 percent had a definite plan to follow in mapping out their careers.

Logical, ordered careers are found more often with increasing levels of education. For example, while 25 percent of high school dropouts took the only job available, this was true for only 8 percent of those with at least some college. But you should not assume this means that such occupational stability is healthy. Many adult developmental psychologists believe occupational change is not only normal, but may even be necessary for sound adult growth and development.

Quick Tip

It is common, even normal, to reconsider occupational roles during your twenties, thirties, and forties, even in the absence of economic pressure to do so.

One viewpoint is that a healthy occupational change allows some previously undeveloped aspect of the self to emerge. The change may be as natural as from clerk to supervisor or as drastic as from professional musician to airline pilot. Although risk is always a factor when change is involved, reasonable risks are healthy and can raise self-esteem.

Whether you are seeking similar work in another setting or changing careers, you need a workable plan to find the right job. The rest of this chapter gives you the information you need to help you find a good job quickly. Short as this chapter is, it does present you with the basic skills to find a good job in less time. The techniques work.

Seven Steps for a Quick and Successful Job Search

You can't just read about getting a job. The best way to get a job is to go out and get interviews! The best way to get interviews is to make a job out of getting a job. I have identified just seven things you need to do that make a big difference in your job search. The following sections cover each of these steps.

Seven Steps for a Quick Job Search

1. Identify your skills.
2. Have a clear job objective.
3. Know where and how to look for job leads.
4. Spend at least 25 hours a week looking for a job—more if you're currently unemployed.
5. Get two interviews a day.
6. Do well in interviews.
7. Follow up on all contacts.

Step 1: Identify Your Skills

An effective career plan requires that you know your skills. Chapters 5 and 6 review the basics of how to identify your key skills. If you have not spent time on this issue, I strongly suggest that you do. It is very important for both planning your career and for presenting yourself effectively throughout the job search.

Most job seekers cannot answer the question, "Why should I hire you?" The consequence of not being able to answer that question, as you might guess, is that your chances of getting a job offer are greatly reduced. Knowing your skills, therefore, gives you a distinct advantage in the job search as well as helps you write a more effective resume.

If you have not done the skills identification activities in Chapters 5 and 6 or are not able to identify your key skills, I suggest that you review those chapters before you go on with your search for a job.

Assuming that you have completed the activities in Chapters 5 and 6, here are some reminder lists on your most important skills.

A Skills Review

Your top five adaptive/self-management skills

1. ______________________________
2. ______________________________
3. ______________________________
4. ______________________________
5. ______________________________

Your top five transferable skills

1. ______________________________
2. ______________________________
3. ______________________________
4. ______________________________
5. ______________________________

Your top five job-related skills

1. ______________________________
2. ______________________________
3. ______________________________
4. ______________________________
5. ______________________________

Step 2: Have a Clear Job Objective

Having a clear job objective is not just an issue for your resume. I realize how difficult it can be to figure out the exact job you want; however, getting as close as you can is essential.

Too many people look for a job without having a good idea of exactly what they are looking for. Before you go out looking for "a" job, I suggest that you first define exactly what it is you really want—"the" job. Most people think a job objective is the same as a job title, but it isn't. You need to consider other elements of what makes a job satisfying for you. Then, later, you can decide what that job is called and what industry it might be in.

Quick Reference

Chapter 7 covers the basics of defining a clear job objective. That chapter also discusses the importance of considering your industry preferences. With that information, and additional study as needed, you should have a clearer sense of the job you want and the industry where you would like to work. So, if you've not done your homework and don't have a clear job objective, I suggest you spend more time with Chapter 7.

Here are a few points from Chapter 7 to summarize the elements to consider in your ideal job.

Your Ideal Job

What skills do you want to use?

1. ______________________________

2. ______________________________

3. ______________________________

(continued)

(continued)

4. ______________________________

5. ______________________________

What special knowledge would you like to use in your ideal job?

____

____

____

What types of people do you like to work with or for?

____

____

____

What type of work environment do you prefer?

____

____

____

Where do you want your next job to be located?

____

____

____

How much money do you hope to make in your next job?

____

How much responsibility are you willing to accept?

____

____

____

What things are important or have meaning to you?

____

____

____

Describe your ideal job:

____

____

____

Step 3: Know Where and How to Look for Job Leads

One survey found that about 85 percent of all employers don't advertise their job openings. They hire people they know, people who find out about the jobs through word of mouth, or people who happen to be in the right place at the right time. While the Internet has changed how some employers find people, getting a solid lead is still too often a matter of "luck." But the good news is that, by using the right techniques, you can learn to increase your "luck" in finding job openings.

Traditional Job Search Methods Are Not Very Effective

Most job seekers don't know how ineffective some traditional job hunting techniques tend to be. For example, the chart on this page shows that fewer than 15 percent of all job seekers get jobs from reading the want ads.

Figure 14-1: How people find jobs.

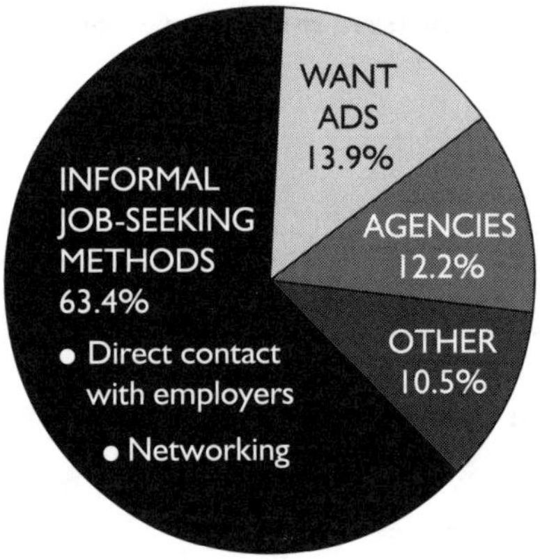

Here is more detail on the effectiveness of seven of the most popular traditional job search methods:

- **Help wanted ads:** Less than 15 percent of all people get their jobs through the newspaper want ads. Everyone who reads the paper knows about these openings, so competition for advertised jobs is fierce. You can get want ads through the Internet for most metropolitan newspapers—but so can everyone else. (Position advertisements on Internet job boards are discussed separately in Chapter 15.) Still, some people get jobs through ads, so go ahead and apply. Just be sure to spend most of your time using more effective methods.

- **State employment services:** Each state has a network of local offices to administer unemployment compensation and provide job leads and other services. These services are provided without charge to you or employers. Names vary by state, so it may be called "Job Service," "Department of Labor," "Workforce Development," "Unemployment Office," or another name.

  Nationally, only about 5 percent of all job seekers get their jobs here, and these organizations typically know of only one-tenth (or fewer) of the job openings in a region. Local openings are posted on a government-funded Internet site at www.ajb.dni.gov, where you can search by occupation and location anywhere in the country.

- **Private employment agencies:** Recent studies have found that staffing agencies work reasonably well for those who use them. But consider some cautions. For one thing, these agencies work best for entry-level positions or for those with specialized, in-demand skills. Most people who use a private agency usually find their jobs using some other source, making the success record of these businesses quite modest.

  Private agencies charge a fee as high as 20 percent of your annual salary to you or to the employer. Because of the high expense, you can require that you be referred only to interviews where the employer pays the fee. Keep in mind that most private agencies find job openings by calling employers, something you could do yourself.

Quick Alert

Never work with a search firm or employment agency that charges you to get a job through them. Legitimate firms are paid only by the employer for whom they fill jobs. There should be no cost to you. (But don't confuse this advice with the fees you pay to private-practice career counselors or coaches; they provide coaching services for a fee and don't promise you a job.)

- **Temporary agencies:** These can be a source of quick but temporary jobs to bring in some income while you look for long-term employment. Temp jobs also give you experience in a variety of settings—something that can help you land full-time jobs later. More and more employers are also using these jobs as a way to evaluate workers for permanent jobs. So consider using these agencies if it makes sense, but continue an active search for a full-time job.
- **Sending out resumes:** One survey found that you would have to mail more than 500 unsolicited resumes to get one interview! Like other traditional approaches, use this method sparingly because the numbers are stacked against you.

  A better approach is to contact the person who might hire you, by phone or via e-mail, to set up an interview directly—then send a resume. If you insist on sending out unsolicited resumes, do this on weekends and evenings and save your "prime time" for more effective job search techniques.
- **Filling out applications:** Most applications are used to screen you out. Larger organizations may require them, but remember that your task is to get an interview, not fill out an application. If you do complete applications, make them neat and error-free and do not include anything that could get you screened out. Never present something in a way an employer would see as a negative. For example, instead or saying you were "fired," say "position eliminated due to corporate downsizing." If the form asks for pay requirements, simply write in something like "flexible" instead of giving a specific number.

Quick Tip

If necessary, leave a problem question or section blank on an application. You can always explain it after you get an interview.

- **Human resource departments:** Hardly anyone gets hired by interviewers in HR or personnel departments. Their job is to screen you and then refer the "best" applicants to the person who would supervise you. You may need to cooperate with the people in HR, but it is often better to go directly to the person who is most likely to supervise you—even if no opening exists at the moment. And remember that many smaller organizations don't even have HR or personnel offices.

The Two Job Search Methods That Work Best

About two-thirds of all people get their jobs using informal methods. These jobs are often not advertised and are part of the "hidden" job market. How can you find them?

There are two basic informal job search methods: networking with people you know (which I call warm contacts), and making direct contacts with an employer (which I call cold contacts). They are both based on the most important job search rule of all:

> ***THE MOST IMPORTANT JOB SEARCH RULE:***
> Don't wait until the job is open before contacting the employer!

Most jobs are filled by someone the employer meets before the job is formally open. So the trick is to meet people who can hire you *before* a job is available! Instead of saying, "Do you have any jobs open?" say, "I realize you may not have any openings now, but I would still like to talk to you about the possibility of future openings.

Develop a Network of Contacts in Five Easy Steps

One study found that about 40 percent of all people found their jobs through a lead provided by a friend, a relative, or an acquaintance. Developing new contacts is called "networking," and here's how it works:

1. **Make lists of people you know.** Develop a list of anyone with whom you are friendly; then make a separate list of all your relatives. These two lists alone often add up to 25 to 100 people or more. Next, think of other groups with whom you have something in common, such as former coworkers or classmates; members of

your social or sports groups; members of your professional association; former employers; and members of your religious group. You may not know many of these people personally, but most will help you if you ask them.

2. **Contact the people on your lists in a systematic way.** Each of these people is a contact for you. Obviously, some lists and some people on those lists will be more helpful than others, but almost any one of them could help you find a job lead.

3. **Present yourself well.** Begin with your friends and relatives. Call or e-mail them and tell them you are looking for a job and need their help. Be as clear as possible about what you are looking for and what skills and qualifications you have. Look at the sample phone script later in this chapter for presentation ideas.

4. **Ask them for leads.** It is possible that they will know of a job opening that is just right for you. If so, get the details and get right on it! More likely, however, they will not, so here are three questions you should ask.

5. **Contact these referrals and ask them the same questions.** For each original contact, you can extend your network of acquaintances by hundreds of people. Eventually, one of these people will hire you or refer you to someone who will! If you use networking thoroughly, it may be the only job search technique you need.

Quick Tip

If you're worried that you don't know enough people to network effectively, concentrate on going to group events where you'll have a large pool of people from which to develop contacts, rather than just meeting people one by one. Attend professional association meetings, lectures, classes, social functions, and anywhere that you can meet a lot of folks.

The Three Magic Networking Questions

1. **Do you know of any openings for a person with my skills?** If the answer is no (which it usually is), ask the next question.
2. **Do you know of someone else who might know of such an opening?** If your contact does, get that name and ask for another one. If he or she doesn't, ask the next question.
3. **Do you know of anyone who might know of someone else who might?** Another good way to ask this is "Do you know someone who knows lots of people?" If all else fails, this will usually get you a name.

Quick Alert

Networking is about much more than asking people if they know of any job openings. The answer is likely to be no, so that question doesn't get you far. Instead, look at networking as a way to build relationships with people who know other people, who may know other people who know of jobs. Networking is also about getting advice about your search and insight into the organizations you're trying to break into.

Figure 14-2: How referrals can expand your network.

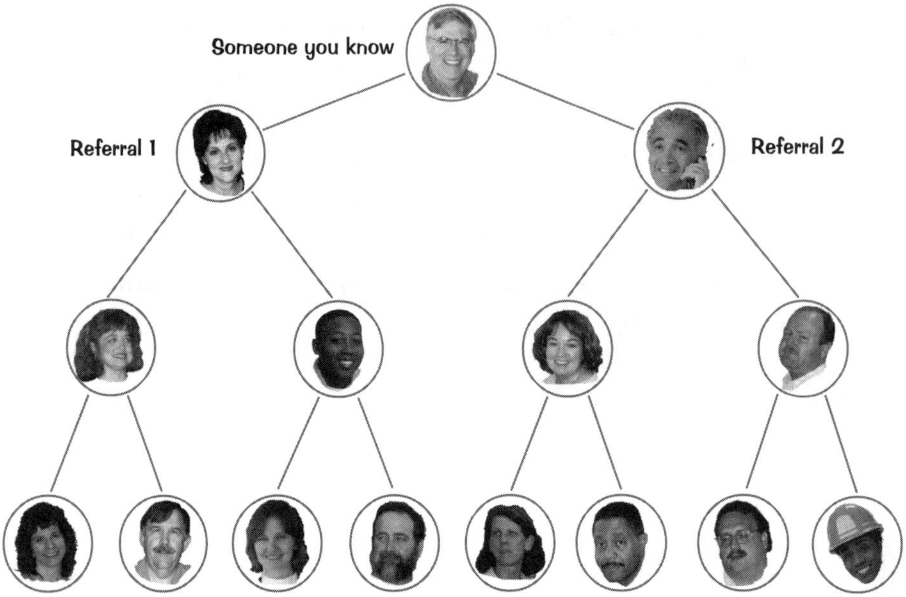

If you ask each referral for two names and follow through, your network will soon look like this:

Quick Reference

For much more advice about this important topic of networking and how to make it work for you, I recommend reading *Networking for Job Search and Career Success* by Michelle Tullier (JIST Publishing).

Use Cold Contacts—Contact Employers Directly

It takes more courage, but contacting an employer directly is a variation on the networking idea and a very effective job search technique. I call these cold contacts because you don't know or have an existing connection with the employers. Following are two basic techniques for making cold contacts.

- **Use the Yellow Pages to find potential employers.** Online sites like www.yellowpages.com and others allow you to find potential employers anywhere, but the print version is best if you're looking for a local job. You can begin by looking at the index and asking for each entry, "Would an organization of this kind need a person with my skills?" If the answer is "yes," then that type of organization or business is a possible target. You can also rate "yes" entries based on your interest, writing an "A" next to those that seem very interesting, a "B" next to those you are not sure of, and a "C" next to those that don't seem interesting at all.

  Next, select a type of organization that got a "yes" response (such as "hotels") and turn to the section of the Yellow Pages where they are listed. Then call the organizations and ask to speak to the person who is most likely to hire or supervise you. A sample telephone script is included later in this section to give you ideas about what to say.

  The Internet provides a variety of ways to do the same thing in a different way. For example, Yellow Pages listings are available online for any geographic area of the country. And many businesses have Web sites where you can get information and apply for job openings. There are also databases of companies that you can search to develop "hit lists." Several of these databases are listed in Chapter 15.

- **Drop in without an appointment.** While building security has become increasingly tight in some locations, you can sometimes simply walk into many potential employers' organizations and ask to speak to the person in charge. This is particularly effective in small businesses, but it works surprisingly well in larger ones, too. Remember, you want an interview even if there are no openings now. If your timing is inconvenient, ask for a better time to come back for an interview.

- **Use the phone to get job leads.** Once you have created your JIST Card (see Chapter 13), it is easy to create a telephone contact script based on it. Adapt the basic script to call people you know or your Yellow Pages leads. Select Yellow Pages index categories that might use a person with your skills and get the numbers of specific organizations in that category. Once you get to the person who is most likely to supervise you, present your phone script.

  While it doesn't work every time, most people, with practice, can get one or more interviews in an hour by making these cold calls. Here is a sample phone script based on a JIST Card:

  Hello, my name is Pam Nykanen. I'm interested in a position in hotel management. I have four years' experience in sales, catering, and accounting with a 300-room hotel. I also have an associate degree in Hotel Management plus one year of experience with the Bradey Culinary Institute. During my employment, I helped double revenues from meetings and conferences and increased bar revenues by 46 percent. I have good problem-solving skills and am good with people. I am also well organized, hardworking, and detail oriented. When may I come in for an interview?

  While this example assumes that you are calling someone you don't know, the script can be easily modified for presentation to warm contacts, including referrals. Using the script for making cold calls takes courage, but it works for most people.

Most Jobs Are with Small Employers

About 70 percent of all people work in small businesses—those with 250 or fewer employees. While the largest corporations have reduced the number of employees, small businesses have been creating as many as 80 percent of the new jobs over the past decade.

Smaller organizations are where most of the job search action is, and do not ignore this fact. Many opportunities exist to obtain training and promotions in smaller organizations, too. Many do not even have HR departments, so nontraditional job search techniques are particularly effective.

Step 4: Spend 25 Hours or More a Week Looking for a Job

On the average, job seekers spend fewer than 15 hours a week looking for work. The average length of unemployment varies from three or more months, with some being out of work far longer (older workers and higher earners are two groups who take longer). There is a clear connection between how long it takes to find a job and the number of hours spent looking on a daily and weekly basis.

Based on many years of experience, I can say that the more time you spend on your job search each week, the less time you are likely to remain unemployed. Of course, using more effective job search methods also helps. Those who follow my advice have proven, over and over, that they get jobs in less than half the average time; and they often get better jobs, too. Time management is the key.

Quick Alert

Of course, if you are currently employed and looking for a better job, you would spend less than 25 hours a week looking—but the principles remain the same.

If you are unemployed and looking for a full-time job, you should look for a job on a full-time basis. It just makes sense, although many do not do so because of discouragement, lack of good techniques, and lack of structure. Most job seekers have no idea what they are going to do next Thursday—they don't have a plan. The most important thing is to decide how many hours you can commit to your job search, and stay with it. If you are unemployed, you should spend a minimum of 25 hours a week on hard-core job search activities with no goofing around, and even more is better. The following worksheet walks you through a simple but effective process to help you organize your job search schedule.

Structure Your Job Search Like a Job

1. **Decide how many hours you will spend a week looking for work.**

   Write here how many hours you are willing to spend each week looking for a job:

   ____

2. **Decide which days and times you will look for work.**

   Answering the following questions requires you to have a schedule and a plan, just as you had when you were working.

   Which days of the week will you spend looking for a job? ______________

   ____

   How many hours will you look each day? ______________

   At what time will you begin and end your job search on each of these days? ______

3. **Create a specific daily schedule.**

   A specific daily job search schedule is very important because most job seekers find it hard to stay productive each day. You already know which job search methods are most effective, and you should plan on spending most of your time using those methods.

The sample daily schedule that follows has been very effective for people who have used it, and it will give you ideas for your own. Although you are welcome to create your daily schedule however you like, I urge you to consider one similar to this one. Why? Because it works.

7–8 a.m.	Get up, shower, dress, eat breakfast.
8–8:15 a.m.	Organize work space; review schedule for interviews or follow-ups; update schedule.
8:15–9 a.m.	Review old leads for follow-up; develop new leads (want ads, Internet, networking lists, and so on).
9–10 a.m.	Make networking or direct employer phone calls or Internet contacts; set up meetings and interviews.
10–10:15 a.m.	Take a break!
10:15–11 a.m.	Make more new calls and Internet contacts.
11–12 p.m.	Make follow-up calls and e-mails as needed.
12–1 p.m.	Lunch break.
1–5 p.m.	Go on interviews and networking meetings; make cold contacts in the field; conduct research for upcoming interviews.
5–8 p.m.	Attend networking events.

4. Get a schedule book and write down your job search schedule.

This is important: If you are not accustomed to using a daily schedule book or planner, promise yourself that you will get a good one today. Choose one that allows plenty of space for each day's plan on an hourly basis, plus room for daily "to-do" listings. Write in your daily schedule in advance; then add interviews as they come. Get used to carrying it with you and using it!

Step 5: Get Two Interviews a Day

The average job seeker gets about five interviews a month—fewer than two interviews a week. Yet many job seekers using the techniques I suggest routinely get two interviews a day. But to accomplish this, you must first redefine what an interview is.

The New Definition of an Interview

An interview is any face-to-face contact with a person who has the authority to hire or supervise someone with your skills. The person may or may not have an opening at the time.

With this definition, it is *much* easier to get interviews. You can now interview with all kinds of potential employers, not just those who have job openings. Many job seekers use the Yellow Pages to get two interviews with just one hour of calls by using the telephone contact script discussed earlier. Others drop in on a potential employer and ask for an unscheduled interview—and they get one. And getting names of others to contact from those you know—networking—is quite effective if you persist.

Quick Tip

Getting two interviews a day equals 10 a week and 40 a month. That's 800 percent more interviews than the average job seeker gets. Who do you think will get a job offer quicker? So set out each day to get at least two interviews. It's quite possible to do, now that you know how.

Step 6: Do Well in Interviews

No matter how you get an interview, once you are there, you will have to create a good impression

- Even if your resume is one of the 10 best ever written.
- Even if you have the best of credentials.
- Even if you really want the job.

Quick Tip

One study indicated that, of those who made it as far as the interview (many others were screened out before then), about 40 percent created a bad first impression, mostly based on their dress and grooming. First impressions count, and if you make a bad one, your chances of getting a job offer rapidly decrease to about zero.

Dress for Success

Although there is more to making a good first impression than your dress and grooming, this is fortunately something that you can change readily. So, for this reason, I have created the following rule (and, I point out, this is one of the very few rules you will see in this book):

> ***Farr's Dress and Grooming Rule:***
> Dress the way you think the boss is most likely to dress—only neater.

Dress for success. If necessary, ask someone who dresses well to help you select an interview outfit. Pay close attention to your grooming, too.

Quick Tip

Written materials such as correspondence and resumes must be neat and error-free as well, since they also create a first impression.

How to Answer Tough Interview Questions

Interviews are where the job search action happens. You have to get them; then you have to do well in them. If you have done your homework, you will seek out interviews for jobs that will maximize your skills. That is a good start, but your ability to communicate your skills in the interview makes an enormous difference.

This is where, according to employer surveys, most job seekers have problems. A large percentage of job seekers don't effectively communicate the skills they have to do the job, and they answer one or more "problem" questions poorly. Trust me, this is a big problem. If you leave the interview without having answered one or more problem questions, your odds of getting a job offer are greatly decreased.

While thousands of problem interview questions are possible, I have listed just 10 that, if you can plan how to answer them well, will prepare you for most interviews.

Top 10 Problem Questions

1. Why don't you tell me about yourself?
2. Why should I hire you?
3. What are your major strengths?
4. What are your major weaknesses?
5. What sort of pay do you expect to receive?
6. How does your previous experience relate to the jobs we have here?
7. What are your plans for the future?
8. What will your former employer (or references) say about you?
9. Why are you looking for this type of position, and why here?
10. Why don't you tell me about your personal situation?

I don't have the space here to give thorough answers to all of these questions, and there are potentially hundreds of additional questions you might be asked. Instead, let me suggest several techniques I have developed that you can use to answer almost any interview question.

A Traditional Interview Is Not a Friendly Exchange

Before I present the techniques for answering interview questions, it is important to understand what is going on. In a traditional interview situation, there is a job opening, and you are one of several (or one of a hundred) applicants. In this setting, the employer's task is to eliminate all but one applicant.

Assuming that you got as far as an interview, the interviewer's questions are designed to elicit information that can be used to screen you out. If you are wise, you know that your task is to avoid getting screened out. It's not an open and honest interaction, is it? This illustrates yet another advantage of nontraditional job search techniques: the ability to talk to an employer before an opening exists. This eliminates the stress of a traditional interview. Employers are not trying to screen you out, and you are not trying to keep them from finding out the bad stuff about you.

Having said that, knowing a technique for answering questions that might be asked in a traditional interview is good preparation for whatever you might run into during your job search. The next section gives you a process for doing that.

The Three-Step Process for Answering Interview Questions

I know this might seem too simple, but the Three-Step Process is easy to remember. Its simplicity allows you to evaluate a question and create a good answer. The technique is based on sound principles and has worked for thousands of people, so consider trying it.

1. **Understand what is really being asked.**

   Most questions are really designed to find out about your self-management skills and personality. Although they are rarely this blunt, the employer's real questions are often directed at finding out the following:

   - Can I depend on you?
   - Are you easy to get along with? Are you a good worker?
   - Do you have the experience and training to do the job if we hire you?

- Are you likely to stay on the job for a reasonable period of time and be productive?

Ultimately, if the employer is not convinced that you will stay and be a good worker, it won't matter if you have the best credentials. He or she won't hire you.

2. **Answer the question briefly, in a non-damaging way.**

   Acknowledge the facts, but present them as an advantage rather than a disadvantage.

   Many interview questions will encourage you to provide negative information. The classic is the "What are your major weaknesses?" question that I included in my top 10 problem questions list. Obviously, this is a trick question, and many people are not prepared for it. A good response might be to mention something that is not all that damaging, such as "I have been told that I am a perfectionist, sometimes not delegating as effectively as I might." But your answer is not complete until you do the last step.

3. **Answer the real concern by presenting your related skills.**

   Base your answer on the key skills that you have identified and that are needed in this job. Give examples to support your skills statements. For example, an employer might say to a recent graduate, "We were looking for someone with more experience in this field. Why should we consider you?" Here is one possible answer: "I'm sure there are people who have more experience, but I do have more than six years of work experience, including three years of advanced training and hands-on experience using the latest methods and techniques. Because my training is recent, I am open to new ideas and am used to working hard and learning quickly."

In the example I presented in Step 2 (about your need to delegate more effectively), a good skills statement might be "I have been working on this problem and have learned to be more willing to let my staff do things, making sure that they have good training and supervision. I've found that their performance improves, and it frees me up to do other things."

Quick Tip

Whatever your situation, learn to use it to your advantage. It is essential to communicate your skills during an interview, and the Three-Step Process gives you a technique that can dramatically improve your responses. It works!

Step 7: Follow Up on All Contacts

People who follow up with potential employers and with others in their network get jobs faster than those who do not. This is another principle that seems too simple to be so important, but it is true.

Four Rules for Effective Follow-Up

1. Send a thank-you note to every person who helps you in your job search.
2. Send the thank-you note within 24 hours of speaking with the person.
3. Enclose JIST Cards with thank-you notes and all other correspondence.
4. Develop a system to keep following up with good contacts.

Thank-You Notes Make a Difference

Within 24 hours of the interview, send a thank-you note or e-mail to each person you spoke with. This gives you a great advantage over all the competing job seekers who don't take time to do this. Thank-you notes can be handwritten or typed on quality paper and matching envelopes or e-mailed. Keep your note simple, neat, and errorless. Following is a sample.

Figure 14-3: Sample thank-you note.

April 16, 20XX

2234 Riverwood Ave.
Philadelphia, PA 17963

Ms. Sandra Kijek
Henderson & Associates, Inc.
1801 Washington Blvd., Suite 1201
Philadelphia, PA 17963

Dear Ms. Kijek:

Thank you for sharing your time with me so generously today. I really appreciated seeing your state-of-the-art computer equipment.

Your advice has already proved helpful. I have an appointment to meet with Mr. Robert Hopper on Friday as you anticipated.

Please consider referring me to others if you think of someone else who might need a person with my skills.

Sincerely,

William Richardson

Quick Reference

Chapter 13 provides more thank-you note samples and tips.

Use Job Lead Cards to Organize Your Contacts

Use a simple 3 × 5-inch card to keep essential information about each person in your network. Buy a 3 × 5–inch card file box and tabs for each day of the month. File the cards under the date you want to contact the person, and the rest is easy. I've found that staying in touch with a good contact every other week can pay off big.

Quick Tip

You can take advantage of technology to help you manage your job search. A contact-management program such as ACT! enables you to create electronic "cards" for each contact and integrate them into your weekly schedule. You might also create a spreadsheet with a program such as Microsoft Excel where you log your activity and keep details on each person and organization. You could also use a PDA such as a Palm Pilot to keep track of your appointments and contacts.

Here's a sample card to give you ideas for creating your own if you use the index card method.

Figure 14-4: Sample job lead card.

ORGANIZATION: Mutual Health Insurance

CONTACT PERSON: Anna Tomey PHONE: 317-355-0216

SOURCE OF LEAD: Aunt Ruth

NOTES: 4/10 Called. Anna on vacation. Call back 4/15. 4/15 Interview set 4/20 at 1:30. 4/20 Anna showed me around. They use the same computers we used in school! (Friendly people.) Sent thank-you note and JIST Card, call back 5/1. 5/1 Second interview 5/8 at 9 a.m.!

The Quick Job Search Review

There are a few thoughts I want to emphasize in closing my brief review of job-seeking skills:

- Approach your job search as if it were a job itself.
- Get organized and spend at least 25 hours per week actively looking.
- Know your skills and have a clear job objective.
- Get lots of interviews, including exploratory interviews through networking.
- Have a good answer to the question "Why should I hire you?"
- Follow up on all the leads you generate and send out lots of thank-you notes and JIST Cards.
- Pay attention to all the details; then be yourself in the interview. Remember that employers are people, too. They will hire someone who they feel will do the job well, be reliable, and fit easily into the work environment.
- When you want the job, tell the employer that you want the job and why.
- Believe in yourself and ask people to help you.

It's that simple.

Chapter 15

Quick Tips for Using the Internet in Your Job Search

Now that you've gotten an overview of the quickest and most efficient job search methods, this chapter focuses on the Internet as one of those job search tools, and one that is gaining in popularity.

This chapter assumes you know how to use the Internet. If the Internet and World Wide Web are new to you, I recommend a JIST book titled *Best Career and Education Web Sites,* by Rachel Singer Gordon and Anne Wolfinger. This book covers the basics of how the Internet works, plus provides information on using it for career planning and job seeking.

A point to note: I will use the terms "Internet" and "Web" interchangeably. While differences between the two matters to technical folks, the terms are casually used to mean the same thing.

Career and job hunting resources are all over the Internet. Telling you all that it contains relevant to your search is just not possible. My objective is not to cover all there is to know about career resources on the Web. My objective instead is to make sure that you make the most of this powerful tool in your search and that you avoid some of the common pitfalls.

The Internet as a Tool for Your Job Search

You hear about the Internet everywhere, and you may use it on a regular basis. But is it a good place for job seeking? Yes and no.

I say yes because people do get jobs through the Internet, and the numbers who do are increasing every day. I am a practical person and have always looked for job search methods that work, and the Internet is another tool to use in your search for a good job. But you should also know that the Internet has its limitations.

The Dangers of Online Job Hunting

While the Internet has worked for many in finding job leads, far more people have been disappointed. Online job hunting can seem like the greatest thing since sliced bread in that it's so easy. You zap your resume out into cyberspace and sit back while it does all the work for you—24 hours a day if you post the resume in a database rather than just applying to jobs one at a time. It's true that the Internet has made job searching much easier in a lot of ways, but using it is often not as effective as you might hope.

The good thing about the Internet is its stupendous amount of information. The bad thing about the Internet is its stupendous amount of information.

It Makes You Too Passive

Many job seekers assume they can simply put resumes in Internet resume databases and employers will line up to hire them. It sometimes happens this way, but not often. This is the same negative experience that people have when mailing lots of unsolicited resumes to human resource offices—a hopeful but mostly ineffective, shot-in-the-dark approach that has been around since long before computers.

There's a Huge Amount of Competition

Many Web sites have thousands of job seekers posting resumes and applying for jobs every day—hundreds of thousands or even more than a million on the biggest sites—so you have huge amounts of competition. The odds of your resume being the one that gets looked at (referred to as "gets a hit" in online job hunting lingo) are slim. You have to make sure your resume has the right keywords (as discussed in Chapter 4) and then hope for the best.

A Threat to Your Personal Security

A major downside to online job hunting is the potential for personal security breaches, ranging from the annoying, as in unwanted spam mail, to the highly invasive, such as identity theft. Many job seekers opt for leaving their phone number and address off of their electronic resume—using only their e-mail address—to minimize the chances that criminals can track down their Social Security number or other personal data.

Quick Alert

As with sending out many unsolicited resumes, putting your resume on the Internet is a passive approach that is unlikely to work well for you. Use the Internet in your job search, but plan to use other techniques, including networking and direct contacts with employers.

An Internet Success Story

Now that I have cautioned you regarding the Internet's limitations, you should know that it works very well for some people. To illustrate this, let me share a real situation I recently uncovered.

I was doing a series of interviews about jobs for a rural and small-market TV station. I asked the staff members—all young people—how they got their jobs. It turned out that many previous employees had recently left for larger markets. That put one recent graduate with just a few months' experience in

(continued)

(continued)

charge—and he desperately needed staff to keep the station running. He had obtained his job by responding to a posting on a broadcasters' Web site, so he listed on that site all the open jobs at his station.

In a few days, new broadcasting graduates from all over the country saw the Web postings and responded. E-mail went back and forth, and the relatively few willing to come to the remote station at their expense were invited to interview. Within a few weeks, most open positions were filled by young people who had responded on the Internet.

The staffing crisis for the TV station ended, and many of those new hires told me that they were getting a great opportunity not attainable by other methods. I have to agree.

Traditional recruiting methods would have created long delays for the employer and the job seekers. And traditional recruiting may have screened out these less-experienced applicants. These people got jobs by using the Internet. While many people surely had better credentials, they did not know about or get these jobs.

Note that the ones who got the jobs were those willing to travel to the employer on short notice and at their own expense. They had to be active and take some chances. They did not simply post resumes in a resume database and hope for the best. The winning applicants were proactive in using the Internet to make direct contact with this employer, and then they followed up aggressively.

There Are Many Ways to Use the Internet in Your Job Search

Job seeking on the Internet involves more than simply visiting job boards and posting your resume in resume banks. The job seekers who got the jobs at the TV station used the Internet in an active way. And they combined a number of methods, both Internet and more conventional ones (such as going to the interview), to get the jobs.

Don't forget that in addition to posting your resume or browsing jobs, you can use the Internet in other ways in your job search such as research, networking, and identifying employers to contact directly. Here are some of the ways the Internet can help you in your job search:

- **Employer Web sites.** Many employers have Web sites that include substantial information plus a list of job openings. Some sites allow you to interact with staff online or via e-mail to get answers to questions about working there.
- **Information.** You can search for information on a specific employer or industry, get job descriptions that list skills and requirements to emphasize in interviews (and on your resume), find career counseling and job search advice, and look up almost anything else you need related to your job search.
- **E-mail.** Most Internet-savvy employers accept resumes via e-mail, and many will correspond with you this way. Many resume database sites will send you e-mail notices of newly added jobs that meet your criteria.
- **Specialty sites.** People in the TV industry have specialized associations and magazines, and the same is true of other fields. Your task is to find the Web sites that specialize in the jobs that interest you. Many have job postings, useful information, and access to people in the know. Also, many geographic-specific sites for cities and towns list local openings. A simple keyword search using a search engine like Google.com or Yahoo.com can broaden your search.

Quick Tip

Save time in your search by typing your search information directly into your Web browser's address bar. You may be led to just what you're looking for without having to go through a search engine.

- **Newsgroups.** Thousands of newsgroups specialize in topics of interest to their respective users and provide excellent networking opportunities. Some are for members of specific organizations, like accountants in a given city. Others are open to those interested in specialty topics. Newsgroups can be a good source of local or field-specific contacts who may be able to give you job leads. Some newsgroups list job openings. To learn more about newsgroups and how to find them, visit www.learnthenet.com, or http://groups.google.com.

The sites listed later in this chapter will help you find additional Internet resources. I encourage you to be creative in using these and other tools to conduct an active job search.

Eight Quick Tips to Increase Your Job Search Effectiveness on the Internet

You could get lucky putting your resume on the Internet and waiting for an employer to contact you. It does happen. But being passive on the Internet—as I've said before—is often about as effective as using other passive job search methods, which is not very effective at all.

You can do far more on the Internet than simply posting your resume in one or more resume databases. The list of Internet sites later in this chapter gives you job search sites to visit, but here are some brief points to use in preparing.

> My advice is to use the Internet in your job search, but be active rather than passive.

1. **Be as specific as possible in the job you seek.** This is important in using any job search method and even more so in using the Internet. I say this because the Internet is so enormous in its reach that looking for a nonspecific job is simply not an appropriate task. So do your career planning homework—reviewing Chapters 5, 6, and 7 again, if needed—and be focused in what you are seeking.

2. **Keep your expectations reasonable.** The people who have the most success on the Internet are those who best understand its limitations. For example, those with technical skills that are in short supply will have more employers looking for these skills

and more success on the Internet. Keep in mind that many listed jobs are already filled by the time you see them and that thousands may apply to those that sound particularly attractive.

Quick Reminder

People do get job leads on the Internet, but be reasonable in your expectations and use a variety of job search methods in addition to the Internet.

3. **Consider your willingness to move.** If you don't want to move, or are willing to move only to certain locations, restrict your job search to geographic areas that meet your criteria. Many Internet databases allow you to view only those jobs that match your geographic preferences.

4. **Seek out relevant sites.** Simply getting your resume listed on several Internet sites is often not enough. Many employers do not use these sites, or they use one but not another. Remember the example that I described earlier—those people found out about TV-related jobs from an Internet site that was run by a trade publication for broadcasters. Many professional associations post job openings on their sites or list other sites that would be of interest to that profession. Check out the resources available to people in the industries or occupations that interest you, since many of these resources also have Internet sites.

Quick Reference

A great place to find sites that are tailored to a specific industry or functional specialty is www.careerxroads.com, or in the book *CareerXroads* by Gerry Crispin and Mark Mehler.

5. **Find specific employer sites.** Most employers have their own Internet sites that list job openings, allow you to apply online, and even provide access to staff who can answer your questions. While larger companies mostly use this approach, many smaller employers and government agencies have set up sites to attract candidates.

6. **Use informal chat rooms or request help.** Many Web sites have interactive chat rooms or allow you to post a message on their online bulletin boards for others to respond to on the board, or privately by e-mail. These methods allow you to meet potential employers or others in your field that can provide the advice or leads you seek.

7. **Use the listings of large Internet browsers or service providers.** While thousands of career-related Internet sites exist, some are better than others. Many sites listed later in this chapter provide links to other recommended sites. Large service providers such as America Online (www.aol.com) and MSN (www.msn.com) offer career-related information and job listings on their sites and links to other sites. Most larger search engines give links to recommended career-related sites and can be quite useful. Some larger such sites include AltaVista (www.altavista.com), Lycos (www.lycos.com), and Yahoo! (www.yahoo.com).

8. **Don't get ripped off online.** Since the Internet has few regulations, crooks use it as a way to take money from trusting souls. Remember that anyone can set up a site, even if the person does not provide a legitimate service. So be careful before you pay money for anything on the Internet. A general rule is that if it sounds too good to be true, it probably is. For example, if a site "guarantees" that it will find you a job or charges high fees, I recommend that you look elsewhere.

The Most Useful Internet Sites

Thousands of career and job-related sites are on the Internet, and more are added every day. You can waste an enormous amount of time finding what you need. So, to help you save time, I have listed sites here that are among the most helpful. Since many of these sites provide links to other sites, I've listed only a few of the better sites in each category. You can find links to many other sites by starting with these. Among many other resources, JIST Publishing's site at www.jist.com has free career and job search information as well as links to other sites. Note that Web sites sometimes change addresses or shut down, so one or more of the sites mentioned here may not be valid in the future.

Quick Reference

Some of these listings come from *Best Career and Education Web Sites* (JIST Publishing) by Rachel Singer Gordon and Anne Wolfinger. The book provides more details on each site than I could provide here, as well as on many other sites, organized into useful categories. But these will give you good places to begin.

Sites with the Best Links to Other Career and Job Search Sites

These sites describe and provide Internet links to other career-related sites. For example, some provide lists of sites by type of job, by employer name, by region, or by other useful criteria.

- **Career Resource Center**—www.careers.org. Provides more than 7,500 links to sites listing job openings at businesses, on job banks, and other resources.
- **CareerOneStop**—www.careeronestop.org. Based on the Department of Labor's vision for America's Labor Market Information System, this site is a gateway to some of the best job listings and free career information sites on the Internet.
- **Catapult on the Web**—www.jobweb.com. Maintained by the National Association of Colleges and Employers.
- **Quintessential Careers**—www.quintcareers.com. An outstanding site with a huge number of resources and helpful links on all career planning and job hunting topics.
- **The Riley Guide**—www.rileyguide.com. One of the first comprehensive career sites on the Web and still considered by many to be one of the best.

Best Resume Banks and Sites Listing Job Openings

These Web sites provide listings of job openings and allow you to add your resume for employers to look at. All allow you to look up job openings in a variety of useful ways including by location, job type, and other criteria. Most get their fees from employers and don't charge job seekers.

Quick Tip

These sites often provide features such as resume and job search advice, e-mail notification to you of new job entries that meet your criteria, and more.

- **America's Job Bank**—www.ajb.dni.us. A big one run by the U.S. Public Employment Service. Lists openings from all 50 state employment services, plus gives employer-maintained listings and other services.
- **Best Jobs in the USA Today**—www.bestjobsusa.com. Features career-related articles and employer-listed jobs.
- **CareerBuilder**—www.careerbuilder.com. Generally considered to be one of the top three Internet job destinations (along with Monster and HotJobs). One feature allows a search of over 40 other sites and listings of a million openings.
- **CareerSite**—www.careersite.com. Includes a large network of professional resume writers in addition to the usual job listing service.
- **DirectEmployers**—www.directemployers.com. A no-frills but excellent site that gives direct access to the job listings of more than 200 employers.
- **Employment Guide**—www.employmentguide.com. An easy to use, good all-purpose site.
- **Exec-u-net**—www.execunet.com. Lists job openings for top-level managers and executives and offers networking opportunities.
- **JobBank USA**—www.jobbankusa.com. Established in 1995, this is one of the more reliable, comprehensive sites.
- **Monster**—www.monster.com. One of the biggest, with lots of features including browsing or keyword searches of the job database, employer profiles, career fair listings, and career information. Also has a great online networking feature, Monster Networking.
- **TrueCareers**—www.truecareers.com. A resume-posting and job search site for degreed professionals.

- **USA Jobs**—www.usajobs.com. The best source for federal government jobs.
- **Yahoo! Hot Jobs**—http://hotjobs.yahoo.com. One of the "big three." A full-featured site well worth a visit.

Best Sites for Occupational Information

These sites provide solid information on the skills, training, work environment, pay, and other important information on all major jobs. Use this to emphasize your most relevant skills and experiences in your resume or prepare for an interview by knowing in advance what skills and other characteristics are most important to an employer. You can also use these sites to identify many jobs that require your skills but that you might otherwise overlook in your job search.

- **CareerOINK**—www.careeroink.com. Descriptions for more than 14,000 job titles plus easy-to-use links to jobs by interest, education, or training needed, and other criteria (operated by JIST Publishing).
- **O*NET Online**—http://online.onetcenter.org/. Funded by the U.S. Department of Labor, this site provides descriptions for the 1,100 or so major jobs the government tracks, with sorts by skills required and other criteria.

Best Sites for Recent Grads or Students

Many good sites exist for students and recent graduates, and here are a few of the best. All provide information, links to other sites, and listings of internships and job openings.

- **College Grad Job Hunter**—www.collegegrad.com
- **JobDirect**—www.jobdirect.com
- **JobWeb**—www.jobweb.com
- **MonsterTrak**—www.monstertrak.monster.com

Best Sites for College, Training, and Financial Aid Information

Many excellent sites provide information on education and training options. Some of the sites I list here will link you to school sites packed with specific information about their programs.

- **College Board**—www.collegeboard.org. Information about the SAT standardized college admissions test.
- **FastWeb**—http://fastweb.monster.com. Matches student profiles with more than 180,000 financial aid awards.
- **FinAid**—www.finaid.org. A site sponsored by the National Association of Student Financial Aid Administrators.
- **National Association of Colleges and Employers (NACE)**—www.jobweb.org.
- **Peterson's Education Center**—www.petersons.com. Information on colleges, financial aid, internships, summer programs for kids, and career and resume sites.
- **U.S. Department of Education's Financial Aid site**—www.fafsa.ed.gov. Allows you to look up and submit applications for various government financial aid programs.
- **U.S. News Education**—www.usnews.com/usnews/edu/eduhome.htm. Includes school rankings, "best education buys," career tips, financial aid information, and links to other sites.

Closing Thoughts: Remember Your Main Purpose

You could spend years browsing the Internet's career-related sites. Some people, in fact, have made a career of doing this—and writing books about it. But, as I say whenever I can, your task is to get interviews and job offers, not hang around working on your resume, or browsing the Internet, or whatever.

So, please, use the Internet in your search for a new job but be active, not passive. Use other job search methods, too. Spend time every week and every day on the job search. And keep the faith. One other thing: The Internet is open 24 hours a day, so keep your daytime hours open for contacting employers directly and use the Internet at night and on weekends.

Appendices

The appendices to this book include more information you will find helpful in your career planning and job search.

Appendix A is a sample job listing from the *Occupational Outlook Handbook,* the U.S. Department of Labor's definitive source of occupational information.

Appendix B is a listing of the contact information for the professional writers who contributed resumes and cover letters to this book. You can contact them or their professional associations if you need more help with your resume.

Appendix A

Sample Job Description from the *Occupational Outlook Handbook*

The *Occupational Outlook Handbook (OOH)* is an important source of information about many jobs. Updated every two years by the U.S. Department of Labor, it provides helpful descriptions for about 270 jobs. These jobs are the most popular ones in our economy and about 88 percent of all people work in one of them.

I have included here the content from one job listed in the *OOH* as an example. I selected the description for school teachers since I felt that most people would be familiar with this job. As you read the description for school teachers, understand that one or more similar descriptions are in the *OOH* for jobs that will interest you.

The *OOH* descriptions can be very helpful in a variety of ways. For example, as you read a description, you can circle key skills the job requires. This will help you to know which skills you should emphasize in your resume and in interviews. If you are interviewing for a job, reviewing the description in advance can help you to do a much better job in the interview.

Another way to use these descriptions is to look up past jobs to identify skills you needed for them. In many cases, those same or similar skills will be needed in the job you want now. You can cite your previous jobs to support your having the skills needed in the new job. For example, you will find that a school teacher needs to keep up with computer skills, which is a requirement in many other jobs.

As you review the sample description, note that it provides other important information such as salary ranges, education or training required, related jobs, and other details that can help you make career decisions as well as look for a job. While the descriptions don't change much between editions, data on salaries and growth projections are typically several years old before they are published, so look for the most recent edition of the book.

I feel strongly about the value of the *OOH* and encourage you to use it routinely throughout your job search. The book is available in most libraries and a bookstore version, titled *America's Top 300 Jobs,* can be obtained directly from JIST by calling 1-800-648-5478 or visiting www.jist.com.

Sample *OOH* Job Description: School Teachers—Preschool, Kindergarten, Elementary, Middle, and Secondary

Significant Points

- Public school teachers must have at least a bachelor's degree, complete an approved teacher education program, and be licensed.
- Many States offer alternative licensing programs to attract people into teaching, especially for hard-to-fill positions.
- Excellent job opportunities are expected as a large number of teachers retire over the next 10 years, particularly at the secondary school level; opportunities will vary somewhat by geographic area and subject taught.

Nature of the Work

Teachers act as facilitators or coaches, using interactive discussions and "hands-on" approaches to help students learn and apply concepts in subjects such as science, mathematics, or English. They utilize "props" or "manipulatives" to help children understand abstract concepts, solve problems, and develop critical thought processes. For example, they teach the concepts of numbers or of addition and subtraction by playing board games. As the children get older, the teachers use more sophisticated materials, such as science apparatus, cameras, or computers.

To encourage collaboration in solving problems, students are increasingly working in groups to discuss and solve problems together. Preparing students for the future workforce is the major stimulus generating the changes in education. To be prepared, students must be able to interact with others, adapt to new technology, and think through problems logically. Teachers provide the tools and the environment for their students to develop these skills.

Preschool, kindergarten, and elementary school teachers play a vital role in the development of children. What children learn and experience during their early years can shape their views of themselves and the world and can affect their later success or failure in school, work, and their personal lives. Preschool, kindergarten, and elementary school teachers introduce children to mathematics, language, science, and social studies. They use games, music, artwork, films, books, computers, and other tools to teach basic skills.

Preschool children learn mainly through play and interactive activities. Preschool teachers capitalize on children's play to further language and vocabulary development (using storytelling, rhyming games, and acting games), improve social skills (having the children work together to build a neighborhood in a sandbox), and introduce scientific and mathematical concepts (showing the children how to balance and count blocks when building a bridge or how to mix colors when painting). Thus, a less structured approach, including small-group lessons, one-on-one instruction, and learning through creative activities such as art, dance, and music, is adopted to teach preschool children. Play and hands-on teaching also are used in kindergarten classrooms, but there academics begin to take priority. Letter recognition, phonics, numbers, and awareness of nature and science, introduced at the preschool level, are taught primarily by kindergarten teachers.

Most elementary school teachers instruct one class of children in several subjects. In some schools, two or more teachers work as a team and are jointly responsible for a group of students in at least one subject. In other schools, a teacher may teach one special subject—usually music, art, reading, science, arithmetic, or physical education—to a number of classes. A small but growing number of teachers instruct multilevel classrooms, with students at several different learning levels.

Middle school teachers and secondary school teachers help students delve more deeply into subjects introduced in elementary school and expose them to more information about the world. Middle and secondary school teachers specialize in a specific subject, such as English, Spanish, mathematics, history, or biology. They also can teach subjects that are career oriented. Vocational education teachers, also referred to as career and technical or career-technology teachers, instruct and train students to work in a wide variety of fields, such as healthcare, business, auto repair, communications, and, increasingly, technology. They often teach courses that are in high demand by area employers, who may provide input into the curriculum and offer internships to students. Many vocational teachers play an active role in building and overseeing these partnerships. Additional responsibilities of middle and secondary school teachers may include career guidance and job placement, as well as followups with students after graduation. (Special education teachers—who instruct elementary and secondary school students who have a variety of disabilities—are discussed separately in this section of the Handbook.)

Teachers may use films, slides, overhead projectors, and the latest technology in teaching, including computers, telecommunication systems, and video discs. The use of computer resources, such as educational software and the Internet, exposes students to a vast range of experiences and promotes interactive learning. Through the Internet, students can communicate with students in other countries. Students also use the Internet for individual research projects and to gather information. Computers are used in other classroom activities as well, from solving math problems to learning English as a second language. Teachers also may use computers to record grades and perform other administrative and clerical duties. They must continually update their skills so that they can instruct and use the latest technology in the classroom.

Teachers often work with students from varied ethnic, racial, and religious backgrounds. With growing minority populations in most parts of the country, it is important for teachers to work effectively with a diverse student population. Accordingly, some schools offer training to help teachers enhance their awareness and understanding of different cultures. Teachers may also include multicultural programming in their lesson plans, to address the needs of all students, regardless of their cultural background.

Teachers design classroom presentations to meet students' needs and abilities. They also work with students individually. Teachers plan, evaluate, and assign lessons; prepare, administer, and grade tests; listen to oral presentations; and maintain classroom discipline. They observe and evaluate a student's performance and potential and increasingly are asked to use new assessment methods. For example, teachers may examine a portfolio of a student's artwork or writing in order to judge the student's overall progress. They then can provide additional assistance in areas in which a student needs help. Teachers also grade papers, prepare report cards, and meet with parents and school staff to discuss a student's academic progress or personal problems.

In addition to conducting classroom activities, teachers oversee study halls and homerooms, supervise extracurricular activities, and accompany students on field trips. They may identify students with physical or mental problems and refer the students to the proper authorities. Secondary school teachers occasionally assist students in choosing courses, colleges, and careers. Teachers also participate in education conferences and workshops.

In recent years, site-based management, which allows teachers and parents to participate actively in management decisions regarding school operations, has gained popularity. In many schools, teachers are increasingly involved in making decisions regarding the budget, personnel, textbooks, curriculum design, and teaching methods.

Working Conditions

Seeing students develop new skills and gain an appreciation of knowledge and learning can be very rewarding. However, teaching may be frustrating when one is dealing with unmotivated or disrespectful students. Occasionally, teachers must cope with unruly behavior and violence in the schools. Teachers may experience stress in dealing with large classes, students from disadvantaged or multicultural backgrounds, or heavy workloads. Inner-city schools in particular, may be run down and lack the amenities of schools in wealthier communities. Accountability standards also may increase stress levels, with teachers expected to produce students who are able to exhibit satisfactory performance on standardized tests in core subjects.

Teachers are sometimes isolated from their colleagues because they work alone in a classroom of students. However, some schools allow teachers to work in teams and with mentors to enhance their professional development.

Including school duties performed outside the classroom, many teachers work more than 40 hours a week. Part-time schedules are more common among preschool and kindergarten teachers. Although some school districts have gone to all-day kindergartens, most kindergarten teachers still teach two kindergarten classes a day. Most teachers work the traditional 10-month school year with a 2-month vacation during the summer. During the vacation break, those on the 10-month schedule may teach in summer sessions, take other jobs, travel, or pursue personal interests. Many enroll in college courses or workshops to continue their education. Teachers in districts with a year-round schedule typically work 8 weeks, are on vacation for 1 week, and have a 5-week midwinter break. Preschool teachers working in daycare settings often work year round.

Most States have tenure laws that prevent teachers from being fired without just cause and due process. Teachers may obtain tenure after they have satisfactorily completed a probationary period of teaching, normally 3 years. Tenure does not absolutely guarantee a job, but it does provide some security.

Employment

Preschool, kindergarten, elementary school, middle school, and secondary school teachers, except special education, held about 3.8 million jobs in 2002. Of the teachers in those jobs, about 1.5 million were elementary school teachers, 1.1 million were secondary school teachers, 602,000 were middle school teachers, 424,000 were preschool teachers, and 168,000 were kindergarten teachers. The majority of kindergarten, elementary school, middle school, and secondary school teachers, except special education worked in local government educational services. About 10 percent worked for private schools.

Preschool teachers, except special education were most often employed in child daycare services (63 percent), religious organizations (9 percent), local government educational services (9 percent), and private educational services (7 percent). Employment of teachers is geographically distributed much the same as the population is.

Training, Other Qualifications, and Advancement

All 50 States and the District of Columbia require public school teachers to be licensed. Licensure is not required for teachers in private schools. Usually licensure is granted by the State Board of Education or a licensure advisory committee. Teachers may be licensed to teach the early childhood grades (usually preschool through grade 3); the elementary grades (grades 1 through 6 or 8); the middle grades (grades 5 through 8); a secondary-education subject area (usually grades 7 through 12); or a special subject, such as reading or music (usually grades kindergarten through 12).

Requirements for regular licenses to teach kindergarten through grade 12 vary by State. However, all States require general education teachers to have a bachelor's degree and to have completed an approved teacher training program with a prescribed number of subject and education credits, as well as supervised practice teaching. Some States also require technology training and the attainment of a minimum grade point average. A number of States require that teachers obtain a master's degree in education within a specified period after they begin teaching.

Almost all States require applicants for a teacher's license to be tested for competency in basic skills, such as reading and writing, and in teaching. Almost all also require the teacher to exhibit proficiency in his or her subject. Nowadays, school systems are moving toward implementing performance-based systems for licensure, which usually require the teacher to demonstrate satisfactory teaching performance over an extended period in order to obtain a provisional license, in addition to passing an examination in one's subject. Most States require continuing education for renewal of the teacher's license. Many States have reciprocity agreements that make it easier for teachers licensed in one State to become licensed in another.

Many States offer alternative licensure programs for teachers who have bachelor's degrees in the subject they will teach, but who lack the necessary education courses required for a regular license. Alternative licensure programs originally were designed to ease shortages of teachers of certain subjects, such as mathematics and science. The programs have expanded to attract other people into teaching, including recent college graduates and those changing from another career to teaching. In some programs, individuals begin teaching quickly under provisional licensure. After working under the close supervision of experienced educators for 1 or 2 years while taking education courses outside school hours, they receive regular licensure if they have progressed satisfactorily. In other programs, college graduates who do not meet licensure requirements take only those courses that they lack and then become licensed. This approach may take 1 or 2 semesters of full-time study. States may issue emergency licenses to individuals who do not meet the requirements for a regular license when schools cannot attract enough qualified teachers to fill positions. Teachers who need to be licensed may enter programs that grant a master's degree in education, as well as a license.

In many States, vocational teachers have many of the same requirements for teaching as their academic counterparts. However, because knowledge and experience in a particular field are important criteria for the job, some States will license vocational education teachers without a bachelor's degree, provided they can demonstrate expertise in their field. A minimum number of hours in education courses may also be required.

Licensing requirements for preschool teachers also vary by State. Requirements for public preschool teachers are generally higher than those for private preschool teachers. Some States require a bachelor's degree in early childhood education, others require an associate's degree, and still others require certification by a nationally recognized authority. The Child Development Associate (CDA) credential, the most common type of certification, requires a mix of classroom training and experience working with children, along with an independent assessment of an individual's competence.

In some cases, teachers of kindergarten through high school may attain professional certification in order to demonstrate competency beyond that required for a license. The National Board for Professional Teaching Standards offers a voluntary national certification. To become nationally accredited, experienced teachers must prove their aptitude by compiling a portfolio showing their work in the classroom and by passing a written assessment and evaluation of their teaching knowledge. Currently, teachers may become certified in a variety of areas, on the basis of the age of the students and, in some cases, the subject taught. For example, teachers may obtain a certificate for teaching English language arts to early adolescents (aged 11 to 15), or they may become certified as early childhood generalists. All States recognize national certification, and many States and school districts provide special benefits to teachers holding such certification. Benefits typically include higher salaries and reimbursement for continuing education and certification fees. In addition, many States allow nationally certified teachers to carry a license from one State to another.

The National Council for Accreditation of Teacher Education currently accredits more than 550 teacher education programs across the United States. Generally, 4-year colleges require students to wait until their sophomore year before applying for admission to teacher education programs. Traditional education programs for kindergarten and elementary school teachers include courses—designed specifically for those preparing to teach—in mathematics, physical science, social science, music, art, and literature, as well as prescribed professional education courses, such as philosophy of education, psychology of learning, and teaching methods. Aspiring secondary school teachers most often major in the subject they plan to teach while also taking a program of study in teacher preparation. Teacher education programs are now required to include classes in the use of computers and other technologies in order to maintain their accreditation. Most programs require students to perform a student-teaching internship.

Many States now offer professional development schools—partnerships between universities and elementary or secondary schools. Students enter these 1-year programs after completion of their bachelor's degree. Professional development schools merge theory with practice and allow the student to experience a year of teaching firsthand, under professional guidance.

In addition to being knowledgeable in their subject, teachers must have the ability to communicate, inspire trust and confidence, and motivate students, as well as understand the students' educational and emotional needs. Teachers must be able to recognize and respond to individual and cultural differences in students and employ different teaching methods that will result in higher student achievement. They should be organized, dependable, patient, and creative. Teachers also must be able to work cooperatively and communicate effectively with other teachers, support staff, parents, and members of the community.

With additional preparation, teachers may move into positions as school librarians, reading specialists, curriculum specialists, or guidance counselors. Teachers may become administrators or supervisors, although the number of these positions is limited and competition can be intense. In some systems, highly qualified, experienced teachers can become senior or mentor teachers, with higher pay and additional responsibilities. They guide and assist less experienced teachers while keeping most of their own teaching responsibilities. Preschool teachers usually work their way up from assistant teacher, to teacher, to lead teacher—who may be responsible for the instruction of several classes—and, finally, to director of the center. Preschool teachers with a bachelor's degree frequently are qualified to teach kindergarten through grade 3 as well. Teaching at these higher grades often results in higher pay.

Job Outlook

Job opportunities for teachers over the next 10 years will vary from good to excellent, depending on the locality, grade level, and subject taught. Most job openings will be attributable to the expected retirement of a large number of teachers. In addition, relatively high rates of turnover, especially among beginning teachers employed in poor, urban schools, also will lead to numerous job openings for teachers. Competition for qualified teachers among some localities will likely continue, with schools luring teachers from other States and districts with bonuses and higher pay.

Through 2012, overall student enrollments, a key factor in the demand for teachers, are expected to rise more slowly than in the past. As the children of the baby-boom generation get older, smaller numbers of young children will enter school behind them, resulting in average employment growth for all teachers, from preschool through secondary grades. Projected enrollments will vary by region. Fast-growing States in the South and West—particularly California, Texas, Georgia, Idaho, Hawaii, Alaska, and New Mexico—will experience the largest enrollment increases. Enrollments in the Northeast and Midwest are expected to hold relatively steady or decline. The job market for teachers also continues to vary by school location and by subject taught. Many inner cities—often characterized by overcrowded, ill-equipped schools and higher-than-average poverty rates—and rural areas—characterized by their remote location and relatively low salaries—have difficulty attracting and retaining enough teachers, so job prospects should be better in these areas than in suburban districts. Currently, many school districts have difficulty hiring qualified teachers in some subject areas—mathematics, science (especially chemistry and physics), bilingual education, and foreign languages. Qualified vocational teachers, at both the middle school and secondary school levels, also are currently in demand in a variety of fields. Specialties that have an adequate number of qualified teachers include general elementary education, physical education, and social studies. Teachers who are geographically mobile and who obtain licensure in more than one subject should have a distinct advantage in finding a job. Increasing enrollments of minorities, coupled with a shortage of minority teachers, should cause efforts to recruit minority teachers to intensify. Also, the number of non-English-speaking students has grown dramatically, creating demand for bilingual teachers and for those who teach English as a second language. The number of teachers employed is dependent as well on State and local expenditures for education and on the enactment of legislation to increase the quality of education. A number of initiatives, such as reduced class size (primarily in the early elementary grades), mandatory preschool for 4-year-olds, and all-day kindergarten, have been implemented in a few States, but not nationwide. Additional teachers—particularly preschool and early elementary school teachers—will be needed if States or localities implement any of these measures. At the Federal level, legislation that is likely to affect teachers recently was put into place with the enactment of the No Child Left Behind Act. Although the full impact of this act is not yet known, its emphasis on ensuring that all schools hire and retain only qualified teachers, may lead to an increase in funding for schools that currently lack such teachers.

The supply of teachers is expected to increase in response to reports of improved job prospects, better pay, more teacher involvement in school policy, and greater public interest in education. In recent years, the total number of bachelor's and master's degrees granted in education has increased steadily. Because of a shortage of teachers in certain locations, and in anticipation of the loss of a number of teachers to retirement, many States have implemented policies that will encourage more students to become teachers. In addition, more teachers may be drawn from a reserve pool of career changers, substitute teachers, and teachers completing alternative certification programs.

Earnings

Median annual earnings of kindergarten, elementary, middle, and secondary school teachers ranged from $39,810 to $44,340 in 2002; the lowest 10 percent earned $24,960 to $29,850; the top 10 percent earned $62,890 to $68,530. Median earnings for preschool teachers were $19,270.

According to the American Federation of Teachers, beginning teachers with a bachelor's degree earned an average of $30,719 in the 2001–02 school year. The estimated average salary of all public elementary and secondary school teachers in the 2001–02 school year was $44,367. Private school teachers generally earn less than public school teachers.

In 2002, more than half of all elementary, middle, and secondary school teachers belonged to unions—mainly the American Federation of Teachers and the National Education Association—that bargain with school systems over wages, hours, and other terms and conditions of employment. Fewer preschool and kindergarten teachers were union members—about 15 percent in 2002.

Teachers can boost their salary in a number of ways. In some schools, teachers receive extra pay for coaching sports and working with students in extracurricular activities. Getting a master's degree or national certification often results in a raise in pay, as does acting as a mentor. Some teachers earn extra income during the summer by teaching summer school or performing other jobs in the school system.

Related Occupations

Preschool, kindergarten, elementary school, middle school, and secondary school teaching requires a variety of skills and aptitudes, including a talent for working with children; organizational, administrative, and recordkeeping abilities; research and communication skills; the power to influence, motivate, and train others; patience; and creativity. Workers in other occupations requiring some of these aptitudes include teachers—postsecondary; counselors; teacher assistants; education administrators; librarians; child care workers; public relations specialists; social workers; and athletes, coaches, umpires, and related workers.

Sources of Additional Information

Information on licensure or certification requirements and approved teacher training institutions is available from local school systems and State departments of education.

Information on the teaching profession and on how to become a teacher can be obtained from:

> Recruiting New Teachers, Inc., 385 Concord Ave., Suite 103, Belmont, MA 02478. Internet: http://www.rnt.org

This organization also sponsors another Internet site that provides helpful information on becoming a teacher:

> http://www.recruitingteachers.org

Information on teachers' unions and education-related issues may be obtained from any of the following sources:

> American Federation of Teachers, 555 New Jersey Ave. NW., Washington, DC 20001.

> National Education Association, 1201 16th St. NW., Washington, DC 20036.

A list of institutions with accredited teacher education programs can be obtained from:

> National Council for Accreditation of Teacher Education, 2010 Massachusetts Ave. NW., Suite 500, Washington, DC 20036-1023. Internet: http://www.ncate.org

For information on vocational education and vocational education teachers, contact:

> Association for Career and Technical Education, 1410 King St., Alexandria, VA 22314. Internet: http://www.acteonline.org

For information on careers in educating children and issues affecting preschool teachers, contact either of the following organizations:

> National Association for the Education of Young Children, 1509 16th St. NW., Washington, DC 20036. Internet: http://www.naeyc.org

> Council for Professional Recognition, 2460 16th St. NW., Washington, DC 20009-3575. Internet: http://www.cdacouncil.org

For information on teachers and the No Child Left Behind Act, contact:

> U.S. Department of Education, 400 Maryland Avenue, SW., Washington, DC, 20202. Internet: http://www.ed.gov

OOH ONET Codes

25-2011.00, 25-2012.00, 25-2021.00, 25-2022.00, 25-2023.00, 25-2031.00, 25-2032.00

Appendix B

Resume and Cover Letter Contributors

The following people contributed sample resumes and cover letters to this book. They are all professional resume writers or career coaches. I acknowledge with appreciation their submissions.

Carla Barrett
Career Designs
6855 Irving Rd.
Redding, CA 96001
Phone: (530) 241-8570
Fax: (530) 248-3351
E-mail: carlab@careerdesigns.com
Web site: www.careerdesigns.com
Member: CMI
Certification: CCM

Beverley Baskin and Mitchell I. Baskin
BBCS Counseling Services
6 Alberta Dr.
Marlboro, NJ 07746
Also at Iselin, NJ, and Princeton, NJ
Toll-free: (800) 300-4079
Fax: (732) 972-8846
E-mail: bbcs@att.net and
info@bbcscounseling.com
Web sites: www.baskincareer.com and
www.job-research.com
Member: NRWA, NCDA, NECA, MACCA,
AMHCA
Certification: Ed.S, MA, LPC, NCCC

Janet L. Beckstrom
Word Crafter
1717 Montclair Ave.
Flint, MI 48503
Phone: (800) 351-9818
Fax: (810) 232-9257
E-mail: wordcrafter@voyager.net
Member: PARW/CC
Certification: CPRW

Alesia Benedict
Career Objectives
151 W. Passaic St.
Rochelle Park, NJ 07662
Phone: (800) 206-5353
E-mail: careerobj@aol.com
Web site: www.getinterviews.com
Member: PARW/CC (Board), CMI (Board),
NAJST
Certification: CPRW, JCTC

Gayle Bernstein
Typing PLUS
2710 E. 62nd St., Suite 1
Indianapolis, IN 46220
Phone: (317) 257-6789
Fax: (317) 479-3103
E-mail: GayleBerns@aol.com
Member: PARW/CC, NRWA
Certification: CPRW

Arnold G. Boldt
Arnold-Smith Associates
625 Panorama Trail, Bldg. One, Ste. 120
Rochester, NY 14625
Phone: (716) 383-0350
Fax: (716) 387-0516
E-mail: Arnoldsmth@aol.com
Web site: www.resumesos.com
Member: PARW/CC, CMI, NRWA, PRW&RA
Certification: CPRW

Patricia S. Cash
Résumés For Results
P.O. Box 2806
Prescott, AZ 86302
Phone: (520) 778-1578
Fax: (520) 771-1229
E-mail: patticash@hotmail.com
Member: PARW/CC
Certification: CPRW

Kristin M. Coleman
Principal, Custom Career Services
44 Hillcrest Dr.
Poughkeepsie, NY 12603
Phone: (845) 452-8274
Fax: (845) 452-7789
E-mail: kristincoleman44@yahoo.com
Member: PARW/CC, NRWA

Teresa Collins, CPRW
Erica Hanson
Quality Résumé
1018 Lincoln Ave.
Evansville, IN 47711
Phone: (812) 421-7280
Fax: (812) 421-7281
E-mail: barbwork@evansville.net

Kristie Cook
Absolutely Write
913 North Sumac
Olathe, KS 66061
Phone: (913) 397-9673
Toll-free: (877) 218-4114
Fax: (913) 397-9273
E-mail: kriscook@absolutely-write.com
Web site: www.absolutely-write.com
Certification: CPRW
Member: PARW/CC, NRWA, CMI

Annemarie Cross
Advanced Employment Concepts
P.O. Box 91
Hallam, Victoria 3803
Australia
Phone: +613 9708 6930
Fax: +613 9796-4479
E-mail: success@aresumewriter.net
Web site: www.aresumewriter.net
Member: PARW/CC, PRWRA, CMI, AHRI, Coachville, MBN
Certification: CPRW, CEIP, CECC, CRW, CCM

Jean Cummings
Concord, MA
Phone: (978) 371-9266
Toll-free: (800) 324-1699
Fax: (978) 964-0529
E-mail: jcummings1@verizon.net
Web site: www.AResumeforToday.com
Certification: MAT, CPRW, CEIP

Becky J. Davis
20 Chamberlain Ave.
Brunswick, ME 04011
Phone and fax: (207) 373-1117
E-mail: RezWriter@aol.com
Certification: CPRW

Deborah Wile Dib
President, Advantage Resumes of New York
77 Buffalo Ave.
Medford, NY 11763
Toll-free: (888) 272-8899
Phone: (631) 475-8513
Fax: (501) 421-7790
E-mail: 100kPLUS@advantageresumes.com
Web site: www.advantageresumes.com
Member: NRWA, PARW/CC, AJST, CMI, CPADN
Certification: CCM, NCRW, CPRW, CEIP, JCTC, CCMC

Beverley Drake
Executive Director, CareerVision Resume & Job Search Systems
1816 Baihly Hills Dr. SW
Rochester, MN 55902
Phone: (507) 252-9825
Fax: (507) 252-1559
E-mail: bdcprw@aol.com
Member: PARW/CC, NAJST
Certification: CEIP, CPRW, IJCTC, Certified Peer Counselor

Patricia Traina Duckers
The Resume Writer
P.O. Box 595
Edison, NJ 08818-0595
Phone: (732) 239-8533
Toll-free: (877) 260-1333
Fax: (732) 906-5636
E-mail: sales@theresumewriter.com
Web site: www.theresumewriter.com
Member: NRWA, CMI, PARW/CC
Certification: CPRW, CRW, CEIP, CFRWC

Dayna Feist
President, Gatehouse Business Services
265 Charlotte St.
Asheville, NC 28801
Phone: (828) 254-7893
Fax: (828) 254-7894
E-mail: gatehous@aol.com
Web site: www.BestJobEver.com
Member: PARW/CC
Certification: CPRW, CEIP, JCTC

Harold J. Flantzer
Professional Career Resources
8344 Lefferts Blvd., Ste. 2N
Kew Gardens, NY 11415
Phone: (718) 846-3027
Fax: (877) 848-3295
E-mail: ProCareers@att.net
Certification: Adult Career Management and Development, NYU

Michelle M. Fleig-Palmer
Director, Dual Career Program
University of Nebraska at Kearney
Kearney, NE 68849
Phone: (308) 865-8404
Fax: (308) 865-8917
E-mail: fleigpalmerm@unk.edu
Web site: www.unk.edu/offices/dcp
Certification: MBA, CCM

Louise Fletcher
Blue Sky Resumes
15 Merriam Ave.
Bronxville, NY 10708
Phone: (914) 337-5742
Fax: (914) 337-1943
E-mail: info@blueskyresumes.com
Web site: www.blueskyresumes.com
Certification: CPRW

Gail Frank
Frankly Speaking: Resumes that Work
Voice: (813) 926-1353
Fax: (813) 926-1092
E-mail: gfrank01@tampabay.rr.com
Web site: www.callfranklyspeaking.com
Member: CMI, NRWA, PARW/CC
Certification: NCRW, CPRW, JCTC, CEIP

Louise Garver
Career Directions, LLC
115 Elm St., Ste. 203
Enfield, CT 06082
Phone: (860) 623-9476
Fax: (860) 623-9473
E-mail: TheCareerPro@aol.com
Web sites: www.ResumeImpact.com and www.CareerEdgeCoach.com
Member: PARW/CC, NRWA, IACMP, NCDA, ACA
Certification: CPRW, CMP, JCTC, CEIP, MCDP

Wendy Gelberg
President, Advantage Résumés
21 Hawthorn Ave.
Needham, MA 02492
Phone: (781) 444-0778
Fax: (781) 444-2778
E-mail: wgelberg@aol.com
Member: NRWA
Certification: CPRW, IJCTC, M.Ed.

E. René Hart
Executive Career Solutions
CareerPlan, Inc.
Kewanee, IL
Phone: (888) 522-6121
Web site: www.executivecareersolutions.com
Member: NRWA
Certification: CPRW

Maria E. Hebda
Managing Executive, Career Solutions, LLC
Trenton, MI
Phone: (734) 676-9170
Fax: (734) 676-9487
E-mail: mhebda@writingresumes.com
Web sites: www.certifiedresumewriters.com, certifiedcareercoaches.com, and www.writingresumes.com
Member: PARW/CC
Certification: CCMC, CPRW

Kim Isaacs, MA
Director, ResumePower.com
4695 Watson Dr.
Doylestown, PA 18901
Phone: (800) 203-0551
E-mail: info@resumepower.com
Web site: www.ResumePower.com
Member: NRWA, PARW/CC
Certification: CPRW, NCRW

Myriam-Rose Kohn
JEDA Enterprises
27201 Tourney Rd., Ste. 201M
Valencia, CA 91355-1857
Phone: (661) 253-0801
Fax: (661) 253-0744
E-mail: myriam-rose@jedaenterprises.com
Web site: www.jedaenterprises.com
Certification: CPRW, CEIP, IJCTC, CCM, CCMC

Louise M. Kursmark
Best Impression
9847 Catalpa Woods Ct.
Cincinnati, OH 45242
Phone: (888) 792-0030
Fax: (513) 792-0961
E-mail: LK@yourbestimpression.com
Web site: www.yourbestimpression.com
Member: CMI, NRWA, PARW/CC, NAJST
Certification: CPRW, JCTC, CCM

Linda Matias
CareerStrides
Phone: (631) 387-1894 or (631) 382-2425
E-mail: linda@careerstrides.com
Web site: www.careerstrides.com
Certification: NCRW, CEIP, JCTC

Diane McGoldrick
Business Services of Tampa Bay
4802 Lastrada Ct.
Lutz, FL 33549
Phone: (813) 935-2700
E-mail: diane@tntpc.com
Member: PARW/CC, NAJST, Who's Who Among Professionals, CMI
Certification: CPRW

Melanie A. Noonan
Peripheral Pro, LLC
560 Lackawanna Ave.
West Paterson, NJ 07424
Phone: (973) 785-3011
Fax: (973) 256-6285
E-mail: PeriPro1@aol.com
Member: PARW/CC, NRWA, IAAP
Certification: CPS

John M. O'Connor
Career Pro Resumes
3301 Woman's Club Dr., Ste. 125
Raleigh, NC 27612
Phone: (919) 787-2400
Fax: (866) 447-9599
E-mail: john@careerproresumes.com
Web site: www.CareerProResumes.com
Certification: CRW, CCM, CECC, CPRW, CFRW

Donald Orlando
The McLean Group
640 S. McDonough St.
Montgomery, AL 36104
Phone: (334) 264-2020
Fax: (334) 264-9227
E-mail: yourcareercoach@aol.com
Member: PARW/CC, CMI Training Master
Certification: MBA, CPRW, JCTC, CCM, CCMC

Sydney J. Reuben
CareerXpress
854 Coleman Ave., #L
Menlo Park, CA 94025
Phone: (650) 323-2643
E-mail: SReubenMA@aol.com
Member: NRWA, PARW/CC
Certification: CPRW, MA

Phyllis B. Shabad
CareerMasters
95 Woods Brooke Circle
Ossining, NY 10562
Phone and fax: (914) 944-9577
E-mail: careermasters@cyburban.com
Member: NRWA, PARW/CC
Certification: NCRW, JCTC

Billie Ruth Sucher
Billie Sucher & Associates
7177 Hickman Rd., Ste. 10
Urbandale, IA 50322
Phone: (515) 276-0076
Fax: (515) 334-8076
E-mail: betwnjobs@aol.com
Member: CMI
Certification: MS, CTMS, CTSB

Susan Britton Whitcomb
Career Coach Academy/Career Masters Institute
757 E. Hampton Way
Fresno, CA 93704
Phone: (559) 222-7474
Fax: (559) 222-0670
E-mail: swhitcomb@cminstitute.com
Web site: www.careerwriter.com
Member: NRWA, ICF, NCDA, CCN,
CMI President
Certification: CCMC, CCM, MRW, NCRW

Pearl White
A 1st Impression Resume
41 Tangerine
Irvine, CA 92618
Phone: (949) 651-1068
Fax: (949) 651-9415
E-mail: pearlwhite1@cox.net
Web site: www.a1stimpression.com
Member: NRWA, PARW/CC, CMI
Certification: CEIP

Kathy Williams
A Career Advantage
P.O. Box 4011
Appleton, WI 54915
Phone: (920) 731-5167; (877) 731-5167
Fax: (877) 576-5424
E-mail: kk@acareeradvantage.com
Web site: www.acareeradvantage.com
Member: NRWA
Certification: NCRW

Professional Associations for Resume Writers and Career Professionals

Contact these organizations directly or see their Web sites for recommendations of resume writers in your area.

Career Masters Institute (CMI)

757 E. Hampton Way
Fresno, CA 93704
Phone: (559) 222-7474
Fax: (559) 227-0670
E-mail: swhitcomb@cminstitute.com
Web site: www.cminstitute.com

National Résumé Writers' Association (NRWA)

P.O. Box 184
Nesconset, NY 11767
E-mail: Secretary@nrwaweb.com
Web site: www.nrwaweb.com.

Professional Association of Résumé Writers & Career Coaches (PARW/CC)

1388 Brightwaters Blvd., NE
St. Petersburg, FL 33704
Phone: (813) 821-2274 or (800) 822 7279
Fax: (813) 894-1277
E-mail: PARWhq@aol.com
Web site: www.parw.com

Professional Résumé Writing and Research Association (PRWRA)

Phone: (321) 752-0442
Toll free: (888) 86-PRWRA (867-7972)
Fax: (321) 752-7513
E-mail: info@prwra.com
Web site: www.prwra.com

Index

A

B

C

D

E

F–G

H

I

J

K–L

M

N–O

P

Q–R

S

T

U–V

W

Y–Z